U   ᴧᴀᴛɪᴠᴇ
                    APPROACH

USING ECONOMICS: A QUANTITATIVE APPROACH

Richard Stead
Senior Lecturer in Economics
Leeds Polytechnic

Mik Wisniewski
Principal Lecturer in Quantitative Methods
Leeds Polytechnic

McGRAW-HILL BOOK COMPANY

London · New York · St Louis · San Francisco · Auckland · Bogotá · Guatemala
Hamburg · Lisbon · Madrid · Mexico · Montreal · New Delhi · Panama · Paris
San Juan · São Paulo · Singapore · Sydney · Tokyo · Toronto

Published by
McGRAW-HILL Book Company (UK) Limited
MAIDENHEAD · BERKSHIRE · ENGLAND

British Library Cataloguing in Publication Data
Stead, Richard, 1948–
   Using economics: a quantitative approach.
   1. Economics
   I. Title   II. Wisniewski, Mik
   330
   ISBN 0-07-084190-X

Library of Congress Cataloging-in-Publication Data
Stead, Richard.
   Using economics: a quantitative approach
   Includes index.
   1. Economics, Mathematical.   I. Wisniewski, Mik.
   II. Title.
   HB135.S725   1988   330′.01′51   88-8907
   ISBN 0-07-084190-X

1234 CUP 898

Typeset by Eta Services (Typesetters) Ltd, Beccles, Suffolk
Printed in Great Britain at the University Press, Cambridge

CONTENTS

PREFACE

The title of this textbook was carefully chosen. It reflects the fact that, although there are a bewildering variety of introductory economics texts and an equally bewildering array of introductory statistics and mathematics texts, there are few serious attempts at presenting these subjects on an integrated basis. This is what this book sets out to do.

All too commonly, economics is taught as an extended exercise in pure logic. Similarly, quantitative methods frequently comes across as a collection of numerical techniques which have no obvious application. The two subject areas thus remain separate in the teaching/learning process: students are often left feeling bemused as to the uses of their economics courses and grateful that maths and statistics are over and can be forgotten.

It is our intention in this textbook to integrate economic theory and the relevant statistical and mathematical techniques. We examine key economic principles and then proceed, with the assistance of the relevant quantitative techniques, to present evidence to determine the validity of those principles. At the appropriate stages in this process the supporting statistical and mathematical methods are developed. Real data sets are used wherever possible to illustrate economic principles and quantitative techniques. Overall, the text covers all the material which would normally be found in introductory courses in economics and in quantitative methods.

As a result of this approach, economics emerges not as a network of assumptions and logical deductions but as a useful body of theory and ideas which can be used to explain and predict changes in the economic behaviour of consumers, business organizations and the economy as a whole. Its ability to be applied in such a way is considerably enhanced by the use of quantitative techniques. Similarly, quantitative techniques emerge as an essential and integral part of the study of economics rather than as a separate, peripheral subject.

Although the text is intended primarily for students of economics, we feel that the approach taken—the integration of economic ideas with their supporting quantitative skills—will be helpful to students following a variety of courses in business, business information technology and the social sciences. This text can be used to support an integrated or joint course in economics and quantitative methods, or two parallel courses in these subjects.

Although the text integrates quantitative methods with economics, it is not intended as an econometrics text, being restricted to introductory work in the two areas. It should be stressed that 'A' level maths (or similar) is not a prerequisite for understanding this book—it presumes no previous knowledge in the field.

The approach to quantitative techniques places as much emphasis on the 'why' as on the 'how'. This is because it is not sufficient to have purely mechanical and computational skills in the modern business world—it is also necessary to understand and appreciate both the potential and limitations of such techniques. To reinforce this we encourage students studying the text to perform the relevant calculations using computer facilities wherever practical and a computer package of direct relevance to much of the material in the text is detailed at the end of Chapter 1.

Additionally, at the end of each chapter, readers will find a variety of exercises relating to the material covered. While it is tempting, and indeed understandable, to regard such exercises as 'optional', they are there for a specific purpose. Not only do they enable readers to ensure they have adequately understood the concepts and techniques introduced, but they also serve as a lead-in to subsequent chapters and topics. They should be seen, therefore, as an integral part of the text.

After completing the text, readers should not only have an adequate grasp of economic and quantitative principles. They should be able to begin to put these principles to work in explaining and predicting economic events.

Richard Stead
Mik Wisniewski

AN INTRODUCTION TO ECONOMICS

1-1 INTRODUCTION

Economics is about business. It is the analysis of the mechanisms by which resources are allocated to meet people's wants.

The attention of economists is frequently directed towards the activities of privately owned businesses selling goods and services for profit. Prices, output, employment and unemployment, investment, the money supply, exchange rates, public expenditure and taxation and a range of similar items are their principle topics of analysis. There is, however, no necessity so to restrict the horizons of economics: state-owned companies like British Rail or the Bank of England, welfare services like the National Health Service and voluntary bodies like Oxfam all attempt, in their respective ways, to meet people's wants and all may therefore be described as different kinds of business organization. All are thus equally legitimate subjects for economic analysis.

An understanding of economics clearly requires some knowledge of the main institutions and practices of business life, and it is fortunate that many of these are familiar to most people through their everyday activities and through the media. Technical terms are, of course, required on occasion, and these will be explained as the need arises. Less familiar to most, perhaps, is a knowledge of the statistical and quantitative dimensions of the economy, such as the level of industrial output, the size of the national income or the rate of company liquidations. Business statistics such as these are far more abundant today than they used to be, and it is obvious that economists will draw upon these sources in their work.

Economists, however, attempt to go beyond the mere recording of facts and statistics about business. This is the work, important in its own right, of statisticians and of business and economic historians. The objective of the economist is rather to go behind the superficial appearances of events and gain an understanding of the underlying mechanisms and processes of the economy by using the theories of economics. For example, the prices of semi-detached houses in Britain and the balance between the revenue and expenditure of the government of the United States may seem quite unconnected. They are, after all, separated by thousands of miles and are located in countries using different currencies. Economic theory, however, can demonstrate that the two phenomena are linked in a fairly direct fashion through the mechanisms of interest rates and exchange rates.

1-2 ECONOMIC THEORIES

Theories in economics fall into two broad categories, depending on their subject matter. The first is *micro-economics*, which may be defined as the analysis of developments and relationships at the level of individual industries or markets. The terms 'industries' and 'markets' can naturally be defined to suit the purpose of the work to be undertaken. An economist may, for example, be concerned with the transport industry in its entirety (air, sea and road travel), with the market for bicycles or even with the market for one particular brand of bicycle. Among the concerns of micro-economics are trends in output, sales, employment and prices of particular goods and services and, of course, the relationships between these trends. Given the detailed nature of micro-economic analysis, work at this level frequently involves the investigation of factors such as the organization of an industry (the number and size of firms), its legal constraints (such as licensing regulations) or technological developments.

The second category of theory comprises *macro-economics*, which can be defined as the analysis of developments and relationships at the level of a national or regional economy considered as a single entity. A list of the principal items for consideration under this heading would include national income, inflation, employment and unemployment, the money supply, interest rates, the balances of trade and payments, the level of consumer spending, investment public spending and aggregate saving.

1-3 ECONOMIC MODELS

Economists undertake their exploration of economic relationships at both micro- and macro-economic levels by means of the construction of *models*. Models derive from economic theories, and are best thought of as expressions or formulations of theories.

The purpose of a model is to reduce the complexities of the real world to a level that can be understood and analysed. Thus a model is restricted to the key features of a situation. For example, to investigate the ways in which people spend their incomes economists use a model of consumer behaviour. This begins by assuming, for simplicity, that there is only a single consumer with a given set of tastes and preferences and a certain income. It is also assumed that there are only two goods which can be purchased and that these goods sell at certain prices. Economists use this model to establish the bundle of goods (how much of the first and how much of the second good) that will yield the most satisfaction to the consumer. The next step is to vary some of the initial conditions by, for example, increasing the price of one of the two goods available. The consumer's reaction to these changes, in terms of the amounts of the two goods consumed, can then be explored. In this instance, an increase in the price of one commodity will, all else equal, lead to a fall in the quantity bought.

This example illustrates the four main stages in the work of building and using models in economics. The first stage is to make *assumptions* which specify the key characteristics of the situation: the people ('economic agents') present, their intentions, and the constraints which they face, such as the number of firms competing in a market. The second stage is to deduce the *implications* which follow logically from these assumptions. Thus, in the example given, it can be deduced that there would be a specific and unique combination of the two goods which would give the consumer maximum satisfaction. Frequently the implication of a set of assumptions is that economic agents would reach some kind of equilibrium position. Thus the consumer in the example above would be expected to settle upon some particular bundle of goods in order to maximize his or her satisfaction. The third stage is to *vary* one of the initial assumptions and then to repeat the process of deduction. In the model of consumer choice, stage three was the change in the price of one of the two goods and the task of deducing the content of the new bundle of goods. The final stage is to *compare* the two outcomes and relate them to the change in the initial conditions. In the example, this meant drawing the conclusion that a rise in the price of a good will, all else being equal, lead to a fall in the quantity that is bought. This stage is thus a statement about a link between two items—here, price and quantity. If this relationship is a supposition that has yet to be tested, it will be known as a *hypothesis*. If, on the other hand, it has been tested and is widely accepted, then it may be known as an *economic law*.

Stages three and four are analogous to performing experiments in a laboratory. The process may, of course, be repeated many times, so that one model may generate a whole series of hypotheses and/or laws. The entire procedure of building models, deducing outcomes and comparing different outcomes under changing conditions is known as *comparative static analysis*. The word 'static' is used because the outcomes are stable situations which contain no inherent forces to make them change. In using the models of economics, this book will follow, either explicitly or implicitly, the above four stages.

This work of constructing economic models has two results. The first is to bring a measure of order and consistency to the investigation of economic and business problems. Economic theory provides a framework within which the relevant factors may be marshalled for examination. The basic division is into *supply-side* and *demand-side* factors, distinguishing between those factors which affect the provision of goods and those which affect their consumption. Other sub-divisions follow: on the supply side, the prices of factors of production, their availability, their productivity and so on; on the demand side, population growth, diet patterns, consumers' income and so on. One corollary of this systematic approach to analysis is that economic theory is able to suggest to the investigator the kinds of evidence which ought to be considered. An economist may, for example, wish to assess the outlook for consumer demand. Economic theory provides a checklist of items to look at. This might well include projections of pay settlements, employment levels, taxation, inflation, lending by banks and building societies and other sources of consumer credit, interest rates, exchange rates and other potentially important factors.

The second result of building models and undertaking comparative static analysis is the formulation of economic laws. An example is the law of demand which states that as the price of a good rises, the quantity demanded will fall. Such an economic law is not meant to be an unqualified prediction of what will happen every time the price of any good changes but rather a general expression as to the likely consequences of a specific change in circumstances. Economic laws, in other words, are thus *conditional predictions* of changes under specific and clearly specified circumstances.

In practice the testing and analysis of economic theories by means of a model is often undertaken by means of computers. A similar emphasis will be developed throughout this text. Although the basic principles and techniques will be introduced so that they can be evaluated without such facilities, the development of skills to deal with the applications of models must, of necessity, include the ability to use computer facilities. Many of the end-of-chapter problems will require access to such facilities.

There are two important features of economic models that deserve further comment. The first relates to the assumptions on which the theories and models of economics are based. Some may be quite plausible: the model of perfect competition, for example, assumes the existence of large numbers of small producers. Others may be reasonable simplifications, like the assumption in the model of consumer choice that there are only two goods. There are, however, some which seem to be entirely at variance with common experience, such as the common assumption that economic agents are endowed with perfect information.

Although the question of whether assumptions in models need to be realistic has periodically troubled economists, it may be observed that the procedure of using hypothetical models is not confined to economics. In physics and mechanics, for example, there are numerous models which employ concepts like 'pure vacuums' or 'perfect spheres'. Scientists construct models using such ideal or limiting cases so as to investigate underlying relationships without having to deal with a clutter of incidental detail. In a similar manner, the purpose of economic models is to simulate the workings of the real economy. By constructing models and by using comparative static analysis, economists attempt to isolate and analyse the fundamental mechanisms of economic behaviour.

The second feature of economic models to be noted is that they can be expressed in a number of different ways. First, like the model of consumer behaviour above, a model may be set out verbally. Second, it may be presented in diagrammatic form. Third, it may be expressed in the form of a set of mathematical equations. These different forms of presentation are *alternative* rather than *competing* approaches, and anyone with an active interest in economics must be able to deal with all three. The skills needed to deal with graphical and mathematical or statistical models will be developed as we progress through the text.

The prospect of developing and dealing with mathematical models in particular may seem, at this stage, somewhat daunting. There is, however, little cause for alarm. Although it is couched in the language of mathematics, a mathematical model is, like any other type, simply a description of the economic system it is intended to represent. The advantage of a mathematical model is that it has greater clarity, being less open to misunderstanding and misinterpretation than a verbal exposition.

It is important to note that the terms we have been using, 'less ambiguous' and 'more precise', do not equate necessarily to 'more accurate', for the accuracy of a model depends on how closely we have perceived the real-world situation. There is nothing inherently more accurate in a mathematical model. A mathematical formulation does, however, have the effect of forcing economists to set out their ideas in a precise and unambiguous manner.

1-4 FACTS AND THEORIES

The relationship between economic theory, on the one hand, and statistical and empirical data, on the other, is of the utmost importance. Without empirical data, economics remains a large-scale exercise in pure logic. All too often, unfortunately, economics is taught without any reference to factual data, and it is indeed perfectly possible for students to go through on entire course in the subject without gaining any knowledge whatever of the dimensions and relationships of the real economy.

The standpoint taken in this text is the exact opposite. It is the belief of the present authors that statistical data are essential to economics. That is to say, economic principles, theories and models need to be set against economic statistics in order both to be fully understood and to be made usable. In a general sense, theories must be supported by factual evidence if they are to have any credence. On the other hand, it should not be imagined that there are original 'brute' facts which exist independently of theories. Rather, facts themselves depend on theories. They do so in the sense that facts can only be gathered by using precise definitions. Without definitions, it would be impossible to make sense of any observations. Indeed it would be impossible to make any meaningful observations in the first place. The work of supplying definitions, of course, is one of the roles of theories.

It may be helpful to illustrate this by using the example of the relationship between income and consumption. Economic theory suggests that there is a direct relationship of some form between the amount of money an individual spends (his or her consumption) and the amount of money the individual has available for spending (his or her income). Although such a relationship seems little more than common sense, it remains at this stage simply a hypothesis, something we *believe* to be the case. To substantiate it, evidence must be presented. You may feel that this could be done by looking at the relationship between your own income and spending patterns. Understandably, however, we generally require more evidence than this—which is simply based on a single individual's behaviour—and we would need to set out and obtain data on a mass of consumption and income patterns. We shall be investigating the methods of doing this later in the text.

Before data can be collected, however, both variables have to be defined. Even a cursory examination of one of the many official statistical publications would quickly reveal that there are a number of differing measures that could be used. There are several different measures of income, for example. Some relate to income before deductions such as income tax, others to income after deductions. Some relate to income which includes such items as interest and profits from savings and investment, others do not and so on. There are similarly a number of different measures of consumption.

Economic theory allows us to identify the key features of the different measures of income and consumption on which we would collect our empirical evidence. In other words, it is economic theory which would tell us the appropriate measures of income and consumption to use to try and identify the nature of the relationship between the two variables in question. Thus a framework of ideas is necessary before empirical observations can be made. Facts, in other words, are 'theory-laden'.

Conversely, theories depend on facts for their acceptance. Facts, that is to say, are often thought to be able to prove that a theory is true. The relationship between facts and theories and the nature of proof is, however, relatively complex and a matter which merits some attention.

The principle point is straightforward enough. It is that factual evidence can *disprove* a theory by showing that something has happened which the theory rules out, but factual evidence can never *prove* a theory to be correct. An example that is frequently used to demonstrate this point concerns the colour of swans. A theory may state that all swans are white. It is clear that no number of observations of white swans will prove whether the remaining, and unseen, swans are all white. That is, the theory cannot be proved without examining every single swan in the universe, and this could never be done since it would never be known if another swan were hidden somewhere. The theory, in short, could never be proved correct. It is, however, fairly easy, in principle, to disprove or to falsify the theory. All that we require is one black swan.

In terms of our previous illustration, let us imagine that our model had suggested that all consumers spent the same proportion, say 80 per cent, of their income. After collecting the appropriate data and undertaking the necessary statistical analysis, we might find that the statistical evidence and the model were consistent. This would not, however, constitute proof that the model was correct. It would simply indicate that we had a working hypothesis about an economic relationship that has not yet been disproved.

It may seem strange at first to learn that theories can never be proved true. After all, textbooks in the natural sciences and social sciences alike contain a large number of laws which are widely accepted as being true. Acceptance, nevertheless, is different from proof. Theories and laws which gain acceptance do so purely on a temporary basis.

The implication of the foregoing discussion might seem to be that the theory ought to be abandoned if it were falsified by the evidence. In practice, it is rare for empirical evidence in economics to provide final, utter and absolute disproof of a hypothesis. To reach the

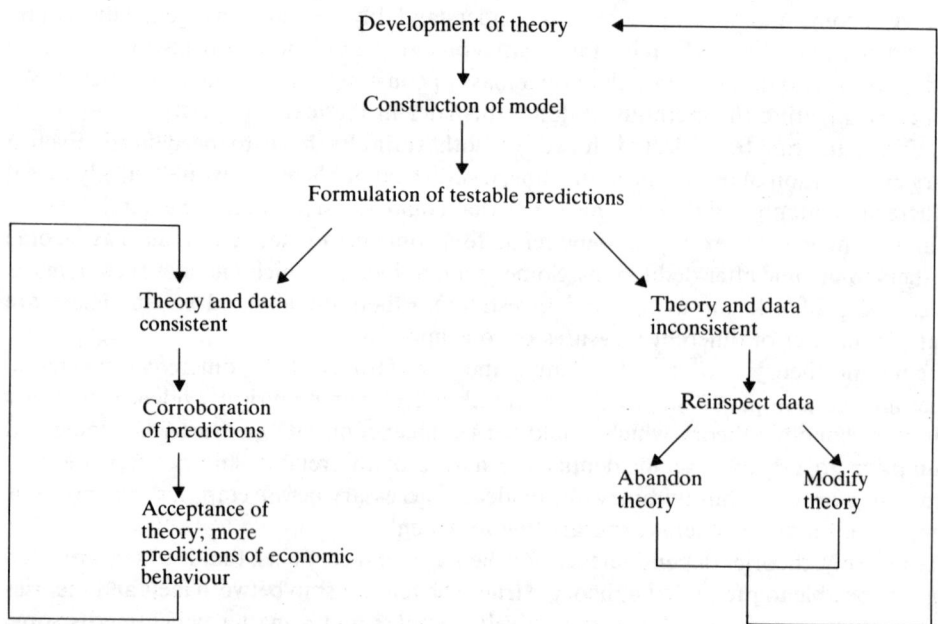

Figure 1-1 Theories and models

conclusion that a hypothesis had been disproved, an economist would have to be satisfied that no extraneous events have influenced the data, that data had been obtained by proper sampling methods, that the data related to the variables defined by the theory and that they had been processed without arithmetical errors. The fact that experiments are not possible in economics means, of course, that these requirements can be extremely difficult to fulfil. Indeed, the most frequent result of any research is not the falsification of an hypothesis but rather the creation of grounds for suspicion that the hypothesis is false. (A complicating factor is the point that a model may generate a number of hypotheses, some of which may be falsified while others may not.)

Economists can, in principle, respond in one of three ways. Each carries markedly different implications for the theory concerned. The first is to discount the theory entirely. The second is to question the evidence by re-examining the data in terms of their accuracy, reliability and suitability. In effect, this second response is a means of defending the theory from the damaging implications of contrary evidence. The third response is to recast the theory to allow for the new evidence, whilst preserving elements of the old theory. Clearly, the modifications can vary from the drastic, which change a theory out of all recognition, to the cosmetic, which allow the theory to live on with only the most minor changes.

Because theories are frequently found to be at odds with the evidence to a greater or lesser extent, there is in economics a continuous process of abandoning or reformulating old theories and of generating new ones. This process is illustrated in Fig. 1-1 and it serves to underline the importance of statistical information for economics. The choice which any economist makes about the truth of any theory will depend upon his or her view of the validity of the data and of the general plausibility of that theory. It will necessarily involve an element of judgement.

1-5 SCHOOLS OF ECONOMIC THOUGHT

Given the importance of judgement in deciding whether to abandon or to retain a theory, it is hardly surprising that economists are divided in their views on the merits of different theories. These divergences of view, moreover, often relate not to particular models but to entire approaches to economic theory, and there are, in consequence, a number of distinct schools of economic thought. Thus all references to 'economic principles' need to be treated with a degree of caution because each school has its own slightly different version of at least some of those principles. Discussion here will be confined to three principal schools, namely neo-classical economics, Keynesianism and Austrian economics.

The three schools divide most importantly over their approach to the idea of equilibrium. This term will be explained in detail in Chapter 9. For present purposes it will suffice to note that a market is taken to be in equilibrium when supply and demand are in balance. This balance is struck by means of the price mechanism. Should the quantity of a commodity supplied to the market be in excess of the quantity demanded, the price will be bidden down. This will at once choke off some supply as traders leave the business and encourage extra customers. Supply and demand will therefore be brought into balance once again. If, on the other hand, the quantity demanded exceeds the quantity supplied, a similar process will operate to restore equilibrium by means of an increase in price. It follows that there is a single equilibrium price and a single equilibrium output level for each market. The price and quantity will only change in response to a change in the conditions which determine supply or demand. Moreover, equilibrium positions are stable in that they contain no forces to cause them to change.

In *neo-classical* economics, markets are generally taken to be in a state of equilibrium. This school of economics could indeed be more informatively renamed 'equilibrium economics'. Hence the prices which may be observed in high-street shops, on the Stock Exchange or elsewhere are taken to be equilibrium prices and the quantities of goods sold are all taken to be equilibrium quantities. Economic statistics which record prices and output levels are therefore assumed, by neo-classical economists, to refer to equilibrium situations. For example, a neo-classical economist would interpret Fig. 1-2 as representing a series of equilibrium prices and quantities in the market for natural gas, that is to say, in spite of the considerable change that took place in domestic gas sales over this period, each year's figure represents an equilibrium between supply and demand according to the neo-classical school. Indeed, virtually every market shows changes in price or quantity or both from year to year, rather than displaying the stability which the notion of equilibrium seems to imply. This might at first sight seem to present neo-classical economists with a problem. Neo-classical economists, however, argue that movements in prices and quantities reflect a series of successive equilibria. These in turn reflect changes in the underlying conditions of supply or demand. The work of the neo-classical economist, therefore, is to search for explanations of changes in price and quantity. In the gas example, the expansion in gas sales could be explained in terms, say, of increasing prices of other fuels or of rising incomes.

This approach is to be contrasted with those of *Austrian* economics and *Keynesianism*. Both these schools of thought assume that markets or economies are frequently *not* in equilibrium, and both proceed to analyse economic behaviour in this light.

For Austrian economics, the focus of interest is upon the activities of entrepreneurs in individual markets (that is, upon *micro-economic* situations). Economists of this school believe that entrepreneurial businessmen are constantly engaged in a process of trying out new products and new production methods. There is, according to Austrian economists, a constant process of exploration, of trial and error.

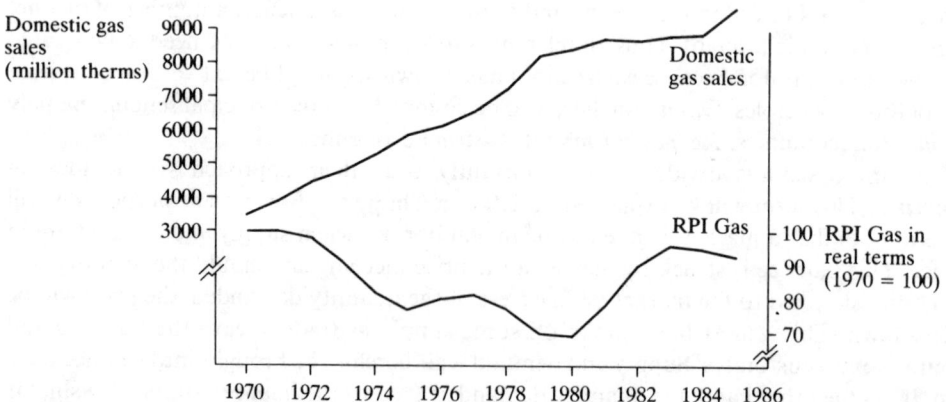

Figure 1-2 Domestic gas sales and RPI Gas, 1970–85 (*Source: Annual Abstract of Statistics; Digest of UK Energy Statistics*)

This view has quite profound implications for the use of data. Prices and quantities which statisticians observe are not, for Austrians, equilibria but merely intermediate points in a dynamic process. There is, therefore, no need to explain why one set of prices and quantities is superseded by another set. The data on gas sales, for example, would be interpreted as recording the way more and more consumers were trying out gas as a fuel. The gas market might only come to an equilibrium after the lapse of several years. For Austrian economists, change is the normal state of affairs. (There is, of course, an interesting corollary to this line of argument in terms of our earlier discussion of proving and falsifying theories. Because Austrian economists take change to be normal, they have difficulty in producing conditional predictions which can ever be falsified.)

Keynesian economics is similarly concerned with disequilibrium situations, but here the focus is upon the *macro-economy*. Keynes's major contribution to macro-economics was made during the 1930s when the world economy was in a prolonged economic depression. The consensus among economists was that the economic system would return to prosperity under its own steam. Keynes disputed this, arguing that the economy had no inherent tendency to pull itself out of a state of depression. Mass unemployment, in other words, might persist indefinitely. Only a policy of active government intervention, he argued, could restore prosperity. Such a policy would plainly have to be based on a detailed knowledge of levels of unemployment, output and so on. The influence of Keynes's ideas, therefore, gave a substantial impetus to the compiling of national accounts and the collection of much other economic information.

1-6 THE CONTRIBUTIONS OF ECONOMICS AND OF ECONOMISTS

The main purpose behind the integration of economics and quantitative technicians in this book is to help students to put economics into use. The subject is, of course, already employed by three broad (and non-exclusive) groups of people: first, professional economists; second, ordinary citizens with some interest in current affairs; and third, administrators, business people and other decision-makers. The ways in which these groups use economics are described in turn.

Professional economists are widely employed in both public and private sectors. Over and above teaching in schools, colleges and universities, economists work in government departments, local government, the nationalized industries, industrial and commercial firms, and financial institutions ranging from banks and building societies to stockbroking houses. They are also to be found in the offices of politicians and of trades unions and other pressure groups, in consultancy and in financial and economic journalism.

Foremost among these organizations is central government. Governments have a general responsibility for the stability and prosperity of the economy and usually come into office having given various undertakings to the voters about controlling inflation, reducing unemployment or rekindling economic growth. They therefore need to be kept informed of economic developments so as to assess the success (or otherwise) of their policies, with a view to recasting them should this be necessary. Economists from the Treasury, the Cabinet

Office and other departments have the job of assembling the relevant information and of exploring the likely effects of any amendments to policy.

Outside government, economists are employed to monitor and interpret macro-economic trends. Some, like the Trades Union Congress (TUC) or the Confederation of British Industry (CBI), employ economists because they wish to modify government policy by offering informed criticism and advice. Others have a more direct commercial interest in these matters. Stockbrokers, foreign exchange dealers and investors, for example, earn their livings by anticipating changes in interest rates, security prices and exchange rates. Similarly, international banks need to pay strict attention to macro-economic events in countries in which they have made loans, for adverse developments like the collapse of the market for a country's main export may mean that the loans will not be repaid. (By the same token, the International Monetary Fund (IMF) and the Organization for Economic Co-operation and Development (OECD) keep a watching brief over trends in the United Kingdom along with those in other industrial countries.)

Micro-economic analysis is also needed for both policy and commercial reasons. Industrial and commercial companies plainly have to monitor trends in various markets as part of the process of launching new products, investing in new capacity or searching for new outlets. The taking over of other firms will obviously depend on the growth prospects for their markets. Though not all industrial firms have their own economists, many make use of the professional services of economic consultants such as the Economist Intelligence Unit (EIU).

Economists are also found working for the media. Some produce specialist material for the financial press (like the *Investors Chronicle*) while others contribute to news and current affairs programmes for wider audiences. This is because the *general public* constitute the second category of users of economics. The reason for public interest in economic affairs is simply that today economic issues form an integral part of political and social debate. The control of inflation, the pursuit of economic growth, privatization, import controls, the maintenance of uneconomic coalmines, the costs of conservation—all these questions and many others on the current political agenda involve, to a greater or lesser degree, the concepts and theories of economics. Indeed, general elections are typically fought over issues of economic policy: monetarism versus Keynesianism, *laissez-faire* versus intervention. The effect is to draw ordinary electors into making decisions upon economic matters, despite the fact that most voters have had little, if any, formal education in economics. Much of the work, therefore, of professional politicians of all parties and of economic commentators in the media consists of presenting economic questions in ways which are intelligible to the layman. In so far as they are successful, ordinary electors are enabled to evaluate the economic policies which rival parties put forward.

Businessmen, senior administrators and other *decision-makers* form the third category of users of economics. Although they are not full-time, professional economists, people in positions of executive reponsibility will generally wish to keep abreast of changes in the environment in which they are operating. Much of the information that is of relevance here concerns economic trends and policies, and the ability to interpret economic reports both from their own economic research departments and from outside will be important. This is not to suggest that a knowledge of economics is all that is required for success in business—far from it! Clearly other areas of expertise, such as engineering, accounting, marketing, personnel management and operations research, are necessary, together with flair and, of course, a little luck. Nevertheless, successful decision-making in business will involve some dependence upon the concepts and theories of economics and the ability to interpret economic statistics. This consideration of the use of economics in the world outside schools, universities and colleges serves to underline two points of great importance. First, economists must be able to offer evidence to back up their theories. It is not sufficient, in other words, merely to be conversant with the principles of economics. The skills of the useful economist also include the ability to gather, process and present economic data. Second, business decision-makers in all organizations need to be conversant both with economic theories and with economic data. In short, both economists and decision-makers ought to be competent in handling economic theory *and* its associated quantitative techniques. This, of course, is the rationale for the integrated approach that has been adopted in this book.

1-7 BASIC ECONOMIC VOCABULARY

Although in general it will be best to consider specialist terms in their own particular contexts, some are sufficiently general to merit an explanation at this stage.

Real terms and money terms

These phrases are used to describe changes in the value of money. For example, consumers in the United Kingdom spent £65 billion in 1975 and £213 billion in 1985. Thus consumer spending rose by 228 per cent in *money* terms, that is, in terms of the money which changed hands during 1975 and 1985 respectively. This might suggest a massive increase in living standards over this period. The years between these dates, however, were marked by severe inflation. When account is taken of higher prices, the volume of consumer goods rose by only 22 per cent between 1975 and 1985. This latter figure describes the change in *real terms*, that is, it measures not the amount of money spent but rather what the money was able to buy.

Positive and normative statements

The distinction between *positive* and *normative* statements is one which is often held to be particularly important for a subject such as economics which is frequently used in policy-making. Positive statements are statements which are objective, scientific and factual. To qualify as positive a statement must be testable, or, more correctly, falsifiable. Thus the statement that 'the rate of inflation in the UK is 3 per cent' is a positive statement. (Positive statements may, of course, be false but they remain, nevertheless, positive statements.) As a basic minimum positive statements must relate to things which can be observed by others. In the example, above the rate of inflation in the UK can be recorded and calculated and the statement verified or falsified.

Normative statements (which may also be described as 'value judgements') have the opposite characteristics. They are subjective and untestable. Thus the statement that 'the rate of inflation is at an acceptable level' is a normative statement for it is clearly subjective. That is, it reveals the feelings of the speaker towards the topic. In this, it bears the hallmark of all normative statements: all convey or at least indicate the emotions, feelings and beliefs of the speaker, and as such cannot be challenged in terms of being true or false. Since normative statements cannot be falsified, they cannot form the basis of economic hypotheses or laws.

In practice, the two sorts of statement can easily become entangled. Economists are frequently called upon to help to formulate economic policies (or to advise on policies) and their responses will typically be admixtures of both positive and normative statements. For example, Conservative economists would tend to advocate the policies of *laissez-faire* and privatization, while Labour economists might argue for price controls or the restriction of imports. Both groups would employ positive statements to analyse the state of the economy, but both would come to their differing normative conclusions. To a large extent this interleaving of positive and normative is unavoidable. It is nevertheless important that economists remain aware of the relative extent of positive and normative elements in their thinking.

Quantity

This is often used without qualification, both in this book and elsewhere. It must be born in mind, however, that it usually denotes *quantity per unit of time*—the number of units sold per month, production per year and so on.

Short run and long run

The factor which distinguishes these time-periods is the degree of mobility which economic resources are assumed to possess. Over the long run, resources are taken to be fully mobile, so that their owners can respond to any change in conditions to the maximum extent. The short run refers to that period of time over which some resources—notably wealth in the form of capital equipment and buildings—are committed to some specific line of business or activity, thus preventing their owners from making complete adjustment to changed circumstances. For example, an increase in the price of petrol may, in the long run, induce car owners to buy vehicles with smaller, more efficient engines. In the short run, however, they may be forced to keep using their existing, inefficient cars and their response to higher petrol prices may be simply to do less driving. It may be of interest to note that the attention of neo-classical economists tends to fall upon the long run, when all adjustments have been made, while that of Austrian economists falls upon the short run.

Marginal units

Economists often focus attention upon the *marginal* units of production or consumption. This refers to the last items to be made or purchased. It is at the margin that adjustments to the flows of production and consumption are made.

1-8 CONCLUSION

This book will pursue the following plan. The models and principles of economic theory will be introduced in turn, beginning with micro-economics and then moving to macro-economics. When relevant, the contrasting views of the different schools of economic thought will be developed. At every stage, the quantitative techniques which are appropriate will be explained and applied to the economic data relating to the topic under consideration. The book should therefore serve as a basis for courses both in economics and in quantitative methods or, indeed, for a single combined course in the two subjects.

It is essential that students attempt the exercises at the end of each chapter as these do not merely rehearse the chapter's ideas and techniques but develop and apply them. In many cases, it will be necessary to use computer software such as that described in the Appendix to this chapter or a suitable alternative. It will, of course, be possible to follow the book without using a computer though readers will be presumed to have access to the principal official sources of economic and business statistics such as the *Annual Abstract of Statistics*, the *Monthly Digest of Statistics* or *Economic Trends*.

The work begins straight away. Having looked at the general nature of economic laws in this chapter, and having stressed the importance of testing hypotheses against the data, the second chapter will be devoted to the gathering and presenting of information that can be used to corroborate or falsify those laws. It is the importance of these links between economics, statistics and mathematics (and between them all and information technology) that has prompted the writing of this book. On completing it, our readers should not merely understand economics. They should also be able to use it.

1-9 SUMMARY

Economics is the branch of social science which seeks to explain how resources are allocated so as to provide people with the goods and services which they want.

Economic models are relatively precise formulations of economic theories. They may be expressed verbally, mathematically or graphically. Their use involves four stages: making assumptions; deducing implications from these assumptions (frequently these implications will relate to the equilibrium position that will be reached); varying one of the assumptions; and deducing the effect of that change.

Comparative statics is the work of comparing the state of a model before the change has been made with the state afterwards. Comparative statics thus generates conditional predictions about the ways economic agents will respond to changes in their circumstances. These conditional predictions may be hypotheses (if they have yet to be tested) or laws (if they have become generally accepted).

Proof and disproof: empirical evidence can, if it is unambiguous, disprove an hypothesis, but no amount of corroboration can ever prove a hypothesis to be true.

Neo-classical economics assumes markets to be in equilibrium as a general rule, while *Keynesian* economics (which describes primarily macro-economic relationships) and *Austrian* economics (which is concerned mainly with micro-economic relationships) assume that markets are more frequently in disequilibrium.

EXERCISES

1-1

(a) Formulate a hypothesis about the relationship you would expect between the level of energy consumption in the UK and the level of total national output.

(b) Using the latest edition of the *Annual Abstract of Statistics* collect data for the last 10 years on total energy consumption by final users and net national product at factor cost, measured in constant prices.

(c) Draw a graph showing the two sets of data.

(d) Do the trends evident in the two variables prove or disprove your hypothesis?

(e) Do you think you chose the correct version of the two variables from those available? Did you search out the definitions used for the variables you selected?

1-2 Explain the main differences in approach between neo-classical economics and Austrian economics.

1-3 Consider the following statements:

'Economic growth in the UK has averaged 3 per cent per year since 1981.'
'Economic growth in the UK during the 1960s and 1970s averaged 2 per cent.'
'Britain's economic growth has been higher than that of West Germany since 1981.'
'Britain's economic growth has been better than that of West Germany.'
'Economic growth in the UK has been rapid since 1981.'
'Economic growth in the UK in the 1960s and 1970s was disappointing.'
'Economic growth in the UK ought to be maintained at a high level.'

Which would you describe as positive statements and which as normative?

APPENDIX: COMPUTER SOFTWARE

As was indicated in Chapter 1, the authors feel that the use of relevant computer software in both quantitative and economic analysis can enhance considerably a student's appreciation and understanding. This is not to argue that such computer programs should be used unthinkingly but rather as a means of relieving the economic analyst and economics student from tedious and repetitive calculations. It is not the intention to review the available software (which in any case is constantly changing). Such a review is published annually in the journal *Economics*. Rather we shall draw the reader's attention to two specific software items.

The first of these is *Quantass*, by Mik Wisniewski, which is available from Social Science Software, Shrewsbury Road, Claughton, Birkenhead, Merseyside L43 8SP, UK. It is currently available for the BBC micro and has been written by one of the authors of this text. The techniques covered are primarily those introduced in this text and the software is ideally suited for much of the analysis undertaken here. Accompanying the programs is a data disk that contains many of the data sets used throughout this text, and many of the quantitative-related exercises are appropriate for use with this software.

The second is *Economics in Action* by C. Attfield and N. Duck, and available from McGraw-Hill Book Company (UK) Limited, Shoppenhangers Road, Maidenhead, Berkshire SL6 2QL, UK. This is a set of BBC software which covers much of basic economics in an interactive way using both text and graphics.

Additionally, it is worth noting that computer spreadsheets are also ideally suited for much of the analysis undertaken in the text. Most such spreadsheets can very easily be used to perform the relevant calculations and to support the techniques introduced. We have indicated where such spreadsheet use may be particularly relevant in the exercises.

DESCRIPTIVE STATISTICS (I)

2-1 INTRODUCTION

The importance of statistical evidence in economic analysis was stressed in Chapter 1 and this chapter will introduce basic techniques that we require for summarizing and describing such statistical information. For our purposes, the role of statistics is to allow us to test the hypotheses which economic models generate by comparing them with the numerical evidence. For, ultimately, it is only those theories that have not been proved false by the evidence that can form the basis for decision-making.

By way of an illustration, let us return to the relationship between income and consumption that was introduced in Chapter 1. Rather than discussing total consumption we may find it more helpful to take one specific relationship: that between income and car ownership. Economic theory (and, again, common sense) would lead us to the conclusion that there should be a strong and definite relationship between the two variables. Other things being equal, we should anticipate that people on higher incomes are likely to spend more on cars and to have, therefore, a higher level of car ownership than those on lower incomes. Naturally, we would not suggest that income is the sole determinant of this consumption but we would expect it to play a major part in determining consumption behaviour.

Quantifying this relationship would clearly be helpful to decision-makers. Public sector bodies with an interest would include central government departments as well as local urban and transport planners. Similarly car manufacturers, designing and pricing vehicles aimed at specific groups of customers, will also require detailed information about such a relationship to allow them to assess the potential success of their decisions. Economists also will wish to test their theories against real-world behaviour patterns—the empirical evidence—in order to establish the accuracy of such theories.

Let us therefore formulate the hypothesis that the higher the income of a particular group of households, the higher will be the proportion of those households owning a car. Figure 2-1 shows data taken from the 1985 *Family Expenditure Survey* (*FES*), which is a comprehensive survey of consumer spending undertaken annually by central government. From Fig. 2-1 we can see that there is an evident relationship between the two variables, as our hypothesis suggested. Later we will be able to quantify relationships like this in precise statistical and mathematical terms. The development of such patently useful analytical techniques, however, is somewhat premature. First we need to examine the statistical principles which underpin such analysis.

This can be illustrated by assuming that we have been commissioned by a local authority to carry out a survey of income levels in a particular city. The local authority might be reviewing its policy of parking provision in different parts of the city or the provision of public transport facilities to different housing estates. Given the evident relationship in the *FES* data between income levels and levels of car ownership, let us assume that the authority has commissioned surveys into the income levels of its residents as a means of predicting car ownership levels. The purpose behind such surveys is to provide information to allow the local authority to prioritize between areas which need public transport facilities and areas which do not.

Let us further suppose that two such surveys have been undertaken: the first was taken in an inner-city area, and the second was taken of residents of a new, privately built development on the edge of the green belt. Income levels for 100 households in each area were recorded. (It should be noted that households can vary in size from those with just one member to those of large families, and that the number of incomes received by households can also vary markedly.) Table 2-1 shows gross weekly income (that is, income received by

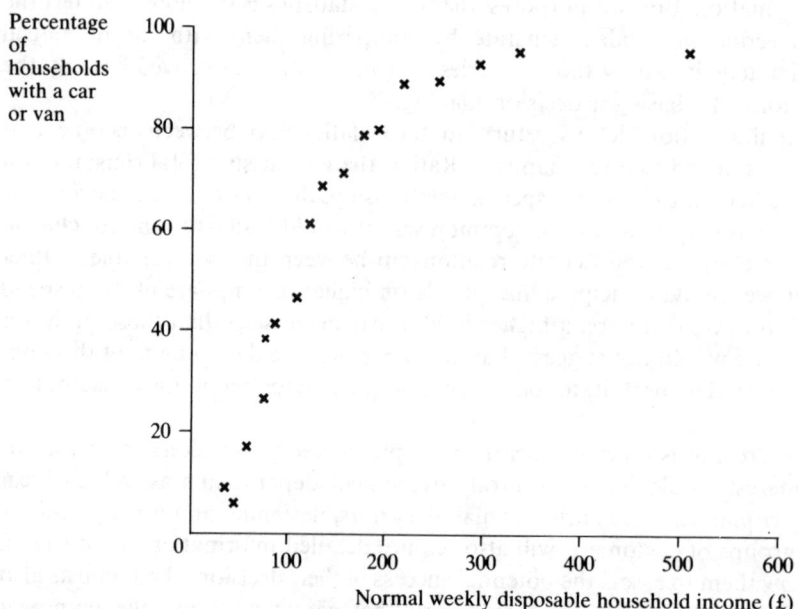

Figure 2-1 Income and car ownership, 1985 (*Source: Family Expenditure Survey*, 1985)

Table 2-1 Gross weekly household income, inner-city area (£)

200.00	57.60	53.60	63.60	388.40	199.62	100.29	252.42	27.60	24.00
340.82	26.80	40.80	61.60	139.62	160.71	184.82	134.40	151.62	104.86
24.00	158.00	54.40	111.20	231.61	172.71	71.20	173.22	62.40	62.41
166.82	311.60	52.40	172.00	226.82	69.50	219.21	106.41	52.81	153.58
140.82	257.60	59.20	98.80	234.82	96.55	101.22	243.61	52.00	25.61
161.62	59.20	101.20	73.62	55.21	58.77	164.82	66.80	150.82	48.80
137.22	94.40	35.20	38.40	97.21	137.93	136.00	65.61	40.41	23.60
223.22	21.20	268.40	37.20	187.62	124.02	130.82	33.60	122.82	145.43
190.42	26.00	98.80	78.80	92.41	104.81	154.00	155.62	52.41	215.38
176.82	38.00	45.60	128.40	258.41	78.81	95.61	66.81	103.21	148.42

Table 2-2 Gross weekly household income, suburban housing development (£)

243.20	257.60	255.60	387.60	272.80	202.40	274.03	318.84	294.84	450.96
212.80	237.60	272.40	251.60	169.20	280.80	372.45	293.24	261.23	470.15
313.60	207.20	338.40	264.40	200.80	368.00	159.62	263.63	340.84	270.45
331.60	212.00	264.40	124.00	316.40	257.60	249.23	269.23	348.85	286.04
281.60	331.20	199.20	171.60	316.80	215.60	146.42	250.83	389.65	226.08
240.03	271.63	361.25	394.05	296.84	381.25	201.49	407.78	325.62	301.64
250.66	380.79	221.88	275.25	289.64	522.92	432.36	434.15	542.71	489.93
274.03	314.44	361.25	333.24	354.04	376.29	203.33	319.64	396.85	268.83
358.00	314.05	391.65	274.83	346.04	318.44	222.43	296.84	372.05	270.03
221.23	340.85	228.43	360.05	346.84	287.24	284.04	224.03	366.05	204.82

the whole household unit before any deductions) for the (hypothetical) inner-city sample. Table 2-2 shows the equivalent data for the (likewise hypothetical) suburban development.

It is difficult to form an immediate impression from the data in the two tables. There is too much information for us to assimilate easily. To assertain the key features of this information we must reduce it to a more manageable form, and this can only be done by using the principles of statistics.

The ability to deal confidently and properly with information provided by statistical methods is clearly essential for two main purposes: to undertake practical research and investigation to try and determine whether a particular model and its supporting theory appear valid; and to evaluate the validity of other people's investigations and research which use mathematical and statistical techniques. This is not to imply that you need to become a statistician but rather than you must develop an adequate working knowledge to allow you to deal competently with information presented in this form. For the basic definition of statistics is *the analysis and interpretation of numerical information.* As you can appreciate from the definition there is a dual emphasis both upon *analysis* (that is, actually performing the calculations) and upon the *interpretation* of the results of the analysis. Increasingly, the analysis of statistical information is undertaken through the use of computers because a computer (if correctly programmed and used) will calculate statistics far faster and more accurately than a human being. Unfortunately, the computer will *not* be able to tell which statistical analysis is appropriate nor will it be able to assess the reliability and usefulness of the statistical information produced. This explains why we need to spend time illustrating the basic calculations which underpin these quantitative techniques. Even though you may rarely, in practice, need to resort to manual calculations, it is necessary to understand how these calculations are performed (either by you or by a computer) so as to be able to evaluate both the uses of such numerical information and its limitations.

2-2 BASIC VOCABULARY

As with economics there are a number of terms in statistics which have a specialized meaning and which need to be defined before we can progress.

In statistical teminology a *variable* is the specified characteristic in which we are interested. In the sample above, we have two variables, income and car ownership. Variables may take one of three general forms:

Discrete.   A variable is discrete if it can take only certain specific values (most often whole numbers). The variable on car ownership is discrete. A household may own one car, for example, or two or three. But it cannot own 1.5 cars or 4.6289 cars and so on.

Continuous.   A continuous variable is one which is not discrete! Effectively, a continuous variable is one which, in theory at least, can take *any* numerical value. So, for example, a person's height or weight is a continuous variable as we could measure the variable to any degree of accuracy. The fact that, very often, we may measure to the nearest whole number does not detract from the fact that the variable is technically a continuous one.

Attribute.   An attribute variable is a characteristic that is not normally expressed in numerical terms. So, for example, a person's sex or marital status is not measured in number form. It makes no sense to say that an individual is of sex 105 or 32.6. To perform statistical analysis on such variables we may need to assign to such variables arbitrary number values but such numbers have no meaning in themselves.

The term *data* refers to the information pertaining to a variable. *Raw* data are data in their original form (like Tables 2-1 and 2-2 above) where the individual numbers are available for analysis. *Aggregated* data relates to data which have, in some way, already been summarized. As we shall see, statistics calculated on raw data are more accurate, and more reliable, than those based on aggregated data. We must also distinguish between *secondary* data, which have been collected by someone other than the person using the information, and *primary* data, which have been obtained at first hand. It is not surprising that, when using secondary data, detailed information will be required on how and for what initial purposes the data were obtained, otherwise we shall be unsure whether the secondary data are suitable for the analysis we wish to undertake. The *FES* data, for example, are secondary data since they have been collected for purposes other than ours.

In statistical terms, a *population* does not necessarily have anything to do with people. It refers rather to the entire set of data that exists for some variable. So, returning to the study of household income and car ownership, the statistical population would refer to the incomes for *all* households. For obvious reasons—of time, cost and availability—

population data are rarely, if ever, available for analysis. Instead we must content ourselves with data on only a representative subset of the population, that is, data on a *sample*. The *FES* relates to sample information—around 7,000 households—from the several millions comprising the population. Naturally, we will need to ensure that the sample is properly representative of the population.

The techniques of *descriptive* statistics are, as the name implies, concerned with organizing and summarizing a set of data in order to describe its main features. *Inferential* statistics is concerned with using information derived from samples to predict the characteristics of the entire population. Again with reference to the *FES*, our real interest lies not in the behaviour of the sample of households but rather in what the sample can tell us about the behaviour of the population.

The rest of this chapter and Chapter 3 will be concerned with introducing basic descriptive statistical techniques, with starting the process of making elementary statistical inferences and with showing how such statistical techniques can be used by economists, business researchers and decision-makers. Wherever possible we will illustrate the basic principles behind the various techniques with reference to some real data set and the exercises at the end of the chapters will reinforce this. In some cases, however, the use of real data is inappropriate, either because data may be confidential or copyright or because real data sets contain a large set of numbers which become tedious to manipulate. In such cases we shall illustrate basic principles with reference to a fictional data set (like the one on sample incomes) which will be at once realistic and manageable. In addition, although we shall show how you can perform the various statistical computations yourself, you will be expected to utilize computer facilities to avoid the repetitive chore of manual calculations.

2-3 AGGREGATING DATA

The first step in the process of identifying the key features of a data set is to aggregate it, that is, to present the raw data, like that in Tables 2-1 and 2-2, in a more intelligible form. This is achieved by constructing a *frequency table*. The frequency table relating to the incomes of the 100 households from the inner city is shown in Table 2-3.

Table 2-3 Frequency table of gross weekly household income, inner-city area (£)

Interval	Frequency
Less than £50 per week	17
£50 but <£100	30
£100 but <£150	20
£150 but <£200	18
£200 but <£250	8
£250 but <£300	4
£300 but <£350	2
£350 but <£400	1
Total	100

The advantage of aggregating the raw data immediately becomes apparent. The frequency table, which simply aggregates the original income figures into broad groups, or intervals, allows us readily to observe the basic pattern of values in the data set. We can see, for example, that more households fall into the second income group, £50 but <£100, than into any other; the bulk of households are calculated in the first four intervals; progressively fewer and fewer households are to be found in the higher income intervals. In other words, the frequency table allows us to pick out the salient features from an otherwise confusing mass of information. But how do we set about constructing such a frequency table? The method is straightforward.

First, we find from the raw data the range of values with which we are dealing. In other words, we identify the minimum and maximum income to allow us to see the spread of incomes the table will have to include. Here, the minimum income is £21.20 and the maximum £388.40. Accordingly, the table must allow for a spread of approximately £400.

Second, we choose the number of intervals to be shown in the table. There is no hard and fast rule that can be applied here. We simply have to use whatever experience we have to produce a table which looks most appropriate for the data. It is conventional to have between 5 and 15 intervals in such a table with fewer intervals for small data sets than for large. With less than five intervals we would tend to find that important details about the data set have been lost in the aggregation process. Conversely, with a large number of intervals no obvious patterns in the data are apparent.

Third, we decide how large each interval should be. In Table 2-3 our intervals are all £50. Obviously this stage and the previous stage are interdependent and we must choose interval sizes and the number of intervals together. This will often be a process of experimentation until a suitable table has been constructed (which is one reason why the use of computer facilities is important). If possible we should choose intervals which are all the same width as this makes the table easier to read and comparison between intervals easier to make. However, it is not always possible, or desirable, to have equal classes and we shall see the effect of unequal classes later.

Fourth, we should ensure that the boundaries of the intervals are clear and unambiguous. In Table 2-3 the intervals are expressed so that there is no possible misunderstanding. A common mistake is to express intervals in the form: 50 to 100, 100 to 150, 150 to 200, 200 to 250 and so on. The problem with this approach is that when we come to construct the frequency table we are uncertain whether to place an observation of exactly 200 in the second category, 150 to 200, or in the third category, 200 to 250. More importantly, other users of your analysis will be unclear as to how you have grouped the data and will have little confidence in the rest of your analysis.

Last, we simply work through the data set, counting up the number of data items in each interval.

Table 2-4, a comparable frequency table for the data on the households in the suburban housing development, shows clear contrasts with the inner-city data. No one in the suburban development has an income of less than £100, whereas there are 47 such households in the inner-city area. Generally, the impression we get is that incomes are consistently higher in the suburban development than in the inner-city area. This is not too surprising as the former is a private development and householders will be owner-occupiers, having taken out mortgages to acquire their homes. In the inner-city area, on the other hand, we are likely to have a mixture of households—some owner-occupiers, others council

Table 2-4 Frequency table of gross weekly household income, suburban housing development (£)

Less than £50 per week	0
£50 but <£100	0
£100 but <£150	2
£150 but <£200	4
£200 but <£250	19
£250 but <£300	31
£300 but <£350	19
£350 but <£400	17
£400 but <£450	3
£450 but <£500	3
£500 but <£550	2
Total	100

tenants or students living in rented bedsits. In short, incomes in our sample of 100 inner-city households are *generally* lower than those among the 100 suburban households. This is, of course, consistent with there being a lower rate of car ownership in the inner city.

Frequency tables are useful in presenting a summary of the raw data. A graphical presentation of this summary can be even more useful, however, as it allows us to identify trends and patterns in the data even more easily. It is to this that we now turn.

2-4 HISTOGRAMS AND OGIVES

Figure 2-2 shows the histogram for the data in Table 2-3 with each bar or rectangle representing a particular interval and the height of each bar showing the frequency of that interval. As you can see, the histogram provides an immediate picture of the overall pattern of the variable. By comparing this with Fig. 2-3, which is the histogram for the data relating to the suburban housing development, we have a useful means of comparing data sets. The histogram for the inner city confirms that we have a considerable number of households at the lower end of the income scale, while that for the suburban area confirms our impression that incomes are generally higher and more evenly distributed.

Constructing a histogram is as straightforward as compiling a frequency table. The important point to remember is that we are trying to present a quick, visual summary of the data that can be interpreted easily and accurately. You will find that the construction of histograms has no hard and fast rules and that there are minor variations in terms of presentation. All are acceptable on the premise that they meet the primary purpose of presenting an accurate visual representation of the data set.

In general, there are only two aspects of histogram construction which, initially, may be problematical. The first of these relates to *open-ended* intervals. These are intervals which have no upper (or lower) limit specified. In Table 2-3 we have one such interval where we group incomes which are less than £50. We have not specified a lower limit to this interval. While this is not a problem in the frequency table it does cause a problem when drawing

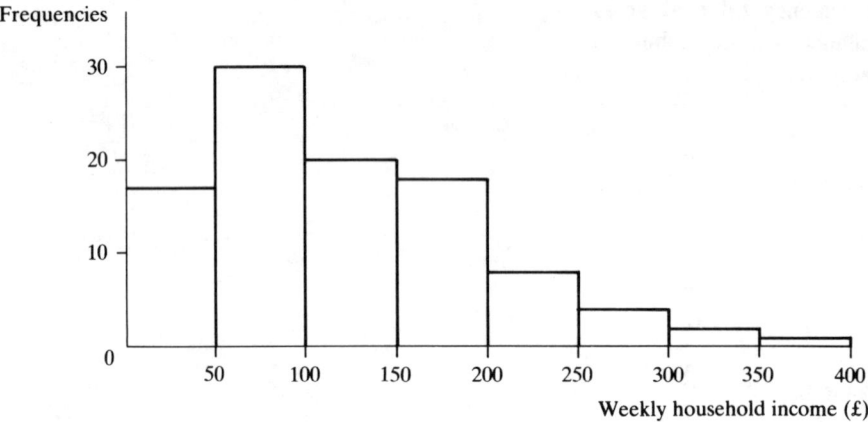

Figure 2-2 Histogram of income distribution, inner-city data set

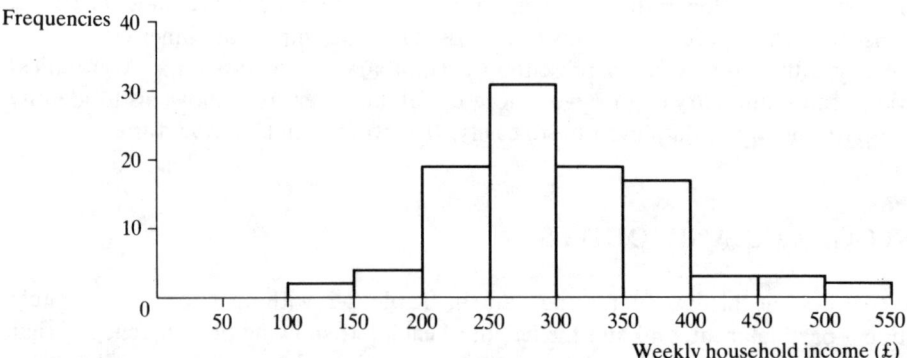

Figure 2-3 Histogram of income distribution, suburban area data set

the histogram as we do not know where to draw the lower limit for the appropriate bar in the diagram. This is frequently a problem if we are using secondary data and we have no access to the original data and, therefore, cannot determine the precise upper or lower limit. The simple solution is to choose an arbitrary, but realistic, limit. Here it would be logical to choose a lower limit of zero. This is a sensible choice for two reasons: common sense would indicate that we will not have any raw data observations falling below this value, and, conveniently, it gives us an interval which has the same width (£50) as all our other intervals.

The second aspect of histogram construction which may cause problems is that of *unequal* intervals. Readers may remember that we said earlier it was advisible to choose intervals that had the same width. This is because intervals of unequal width run the risk of giving a distorted view of the data distribution as the following simple example illustrates.

Table 2-5 Example of unequal classes

Interval	Frequency
100 but <200	50
200 but <300	30
300 but <400	20
Total	100

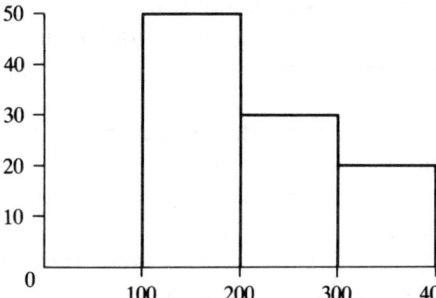

Figure 2-4 Interval adjustment, original frequencies

Table 2-5 shows a frequency table and Fig. 2-4 the associated histogram. There are three intervals of equal width and an obvious pattern in the data. But let us show the same data in different groupings. Table 2-6 shows the same frequencies but now the last two intervals have been grouped together into an interval which has twice the normal width. Figure 2-5 shows the histogram that we might, at first, construct for this frequency table.

Table 2-6 Example of unequal classes

Interval	Frequency
100 but <200	50
200 but <400	50
Total	100

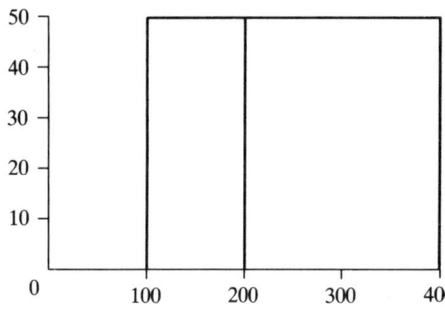

Figure 2-5 Interval adjustment, unadjusted frequencies

It is immediately apparent that Fig. 2-5 gives a distorted picture. This has occurred because we have made no allowance for the fact that our second interval is twice the usual width. We can make an appropriate adjustment with ease. What we are trying to show in a histogram is the *relative* frequency of each interval. If an interval is larger than usual we need to scale the *actual* frequency of that interval downwards to bring it into line with our standard interval width. Conversely, if an interval were smaller than usual we would scale the frequency upwards. We do this by ensuring that the area of each of the bars in the histogram is proportional to the frequency and interval width. The area is calculated simply by multiplying the height times the width. So in Table 2-7 the first interval has a frequency of 50 and a width of 100 and, therefore, an area of 5000. The second interval has the same frequency so it must have the same area. But now the interval width is 200 and we must adjust the height (frequency) to 25 to give an area of 5000. Figure 2-6 shows the histogram with the first interval having a frequency of 50 and the second, larger, interval with an adjusted frequency of 25. As you can see this produces a histogram which is somewhat fairer than Fig. 2-5. What we have done is to scale down the frequency of the unequal interval by a factor of two as the interval is twice the normal width. If the interval had been three times the normal width we would scale down the frequency by a factor of three and so on. Figure 2-6 is obviously still not as accurate a picture of the data as the original histogram, Fig. 2-4. This reinforces the point that, even though they are easy to adjust, it is better not to use unequal intervals given the choice.

Histograms may also be constructed to show relative, rather than absolute, frequencies, that is, percentages or proportions. This may be more useful if we wish to compare two or more data sets of different sizes. We might have one set of data with, say, 500 observations and another with 5000. Relative frequencies allow us to compare the two distributions directly.

It is also often useful to present the frequency table in a different way altogether, in the form of a diagram showing *cumulative* frequencies. This diagram is known as an *ogive*. Such a presentation is useful when we wish to ascertain the number of observations falling below or above a certain limit. For example, in our data set relating to weekly incomes we might wish to ascertain the number of households with an income, say, less than £100 per week. While this is easy to identify directly from the frequency table, there may be other values we are interested in, say, £90, which cannot easily be identified from Table 2-3. They can, however, be estimated from the ogive.

Table 2-7 shows both the frequencies and the cumulative frequencies, that is, the number of observations up to and including that interval. Although we can see that there

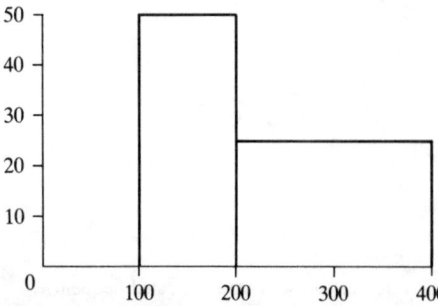

Figure 2-6 Interval adjustment, adjusted frequencies

Table 2-7 Cumulative frequency table of gross weekly household income, inner-city area (£)

Interval	Frequency	Cumulative frequency
Less than £50 per week	17	17
£50 but <£100	30	47
£100 but <£150	20	67
£150 but <£200	18	85
£200 but <£250	8	93
£250 but <£300	4	97
£300 but <£350	2	99
£350 but <£400	1	100
Total	100	

are 47 households on a weekly income of less than £100, the number of households on a weekly income of less than £90 is less obvious. But Fig. 2-7 shows the cumulative frequencies used to construct a histogram. On the diagram the ogive is shown by joining the endpoints of the intervals with straight lines and, in fact, this is the more usual way of showing the cumulative frequencies, as in Fig. 2-8. From the ogive we can estimate the number of observations falling below (or indeed above) a particular value. In this case we can see that there are approximately 43 households with a weekly income of less than £90.

Ogives may also be constructed for relative frequencies, in the same way as histograms. In such a case the ogive would show the percentage of observations falling below a specified value.

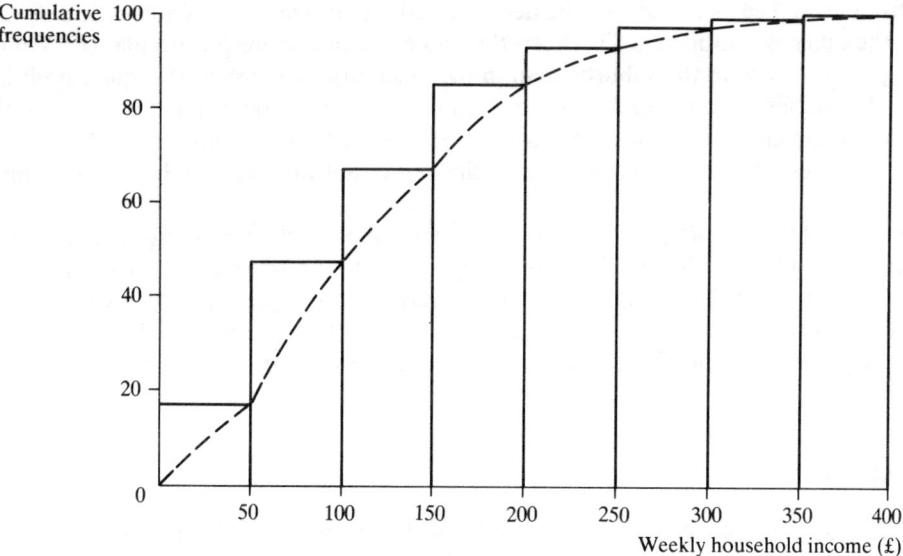

Figure 2-7 Cumulative frequencies and ogive: inner city data set

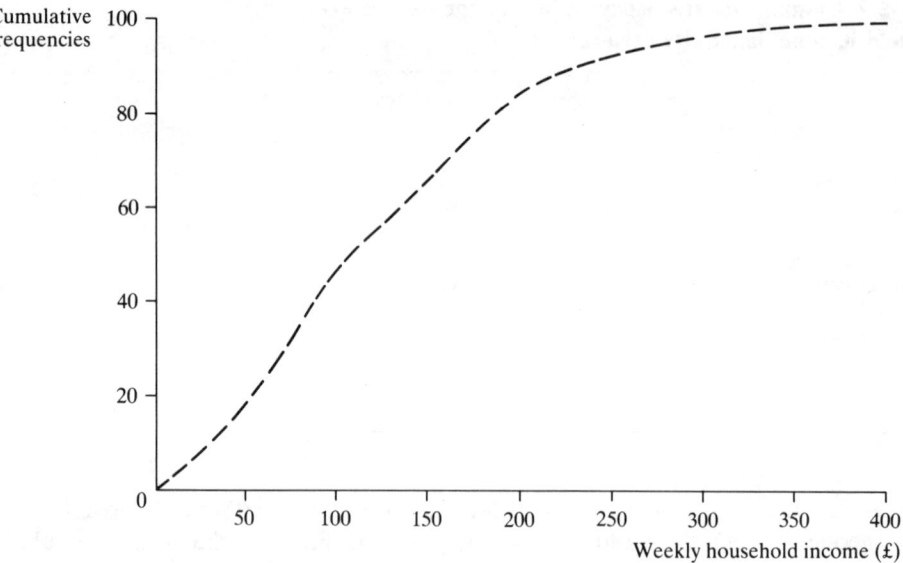

Figure 2-8 Ogive, inner city data set

2-5 CONCLUSION

Frequency tables, histograms and ogives are very useful means of ordering a mass of information into an intelligible form. By using them we were able to see that incomes in the suburban area tended to be higher than those in the inner city.

While this interpretation is undoubtedly correct, it is but an impression. As such, it is hardly likely to suffice as a basis for the decision-making. It would be useful to be able to *quantify* the difference in incomes between the two areas in a more precise manner. How much higher is income in the suburbs than in the inner city? To answer this question it is necessary to establish two major features of each data set: first, a description of the typical or average value; and second, a description of how the data varies around this average value. It is to these statistical means of describing a data set that we turn in the following chapter.

At the end of this chapter, and most of the other chapters in the text, there are a number of exercises intended to illustrate the major points introduced thus far. They are an important part of using this text in that, besides reinforcing the topics already covered, they also lead into some of the topics that are covered in the following sections. If you do not attempt these exercises, therefore, you are likely to miss out on important aspects of the subject.

2-6 SUMMARY

Descriptive statistics is concerned with quantifying the key features of a data set.

A *frequency table* shows the number of data items, either as numbers, percentages or as a cumulative total, that fall in a specified range of values.

A *histogram* is a diagrammatic representation of a frequency table.

Inferential statistics is concerned with formulating and testing hypotheses about the population based on sample data.

An *ogive* is a diagrammatic representation of the cumulative frequencies.

A *sample* is a part of some total set of data—the statistical *population*—selected to represent the population.

EXERCISES

1-1 Using the raw data set for the inner-city sample construct frequency tables and corresponding histograms by summarizing the data into:

(a) five intervals;
(b) fifteen intervals.

Compare your results with the frequency table and histogram used in the text. Which do you think is best?

2-2 Data from the 1985 *Family Expenditure Survey* are given below, showing normal weekly disposable household income for two groups in the survey: households in London and the South-East and households in the North (defined as Yorkshire and Humberside, the North-West and the North).

Normal weekly disposable household income	Number of households in The North	London and the South-East
Less than £40	94	92
£40 but <£50	107	77
£50 but <£65	103	98
£65 but <£100	225	213
£100 but <£150	276	323
£150 but <£200	260	311
£200 but <£250	174	269
£250 but <£300	96	204
£300 but <£350	60	157
£350 but <£400	31	84
£400 but <£450	16	55
£450 or more	18	90
Total	1460	1973

Construct suitable histograms and ogives for the two data sets.

(a) Ensure that you understand what is meant by 'normal disposable household income' in this context.
(b) What evidence is there, based on this data, of a 'North–South' divide? What factors can you suggest that might account for such differences?
(c) Do you think it right to conclude, based on this information, that people in London and the South-East are better off than those in the North? What other factors would you wish to take into account?

2-3 The data shown below are taken from the *Annual Abstract of Statistics* and show the distribution of total income before and after tax for the year ending 5 April 1985.

Income group	Number of tax units (thousands)	
	Before tax	After tax
Less than £2000	2 778	2 778
£2000 but <£3000	4 727	5 013
£3000 but <£4000	3 833	4 750
£4000 but <£5000	3 206	3 652
£5000 but <£6000	2 386	2 908
£6000 but <£7000	2 043	2 309
£7000 but <£8000	1 921	1 866
£8000 but <£9000	1 656	1 542
£9000 but <£10 000	1 329	1 351
£10 000 but <£12 500	2 752	2 381
£12 500 but <£15 000	1 792	1 354
£15 000 but <£17 500	1 084	632
£17 500 but <£20 000	662	349
£20 000 but <£25 000	601	309
£25 000 but <£30 000	286	116
£30 000 but <£35 000	130	48
£35 000 but <£40 000	71	22
£40 000 but <£50 000	77	19
£50 000 or more	81	17
Total	31 416	31 416

Source: Annual Abstract of Statistics.

Construct suitable histograms and ogives for these data and then answer the following questions.

(a) Why are open-ended intervals a problem when using this type of information? How would you resolve the problem for these data?

(b) Why are unequal intervals a problem when using this type of information? How would you resolve the problem for this data?

(c) Is it better to represent the data in terms of absolute frequencies or in percentage terms?

(d) Were you able to construct a 'reasonable' histogram for either of the two distributions? If not, what were the problems and how could they be resolved?

DESCRIPTIVE STATISTICS (II)

3-1 INTRODUCTION

In Chapter 2 we began to see how data could be used as evidence to support, or to falsify, a hypothesis—in our case that car ownership rates and income levels are related. Principles of descriptive statistics were used to process two hypothetical data sets. The results of this processing—frequency tables, histograms and ogives—showed that incomes in the inner-city were generally lower than incomes in the suburban area (with the inference that the associated rates of car ownership would also differ). This processing, however, is but the first stage. It would clearly be of use to be able to state in more exact terms the difference in income levels between the two samples. In other words, it would be helpful to establish the typical, or average, income in each data set. It would also be useful to know the extent to which such an average income was representative of the sample, that is, the extent to which incomes in the sample vary around the average. This chapter will be devoted, therefore, to examining these two important features of a data set: measures of average and measures of variation.

3-2 AVERAGES

There are three common measures of average—or *central tendency* as statisticians refer to them. These are the *arithmetic mean*, the *median* and the *mode*. We shall look at each in turn.

Arithmetic mean

Besides being the most common, and potentially most useful, measure of average, the arithmetic mean is also the most familiar. Whether you use the name or not, it is a measure of average which you will already have used. By definition, the mean of a data set is simply the sum of all the values divided by the number of observations. In our example of weekly incomes, to calculate the arithmetic mean of the raw data, we would simply add together the observations we have for income and divide by 100, the number of observations in the set. For the inner-city data, the statistic is calculated as follows:

$$\frac{\text{Total of values}}{\text{Number of values}} = \frac{£12\,025.26}{100} = £120.25$$

That is, the mean income for those households in the inner-city area is £120.25 per week. In general, the formula for calculating the arithmetic mean is:

$$\bar{X} = \frac{\sum X}{n}$$

where X refers to the values and n to the number of values. The symbol $\sum$ is one which we shall encounter frequently. It is known as a 'mathematical operator' and is simply a shorthand way of describing a common calculation. The symbol is referred to as 'sigma' and simply means 'the sum of'. So, the arithmetic mean is the sum of the X values divided by n.

In the example above we used the *raw* data to calculate the mean. Frequently, data available for analysis are already aggregated (as in the exercises in Chapter 2). We are still able to calculate the mean value, however, though the method of calculation differs as we can no longer sum the individual data values. The reason for this becomes apparent if we examine Table 3-1. This shows the frequency table for the data set we have been analysing. The difficulty in calculating the mean from these data arises because we need to add the values (incomes) together. The problem is that we no longer know what the individual values are because they have been grouped. We know, for example, that there are 30 households with an income of between £50 and £99.99, but we do not know *precisely* how much each household's income is. To resolve the problem we make a simplifying assumption: that all households in a particular interval have the same income and that this income is in the middle of the interval (referred to as the midpoint). So, for the second

Table 3-1 Calculation of mean for grouped data

Gross weekly household income (£)

Interval	Midpoint	Frequency	Frequency × midpoint
	X'	f	fX'
0 but <50	25	17	425
50 but <100	75	30	2 250
100 but <150	125	20	2 500
150 but <200	175	18	3 150
200 but <250	225	8	1 800
250 but <300	275	4	1 100
300 but <350	325	2	650
350 but <400	375	1	375
Total		100	12 250

interval in the table we assume that all 30 households have an income of £75. The arithmetic mean can now be calculated, as before, by adding all the values together and dividing by the number of values. Denoting the mean by $\bar{X}$, this can be simplified to:

$$\bar{X} = \frac{\sum fX'}{n}$$

where X' now refers to the midpoint of each interval and f to the frequency of each interval. The term $\sum fX'$ is simply the total of the values in a particular interval, assuming they all have the midpoint value. Table 3-1 shows the appropriate calculations. Here, the mean is calculated as:

$$\bar{X} = \frac{£12\,250}{100} = £122.50$$

As can be seen, the mean on the basis of the grouped data gives a slightly different value from that based on the raw data. This is hardly surprising as we had to make a simplifying assumption about values within each interval in order to be able to calculate this average. It is apparent that the mean calculated from the raw data will be more accurate than that calculated from grouped data and if only grouped data are available we should use the grouped mean *with caution*. An additional point about the grouped mean is that it will be influenced by the intervals, and therefore the midpoints, that have been chosen. A different choice of intervals will tend to lead to a slightly different mean value.

The arithmetic mean is easy to interpret. It represents an *average* income in the sense that it would be the income that each household would receive if incomes were shared out equally. Unfortunately, the mean may not always give a realistic picture of the values in the data set. That is, it may not reflect the *typical* income level. For example, suppose we have a simple data set of 11 observations, representing the annual incomes of the employees of a small business:

3500   4000   4500   5000   5500   6000   6500   7000   7500   8000   25 000

The mean for this data set would be:

$$\frac{£82\,500}{11} = £7500$$

However, as we can see, this average value is by no means representative. Only one person, in fact, actually earns an income of £7500. Indeed, only two observations lie above the mean, with the other eight observations falling below the average. It is obvious that the mean has been distorted by the one extremely high value. For this reason it is often useful to have an alternative statistic to the mean to represent the average.

Median

The median is an average in the sense that it is the *middle* value in the ordered data set: a value such that there is an equal number of values above the median and below it. Unlike the mean, the median always splits the ordered set of data into two equal parts. In the case of the salaries of the 11 employees, the median salary is the sixth—there are five below it and five above it. The data set is already ordered from low to high so we can simply count along until we get to item 6, which has a value of £6000. This is the median value. In general, if there are n ordered values, then the median value is the $\frac{1}{2}(n + 1)$th value.

We could calculate the median for our major data set, relating to gross weekly incomes, in the same way. Given that there are 100 observations it would obviously take a little longer if we were to sort the data manually, so you are advised to use a computer package to confirm that the median for the raw data is £102.22. That is, half of the group have a weekly income less than this value and half have an income more than this. If we were to calculate the median manually we would have to make a slight alteration to our method of identifying the median item. By the method just established, if $n = 100$ then $\frac{1}{2}(n + 1) = 50.5$, which is not a whole number. In this case we must find *two* central items: the $\frac{1}{2}n$th and the $(\frac{1}{2}n + 1)$th. Here, the two central items are items 50 and 51. The median value will then be the mean of these two items. This value will then divide the data into two equal parts.

We do not, however, always have access to the raw data and we may need to calculate the median for grouped data. Again, we must remember that in such a case the value we obtain will only be an estimate of the true median value. Let us calculate the median for the data on gross weekly household income, shown previously in Table 2-7.

First, we must identify the interval in which the median item falls. Remembering that the median item will be item 50.5 we can see from the cumulative frequencies that this will fall in the interval £100 < £150. We know, therefore, that the median item is one of the 20 values falling in this interval but we do not know which one. Without the raw data we have no way of knowing and, as with the grouped mean, we must make a simplifying assumption as to how the data within this interval are distributed. It is conventional to make the same assumption as we did for the mean but expressed in a different way. We assume that the 20 values occurring in the interval are spread equally over the width of the interval. That is, they are spaced an equal distance apart over the £50 that the interval covers. It follows that each value is £2.50 (that is, £50/20) away from its neighbours within the interval. Since we are looking for item number 50.5 and since there are 47 items up to the start of this interval, it is clear that item 50.5 will be 3.5 items from the start of the interval. Each value we assume to be £2.50 apart so the median item will have a value of £108.75: £100 + (3.5 × £2.50). Denoting the median by M, we can simplify the procedure into a formula:

$$M = LCV + (I - CF) \times \frac{W}{F}$$

where LCV is the lower class limit of the median interval; I is the value of $\frac{1}{2}(n + 1)$; CF is the cumulative frequency up to the median interval; W is the width of the median interval; and F is the frequency of the median interval. For our data set we would have:

$$M = 100 + (50.5 - 47) \times \frac{50}{20}$$

$$= 100 + (3.5 \times 2.50) = 108.75$$

As with the mean there is a slight difference between the median for the grouped data and that for the raw data.

A comparison of the mean and median for the inner-city sample shows that the mean income is approximately £20 above the median income. It is apparent that a small number of higher incomes in the sample have pulled the mean above the median income. These high incomes are included in the calculation for the mean but not in that for the median. Indeed, we can often compare the mean and median for a data set to provide information about the distribution of the data within the data set.

Mode

This third measure of central tendency is the mode. Though employed relatively infrequently, it is nevertheless a useful measure of central tendency particularly when dealing with discrete variables. The mode is simply the value that occurs most frequently in a data set. To illustrate its potential we can envisage the situation where the construction company responsible for developing the suburban housing estate needed to ensure that the houses it planned to build would meet the requirements of its customers. One decision the company would have to take would relate to garage space. Should it build houses with single or double garages as standard? To assist the company in its decision-making market research could have been undertaken to identify the average number of cars per family among its potential customers. It can be seen that the arithmetic mean would be of little use for this purpose as we have seen that it may well be unrepresentative. The median, similarly, would only indicate that an equal number of households occurred either side of the median value. The mode, however, the most frequent value would indicate the 'typical' number of cars per family in the sense that this number of cars will occur more than any other. If we were dealing with a continuous variable like income then the mode would be of little use, given the large variety of individual values that can occur for a continuous variable.

3-3 CHOOSING A MEASURE OF AVERAGE

A frequent question asked by students at this stage is: which measure of average should I use? The answer, as always, is that it depends. All three have their particular uses and disadvantages, and the only effective answer is to consider carefully which characteristic of the data set you are interested in describing.

The mean is the most common statistic if only because it is the only one which uses all the data in its calculation, and this is essential if we are to undertake further analysis on the full set of data. The mean, however, is easily distorted by relatively few extreme values. The median, by contrast, is more stable in this context and, at this stage, provides more information about the spread of values in the data set. The mode, finally, tends to be useful for discrete variables.

By calculating and comparing these different measures of average we are often able to highlight key features of the data set and compare one data set with another. Useful though an average is, it does not provides a full description of the data set under investigation. For example, returning to the data set on gross weekly household incomes, we know that mean income is £120.25. Without the raw data or the frequency table, however, such a statistic reveals little about the distribution of the data. We would not know, for example, from this statistic whether all 100 households receive this weekly income or whether 99 out of the hundred earn less than this, with one extremely high income, perhaps from a millionaire, pulling the average above the bulk of the data. In other words, we would have no idea of the *variability* of the data around the average. It is to this area of descriptive statistics that we now turn.

3-4 VARIABILITY

There are two basic measures of variability that can be used to give an indication of the *spread* (or *dispersion*) of the data values around the average. The first relates to dispersion around the mean and the second to dispersion around the median.

Standard deviation

The standard deviation is the measure of dispersion most frequently used. It measures dispersion around the arithmetic mean. Let us return to the data set in Table 3-2 which related to 11 values of gross annual salary. In looking for a statistic which measures the spread of data around the mean, the first logical step would be to calculate the deviations from the mean: the amount by which each value in the data set differs from the average. If we denote the mean with the symbol $\bar{X}$, the deviations will be $(X - \bar{X})$, and these are shown in Table 3-2. These simple differences—deviations from the mean—indicate the dispersion of the data from the average. As can be seen, the further away from the mean value lies the larger the deviation. It might initially appear logical, given that we are interested in measuring variability for the total data set, to sum these deviations. If we were to do this, however, we would invariably find that the sum of these deviations equals zero! This must be the case because the positive deviations from *above*-average values would always be cancelled by the negative deviations of the *below*-average values. This difficulty is easily resolved. In fact, we are not interested in whether a particular value is above or below the mean (that is, whether it is plus or minus) but rather *how far away* from the mean it is. In this example, we would not distinguish between £7000 and £8000 as both are the same distance away from the mean. Thus an easy way round the difficulty is simply to *square* the individual deviations (remembering that the square of a negative number will give a positive number). These squared deviations are also shown in Table 3-2.

Table 3-2 Gross annual salary, deviations from mean

X	$\bar{X}$	$X - \bar{X}$	$(X - \bar{X})^2$
3 500	7 500	−4 000	16 000 000
4 000	7 500	−3 500	12 250 000
4 500	7 500	−3 000	9 000 000
5 000	7 500	−2 500	6 250 000
5 500	7 500	−2 000	4 000 000
6 000	7 500	−1 500	2 250 000
6 500	7 500	−1 000	1 000 000
7 000	7 500	−500	250 000
7 500	7 500	0	0
8 000	7 500	500	250 000
25 000	7 500	17 500	306 250 000
Total		0	357 500 000

We can now find the average of these squared deviations by dividing by the number of values, 11, to give 32 500 000.00. This number is known as the *variance*, and is expressed in units of £-squared. To derive a statistic in our original units of measurement we can simply take the square root of the variance to give £5 700.88. This is the standard deviation (denoted s): a statistic measuring average dispersion of the data around the mean. The formula we have derived can be expressed as:

$$s = \sqrt{\frac{\Sigma(X - \bar{X})^2}{n}}$$

How can this statistic be interpreted? It indicates the spread of data around the mean and, other things being equal, a larger value for the standard deviation implies more dispersion. You should be able to see that the lowest value that the standard deviation could ever take would be zero, implying that all values in the data set took the mean value (that is, there were no deviations from the mean). Larger values for the standard deviation, therefore, imply more variability around the mean: a greater difference between the average and the individual items in the data set.

As with the mean and median there are frequent occasions when we wish to compute the standard deviation for grouped, rather than raw, data. Again, we have to amend the basic formula even though the principle and interpretation of the statistic remain the same. The approach taken to calculating the standard deviation for grouped data uses the *midpoint* values to estimate the individual values falling in a particular interval. The formula used is:

$$s = \sqrt{\frac{\Sigma f X'^2}{\Sigma f} - \left(\frac{\Sigma f X'}{\Sigma f}\right)^2}$$

For the data set on household incomes for the inner-city sample, we need the figures calculated in Tables 3-1 and 3-3, and the standard deviation is calculated as follows:

$$s = \sqrt{\frac{2\ 102\ 500}{100} - \left(\frac{12\ 250}{100}\right)^2} = \sqrt{21\ 025 - 15\ 006.25} = £77.58$$

Table 3-3 Calculation of standard deviation for grouped data

Gross weekly household income (£)

Interval	X'	X'^2	Frequency f	Frequency $\times$ (midpoint)^2 fX'^2
0 but <50	25	625	17	10 625
50 but <100	75	5 625	30	168 750
100 but <150	125	15 625	20	312 500
150 but <200	175	30 625	18	551 250
200 but <250	225	50 625	8	405 000
250 but <300	275	75 625	4	302 500
300 but <350	325	105 625	2	211 250
350 but <400	375	140 625	1	140 625
Total			100	2 102 500

Readers who have been following these calculations for the standard deviations using an appropriate computer package may have realized by now that the answers given here for the standard deviations in the two examples differ slightly from those given in a package. In the case of the second example of grouped data the package accompanying this text would compute the standard deviation as £77.97. This is not a large difference, you will admit, but why should there be a difference at all? The data we have analysed—and most data that we will analyse—are *sample* data rather than data referring to the statistical population. In such a case, for reasons that can only be explained in formal mathematical terms, we must use the term $n - 1$ (or its equivalent $f - 1$) rather than n or f when calculating the standard deviation either for raw or grouped data. Most computer packages will do this automatically.

We are now in a position to begin comparing our two data sets, for the inner-city area and for the suburban area, using these statistics. At this point you may wish to calculate for yourself the equivalent statistics—the mean, the median and standard deviation—for the data set relating to income of households in the suburban housing development before reading the subsequent section of this chapter.

The statistics for the two data sets are shown below. In both cases, the statistics have been calculated for the grouped data sets.

	Inner-city area (£)	Suburban area (£)
Mean income	122.50	300.50
Median income	108.75	291.13
Standard deviation	77.97	77.69

Using either of our measures of average we can see that average income is considerably lower in the inner-city area than in the suburban area. We can also see that in both areas there are some households with an income considerably higher than the average. This is indicated by the mean taking a higher value than the median. We have also seen, however, that an average by itself may be misleading and we would also want to compare dispersion in the two data sets. At first sight, using the standard deviations, it appears that both areas have more or less the same dispersion of income about the mean. In general, however, standard deviations for different data sets cannot be compared directly as the two statistics will measure dispersion around their respective, and different, means. In order to compare dispersion using standard deviations we use instead a statistic known as the *coefficient of variation* (V) which is simply:

$$V\% = \frac{\text{standard deviation}}{\text{mean}} \times 100$$

Other things being equal, a higher CV implies more variability. For the inner-city data set the CV is 64 per cent and for the suburban area 26 per cent. This indicates that, in relative terms, there is a greater variability of incomes in the inner-city than in the suburban area. This is not too surprising, as we might expect a more homogeneous group of households on a new suburban housing development—with most in similar income groups—whereas, in the inner-city area, we might reasonably expect much more variation in the type of households and their income. This implies, of course, that it is much more difficult to speak accurately of an average income for such a diverse group.

Interquartile range

We saw earlier that the mean is not always the most appropriate measure of average: we may prefer to use the median as an alternative. In this case the standard deviation would obviously be inappropriate as the measure of dispersion. Instead we use the *interquartile range* to indicate variability around the median. The median, you will remember, divides the distribution into two equal parts. To calculate the interquartile range we identify two additional points in the distribution: the *lower quartile* (Q_L) which divides the distribution so that 25 per cent of observations fall below this value and 75 per cent above it; and the *upper quartile* (Q_U) which divides the distribution so that 75 per cent of observations fall below this value and 25 per cent above it. The interquartile range is then simply the difference between the upper and lower quartiles, as illustrated in Fig. 3-1. It can be seen that the interquartile range always covers the central 50 per cent of a distribution. The quartiles, and hence the interquartile range, are calculated using the same approach as was taken in calculating the median. The formula that was used to find the median is amended as we are now looking for item $n/4$ for the lower quartile and item $3n/4$ for the upper quartile. (Remember that we add 1 to n for even data sets.) Returning to the two data sets the lower quartile can be calculated as follows:

	Inner-city area (£)	Suburban area (£)
Lower quartile	63.75	250.40
Median	108.75	291.13
Upper quartile	174.31	352.21

Interpretation is straightforward. In the inner-city area, a quarter of the group have a weekly income less than £63.75 while a quarter have an income above £174.31. The central 50 per cent of the group have an income between these two figures, and the range separating the top quarter from the bottom quarter is (£174.31 − £63.75) = £110.56. In the suburban

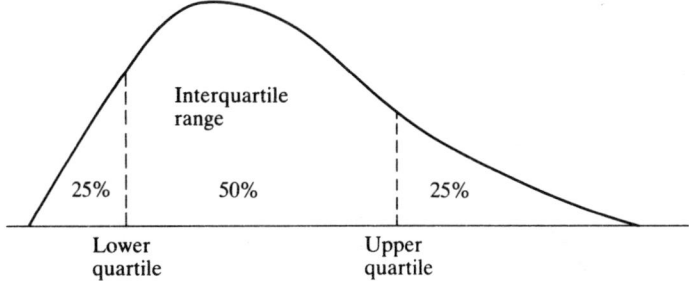

Figure 3-1 Interquartile range

area, the quartiles are considerably different. The lower quartiles indicate that 25 per cent of households have an income of less than £250.40. Compare this with the *upper* quartile for the inner-city area of £174.31 and we again confirm that incomes generally are higher in the suburban area. The corresponding interquartile range is (£352.21 − £250.40) = £101.81 which supports the result we obtained using the coefficient of variation that relative dispersion is higher in the inner-city area.

3-5 SKEWNESS

Notice that the median will not necessarily lie mid-way between the two quartiles. Its position will effectively be determined by the shape of the distribution, in statistical terms referred to as the *skewness* of the distribution. To measure skewness an additional statistic can be calculated: *Pearson's coefficient of skewness* (Sk).

$$Sk = \frac{3(\bar{X} - M)}{s}$$

This statistic provides a quick indication of the distortion in the distribution without the need for histograms or frequency tables. As we have seen, the mean and median for a data set may well be different. The difference will be largely due to extreme values at one end of the distribution. Extremely high values, included in the mean but not in the median, will pull the mean higher than the median, that is, away to the right as illustrated in Fig. 3-2. In such a case the skewness coefficient will be positive: hence this type of distribution is known as *positive skew*. The more extreme the higher values the larger the skewness coefficient will become. On the other hand a distribution with extremely low values will have the mean lower than the median giving a *negative skew*, as in Fig. 3-3. A symmetrical distribution, as in Fig. 3-4, however, will have a zero skew, with the mean and median equal.

The skewness coefficient for the inner-city data set we have been analysing can be calculated for the grouped data as +0.53 and for the suburban area as +0.36. Both areas have income distributions that are positively skewed although this skewness is more pronounced in the inner city. That is, both areas have a few high-income households stretching the income distribution to the right.

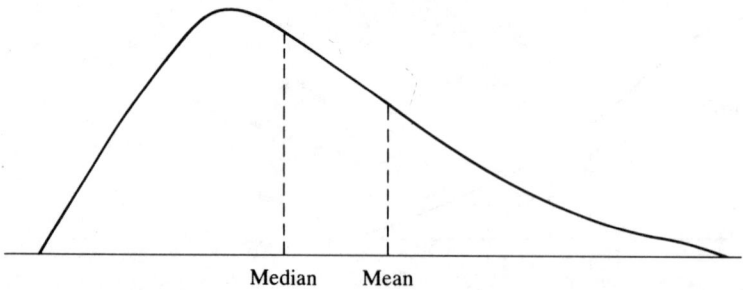

Median   Mean

Figure 3-2 Skewness: positive skew

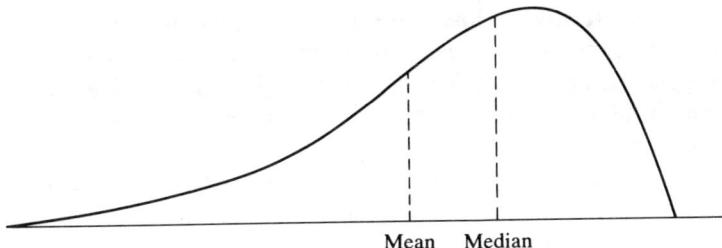

Mean   Median

Figure 3-3 Skewness: negative skew

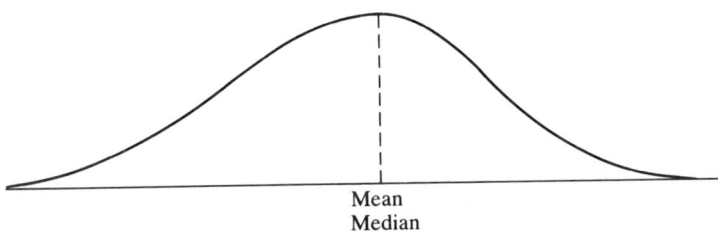

Mean
Median

Figure 3-4 Skewness: zero skew

3-6 CONCLUSION

In Chapter 2 we saw that there appeared to be a link between rates of car ownership and income levels. As part of our investigation into this relationship we hypothesized that higher incomes, other things being equal, would tend to lead to higher rates of car ownership. To this end we have examined incomes in two different samples to determine by how much income levels differed. Chapter 3 showed that there are three common statistical measures that can be used to determine average income. The economist or decision-maker will need to exercise considerable judgement in choosing which measure of average to use. The selection may be based on the measure that most closely corresponds to the underlying economic hypothesis or theory. In this case, the choice may well be the median, as this shows the income of the 'middle' household in each area. The mean income, by contrast, can easily be influenced by a few extreme values. For example, the inclusion of a millionaire in one sample is hardly likely to alter the rate of car ownership in the area but would affect the mean income value dramatically.

If the local authority were to put such statistics to use it would be able to estimate car ownership in a particular area from the average income (see Fig. 2-1). We have calculated the mean income of households in the inner area as £122.50. From Fig. 2-1 we can estimate that the corresponding car ownership figure will be approximately 60 per cent. In the suburban area, by comparison, with a mean income of £300.50 we would expect car ownership to be about 94 per cent.

The measures of variation that were introduced in this chapter showed that whichever measure of average was chosen it should be used and interpreted *with caution*. In the suburban sample the statistics reveal that we had a relatively homogeneous group of households with incomes grouped relatively closely around the average. In the inner-city area, by contrast, households are far more heterogeneous and measures of variation around the average income much higher. It becomes, therefore, far more difficult to talk about an 'average', or typical, income in the inner city and, accordingly, more difficult to infer the probable levels of car ownership.

As we have illustrated in this chapter, basic statistical measures are easy to calculate and understand. As we have also shown, their use requires considerable judgement on the part of the economist. Such statistical measures are extremely common in business decision-making and an adequate grasp of such statistics can only be acquired through sufficient practice. To this end the following exercises should, once again, be seen as an integral part of the text.

3-7 SUMMARY

The *coefficient of variation* is a measure of relative dispersion expressing the standard deviation as a percentage of the arithmetic mean.

The *interquartile range* measures dispersion around the median value and is the difference between the upper and lower quartiles.

The (arithmetic) *mean* is the average value in a data set found by dividing the sum of all the values by the number of values.

The *median* is the value in the middle of a data set when the data are arranged in numerical order.

The *mode* is the most frequently occurring value in the data set.

The *quartiles* (the lower quartile, the median and the upper quartile) divide a data set into four equal parts.

Skewness is an indication of the symmetry (or lack of it) of a distribution.

The *standard deviation* measures dispersion around the arithmetic mean.

EXERCISES

The exercises for this chapter are largely based on the end-of-chapter problems of the previous chapter.

3-1 In Exercise 2-1 you were required to construct different frequency tables for the inner-city data set. For each of these tables determine the mean, standard deviation, median and interquartile range. Compare these with the same statistics calculated for the raw data set. What effects does the choice of intervals in your frequency table have on the accuracy of the statistics? How do you explain this?

3-2 Assume that a new household has arrived in the inner-city area on which we based our sample. The household comprises a married couple who have refurbished a penthouse flat in the area. Both work as company executives and their weekly household income is £750. Add this observation to the raw data set and recalculate the statistics. What effect has this had on the two measures of average and the two measures of dispersion? How do you explain these differing effects?

3-3 For the *FES* data on incomes for households in the North you were required to determine an upper limit for the last open-ended interval in the data set. Use the following upper limits and determine the effects each new limit has on the appropriate statistics:

(a) an upper limit of £500;
(b) an upper limit of £600;
(c) an upper limit of £750.

3-4 For the data on incomes before and after tax answer the following questions:

(a) what is the average amount of tax paid?
(b) assess the tax paid by someone on the lower quartile income, the mean income, the median income, the upper quartile income;
(c) The UK income tax system is often described as 'progressive'. Find out what this means and, using the statistics calculated, determine whether you agree that it is.

4

BASIC MATHEMATICS:
LINEAR GRAPHS AND EQUATIONS

4-1 INTRODUCTION

Chapters 2 and 3 have provided an introduction to the basic *statistical* concepts and techniques that are essential when using economics. In this chapter we shall introduce some of the fundamental *mathematics* that will be required. Mathematics offers the economist a system of analysis through which large-scale economic problems can be resolved and a student of economics needs to be fully conversant with these techniques and to be confident when using numerical information derived from such techniques.

In the previous chapters we examined data relating to income and levels of car ownership. It would clearly be useful not only to be able to describe but also to *quantify* economic relationships such as this. That is, to be able to establish the precise mathematical relationship between the two variables. If we considered, for example, that average income is likely to rise by, say, 10 per cent we would be interested in being able to predict the subsequent change in the rate of car ownership. This can only be achieved using the techniques of mathematics which we will now examine. To illustrate the fundamental principles of the appropriate mathematics we will use data relating to two variables: the number of new registrations of cars, measured in thousands and expressed as an annual average of the monthly figures; and the level of personal disposable income measured in pounds. This is expressed in real terms (i.e. with inflationary effects removed) and in *per capita* terms. Data for both variables are taken from the *Economic Trends Annual Supplement* and cover the period 1956–85.

4-2 FUNCTIONS

The first step is to express the relationship between the two variables in mathematical form:

$$\text{Cars} = f(\text{PDI})$$

where Cars is the number of new car registrations and PDI is *per capita* personal disposable income. The term $f(\ )$—'a function of'—is the symbolic way of expressing a functional relationship between two or more variables. In economics the concept of a functional relationship between variables implies some sort of dependency or causal relationship. Here, in expressing the relationship in this way we are suggesting that the level of income in some way determines or 'causes' the level of consumption. Again, in terms of mathematical notation, Cars would be referred to as the *dependent* variable and PDI as the *independent* or *explanatory* variable. Other simple examples of such relationships would be:

$$\text{Costs} = f(\text{Production})$$
$$\text{Quantity demanded} = f(\text{Price})$$
$$\text{Quantity supplied} = f(\text{Price})$$
$$\text{Employment} = f(\text{Output})$$

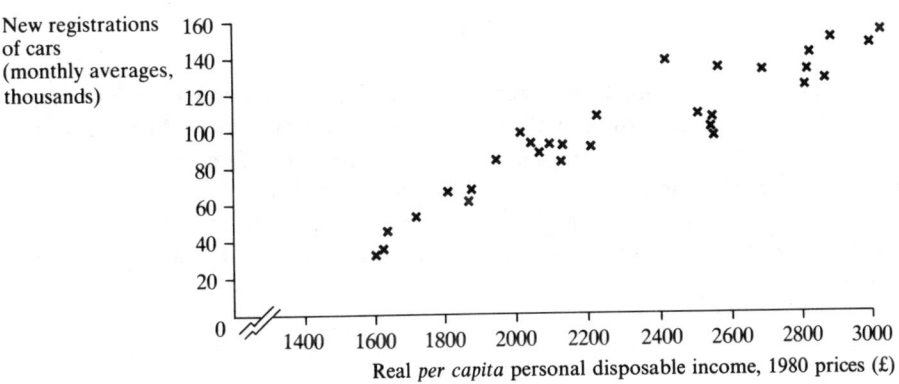

Figure 4-1 Scatter plot of new car registrations versus *per capita* income, 1956–85 (*Source: Economic Trends Annual Supplement*)

The data for the two variables Cars and PDI are shown in Fig. 4.1. We see that there is a strong and evident relationship between the two variables with the number of new registrations increasing as PDI increases. Using regression techniques, which we will examine later in the text, we are able to quantify mathematically the relationship between income and car registrations as:

$$\text{Cars} = -67 + 0.073\text{PDI}$$

We shall now examine this mathematical relationship in detail.

4-3 GRAPHS OF LINEAR FUNCTIONS

This information can also be presented visually in the form of a graph (Fig. 4-2). The graph shows the precise relationship between the two variables and both the graph and the

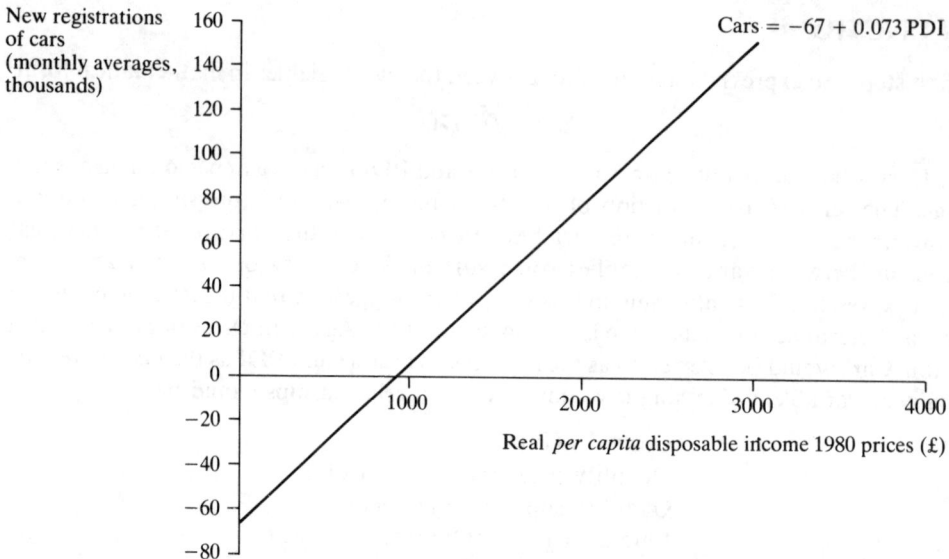

Figure 4-2 Graph of new car registrations versus *per capita* income

equation can be used to predict the level of car registrations at any income level. The graph and equation, in other words, show exactly the same information, but in different forms. Graphical analysis is extremely common in economics and you should ensure that you fully understand the information provided in Fig. 4-2 before proceeding.

In general, any graph comprises four differing areas, or quadrants, as shown in Fig. 4-3. The two axes of this graph intersect at the origin, at which point both scales take a zero

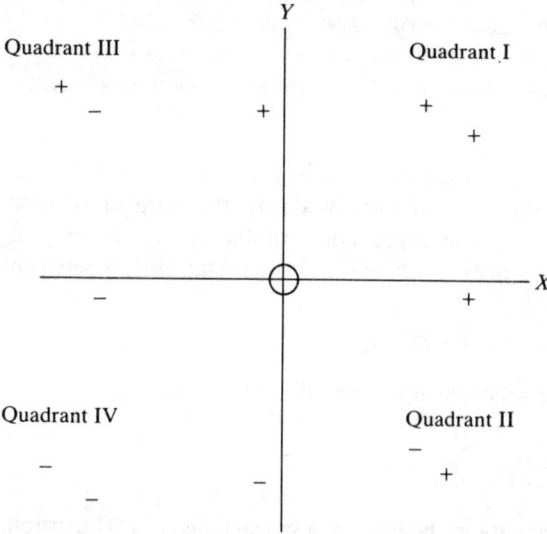

Figure 4-3 The quadrants of a graph

value. By convention the scale on the vertical axis takes positive values above the origin and negative values below while the horizontal axis takes positive values to the right of the origin and negative values to the left. The four quadrants, therefore, are associated with different combinations of values for the two axes. In Quadrant I both axes take positive values, while in Quadrant IV both take negative values. Quadrants II and III, on the other hand, have one axis taking positive values with the other taking negative. Quadrant II has the vertical axis with negative values and Quadrant III the horizontal axis. In economic analysis we are generally (but not always) performing analysis in Quadrant I with both variables positive.

Again by convention, the dependent variable is placed on the vertical axis and the independent variable on the horizontal.

4-4 LINEAR EQUATIONS

You will have realized from Fig. 4-2 that the graph represents the relationship between the two variables as a straight line. Such a relationship, and the equation associated with it, is known as a *linear* function. This type of function is popular with economists and in economic models because it has a number of features which are useful in terms of economic analysis (though linear functions are not always realistic representations of economic behaviour, as we shall see later). In general mathematical form a linear equation can be expressed as:

$$Y = a + bX$$

where Y is the dependent variable, X is the independent variable and a and b are the *parameters* of the equation: the specific numbers that give the linear function its precise shape and form. In our example, Y would represent the level of new car registrations and X PDI, while a takes the value -67 and b the value $+0.073$. The two parameters are also referred to as the *constant* or *intercept* and the *slope* or *gradient*, respectively.

The constant or intercept

Let us look in more detail at the general features of this linear expression, starting with the a parameter. It is apparent that the number -67 in the equation represents the value that Cars will take when PDI is set to zero:

$$\begin{aligned} \text{Cars} &= -67 + 0.073 \text{ PDI} \\ &= -67 + 0.073(0) \\ &= -67 \end{aligned}$$

In the economic context this value for a represents the level of car registrations when income is zero. In other words, the equation states that -67 (thousand) new car registrations will take place when real per capita personal disposable income is zero. At first sight this may seem difficult to understand as we might expect zero registrations at zero income. We can, however, rationalize this value readily on economic grounds.

From Fig. 4-2 we can see that the level of new car registrations will remain below zero until PDI rises to £918, that is where the line crosses the X axis. In an economic context this

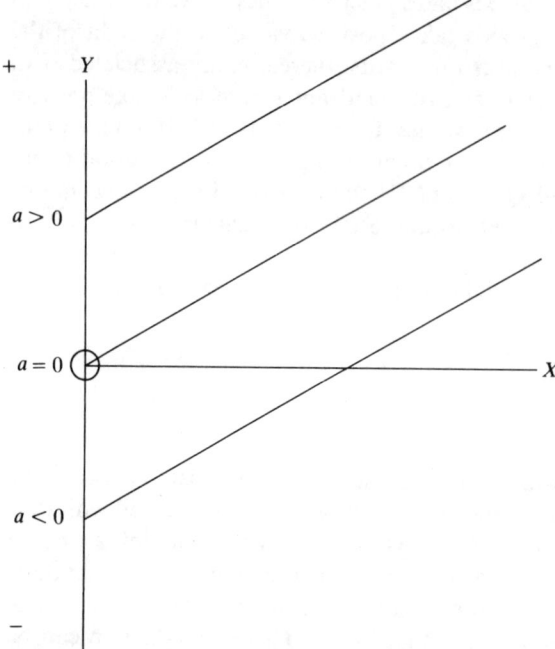

Figure 4-4 Changes in the intercept term

implies that those on a real *per capita* income of less than £918 will not buy a new car. Only those with a real *per capita* income above this level would purchase a new car. (Remember also that we are still dealing with averages. We are not saying that *everyone* with an income over this level will buy a new car or that *no one* on an income below this will not.)

The data suggest that those on low incomes will, for reasons that we may wish to infer, not buy a new car. Instead they may buy a second-hand car (which is cheaper and therefore within their income range) or perhaps a bicycle or use public transport to travel.

It is also clear from the graph that the value of *a*, at −67, is also the point where the straight line crosses or *intercepts* the axis on which we are measuring the dependent variable, Cars. Obviously, in mathematical terms the *a* value could fall into one of three general categories: it could be positive, as in this example, or negative or zero. The implications for the graph of such functions are shown in Fig. 4-4. The *a* parameter, therefore, determines the general position of the line, in terms of where the line crosses the vertical axis. Should the *a* term change its value for any reason (perhaps because of a change in the price of new cars, for example) the function would shift across the graph from one position to another.

The slope or gradient

The second parameter of the linear function is the *b* term, here taking a value of +0.073. This parameter is referred to as the *slope* or *gradient* of the function and, as we shall see throughout much of the text, it is particularly important in an economic context. The *b* parameter in a linear equation indicates the change in the dependent variable that will occur as a result of a change in the independent variable and, in principle, allows us an easy means of prediction.

Let us assume that per capita real personal disposable income is currently £2000, i.e. PDI = 2000. From the equation the predicted level of car registration (in thousands) will be:

$$\begin{aligned}
\text{Cars} &= -67 + 0.073\text{PDI} \\
&= -67 + 0.073(2000) \\
&= -67 + 146 \\
&= 79
\end{aligned}$$

Let us now assume that PDI is expected to increase by £100 to £2100. The new level of car registrations (in thousands) will be:

$$\begin{aligned}
\text{Cars} &= -67 + 0.073\text{PDI} \\
&= -67 + 0.073(2100) \\
&= -67 + 153.3 \\
&= 86.3
\end{aligned}$$

Cars has increased, therefore, by 7.3 as a result of PDI increasing by £100. The change in Cars, in other words, was 7.3 per cent of the change in PDI. Expressed as a decimal, this is 0.073, which is the value of the b parameter in the equation. Simply, the b parameter shows the change that will occur in Cars for a given change in PDI.

The b parameter can also be identified from the graph of the function. The slope, or gradient, of the line indicates the relationship between a change in the independent variable and the subsequent change in the dependent variable:

$$\text{Slope} = \frac{\text{Change in dependent variable}}{\text{Change in independent variable}}$$

This is often expressed as:

$$\frac{\Delta Y}{\Delta X} = \frac{Y_2 - Y_1}{X_2 - X_1}$$

remembering that we are using X and Y as our general notation for any two variables. The symbol Δ is often used in both mathematics and economics to indicate a *change* in some variable (and is pronounced 'delta').

In Fig. 4-5 the income level of £2100 is identified as point X_1 and the corresponding Cars value as Y_1. X_2 and Y_2 correspond to the values when PDI is £2000. Using the slope formula given above we have:

$$\text{Slope} = \frac{86.3 - 79}{2100 - 2000}$$

$$= \frac{7.3}{100}$$

$$= 0.073$$

confirming that the b parameter in the function measures the slope. You can also see from

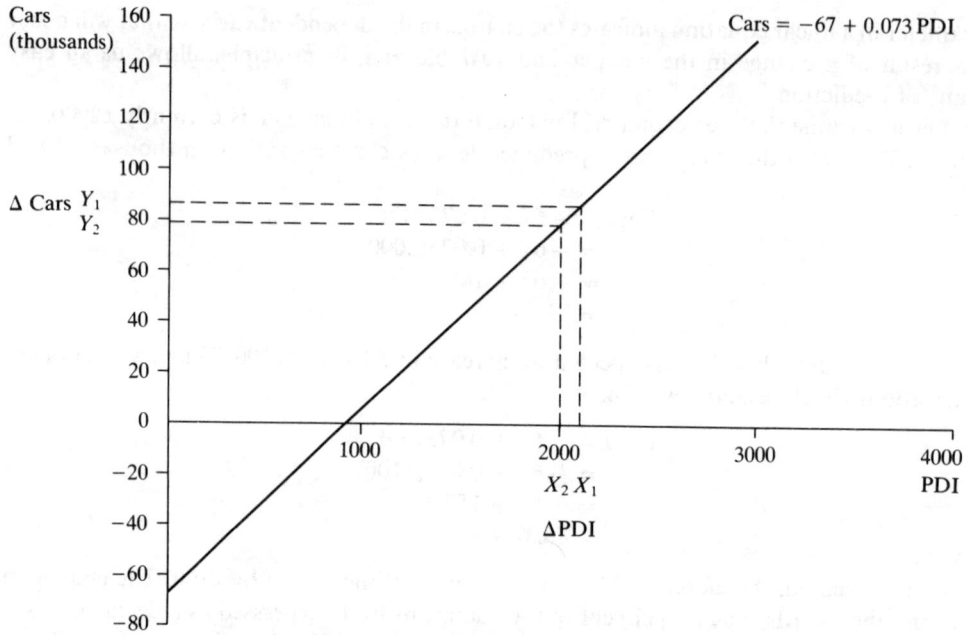

Figure 4-5 Slope of a linear function

the graph that it will not matter *where* on the line we measure the slope, as we will always get the same result. The slope of a linear function, in other words, is constant, implying that the relationship between a change in X and Y always remains the same.

As with the a parameter, the b term may take one of three general forms: it may be either positive, negative or zero. The general features of these three forms are illustrated in Fig. 4-6.

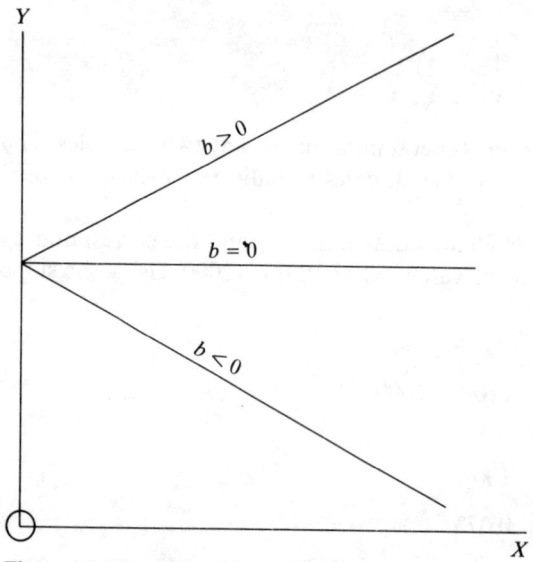

Figure 4-6 Changes in slope

A line with a *positive* b-value slopes *upwards* from left to right, implying that an increase in X will lead to an increase in Y. A Line with a *negative* b-value slopes *downwards* from left to right, implying that an increase in X will lead to a decrease in Y. A line with a *zero* b-value is parallel to the X axis, and implies that as X changes there will be no change in Y. X and Y, in other words, are independent of each other.

4-5 CONCLUSION

Linear functions are very convenient in terms of their ease of use and interpretation, which explains why they are extensively used in economic analysis and model-building (as much of the rest of this text demonstrates). However, they cannot always be used to describe economic relationships with great accuracy. In particular there are two aspects of linear functions which are inadequate for some aspects of economics.

The first is that the linear function we have introduced only allows for *one* independent variable. While there are many instances when such an assumption is reasonable in an economic model, there are others when it is plainly inadequate. In our example, while the hypothesis that PDI is the prime factor behind the purchase of new cars is reasonable, there will be other variables influencing the level of car registrations such as price, public transport fares, availability of imported cars and so on. It is, however, straightforward to incorporate such additional variables into the functional relationship. This is demonstrated in Chapter 5, on demand.

The second aspect is that not all relationships are linear. A considerable number of economic variables are related in a *non-linear* way. This is evident if we return to Fig. 2.1, which showed the level of car ownership against household income. Clearly the relationship between these two variables cannot be quantified by a straight line. For this reason the treatment of *non-linear* functions and equations will also be developed later in the text.

4-6 SUMMARY

The *constant* or *intercept* value indicates where on the vertical axis the line will cross. It is denoted in the equation by the *a* term.

A *functional* relationship expresses two or more variables in terms of cause and effect.

A *linear* function is represented as a straight line on a graph.

The value of the *slope* or *gradient* indicates the steepnes of the line. It is denoted by the *b* term and shows the change in the Y value that will occur for a unit change in the X value.

EXERCISES

4-1 Referring to the equation

$$\text{Cars} = -67 + 0.073\text{PDI}$$

assume the following changes take place:

(*a*) the average price of cars increases;
(*b*) the average price of cars decreases;

(c) the cost of using public transport increases;
(d) the cost of using public transport decreases.

Determine the effect you would expect each of these changes to have on the intercept and slope of the equation. Provide an explanation for each effect.

4-2 In Chapter 4 the linear equation relating new car registrations to PDI for the period 1956–85 was given as:

$$\text{Cars} = -67 + 0.073\text{PDI}$$

The corresponding equation for the same variables for the period 1976–85 is given by:

$$\text{Cars} = -110 + 0.087\text{PDI}$$

(a) Draw this second function on the same graph as the first. Compare the intercepts and slopes both graphically and mathematically.
(b) Assume that PDI takes a value of £3000. Predict the level of new car registrations using each of the two equations.
(c) Formulate a hypothesis to explain why the intercept term for the period 1976–85 is different from that of the period 1956–85.
(d) Formulate a hypothesis to explain why the gradients of the two equations are different.
(e) How could you test whether your hypotheses in (c) and (d) were corroborated by statistical data?

4-3 A retired statistics lecturer has analysed information relating to his total expenditure and disposable income (income after tax) on an annual basis and derived the following equation:

$$C = 1000 + 0.9\text{PDI}$$

where C is expenditure and PDI is disposable income (both measured in thousands of pounds). Such a function, relating consumption expenditure to income, is referred to in economic analysis as the 'consumption function'.

(a) Plot this function up to an income of £12 000.
(b) What is expenditure when income is zero? How do you explain this?
(c) At what level of income is the individual spending all his income?

4-4 A second individual, working in a well-paid managerial position, has also kept records of her expenditure and disposable income. She has noted that last year when her disposable income was £8000 her consumption was £7100. This year her disposable income is £10 000 and her consumption expenditure £8500. From this information determine:

(a) the slope of the linear function;
(b) the intercept.

Plot this function on the same graph as Exercise 4-3 above. Comment on the differences in consumption patterns for the two individuals. What reasons can you suggest for these differences?

4-5 Given that, in economic terms, a person's income must either be spent or saved, determine, for each of the two individuals above, a savings equation of the form: Savings $= f(\text{PDI})$. Plot these two functions on your graph. What conclusion do you come to about:

(a) the constants of the consumption function and savings function for each of the two individuals?
(b) the slopes of the two functions?

5

DEMAND AND PRICE

5-1 INTRODUCTION

Chapters 2–4 have been spent marshalling evidence—some real, some hypothetical—about incomes and car ownership. The conclusion seemed to be that the consumption (in the form of expenditure on cars) was indeed related to the average income of a community or group: in the language of economics, income levels were found to influence the *demand* for cars. This chapter will begin a more systematic examination of the theory of consumer demand in general. The need for such an examination is easily appreciated. Our hypothesis on income and car ownership was formulated largely on the basis of common sense. It is obvious that this procedure cannot be relied upon to work every time.

Demand is one of the most important concepts in economics. It is used in theories at both micro and macro levels, though our discussion in this section of the book will be confined to its micro-economic aspects. Here, economists generally classify the factors that influence a market or industry under one of two headings: *supply-side* factors and *demand-side* factors. The former category consists of things which influence the decisions of *sellers* and would typically include the costs of production, technology and so on. The latter category comprises those factors which bear upon the decisions of *buyers* and would usually take in consumers' tastes and incomes, for instance.

Our examination of demand will involve constructing a model of consumer choice, because it is consumers (whether private households or public authorities) who are ultimately responsible for the demand side of all markets. Even capital goods like the robots used to assemble cars are only demanded because of the consumer goods which they can be used to make.

Our use of the model will follow the steps set out in Chapter 1: first, assumptions are specified; second, implications are deduced; third, one of the initial assumptions is varied and new implications deduced; and fourth, the two outcomes are compared in order to establish the effects of the change in conditions. The model will be described in the three ways at our disposal: verbal, diagrammatic and mathematical.

The purpose of investigating the theory of demand is to equip the reader to formulate his or her own hypotheses on economic behaviour. After completing this chapter and Chapter 6 the reader will be able to formulate a hypothesis relating the demand for any product to any one of a whole range of factors. Any hypothesis would, of course, need to be tested and this could only be done using techniques like those described in Chapters 2–4. That is to say, data would need to be gathered and summarized, averages computed and the degrees of variation measured. Summary information would have to be presented in the form of charts, tables and graphs before any further mathematical analysis—to corroborate or falsify the hypothesis—could be attempted.

5-2 A MODEL OF CONSUMER CHOICE

It might be useful to begin the construction of a model by enumerating the factors which it ought to include. These are: the price of the good under analysis; the incomes of consumers; the price of substitutes, that is, other goods which can be used in place of the good under analysis (for example, public transport can be substituted for cars); the price of complementary goods, that is, those goods consumed along with the good under analysis (for example, petrol in the case of cars); the tastes of consumers; expectations concerning the future price or availability of the good; and advertising. This may be expressed in mathematical notation as:

$$Q_d = f(P_x, Y, P_s, P_c, T, Exp, Adv, Z, e)$$

This expression simply states that the volume or quantity of a good—let it be good x—that is demanded by consumers will depend upon its price (P_x), incomes (Y), the price of substitutes (P_s) and complements (P_c), tastes (T), expectations (Exp) and advertising (Adv). There will often be other factors (aggregated together and denoted as Z) in any specific situation, depending on the nature of the good under discussion. If the good in question were cricket bats, for example, then Z might stand for some indication of weather conditions. Last is the error term (e) which is used to denote any change in demand which does not seem to be related to any of the other variables identified in the functional expression. This expression (and the relationships which it describes) is known as the *demand function*. This chapter will focus on the relationship between quantity demanded and the first variable in the function, price, while Chapter 6 will look at the other factors in the demand function.

Identifying the relevant factors is naturally only the beginning. It is clearly important to try to *quantify* the relationships between each individual factor and the quantity of the good that is demanded if only because a knowledge of the factor to which demand is most sensitive has clear implications for anyone trying either to forecast or to influence sales. Firms will want to raise their sales and profits by strengthening the demand for their products and the means by which this can be done depend upon the main determinants of demand. It price is the main determinant of demand then prices and costs must be cut ruthlessly. If demand is income-sensitive, then high-income markets must be sought out, for example either by opening outlets in prosperous parts of the country or by placing advertisements in the magazines that tend to be read by the better-off. Public authorities also have to attempt to meet the demands placed upon them. For example, roads have to be planned, and for this purpose projections of car-ownership rates have to be made. These, in turn, require some analysis of the major determinants of car sales. Similar considerations apply to the provision of leisure facilities, adult education, water and other public services.

The manner in which these various factors affect the demand for a product can only be assessed by looking at each in turn. That is to say, the effects of each one must be isolated. For example, the relationship between quantity demanded and income could not be investigated if consumer tastes or prices were changing at the same time. To remove this possible interference, economists make the assumption that every other factor in the situation remains unchanged. This is the assumption of *ceteris* (pronounced 'keteris') *paribus*, which means 'all else equal', and conditions which are being held constant are sometimes said to be *in the ceteris paribus pound*.

The first stage in the process is to specify our assumptions. There are as follows:

1. There is only one consumer.
2. There are only two commodities on offer in the market: 'motoring' and 'all other goods' (AOG). Motoring is measured by the number of trips (all of the same length) taken by the consumer. AOG includes commodities which act as substitutes for motoring, such as public transport fares.
3. Our consumer derives pleasure from consuming: she positively enjoys taking trips in the car and having other goods. To use slightly dated but easily understood terminology, consumption provides her with 'utility'. As a result, she prefers having more goods to having less.
4. Each unit of any commodity provides our consumer with a certain 'marginal utility'. As she buys more units of any commodity, so the marginal utility of those successive units declines. In other words, consuming more and more of any particular sort of good yields less and less extra satisfaction. Thus, having bought, say, two pairs of shoes one month, our consumer is likely to spend her next £30 on something other than footwear.
5. The two goods have certain prices. Ignoring, for simplicity, items such as vehicle excise duty and insurance, we may assume that the cost of a car trip is £5. AOG may be thought of as being available in units which cost £10 each.
6. Our consumer has a fixed money income. Let us take it to be £100 per week.
7. Our consumer is fully informed about both her own tastes and about the prices of goods on offer in the market. (Austrian economists, of course, would take issue with this assumption on the grounds that information is never perfect. Consumers, they would argue, are constantly trying out new goods which are being offered and are continually having to update their information on prices.)

The second stage is to deduce some implications from these assumptions. The first would be that there are a number of ways in which the consumer can spend her income: £100 will buy 20 trips or 10 units of AOG; alternatively, it will buy various combinations of the two, for example, 6 trips and 7 units of AOG, or 10 trips and 5 units of AOG. The possibilities are shown graphically in Fig. 5-1. The various combinations of motoring and AOG which our consumer could, in principle, choose are defined by the triangle *ABC*. The line *AB* shows the points at which the consumer spends all her income (and is known as the

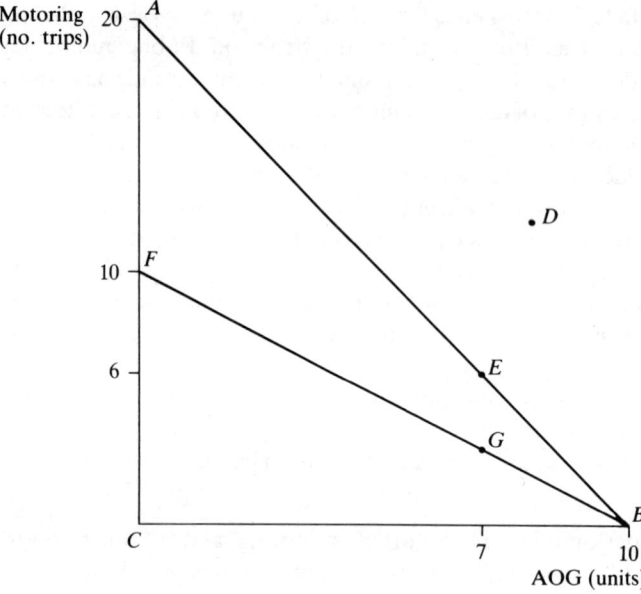

Figure 5-1 Consumption possibilities

budget line), while all points inside the triangle and those on the edges *AC* and *BC* imply that she has some money left over. Points above *AB*, such as *D*, are beyond our consumer's means, given the prices of the products and her fixed income.

Although the consumer could select any point in *ABC*, the third assumption above suggests that she would buy as many goods as possible and would therefore settle upon some point on the line *AB*, thus spending all her income. It is not possible to say which point any particular consumer would be likely to select, since the matter is one of personal taste. The fourth assumption above might suggest that our consumer would be unlikely to settle at either endpoint of the line *AB* since this would imply that she was concentrating on one good despite its declining marginal utility. Point *E*, therefore, with six trips and seven units of AOG, indicates a likely selection. That point having been chosen voluntarily by our consumer, it represents the combination of motoring and AOG that yields her maximum satisfaction, and must accordingly be described as the *equilibrium* point, that is, the position from which there is no tendency to change.

The model is now ready for the third stage, that is, the alteration of our consumer's circumstances in various ways in order to show how these will affect her choice of consumer goods.

5-3 PRICE AND QUANTITY DEMANDED: THE DEMAND CURVE

The first relationship to be examined is that between quantity demanded and price. To the seven assumptions above it will be necessary to add another, to the effect that everything else in the demand function—the prices of substitute and complementary goods, incomes, tastes, advertising, expectations and everything else—remains constant (*ceteris paribus*).

The next stage in our process is to alter the price of one of the goods that the consumer buys, by, say, assuming that the government imposes extra taxes on motoring, raising the price of a trip from £5 to £10. This will naturally cause the consumer's budget line to shift from *AB* to *FB*, with the effect that the previous equilibrium point, *E*, is now unattainable. It is reasonable to assume that a new equilibrium will be established at, say, *G*, with our consumer now consuming 3 trips per week (at a cost of £30) and 7 units of AOG.

The final step is simply to compare the previous position with the new one to see how the consumer has reacted to the increase in price. It is clear that the effect of the increased price of motoring has been to reduce the demand for it from six trips to three. Economists argue that this response is the result of two distinct mechanisms, the *income effect* and the *substitution effect*. The argument is that a price rise affects the consumer in two ways. First, it reduces the total volume of goods which the consumer is able to afford. In effect, the consumer's *real* income falls—she is able to command fewer real resources. Second, a price rise for one good alters the relative prices of the two goods in our model: whereas a trip in the car used to cost half as much as a unit of AOG, it now costs the same.

To isolate the effect of the change in relative prices from all other changes, economists construct a hypothetical budget line *ST*, as shown in Fig. 5-2. This line allows the consumer enough money to buy her old equilibrium bundle at the new prices of £10 for both a car trip and unit of AOG. (*ST* would require a money income of £130 and it would run from 13 trips on the *vertical* axis to 13 units on the other.) The question to be asked is, if the consumer were to find herself on *ST*, that is, able to buy her old bundle at the new prices, what bundle would she in fact choose?

Although it is not possible to say with certainty what our consumer would do, it is nevertheless possible to deduce what she would *not* do. When she was on budget line *AB*, she chose *E*, rejecting all other points in the triangle *ABC*. It seems reasonable to conclude

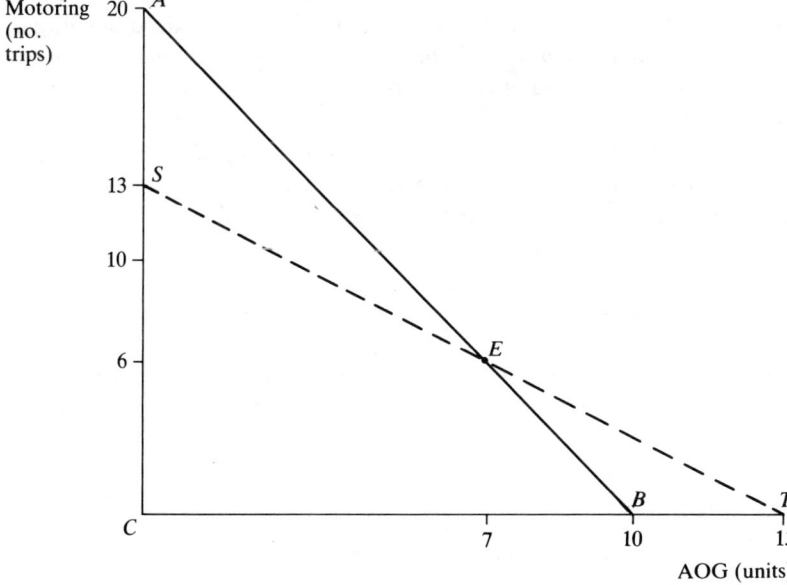

Figure 5-2 The substitution effect

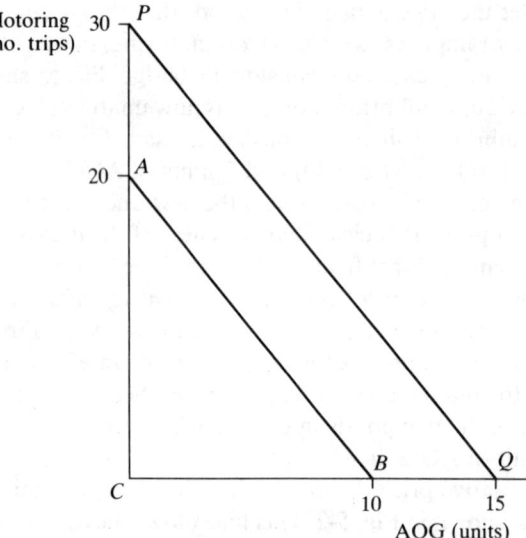

Figure 5-3 The effect of higher money income on consumption possibilities

that she would reject them again. She would therefore prefer E to all points on ST which lay above E, that is, all points on SE. This would leave her with only point E and those below it, that is, the section ET. In all likelihood, of course, she would tend to locate at some point further down ST, that is, to take fewer trips and to buy more units of AOG. This mechanism is the *substitution effect*. Its central point is that, regardless of the level of real income, consumers will react to a change in relative prices by switching expenditure away from expensive items and towards the cheaper ones.

The *income effect* describes the effect of changes in real income on consumer decisions. It is clear that the rise in the price of motoring reduced our consumer's standard of living in that she could afford to buy less of both motoring and AOG. Changes in income are shown by parallel shifts in budget lines. For example, a 50 per cent pay rise for our consumer (before the rise in the price of motoring) would have shifted her budget line from AB to PQ, as shown in Fig. 5-3. An investigation of the likely consequences of a price rise is, in effect, like asking how our consumer would react to a reduction in income, ignoring any changes in relative prices. It seems reasonable to conclude that the probable reaction of the consumer to a reduction in income would be to reduce her consumption of every good to some degree.

In summary, economists argue that an increased price for a good will lead to lower quantities being demanded for two reasons. First, the substitution effect will induce consumers to switch expenditure away from the good in question. Second, the income effect will tend to make consumers reduce their consumption of all goods including that under examination. Thus the *price effect* is the outcome of the income effect acting together with the substitution effect. The conclusion of our analysis is, therefore, the law of demand: *if the price of a good is raised then*, ceteris paribus, *the quantity that is demanded will fall*.

Like many other ideas in economics, this conclusion is capable of being expressed both graphically and mathematically as well as verbally. A graphical expression of the law of demand is shown in Fig. 5-4. Readers will recall from Chapter 4 that the conventional

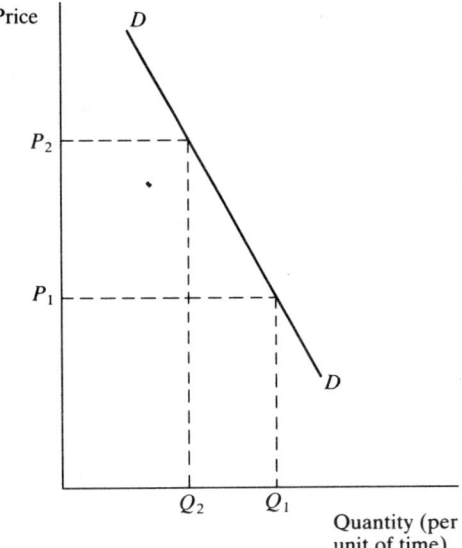

Figure 5-4 The law of demand: the demand curve

practice is to put the independent variable of a relationship on the horizontal axis and the dependent variable on the vertical axis. In micro-economics, however, this convention is violated: price, which is usually the causative, independent variable, goes on the vertical axis while quantity, which is normally in the role of the dependent variable, goes on the horizontal. Bearing this point in mind, it can be seen that the line DD shows that a rise in price (from P_1 to P_2) induces a fall in the quantity demanded (from Q_1 to Q_2). This curve is known as the *demand curve*.

There are two aspects of any demand curve which require attention: first, its general position on the graph and, in particular, the value taken by the intercept; and second, its slope (which, though negative, may be steep or shallow).

Listing the factors which influence the *position* of the demand curve is a straightforward task. They are, quite simply, the items which we have been holding constant: income, the prices of substitutes and complements, tastes, expectations, advertising and other factors. The demand curve is constructed on the assumption that all these items (collectively termed the underlying 'conditions of demand') remain constant and a change in any of them will therefore cause a shift in the demand curve. Such a shift—which is tantamount to changing the constant term in the mathematical expression of the function—is illustrated in Fig. 5-5.

The shift from D_1D_1 to D_2D_2 could have been caused by a change in any of the factors in the *ceteris paribus* pound, that is, by a rise in income, a rise in the price of a substitute, a fall in the price of a complementary good, a switch in tastes in favour of the good, the generation of expectations of a price rise or a successful advertising campaign. That is to say, any one of these changes would lead to a greater volume of the good being demanded at any given price. Conversely, a movement in the opposite direction, from D_2D_2 to D_1D_1, implying that a smaller volume would be demanded at every price, would be brought about by a fall in income, a fall in the price of a substitute, a rise in the price of a complementary good, a switch of tastes away from the good, expectations of a price fall, a bout of negative publicity or a fall in advertising effort. The precise extent of the shift in the demand curve

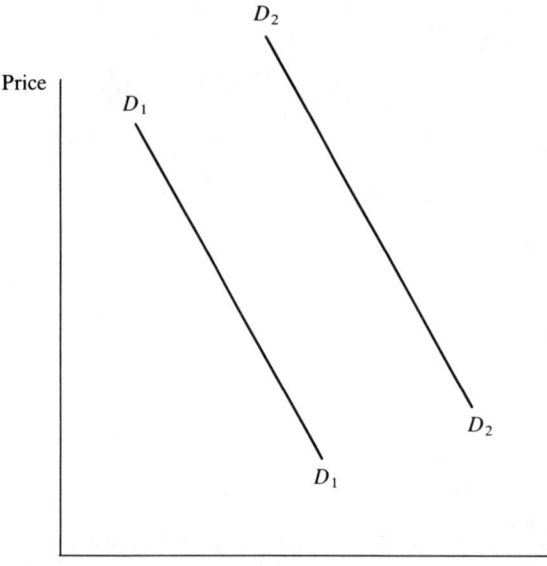

Quantity   **Figure 5-5** Shifts in the demand curve

induced by a change in the various underlying conditions of demand is best analysed by looking directly at those particular relationships, and this will be the task for Chapter 6.

The focus of interest here is upon the relationship between price and quantity demanded. This is plainly of much importance to anyone selling goods and services. Although lower prices can be expected to bring in extra sales, total revenue from these sales will not necessarily increase. The critical question is, of course, how much the quantity demanded will vary with changes in price.

The responsiveness of quantity demanded to price changes is known as the the *price elasticity of demand* (though this is often shortened to 'elasticity of demand' or even 'demand elasticity'). Demand is described as being *elastic* if the volume of demand is highly sensitive to changes in price, and *inelastic* if it is relatively insensitive. Thus the question 'How

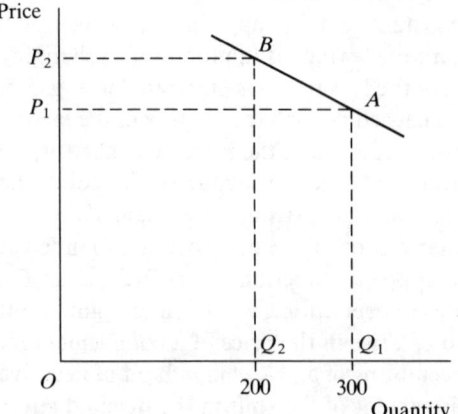

Quantity   **Figure 5-6** Elastic demand

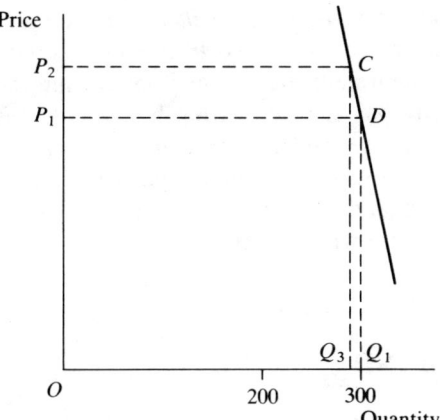

Figure 5-7 Inelastic demand

sensitive is demand to changes in price?' may be rephrased as 'Is demand for this product elastic or inelastic?'.

These two possibilities, elastic and inelastic demand, can be illustrated graphically. Figures 5-6 and 5-7 show two demand curves with differing elasticities. In both cases, demand contracts in response to a rise in price from P_1 (£100 per unit) to P_2 (£120 per unit) in accordance with the law of demand. The extent of the fall in quantity demanded, however, differs markedly. In Fig. 5-6, demand contracts from 300 units to 200 units, a fall of 100, because demand is elastic, while in Fig. 5-7 demand falls by a mere 10 units, from 300 to 290, since demand is inelastic.

Figures 5-8 and 5-9 illustrate two limiting cases. In the first case (Fig. 5-8), demand is *infinitely elastic*, in that consumers appear to have a capacity to absorb infinite amounts of the good at a certain price. Any increase in price, however, will reduce sales to zero. This demand curve most usually applies at very fine levels of disaggregation, such as those relating to the demand for the output of a single firm selling a standarized commodity like timber, sand or wheat. Should such a firm set its prices out of line with those ruling in the market, it would lose its customers to its competitors and fail to sell its wares altogether.

Figure 5-8 Infinitely elastic demand

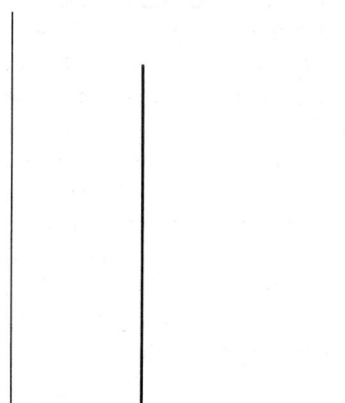

Figure 5-9 Infinitely inelastic demand

In the second case, shown in Fig. 5-9, demand is *infinitely inelastic*. Buyers are completely insensitive to price changes, and appear to be committed to buying a certain volume of the good, come what may. Such a commitment may arise from consumers' investing in complementary goods: households with gas central heating boilers and gas cookers will have a fairly inelastic demand for gas, for example, at least in the short run. Similarly, having a certain make of car can commit a consumer to buying particular kinds of replacement parts. Alternatively, inelasticity of demand may arise from a psychological dependence upon a particular good, as is often the case with tobacco.

5-4 MEASURING ELASTICITY OF DEMAND

Elasticity can also be expressed in mathematical terms and in principle be given a numerical value. That is, it can be measured. The general formula for calculating the elasticity of demand is

$$\text{Elasticity of demand} = \frac{\%\Delta Q}{\%\Delta P}$$

where $\%\Delta$ is the term for 'percentage change in'.

Although demand elasticity should, strictly, take a negative value because quantity falls in response to a price rise, it is conventional to omit the negative sign and to take note solely of the absolute numerical value. Inelastic demand is indicated by values between 0 and 1, where the change in quantity demanded is smaller than the change in price. Values greater than 1 indicate that demand is elastic. Thus if a 1 per cent change in price gives rise to, say, a 5 per cent change in quantity demanded, demand would be described as being 'highly elastic'. Were the change in quantity to match the change in price exactly the result would be a value of 1. This is described as 'unit elasticity'.

The formula can be applied in a rough and ready way when a researcher or decision-maker knows about two price–quantity combinations (like points A and B in Fig. 5-6). (There must also be grounds for supposing that they lie on the same demand curve. The two observations of price and quantity will necessarily relate to different dates—perhaps two consecutive months—and the investigator must be sure that the demand curve has not shifted, because of changes in other variables in the demand function, for this would imply that the two points related to two different curves.)

It is then possible to work out an *average* elasticity value for the range of the demand curve between the two known points. The first step is to establish the absolute changes by subtraction. In the example, ΔQ is -100 and ΔP is 20. Calculating the figures for the percentage changes requires, of course, the investigator to divide the absolute changes by a base figure (before multiplying by 100). It is not immediately obvious, however, what that base figure should be. For price, it could either be £100 or £120, while for quantity the choice seems to lie between 200 and 300. It is conventional simply to take the average of the two possibilities. Thus the formula becomes:

$$\frac{\%\Delta Q}{\%\Delta P} = \frac{-100/(\frac{1}{2}(200 + 300))}{20/(\frac{1}{2}(100 + 120))}$$

$$= \frac{-100/250}{20/110}$$

$$= \frac{-0.4}{0.182}$$

$$= -2.2$$

This application of the general formula is known as the calculation of *arc elasticity* because it relates to elasticity over a whole section of the demand curve (in Fig. 5-6, the section between points *A* and *B*). More precisely, it gives an average value which is accurate only at the mid-point of the arc. There is, therefore, an element of imprecision in this application.

An approach which is mathematically more refined will be introduced in Chapter 16, but the above method is adequate for our purposes at this stage.

5-5 ELASTICITY OF DEMAND AND TOTAL REVENUE

The relationship between the total sales revenue and the elasticity of demand is a matter of some importance, as businessmen who are contemplating a price change will want ultimately to gauge its effects in terms of revenue. Total revenue is easily shown on a demand-curve graph, for revenue is simply the product of revenue per unit (price) and the number of units demanded. These factors are both represented: price on the vertical axis and quantity on the horizontal. Thus, referring back to Figs 5-6 and 5-7, multiplying price (on the graphs, OP_1) by quantity (OQ_1) gives, in each case, the shaded rectangle OP_1AQ_1, which represents the total revenue obtained at price P_1.

In both cases, sales stand initially at 300 units, price at £100 and revenue at £30 000 (area OP_1AQ_1). Again in both cases, price goes up from £100 (P_1) to £120 (P_2), a rise of 20 per cent. In Fig. 5-6, demand elasticity is high and the volume of sales falls substantially to 200 units (Q_2). The new level of total revenue is $200 \times £120 = £24\,000$—a fall of £6000. The fact that revenue has decreased can be deduced by comparing the two rectangles OP_1AQ_1

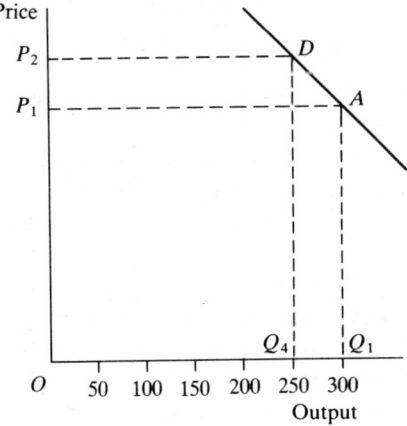

Figure 5-10 Unit elasticity

and OP_2BQ_2. In Fig. 5-7, by contrast, the elasticity of demand is low and the volume of sales is down only marginally to 290 units. In consequence, revenue actually rises even though quantity falls, climbing from the initial £20 000 to £31 200 as indicated by the rectangle OP_2CQ_3.

It is perfectly conceivable for a price change to leave total revenue completely unchanged. This would have occurred in one of the above examples if sales had fallen to exactly 250. This case is illustrated in Fig. 5-10, where rectangular OP_1AQ_1 is equal in area to rectangle OP_2DQ_4. Here, demand is of unit elasticity.

5-6 THE DETERMINANTS OF THE ELASTICITY OF DEMAND

Having explored the quantitative implications of demand elasticity it may now be useful to inquire what factors determine elasticity, making the demand for one product elastic while that for another is inelastic.

The answer to this question turns largely upon one fundamental principle: the availability of substitute products. If alternative commodities are readily available and if consumers are willing to buy them in place of the item in question, then an increase in its price will mean a large-scale loss of customers and the elasticity of demand will be said to be high. Conversely, of course, price cuts in this situation will bring in large numbers of new buyers. As an example, one could cite the petrol sold by one service station in a large conurbation. The service station increases its price. Given the availability of alternative sources of supply there will be a large decrease in quantity demanded. On the other hand, if the petrol station were in a rural area, the absence of substitutes would mean that consumers were, to some degree, committed to consuming the good and would continue to buy even if its price increases. In such a situation, conversely again, price cuts would not be a successful means of persuading more people to start consuming the product.

The question of whether substitute goods are available is to a large extent a subjective one. In the example used earlier, the consumer could switch between service stations when one increased the price of petrol. Whether many people would make such a switch turns ultimately upon their attitudes. While the choice might be a matter of indifference to some, others may have some commitment to their existing service station (perhaps because of convenience of location, attitudes of the staff or through advertising). Marketing executives describe this as 'consumer loyalty' and companies try to foster it by gaining a reputation for quality and service. This reputation may of course be reinforced or even created by advertising. Its effect is to make customers believe that its products are unique in some sense, that is, that other firms' goods are merely poor substitutes.

The availability of substitutes for any product—and thus the elasticity of demand for it—naturally changes over time. As a general rule, the elasticity of demand will tend to be relatively higher when shorter periods of time are considered and relatively lower when the analysis is based on a longer period of time. In other words, consumers are likely to remain loyal in the face of a price rise in the short term but, as time passes, more and more of them will tend to seek out alternative sources of supply. The example of households with gas central heating and gas cookers was noted earlier. In the short run consumers will have little option but to pay whatever price the gas company asks—their demand will be highly inelastic. This does not mean, however, that a gas company can charge whatever price it likes indefinitely. Higher tariffs will induce consumers to save money by installing double-glazing, fitting draught excluders and wearing sweaters indoors. Over the longer term the range of possibilities will expand to include changing the central heating boiler to one using a different fuel. Thus the elasticity of demand for gas over a period of, say, 10 years, will be very much higher than it is over a period of three months.

The importance of the availability of substitutes in determining the elasticity of demand is shown again when considering the *level* of the investigation. That is to say, an economist may try to analyse the demand for a single product (such as a brand of marmalade), for a class of such products (like all jams, preserves and spreads), for an entire sector of industry (such as the food industry) or, indeed, for anything in between. It is clear that the availability of substitutes will change quite substantially as larger and larger groups of products are considered. When the subject of analysis is one product, substitutes in the form of rival brands will be available in abundance and the elasticity of demand will accordingly be high. When, however, the focus of attention is upon larger aggregations of products, like all foodstuffs, the elasticity of demand will be found to be rather lower. There is, after all, no substitute for food.

Besides the availability of substitutes, the elasticity of demand is also influenced by the proportion of income that is spent on the product. Goods which absorb only an insignificant share of a consumer's budget, like salt, may well be in inelastic demand simply because even a large rise in price is so small in absolute terms that consumers do not respond. In the case of goods which absorb a relatively high proportion of spending, the same principle can work in a rather different way. Here the important factor is the number of new users who may be attracted to the product by a price cut. This may bring it within the reach of groups of people who previously could not afford it. Thus the increase in sales which a price cut will induce may well vary with the numbers of people in different income groups. For example, the holiday industry has reduced the prices of Mediterranean holidays to the point at which ordinary working families can afford them and this has raised the demand for them very substantially. In this range, elasticity of demand proved to be fairly high. The same is true of the demand for cars.

On the other hand, cutting the price of meals at the Ritz would probably not raise demand greatly, as the number of people who are wealthy enough to pay even the reduced prices will not be very much greater than the numbers of those able to pay them at present. It seems reasonable to hypothesize, in other words, that there is a low elasticity of demand in this case.

5-7 SUMMARY

Ceteris paribus is the assumption that all other factors remain the same. This assumption allows the economist to examine the various influences upon demand one at a time.

The *demand curve* illustrates the relationship between quantity demanded and price. This curve shifts in response to changes in any of the non-price factors in the demand function, these factors being termed the 'underlying conditions of demand'.

The *demand function* is the relationship between, on the one hand, the quantity of a good or service that is demanded and, on the other, the factors which influence it: its price, the prices of other goods, the incomes of consumers, tastes, expectations and advertising.

Elasticity of demand measures the responsiveness of quantity demanded to changes in price. The elasticity of demand for a product depends on the preferences of consumers for that product and the availability of substitutes. The number of substitutes can naturally be expected to increase as longer periods of time are considered, while the definition of the product will also be important in that widely defined products have few substitutes while narrowly defined ones have rather more.

EXERCISES

5-1 A demand curve takes form $P = 90 - 10Q$, where P is price and Q is quantity demanded.

(*a*) Plot this on a graph, with quantity from 0 to 9.
(*b*) Compile a table showing total revenue at the following prices: $P = 70$; $P = 50$; $P = 30$; $P = 10$.
(*c*) Calculate arc elasticity for the following price ranges: $P = 10$ to 20; $P = 40$ to 50; $P = 70$ to 80.
(*d*) Although the slope of the curve is constant, the elasticity varies along it. Explain why this is.

5-2 A business has monitored its sales and prices over the last few months and made the following observations:

Price	5	10	15
Quantity sold	55	30	5

(*a*) Plot these points on a graph.
(*b*) On the assumption that the three points are from the same linear demand function obtain the demand equation.
(*c*) Calculate the elasticity of demand for the price range 12 to 13. Comment on your result.

5-3 A consumer has only two goods upon which to spend his income: food, priced at £5 per unit; and clothing, priced at £10 per unit. His income is £100.

(*a*) Draw a graph to show his budget line.
(*b*) Show the effect of a fall in the price of clothing to £5.
(*c*) Show the effects of a 25 per cent rise in his income.
(*d*) Show the effects of simultaneous fall in the price of food to £4, and in clothing to £8.

5-4 Describe the operation of the income and the substitution effects in the context of Exercise 5-3.

5-5 Explain why many manufacturers of consumer goods use brand names.

5-6 Which do you consider would have the more elastic demand, and why?

(*a*) shoes;
(*b*) trainers;
(*c*) Adidas trainers.

DEMAND: FURTHER ANALYSIS

6-1 INTRODUCTION

In Chapter 5 we began to discuss the theory of demand. It was suggested that the demand for a product would be influenced by a range of factors, whose effects could only be gauged by examining them individually. This process began by looking at the relationship between quantity demanded and price. In this chapter we will carry this discussion of demand forward by analysing the ways in which consumers might react to changes in other factors in the demand function: incomes, the prices of complementary goods and of substitutes, tastes, advertising, expectations and so on. Our conclusions represent the results of a series of 'comparative statics', that is, of changing the initial conditions under which our imaginary consumer selects her goods, and deducing how she might adjust to the new circumstances.

It is most important to bear in mind the fact that the factors discussed in this chapter bear a very different relationship to the demand curve than does price. The demand curve shows the link between quantity demanded and price on the assumption of *ceteris paribus*. Thus changes in price give rise to movements *along* the curve. Changes in other factors, however, amount to a violation of the *ceteris paribus* assumption and thus give rise to *shifts* in the demand curve. That is, changes in these factors have the result that more (or less) of the good will be bought at every price.

6-2 INCOME AND DEMAND

The relationship between income and quantity demanded (*ceteris paribus*) has already been mentioned in Chapter 5 as the income effect. There it was suggested that higher real incomes

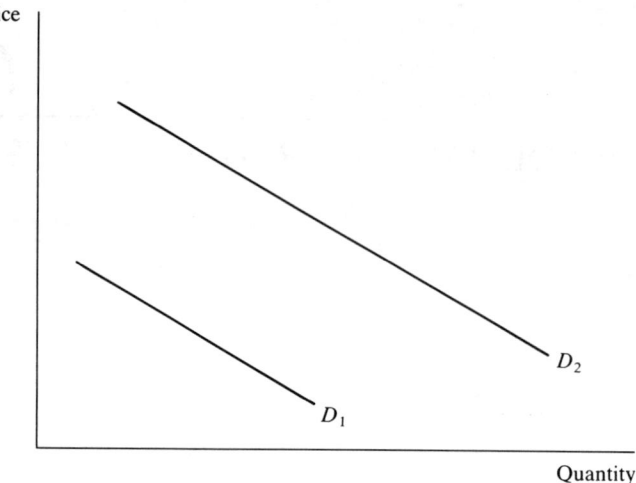

Figure 6-1 An income-induced upward shift in demand

would mean an increase in the consumption of all goods in general and thus of the good under examination as well. Conversely, a lower real income would mean a fall in quantity demanded. It seems reasonable, in other words, to suppose that there will in general be a positive relationship between income and the demand for a good, and it is easy to think of examples like cars, fitted kitchens and cameras. The effect of a rise in income on the demand curve for such a good is shown in Fig. 6-1, which indicates that, at every price, more of the good will be demanded.

Despite the general plausibility of a positive relationship, there are numerous examples of *negative* relationships between income and quantity demanded. The same affluence which has raised the demand for cars has reduced the sales of black and white TV sets and new terraced houses and has cut the use of public transport. Economists thus distinguish between *superior goods* (sometimes called *normal goods*), for which demand increases with income, and *inferior goods*, for which demand diminishes with income.

Graphically, the relationship between income and demand can be expressed by income–consumption curves, like those in Fig. 6-2. These are sometimes referred to as *Engel curves* after Ernst Engel, the nineteenth-century German economist who first drew attention to the relationship. In Figure 6-2, good *A* is a superior good while good *B* is an inferior one.

Engel curves are plotted on the assumption that all else is equal. A change in any one of the other factors in the demand function would shift the curve in its entirety across the graph. The direction of the movement would depend, of course, upon whether the change favoured demand for the good or not. Thus, a fall in the price of the good would shift the Engel curve to the right.

The responsiveness of demand to income changes (and, indeed, whether demand increases or decreases when income increases) is indicated by the slope of the Engel curve. A steep curve would show the demand for a good to be rather insensitive to changes in income. A shallow curve, by contrast, would show that a given change in income would induce a large change in demand. Analysis of the FES data on cars and household income,

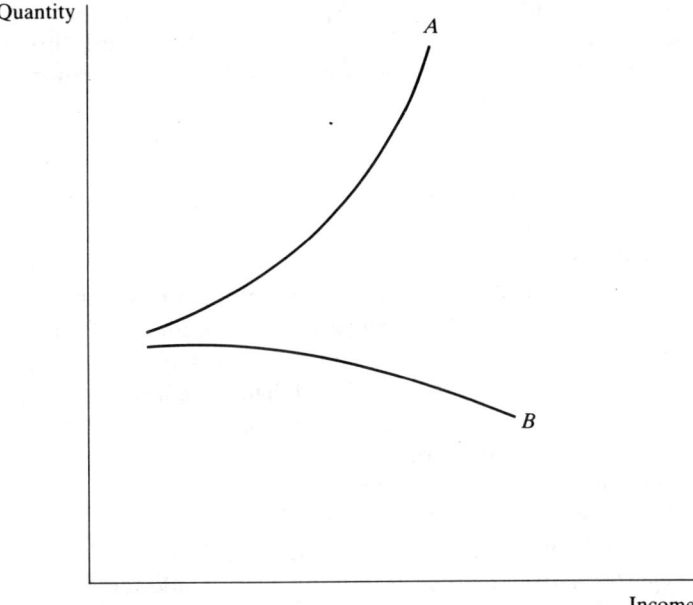

Quantity

Income

Figure 6-2 Income–consumption curves

for instance, indicates that, for groups with an average income over £200, an increase in income of £100 would raise car ownership rates from 85.6 per cent to 89.6 per cent. The sensitivity of quantity demanded to income is called the *income elasticity of demand*. Following the same general approach as was used in the case of price elasticity, the formula for income elasticity is

$$\text{Income elasticity} = \frac{\%\Delta Q}{\%\Delta Y}$$

where Y is income. For car ownership in the range indicated above, the calculation would be

$$\frac{\dfrac{4}{85.6} \times 100}{\dfrac{100}{250} \times 100} = \frac{4.7}{4.0} = 0.118$$

If the formula produces a number greater than 1 income elasticity is said to be high because an increase in income will produce a large effect on quantity demanded. If the result is between 1 and 0, as in the example above, elasticity is described as being low, for changes in income have little effect on demand.

The magnitude of income elasticity of demand for particular goods will depend, ultimately, upon the attitudes and behaviour of consumers, and these will naturally differ from case to case. Perhaps the only general rule is that, like price elasticity, investigations that are conducted at different levels of disaggregation will produce different answers. For instance, the income elasticity of demand for 'durable household goods' (a fairly broad category) is hardly likely to be the same as that for one of its sub-categories like compact disc players.

One item with an extremely large—and negative—income elasticity was noted by Sir Robert Giffen, a statistician who observed the Irish famine of the 1840s. The item in question was the potato, which made up a large proportion of the diet of many people. Its price greatly affected their real income levels: cheap potatoes meant that money wages would go further. Indeed, the result which Giffen noted was that, when potatoes went down in price, people would tend to use their extra spending power to buy superior goods which were, in many cases, other foodstuffs like bread. Thus the paradoxical result of a *fall* in the price of potatoes was a *fall* in the quantity of potatoes demanded. Conversely, an increase in the price of potatoes, as actually occurred when the crop failed, had the effect of reducing real incomes and inducing people to switch back to the inferior good, potatoes. Thus the demand for them actually *increased* as their price rose.

Figure 6-3 illustrates the demand curve for a *Giffen good* as cases of this kind have come to be called. The explanation for this unexpected relationship between price and quantity is that, first, the most important determinant of quantity demanded in this case is income, and, second, the income effect is negative. Normally the substitution effect would tend to raise demand as price falls. In the case of a Giffen good, it is swamped by a large and negative income effect.

This, clearly, is an abnormal case. Giffen goods are only likely to be found in situations similar to Ireland of the 1840s, that is, where poverty is compounded by famine. For most goods, income elasticites take less extreme values. Income remains, nevertheless, an important influence upon the demand for many products.

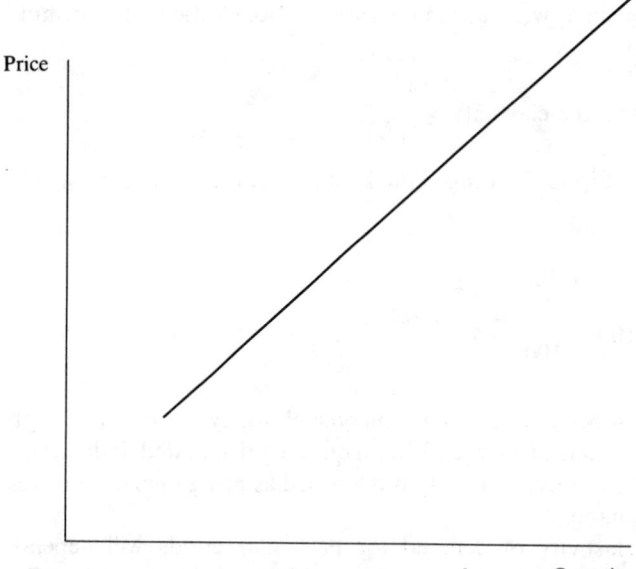

Figure 6-3 Demand for a Giffen good

6-3 THE PRICES OF COMPLEMENTARY GOODS

Changes in the prices of complementary goods will usually influence the demand for any product. Lower petrol prices, motor insurance premiums, parking fees and garage charges will tend, *ceteris paribus*, to make our imaginary consumer more likely to buy a car, because these are all goods and services which are consumed jointly with cars. In effect, all are constituent elements of a larger bundle, 'motoring'.

The relationship between the quantity of cars demanded and the price of one of its complementary goods could be plotted on a graph. Fig. 6-4, for example, relates the demand for cars to the prices of tyres. Like the demand curves and the Engel curves which have already been examined, this curve will undergo a shift in response to a change in any item in the *ceteris paribus* pound. The slope of the curve indicates the responsiveness of the quantity demanded of one good to changes in the price of a complementary good, a shallow curve showing the demand to be highly responsive to changes in the price of the complement and a steep curve showing a low level of responsiveness. The relationship is termed the *cross-elasticity of demand* and its formula is

$$\text{Cross-elasticity of demand} = \frac{\%\Delta Q_x}{\%\Delta P_c}$$

where Q_x is the quantity of good X demanded and P_c is the price of a complementary good; it will generally take a negative value.

The value—high or low—that cross-elasticity takes in any particular case will depend primarily upon the two goods' relative importance in the larger bundle of which they are elements (like motoring). The demand for an important item is unlikely to be much affected by changes in the price of one of the relatively minor constituents. For example, the demand

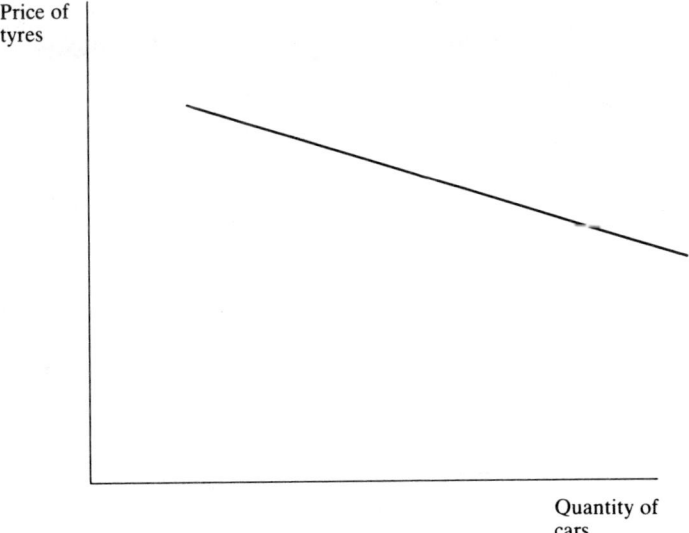

Figure 6-4 Demand for a complementary good

for cars will not, in all probability, be reduced very much by an increase in the price of anti-freeze because anti-freeze, while essential, is but a small element in the total motoring budget. One would expect the cross-elasticity of demand for cars with respect to the price of fuel to be rather higher.

6-4 THE PRICE OF SUBSTITUTES

The demand for any product will also be influenced by the prices of goods and services which may be used in its place. We may enquire into the general nature of this relationship by asking how our consumer would react, in terms of her demand for cars, to a rise in, say, bus fares (*ceteris paribus*). It is reasonable to suppose that, by virtue of the substitution effect, she might tend to use the car more often and the bus less often. There might well, in other words, be a positive relationship between demand for one good and the price of its substitutes, as Fig. 6-5 illustrates. Like the link between demand and the price of complementary goods, this relationship is also known as the *cross-elasticity of demand*. Its algebraic formula is the same, the sole difference being that here the result will be positive rather than negative.

The influence upon demand of the availability of substitutes was mentioned in the previous chapter in the discussion of the price elasticity of demand. The general conclusion was that if substitutes were readily available then elasticity of demand would be high. This relationship can now, in principle at any rate, be quantified using the above formula. Provided that adequate data can be gathered, the formula can tell us in quantitative terms how demand for one good will move in response to changes in the price of another. That is, it can be used to assess quantitatively the readiness of consumers to switch from one good to

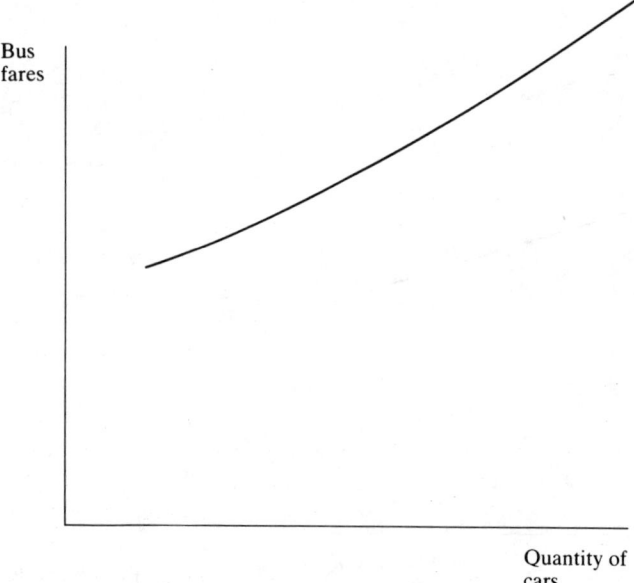

Figure 6-5 Demand for a substitute good

another: a low cross-elasticity of demand for one good with respect to the price of another would show that they were fairly *close* substitutes.

6-5 ADVERTISING

An inescapable aspect of the modern economy, advertising absorbs billions of pounds' worth of resources. Indeed, expenditure on advertising in a typical year amounts to some 40 per cent of the amount spent on new plant and equipment for manufacturing industry.

Again, some assessment of the effectiveness of advertising would clearly be of use, and the expression $\%\Delta Q/\%\Delta Adv$ might suggest itself as a broad indication of the responsiveness of demand to advertisments. The resultant figure would need to be treated with caution, of course, because there could be no guarantee that future campaigns would be as effective as past ones, if only because so much depends on the ability of the advertising agency to devise a successful strategy.

6-6 EXPECTATIONS, TASTES AND OTHER FACTORS

The effect of changed *expectations* on demand may be established by enquiring how, *ceteris paribus*, our imaginary consumer might react to news that the price of something she usually bought was likely to go up in the near future. She might well decide to stock up a little at the next opportunity—that is, to increase her present demand for the good. When many consumers decide on this course of action, demand can alter radically. For example, in the winter of 1973–4, oil supplies from the Middle East were disrupted and Western consumers were unsure when they would be resumed. In consequence, motorists bought as much petrol as they could, filling spare tins and drums as well as their vehicle fuel tanks. Demand, in other words, rose abruptly—serving, of course, to exacerbate the shortage. Similar considerations apply to the demand for shares in particular companies and to foreign exchange dealings. In these cases, the expectation that prices or exchange rates might rise in the future will have the effect of raising demand in the present, while expectations of future price falls will reduce present demand.

Tastes, that is, consumers' perceptions of a product, are another factor which can bring about a shift in a demand curve. In many cases these change as lifestyles evolved. There has, for example, been a general trend towards more informality of dress over the years, and the demand for three-piece suits has tended to decline. As incomes grow, the luxuries of one period, like central heating, become the necessities of another. Social views also change: healthy eating has become more important in recent years, leading to a reduction in the consumption of meat and processed foods. Advertising, of course, must take account of these trends, either reinforcing them or trying to counter them.

One feature separates tastes and expectations from the other elements in the demand function. While prices, incomes and the prices of other goods can be observed, tastes and expectations cannot. At least one implication of great importance derives from this distinction. While economists can formulate hypotheses to explain past changes in demand by referring to any item in the demand function (including the error term, of course), the only ones which can be tested are those which involve observable phenomena. For example, anyone investigating the downward trend in bread consumption that has been evident for several years in the United Kingdom might hypothesize that the change had been caused by, first, the rise in the price of bread relative to other foods; second, the increase in incomes in the context of bread being an inferior good; and third, a switch in tastes away from bread. Although the first and second elements in the hypothesis can be tested, the third cannot. No evidence can be brought to bear to substantiate or to refute the idea. In the terms of our discussion in Chapter 1, there is no means by which it can be falsified. An investigator who can only explain a change in consumption by reference to alterations in tastes is therefore making a statement which is not strictly scientific.

The next factor in the demand function to be considered is Z, which stands for factors which apply only in particular cases. For example, temperature and weather conditions in general affect the demand for all manner of goods ranging from electricity to wellington boots. In other markets, Z might stand for legal requirements. The demand for motor insurance, for instance, is kept at a high level because it is compulsory for drivers to be insured. Although it could be argued that legislation reflects the views or tastes of voters, and is thus already included in the demand function under the heading 'tastes', it is often of sufficient importance to merit explicit and individual consideration. The Z factor is therefore put into the general demand function as an unspecified category which may be used or ignored depending on the circumstances.

It is conventional also to include in the demand function an error term. This stands for changes in demand which cannot be explained by the other factors specified in the function. In practice, of course, researchers usually attribute any unexplained change to such unquantifiable factors as tastes and expectations.

6-7 EXPLAINING AND PREDICTING CHANGES IN DEMAND

The purpose of our analysis has been to provide a framework for explaining and predicting demand. That is to say, our intention has been to allow readers to formulate hypotheses which explain past levels of demand for particular products and which will (hopefully) allow them to predict future changes.

To explain past changes in the demand for a particular product, it would first be necessary to gather data on past changes in consumption. The next step would be to examine all the elements in the commodity's demand function to see if they had undergone any changes over the same period. For example, an investigation of the demand for bread— consumption of which has been on a downward trend, as noted above—would begin by gathering data for a number of years on average bread consumption, the price of bread, the prices of substitutes like potatoes or pasta, the prices of complementary goods like butter, margarine, jam and so on, incomes, advertising expenditure, tastes, expectations and other relevant factors. It would then be necessary to try to establish whether any relationships can be discerned between these various changes. In Chapter 10 we will put the theory of demand (and of supply) to use to investigate such market changes in detail.

6-8 DEMAND IN AUSTRIAN ECONOMICS

The Austrian view of the demand function has been touched upon earlier. Austrian economists lay great stress on the process of discovering new information, new techniques of production, new products and new sources of supply. They would therefore contest the idea that consumers were fully aware both of the prices of goods on offer and of their own tastes. After all, they would argue, prices change continually as new discount warehouses open, as shops hold sales and so on. The task of knowing one's own tastes is arguably even more demanding, since it requires a consumer to sample every good and service on offer: every vintage of wine, every holiday resort, every model of car and so on. Since consumers are unlikely to have undertaken so comprehensive a review, it is far more realistic, Austrian economists argue, to consider consumers as engaged in a process of experimentation, of trying out particular vintages of wine or different brands of marmalade. For them, consumer behaviour is intrinsically far more fluid and far less predictable than it is for neo-classical economists. In consequence, Austrian economists tend to be far more reluctant to make predictions of demand than are their neo-classical colleagues.

6-9 SUMMARY

Shifts in demand curves are caused by changes in any other element in the demand function. Movements *along* the demand curve are caused by changes in price.

Engel curves show the relationship between income and quantity demanded at constant prices. If higher income means higher demand, the good is described as being *superior* or *normal*, while if higher income leads to lower demand, the good is termed *inferior*. This is measured by the good's income elasticity of demand.

Substitutes and *complements* are goods whose prices influence the demand for the item under consideration. The nature of these relationships is indicated by their cross-elasticities of demand: a *positive* cross-elasticity shows that the two goods are *substitutes*, a *negative* one showing them to be *complements*. *Tastes* and *expectations* cannot be *observed* and thus no hypotheses about them can be tested.

EXERCISES

6-1 Give two examples of inferior and superior goods.

6-2 Identify substitute and complementary goods whose prices might influence the demand for the following:

(*a*) suntan oil
(*b*) dried cat food
(*c*) bicycle puncture-repair kits
(*d*) gardening tools.

Illustrate on a graph the effects of changes in the prices of the goods you have selected on the demand curves for the four goods above.

6-3 How do you imagine international trading firms would react to news that the coffee crop in a major supplying nation was likely to fail because of poor weather?

6-4 Identify the major variable factors which would influence the demand for

(*a*) camping equipment
(*b*) fountain pens
(*c*) paraffin heaters.

Formulate hypotheses (following the general format 'If ... then ... ') linking these factors with the demand for the three goods. Describe the statistics which you would need to confirm or falsify these hypotheses.

6-5 Using appropriate sources (such as *Monthly Digest of Statistics, FES, General Household Survey, Economic Trends Annual Supplement*) collect data on the following variables: the price of bread; the Retail Price Index; real *per capita* income; *per capita* consumption of bread; the price of butter; the price of margarine; the price of jam; and the price of potatoes. Collect the data for 1970, 1975, 1980, 1985 and the latest year available. Assess the changes in the demand for bread and determine which factors appear to be at work in causing such changes.

CONSUMER STATISTICS

7-1 INTRODUCTION

In Chapters 5 and 6 we looked at the theory of demand. We itemized the various factors likely to affect the demand for an individual good or service—its price, the prices of substitutes and complementary goods, consumer income and so on—and went on to explore their respective relationships with the quantity of the good demanded. An understanding of demand is clearly essential for business organizations in all sectors. In the private sector industrial and commercial companies have to take a view of the prospects for demand for their products when investment decisions are being taken. Companies will also, of course, try to assess the outlook for the industry in which they are operating, for if demand is likely to contract, for example, competition will become more intense and profits will be harder to earn. Similarly, banks and other financial institutions are obliged to assess the prospects for security prices and interest rates when deciding how to deploy their funds. The same necessity is felt again in the public sector, where resources have to be allocated between competing uses such as health care, education and so on.

What all these organizations require is a reliable indication of the importance of the various factors influencing demand for their particular good or service. The necessity, in short, is for a quantification of the relationships between quantity demanded and its various determinants. This, of course, can only be established by examining the relevant data. Organizations often have to gather the relevant information themselves. One source is their own sales records. If their sales go to a few large buyers, it may be possible to forecast demand and analyse the effect of price changes by meeting their customers to discuss their future requirements. If, on the other hand, their products are sold largely to the public it might be necessary to undertake a survey of consumer attitudes by means of a questionnaire. The survey might be done either by the firm itself or by a market research agency. Apart from these private sources, information can be obtained from government statistical sources like the *FES* and Appendix A details the more important of those available.

The purpose of this chapter is to examine some of these information sources so as to investigate some of the ideas introduced in Chapter 5 and 6, such as Engel curves and elasticities.

7-2 THE *FAMILY EXPENDITURE SURVEY*

One of the biggest surveys in the United Kingdom is the *Family Expenditure Survey* (to which reference has already been made in the text) which is carried out by the Department of Employment. Though published only once a year, the survey work goes on continually. Every year some 7000 households, selected at random, keep records of their daily expenditures over a two-week period. These data are supplemented by information on their less frequent payments such as fuel bills and rates. The basic objective is to obtain a representative picture of expenditure patterns in the statistical population.

Efforts are naturally made to overcome possible errors. One source of bias, for instance, might be the refusal of some households to participate in the survey, for this might cause certain categories of household to be underrepresented in the survey. In the event, it has been found that the households which refuse to cooperate tend to be headed by older people and by self-employed workers. To the extent that these people have different expenditure patterns from the average, the *FES* results will contain an element of bias. Errors may also arise from people failing to report all their expenditure, a fault which seems to apply principally to alcohol and tobacco. The reported expenditure can, however, be checked against data from the Customs and Excise Service on the amounts which have actually been sold. These latter figures suggest that consumption is one-third larger than households usually claim. Since the Customs and Excise information is felt to be reliable, this error can be eliminated.

The *FES* includes virtually every household payment on consumer items, from house repairs to hairdressing. Excluded are expenditures which are not related to consumption, like income-tax payments and savings such as life assurance premiums. Mortgage payments are also excluded because they are deemed to be investment expenditures rather than consumption. Owner-occupiers are, however, counted as spending a sum equal to the rateable value of their houses. Since this figure is supposed to reflect the rental value of a house, they are in effect treated as renting.

The results of the survey are compiled into a statement of average weekly consumer expenditure. The 1985 *FES* showed, for example, that on average households spent £24.56 on transport and vehicles, £32.70 on food and £1.22 on animals and pets per week. Figures are also given for different income bands. Expenditure on transport and vehicles, for instance, varied from £4.08 for those receiving less than £40 per week to £66.87 for those receiving £500 or more. Other tables show how expenditure patterns vary between regions and between households of different size and structure. Comparison with previous surveys also reveals the ways in which spending patterns have altered over the years.

Since the *FES* contains information on family size, incomes, occupations and housing tenure it is widely used to gauge trends in income distribution, changes in family structure and so on. For the working economist, however, its primary interest lies in the information it contains on consumer expenditure. To see why, three particular applications of the *FES* data will now be examined: the construction of the Retail Price Index, the identification of growth markets and Engel curves and the investigation of demand elasticities.

7-3 THE RETAIL PRICE INDEX

There is a clear need to measure the rate at which average prices are increasing. In the United Kingdom this requirement is met by the publication of the General Index of Retail Prices, more commonly known as the Retail Price Index (RPI). Like the *FES*, the RPI is compiled by the Department of Employment, which records each month the price of every item, or category of items, covered in the *FES*. This information is published not as conventional prices in pounds and pence but as a price *index*. Such an index is calculated by selecting a certain base date, noting the prices which prevailed at that date and arbitrarily setting them equal to 100. Prices in subsequent months are expressed as percentages of that initial price (though the percentage sign itself is omitted). For example, let us suppose that the average price of refrigerators on the base date was £200. If it were to increase to £240, the price indicator would rise to 120. If it were to fall to, say, £190, the price indicator would fall to 95. Current indices are published in the *Monthly Digest of Statistics* and in the *Annual Abstract of Statistics*. They show the widely varying pattern of price changes for different goods and services. During 1984, for instance, radios, TVs and other appliances fell in price by 1 per cent while the price of tea went up by 47 per cent.

The problem in constructing a suitable index for *all* price changes is how to combine the price indicators together to provide some average measure of changes in the general level of consumer prices. It is clear that it would be inadequate to take a simple arithmetic mean of all price changes because some goods are more important in terms of consumer spending than others.

The procedure that is adopted is to construct a *weighted average*. The various price indicators are weighted according to their importance in total consumer spending with the weights derived from the *FES*. In practice, there are two alternative ways of weighting. One produces what is called a *Laspeyres* index, the other a *Paasche* index.

7-4 LASPEYRES AND PAASCHE INDEX NUMBERS

The Laspeyres index method uses a constant set of weights for all the calculations, with the weights relating to some chosen base period. The Paasche index, on the other hand, uses a changing set of weights relating to the current period. We shall illustrate the calculation of the two alternatives using the data in Table 7-1. The table shows the changes in the demand for the different types of fuel available to the domestic consumer and the changes in average prices between 1980 and 1985. We wish to calculate an index to show how fuel prices have changed between the two years. It would be grossly inaccurate simply to work out an average price change as it is apparent that the different fuels have changed prices at different rates. Instead, we work out an average price change where we take the relative importance of each fuel into account. That is, we *weight* the prices by the market shares of the competing

Table 7-1 Domestic energy consumption and prices by fuel type

| Fuel type | Domestic energy consumption (percentage of total) | | Average price per therm equivalent (pence) | |
	1980	1985	1980	1985
Solid fuel	20.9	18.1	27.8	37
Gas	53.4	58	22.2	42.2
Electricity	18.6	18	112.6	162.6
Petroleum	7.1	5.9	45.3	58.3

Source: Digest of UK Energy Statistics
(Percentage figures are taken from Energy Consumption by Final Users, measured in millions of therms on a heat-supplied basis. Prices are calculated from the Estimated Expenditure on Domestic Energy by Final Users.)

fuels. The problem then becomes: which year's market shares to use for weighting—those for 1980 or for 1985? In fact, the Laspeyres method uses the 1980 data (the base weights) and the Paasche method uses the 1985 data (the current weights).

For the Laspeyres index we weight the 1980 prices by the 1980 market shares—that is we multiply each price by its respective market share. We then do the same for 1985 but still using the 1980 weights—that is multiply the 1985 prices by the 1980 market shares. We are trying to monitor price changes so all other variables—here market share—must stay constant. We can summarize this in a formula:

$$\text{Index} = \frac{\Sigma P_{85} W_{80}}{\Sigma P_{80} W_{80}} \times 100$$

This gives an index of

$$\frac{6465.07}{4182.49} \times 100 = 154.6$$

That is, our Laspeyres index shows that between 1980 and 1985 fuel prices to the domestic consumer rose by 54.6 per cent.

Alternatively, we could have chose to use the 1985 market share as weights. The Paasche formula can be expressed as:

$$\text{Index} = \frac{\Sigma P_{85} W_{85}}{\Sigma P_{80} W_{85}} \times 100$$

This gives an index of

$$\frac{6388.07}{4084.85} \times 100 = 156.4$$

That is, the Paasche index shows that between 1980 and 1985 fuel prices to the domestic consumer rose by 56.4 per cent.

Although, in this instance, there is not a large arithmetic difference between the two methods, such differences may be important to the decision-maker. If the government is thinking of increasing social security payments because of rising fuel prices or if it is thinking of giving pensioners a supplementary payment to cover fuel costs in the winter then small arithmetic differences become important. But why are there differences at all?

It is apparent that the Laspeyres index will typically tend to overestimate the price increases. As it uses base weights it ignores the fact that people will tend to shift consumption (and hence base weights will change) away from high-price-increase items towards low-price-increase items wherever possible. The Paasche index, on the other hand, will reflect such changing patterns of consumption as it uses current weights. (The fact that, in this example, the Laspeyres index is lower than the Paasche would lead us to infer that energy consumers had not reacted in this way.)

Why then use the Laspeyres at all? The answer is one of convenience. Once we have chosen a set of base weights for the Laspeyres index we can continue using them for successive years until the weights become obviously outdated. Thus, once we have average prices for 1986, 1987, 1988 and so on the Laspeyres index is easily updated. For the Paasche index, however, we would also need a full set of weights for each year and we would have to recalculate the set of indices afresh each year. The Paasche index constantly requires new data for the weights, the collection of which is both costly and time-consuming. Additionally, because weights are changing, the Paasche method allows comparison of the current index only with the base year.

The procedure for compiling the RPI is, in fact, something of a hybrid of the Paasche and Laspeyres methods. The weights are set annually using data from the previous year's *FES* (often before it is published). Those weights remain in use throughout the year for each month's compilation, and to this extent the index follows the Laspeyres methods. When reference is made not to the monthly data but to the figures for whole years, the RPI resembles a Paasche index in that each year's index figure is compiled on the basis of different (updated) weights.

7-5 REBASING AN INDEX

Periodically, an index is *rebased* by setting all the price indicators back to 100 and starting again. Thus the RPI figure for January 1974 stood at 191.8 with 1962 as the base ($= 100$), but the month was simultaneously given the value of 100 as the start of a new index. It is still possible, with care, to calculate price changes for periods that span the rebasing date. This is known as *chaining* and it involves multiplying together the appropriate index numbers expressed as numbers over 100. For example, let us ascertain the rate of inflation between 1969 and 1980.

In 1969, the RPI stood at 131.8 (January 1962 = 100). The index stood at 191.8 in January 1974 when it was rebased (reset to 100), and by 1980 the new index had reached 263.7 (January 1974 = 100). The percentage change between the two dates was therefore:

$$\frac{191.8}{131.8} \times 263.7 = 383.7$$

That is, prices by 1980 had risen *to* 383.7 per cent of their 1969 level. (They had therefore risen *by* 283.7 per cent.)

7-6 ENGEL CURVES, GROWTH MARKETS AND DECLINING MARKETS

From the point of view of the business analyst or economic researcher, one important use of publications such as the *FES* is the identification of changes in the pattern of consumer spending and the implications these have for a business organization. For example, the purchase, maintenance and running of motor vehicles absorbed 8.3 per cent of household spending in 1963, 10.9 per cent in 1973 and 12.3 per cent in 1983—an advance of 48 per cent. By contrast, 'seeds, plants and other gardening items' held constant at 0.4 per cent from 1963 and 1983, while food's share in the average family budget fell from 29.2 per cent to 20.7 per cent.

These relative movements are not to be confused with absolute changes. Food's falling share of family budgets is simply a decline in relative terms, reflecting the fact that food purchases have remained broadly constant in real terms while real incomes have risen. The figures for motoring's share, meanwhile, tend to understate its real expansion since the item has taken a larger share of a total which has itself increased. Other goods, such as rail travel, cinema admissions and domestic help, however, have suffered declines in absolute terms.

One of the major factors behind these changing consumption patterns is, of course, rising incomes: average real personal disposable income (that is, income after the deduction of income tax and national insurance contributions and after adjusting for inflation) rose by 51 per cent in the 20 years to 1985. This mounting affluence has permitted people to afford new commodities (like cars) which often displace previous lines of expenditure (like rail travel). In the vocabulary of Chapter 6, rising incomes have allowed people to move along their Engel curves, increasing their consumption of superior goods and decreasing their consumption of inferior ones. A recognition of these trends is clearly of some concern to business decision-makers, who will normally wish to differentiate between growth markets, stagnant markets and declining markets. Given that average income is likely to continue to rise, it is possible that past trends will serve as a guide.

Readers will recall that an Engel curve describes the relationship between income and the consumption of a good expressed in physical terms—grams of beef, litres of oil and so on. Since it does not relate income to expenditure, it cannot be constructed on the basis of *FES* data alone: other information is necessary. If data on the physical volume of sales of the product concerned are available—as they are with respect to cars—then the most straightforward procedure is simply to plot them against average income levels.

In other cases, the analyst may be obliged to construct his or her own measure of volume changes. This may be because no such information is available, or it may be because the analyst is concerned with a heterogeneous collection of goods (like, say, food) which it would be difficult to measure meaningfully in physical terms. It would first be necessary to establish how much had been spent on the goods in question over the period by looking at the *FES*. Table 7-2 relates to food expenditure. The first column of data shows expenditure on food in current terms, that is in terms of the amount of money actually spent at the time. From the current values it looks as if food expenditure has risen rapidly. *Current* expenditure obviously has, that is, in terms of the amount of money that changed hands. But the key question is: has food expenditure risen in *real* terms?

In Table 7-2, in addition to current expenditure we also have the RPI for food items only. As can readily be seen prices in general have increased over the period. It seems

Table 7-2 Expenditure on food, 1975–85

Year	Food expenditure per household per week (£, current prices)	RPI Food (1975 = 100)	Food expenditure per household per week (£, constant prices)	Index of food consumption per household (1975 = 100)
1975	13.52	100.0	13.52	100.0
1976	15.36	120.1	12.79	94.6
1977	17.74	142.9	12.41	91.8
1978	19.31	153.0	12.62	93.3
1979	21.83	171.4	12.74	94.2
1980	25.15	192.1	13.09	96.8
1981	27.20	208.3	13.06	96.6
1982	28.19	224.7	12.55	92.8
1983	29.62	231.8	12.78	94.5
1984	31.43	246.8	12.74	94.2
1985	32.70	252.5	12.95	95.8

Source: FES; Monthly Digest of Statistics.

sensible, therefore, to look not at actual spending on food but at spending on food relative to price increases. This is achieved by calculating expenditure in *real* terms, that is with the effects of price changes removed. This is shown in the third column in the table which gives expenditure at constant prices. Such a series is easily calculated by taking actual expenditure, dividing by the appropriate index value and multiplying by 100 (remembering that the index is arbitrarily set to 100 at its base). This process is referred to as *deflating* the time series.

The final column expresses expenditure in constant prices as another index. This is arrived at by setting 1975 = 100, dividing all the numbers by 13.52 and then multiplying by 100. This series traces changes in the volume of food consumed per household in purely physical terms.

It is clear that, after the effects of price changes have been removed, household spending on food fluctuated over a fairly narrow range during the period in question.

7-7 ELASTICITY OF DEMAND

The importance of elasticity of demand was discussed in detail in Chapters 5 and 6. To measure the elasticity of demand, it is necessary to compare price changes with changes in the physical volume of sales. For many goods, the latter figure is often available directly from published sources and can be used without further ado. In other cases, it may be necessary to produce one's own estimate of trends in sales volumes by undertaking calculations of the kind used in Section 7-6. Information on prices can often be gleaned from the RPI or some other published or private source. What is important, of course, is not the *absolute* price changes of the product or product group but these price changes *relative* to the general level of prices. This is known as a good's relative price, and for a consumer good it is found by deflating its price indicator by the figure for the RPI. Thus, as can be seen from Table 7-1, the price of electricity rose by 44 per cent from 1980 to 1985. Over the same period the RPI advanced by 42 per cent, showing that the relative price of electricity had risen by $144/142 = 1.5$ per cent. Combined with a fall in sales of electricity to domestic consumers of 3.2 per cent, this figure suggests an elasticity of demand for electricity of approximately -2.1 (that is, demand was fairly elastic).

Austrian economists would tend to query the validity of investigations such as these. They would argue that the information of greatest use to business is never collected because the categories that are used in the *FES* are too broad—it lumps together all expenditure on radio, television and musical instruments, for example, whereas entrepreneurs are interested primarily in sales of particular items like video recorders or micro-computers. They would also tend to take the view that past trends are of little help in predicting future changes because of the inherently volatile nature of economic life. The truth of this view is, to a degree, a matter of judgement. It can, however, be investigated to an extent by carrying out the kinds of analysis which this chapter has discussed.

7-8 SUMMARY

Deflating a time series involves removing the effects of inflation from the variable.

Index numbers show the movement in the value of some aggregated variable over time against a selected base period.

The *Laspeyres index* uses base-period weights in calculating an index.

The *Paasche index* uses current period weights in calculating an index.

Rebasing an index involves calculating a continuous index for some variable from a set of indices with different base dates.

Weights show the relative importance of groups of items that make up an index.

EXERCISES

You are recommended to use a suitable computer spreadsheet for the appropriate calculations for these exercises.

7-1 Update Table 7-1 with the latest data from published sources (you will have to calculate comparable statistics from the published data available).
(*a*) Using 1980 weights, calculate a Laspeyres index for domestic fuel prices for the data you have collected.
(*b*) Using the latest set of market-share figures as weights calculate a Paasche index.
(*c*) Assume you are working for Age Concern and lobbying the Department of Energy to provide fuel supplements for pensioners. Which of the two indices you have calculated would you use and why?

7-2 Using the *Monthly Digest of Statistics* collect data on the RPI for the major groups used in its construction (food, drink, tobacco, etc.) in terms of:
  (*i*) the total index;
 (*ii*) the index for each group;
(*iii*) the weights used for each group.

Collect these data for the latest year available and for the annual period 10 years ago. Answer the following questions:
(*a*) Which group has shown the largest price increase over the last decade?
(*b*) Which group has shown the smallest?

(c) Formulate a hypothesis to explain these different rates of increase. How could you test this hypothesis?
(d) Which group's weight has changed most over the period?
(e) What reasons can you suggest for this?

7-3 Consider the category of expenditure 'Meals bought and consumed outside the home'.

(a) Do you think the elasticity of this expenditure group would be elastic or inelastic?
(b) Collect data on the following series from the *Annual Abstract of Statistics* for the last 10 years:
  (i) RPI all items
  (ii) RPI on the defined 'Meals' group
  (iii) weights used each year for (ii).
(c) Calculate the trend in real expenditure on 'Meals'.
(d) What evidence is there to support your answer to (a) above?

7-4 The data below are taken from the *Monthly Digest of Statistics* and show the weekly rates of two types of social security benefit and the RPI, at the rate prevailing in the November of each year:

Year	Unemployment benefit, men, single women and widows (£ per week)	Retirement pension, single person (£ per week)	RPI (Jan 1974 = 100)
1976	12.90	15.30	165.8
1977	14.70	17.50	187.4
1978	15.75	19.50	202.5
1979	18.50	23.30	237.7
1980	20.65	27.15	274.1
1981	22.50	29.60	306.9
1982	25.00	32.85	326.1
1983	27.05	34.05	341.9
1984	28.45	35.80	358.8
1985	30.45	38.30	378.4

(a) Compare, and comment upon, the difference in the trends of the two payments.
(b) In which year was a single pensioner best-off?
(c) In which year was an unemployed male worst-off?
(d) Update the table with the latest information and identify any change in the two trends.

7-6 The Central Statistical Office (CSO) regularly publishes the Index of Industrial Production. Find out how the index is constructed and how the weights are derived.

8

SUPPLY

8-1 INTRODUCTION

We saw in Chapter 7 that over the past few years consumers had reacted to price changes in domestic fuels by switching between the alternatives as relative prices altered. The implied direction of cause and effect, however, is that consumption patterns responded to a change in price. The question then arises: what factors caused the price to change? To answer such a question we must supplement our analysis on demand with a complementary analysis of the other side of the market—supply. This chapter will outline the theory of supply and will look briefly at some relevant sources of statistical information. It will follow the format laid down in Chapter 1: a model will be assembled by setting out a number of assumptions and by deducing some implications; the initial conditions will then be altered and comparisons will be made. This is intended to allow the formation of hypotheses which can be tested against the evidence. It will be useful to begin the analysis by examining the resources used in the process of production or, as economists call them, the *factors of production*.

8-2 FACTORS OF PRODUCTION

'Factors of production' is the term used to denote economic resources. They may be grouped under the four headings of land, labour, capital and enterprise. The rewards which they earn are, of course, the costs which business organizations are forced to incur in the production process.

Land

Land denotes both land proper and all natural resources like mineral deposits, oil, water and forests. Producers use land, therefore, both in the form of the ground upon which their premises stand and in the form of raw materials. Landlords who let their property out are rewarded with rent. The way in which rent is determined will be examined in Chapter 19, which is devoted to the theory of distribution. For present purposes, it is sufficient to note that, for producers, rent is a cost.

Capital

Capital refers to man-made aids to production. It includes all tools, plant and equipment, stocks of work-in-progress, industrial and commercial buildings and the 'infrastructure' of roads, docks and so on. It does *not*, it should be noted, include money. This is one instance of the terminology of economics differing from the vocabulary of business. For the economist, money is not a real resource but merely a potential claim upon real resources, and is therefore excluded from the definition.

Capital is used up in the process of production: tools and equipment wear out and buildings become unsafe. Capital items can also lose their value as better, more advanced versions become available and equipment is sometimes scrapped because it is obsolete rather than because it is worn out. This process of losing value is known as depreciation, and it will be examined again when our attention turns, in Chapter 14, to costs.

The process of adding new capital items to the current stock is known to economists as *capital formation* or *investment*. This specialist use of the word 'investment' by economists does not therefore cover financial transactions like placing funds in building societies or buying shares on the Stock Exchange. Financial transactions are, however, connected with investment in physical assets in that firms usually borrow money in order to buy equipment and buildings. The interest which lenders charge represents, therefore, a cost to users of capital assets.

Consumer durables like houses, cars and radios have many of the characteristics of capital in that they yield a flow of services over time, and are therefore sometimes called *consumer capital*.

Labour

Labour denotes all human productive effort, both mental and physical, though economists usually restrict their attention to work that is paid. The number of people available for paid employment is, of course, far less than the total population: schoolchildren and old people do not work, and many people work at home looking after their families. The ratio of those *economically active* (i.e. workers, employers and the unemployed) to the whole population is termed the *activity rate* or *participation rate*, and it currently stands at about 45 per cent in the United Kingdom. It will clearly vary with changes in the relative sizes of the different age groups and with changes in social conventions such as whether married women should work.

Labour costs exceed wages and salaries by a substantial margin because of costs like employers' national insurance contributions, superannuation contributions and any fringe benefits paid to employees.

Enterprise

Enterprise is the activity of recognizing and exploiting new market opportunities. Entrepreneurs are the initiators of economic change. They look for the chance to bring new products and services to the market, or perhaps to bring established products to new markets. Usually their recognition of these openings arises from some specialist information: knowledge that technology has recently made possible the manufacture of some particular item or knowledge that consumers' tastes in a particular market are moving in a certain direction. Their response is to marshall the necessary resources—land, labour and capital—to take advantage of the new possibilities.

It must be emphasized that enterprise is inherently speculative. In breaking new ground, entrepreneurs have little to guide them by way of past trends. There can be no guarantee that the new enterprise will succeed, and most entrepreneurs sustain the odd failure. When they are successful their reward is *profit*.

There is an important difference between profit and other factor rewards. While rent, interest, wages and salaries are normally specified in advance, the amount of profit (if there is any!) can only be ascertained when the transaction is completed. It is not, therefore, possible to specify in advance how much profit a transaction will earn. Thus, profit cannot be considered to be a cost to a business in the same way as other factor rewards.

For economists of the Austrian school, enterprise is the key factor of production. Although natural resources and the skills of the workers will influence the prosperity of any national economy, they believe that the crucial factor will be the dynamism of its entrepreneurs whose role is to find ways to apply those resources and skills.

It is—as always—easier to distinguish the various factors of production in a textbook than it is in the real world: the four categories above interpenetrate. For example, land can be similar to capital in that its value can be enhanced by, say, irrigation schemes, which make it in part a man-made aid to production rather than a gift of nature. Similarly, the value of labour can be increased by 'investment' in training. Likewise, capital and enterprise are sometimes difficult to distinguish in that entrepreneurs usually provide both the capital assets and the ideas for their business ventures.

8-3 A MODEL OF SUPPLY

As with demand, we can begin by constructing a model of supply or, perhaps, of producer choice. The fundamental point is that supply will be determined by the profits which producers expect to make by bringing goods to the market. These expectations of profit will in turn be influenced by a range of other factors. These are: the price of the goods or service (P_x); prices of factors of production (F); technology (T); and the profitability of alternative products (R_a). Algebraically, this may be expressed as:

$$S = f(P_x, F, T, R_a, Z, e)$$

where S stands for the quantity supplied, Z stands for any other, unidentified factors which might merit inclusion in any particular analysis and e is an error term. This is the *supply function*, and it is clearly similar to the demand function. As with demand, each relationship in the expression will be examined individually, with the remaining factors being held constant. Before examining these items, however, we shall construct a formal model of producer choice.

Let us assume, first, that all producers seek to maximize their profits; second, that factors of production are available at given prices; third, that factors may move freely from one industry to another; and fourth, that factors of production have varying levels of efficiency. The last assumption is simply the idea that factors of production differ in their various capabilities. Land may be more suitable for one crop than for another, some factories may have better equipment, better transport links or better-trained workers than others while, of course, people differ in their natural aptitudes.

A deduction which may reasonably be made from the above is that firms (producers) will distribute themselves across various industries depending on the profits which they are able to make with the factors of production at their disposal. In other words, some sort of equilibrium will obtain, with different numbers of firms in different industries. This implies, of course, that each industry will have a certain level of output. As with demand, the model can now be used to examine the way in which that output will change in response to changes in the various elements in the supply function.

8-4 SUPPLY AND PRICE: THE SUPPLY CURVE

A higher price for a commodity would naturally alter the above equilibrium, in that producers with rather lower efficiency would now be able to enter the industry and trade profitably. Economists thus conclude that there is a *positive* relationship between price and quantity supplied: the higher the price of any commodity, the more will be supplied to the market. This relationship is known as the *supply curve* and it describes the quantity of the good which producers will plan to bring to market at various prices during a specified period of time (Fig. 8-1).

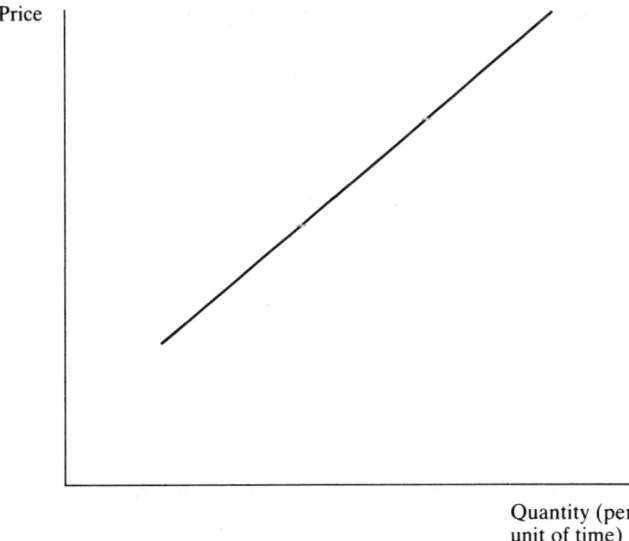

Price

Quantity (per
unit of time)

Figure 8-1 Supply curve

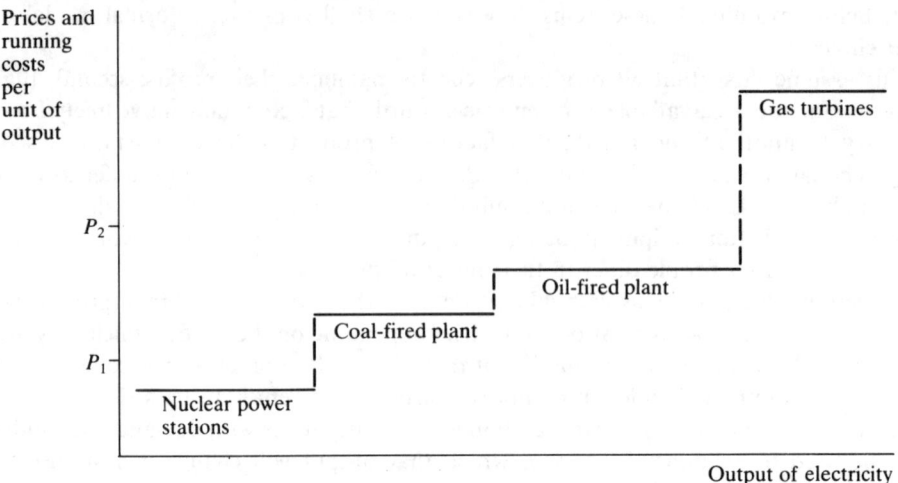

Figure 8-2 Illustrative supply curve of the CEGB

This can be illustrated by considering the position of the Central Electricity Generating Board (CEGB). As well as conventional oil- and coal-fired power stations, the CEGB has nuclear stations and small gas-turbine stations. Some are newer than others, and some have the advantage of being located close to cheap fuel supplies. The stations are run in a 'merit order': the most efficient stations run virtually all the time (the 'base-load stations'), those of medium efficiency are brought into use as demand builds up, and the stations with the highest running costs (the gas-turbine stations) are used only to meet peak demand. The merit order, combined with information on the capacities of the different stations, could produce the curve shown in Fig. 8-2. If the CEGB were a private company seeking to make maximum profits, it would only generate electricity upon which it could make a profit. Thus at price P_1 it would only run the nuclear stations, while at price P_2 it would be able to run much more plant at a profit. Fig. 8-2 would thus show its supply curve.

It was assumed above that the CEGB's stock of power stations was fixed, meaning that supply could only be changed by altering the use of existing plant. Given that it may take typically anything from 5 to 15 years to build a new power station, this is a fair approximation to use when analysing events over a short period. For longer periods, it would be necessary to take account of the CEGB's ability to build new power stations and to scrap unwanted plant.

Economists therefore distinguish between the *short-run* supply curve and the *long-run* supply curve, where the short run is defined as the period over which some resources are fixed. Over the long run, by definition, all resources are mobile. Thus if the CEGB found that electricity demand was rising, its response would be twofold: in the short run (that is, until extra stations could be built) it would run all its plant, even the high-cost gas turbines, while in the long run it could build extra stations. This is illustrated in Fig. 8-3. Note that point C is lower than B, because the new stations will be more efficient than the peak-capacity gas-turbine stations. Conversely, the industry would react to a fall in demand by, first, ceasing to run plant at the bottom end of the merit order altogether and, second, by reducing capacity by closing unwanted power stations.

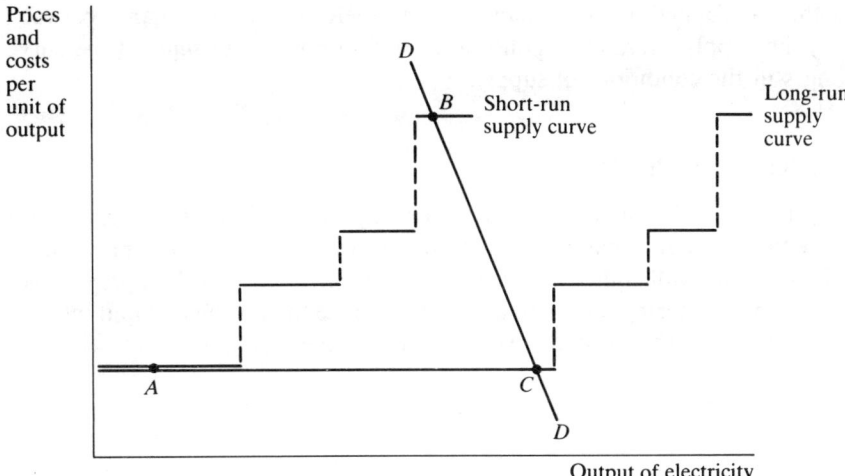

Figure 8-3 Short- and long-run supply curves

These principle are assumed to apply to all industries. All use some resources which are relatively immobile—usually plant and premises but possibly another factor like skilled manpower—and therefore have both long- and short-run supply curves.

The two curves clearly have different slopes. The short-run supply curve is said to be less elastic than the long-run supply curve, reflecting the greater mobility of resources over the long run. The use of the word 'elastic' is analagous to its use in demand theory and it is measured in a similar manner.

$$E_s = \frac{\%\Delta Q}{\%\Delta P}$$

The *duration* of the short run naturally varies from industry to industry. The CEGB lies toward one end of the spectrum: the short run lasts up to 15 years because it uses resources which are not readily available. Large power stations cannot be bought second-hand, nor can nuclear engineers be recruited easily on the open labour market. In the terminology of economics, these resources are *specific*: they have few uses outside one particular industry. When expanding, therefore, the CEGB has to order new power stations and to train its own senior workers. Both processes take time. Light engineering, by contrast, uses standard factories, general-purpose equipment and semi-skilled workers and thus has a short run which may be measured in months rather than years. The motor-vehicle industry, which uses relatively specialist equipment such as robots and assembly lines, lies between these two extremes.

8-5 THE CONDITIONS OF SUPPLY

The supply curves were constructed on the assumption that the other factors in the supply function were constant. Changes in these factors—they may be termed the *conditions of supply*—will shift the supply curves just as changes in income and so on shifted the demand curve. There is thus a distinction to be made, just as there was with demand, between movements *along* the supply curve in response to changes in price and *shifts* of the curve induced by changes in the conditions of supply.

The prices of factors of production

Increases in the price of the factors of production used by an industry will clearly induce some of its firms either to shut down or to enter another market. Thus the supply curves (both long- and short-run) will shift to the left. For example, the CEGB's supply curves must have shifted to the left during the 1970s as fuel prices rose (fuel being an input into the industry's production process) and would have shifted out to the right as oil prices fell in the mid-1980s.

Technology

In the context of economic analysis, technology refers to the process of combining inputs and transforming them into outputs. This can mean a literal transformation—like turning flour and yeast into bread—or transportation—like turning crude-oil-in-Alaska into crude-oil-in-California. It can also, of course, refer to both.

Changes in technology affect the rate at which inputs are transformed into output. Better machines or forms of organization can generate more output (or output which has greater value) from given inputs. Better boilers can make fuel produce more heat, for example, and there is often scope for trimming a firm's labour force by using new technology.

Technology is measured by *productivity ratios* of output per unit of input. The input which is chosen will depend on the purposes of the analysis. Output per unit of labour (*labour productivity*) is often seen as important and British Coal, for example, measures it in terms of tonnes mined per manshift. The productivity of farming, by contrast, is usually measured in yields per hectare.

Productivity ratios combined with data on costs provide information on costs per unit of output (or *unit costs*). Thus a knowledge of both the cost and the output per manshift would allow the NCB to compute the average labour cost per tonne of coal produced. Changes in technology which raised productivity would reduce unit costs. *Ceteris paribus*, such changes would make it easier for more firms to make profits in the industry and would thus have the effect of shifting supply curves to the right.

Profits on alternative goods

Most producers make a range of products and sell in several different markets. They are thus in the position of having to allocate their resources between their different lines of business. For example, department stores have to decide how much floor space to give to each of their different departments. This decision will naturally be taken by examining their respective profit opportunities. If, say, sportswear shows high returns it may be expanded at the expense of the neighbouring food department. Thus the food-retailing industry will contract—its supply curves shifting to the left—because of better profits elsewhere.

Other relevant factors

As with demand, a variable must be included to allow for the specific circumstances which might influence the supply of a particular commodity other than those already discussed. These might relate, for example, to the industry's objectives or obligations. While privately owned firms' primary objectives will be to maximize profits or to expand, the nationalized industries are sometimes obliged by statute to offer certain services. For example, British Rail keeps open several loss-making lines and receives a grant in compensation. Furthermore, any industry can be affected by legislation on safety, advertising or environmental protection, by selective taxation or by subsidies, and these may require special attention in any particular piece of analysis.

The supply function includes the error term e on the grounds that no theory could hope to capture every single influence on supply. In practical terms, the e factor will also have to stand for anything which cannot be measured, such as firms' objectives. Theories based on such factors cannot, of course, be tested.

The effect of changes in the conditions of supply on the position of the supply curve—perhaps we may confine our attention to the short-run curve—is illustrated by the algebraic expression:

$$Q_s = (a_1 + a_2 + a_3 + a_4) + b \times P$$

where Q_s = quantity supplied, P = price, and a_1–a_4 = the various conditions of supply. Graphically, changes in, say, technology would alter one of the a terms and so give the supply curve a new intercept on the vertical axis. In Fig. 8-4 the move from S_1 to S_2 could, for example, have been caused by a fall in factor prices, an advance in technology or a reduction in producers' profits on alternative goods.

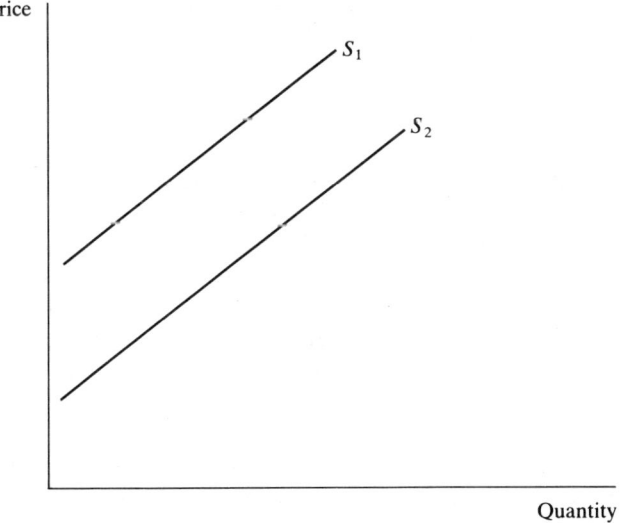

Figure 8-4 Shifts in supply

8-6 USING THE MODEL

This, then, is an outline of the elementary model of supply. In later chapters we shall develop it by looking more closely at the relationship between costs and production. Even as it stands, however, it can be used to explain past changes and to predict future changes. To see the model in operation, let us return to developments in the gas industry in the 1970s. Figure 1-1 in Chapter 1 showed that between 1970 and 1979 the industry raised its sales of gas to domestic consumers by over 150 per cent *and* cut its tariffs by 30 per cent in real terms. This is a fairly substantial change demanding a powerful explanation and will form the basis for a rigorous investigation in Chapter 10. For the present, however, we can pick out the salient points relating to the supply model.

On the demand side, there is evidence of various forces which might have caused the demand curve to shift: real incomes rose by 28 per cent, the price of coal rose by 242 per cent and that of electricity went up by 274 per cent. It is unlikely, however, that these would have been of sufficient magnitude to have caused gas consumption to more than double. The hypothesis must therefore be that the (long-run) supply curve shifted downwards.

Descriptions of the gas industry since 1970 suggest that the conditions of supply did indeed alter markedly. In 1970 the industry was largely a manufacturer of town gas in local gasworks using coal and coke, whereas ten years later it supplied natural gas through a country-wide distribution grid. Labour productivity in terms of therms sold per worker rose more than threefold. Whether the increase in supply should be classed as deriving from changes in the availability of natural resources or from advances in technology is perhaps a moot point. At any rate, there is clear evidence that the supply curve shifted downwards, and that this was the primary cause of lower prices and thus of higher consumption.

However, it is more usual to find that supply-side and demand-side factors are changing simultaneously in a particular sector, making the work of analysis rather more complex. The next chapter will begin to look at this by examining the way supply and demand interact to produce equilibrium.

8-7 SUMMARY

The *conditions of supply* are the non-price elements in the supply function. A change in any of these will induce a shift in the supply curves (long- and short-run).

Factors of production are the various resources used in the process of producing goods and services: land (natural resources), labour, capital and enterprise.

The *supply curve* indicates the quantities of a good which producers will plan to bring to market at different prices. *Short-run* supply curves show how this relationship will operate while certain elements of the production process are fixed, while *long-run* supply curves indicate the nature of the relationship when all factors are mobile. Long-run curves are consequently more elastic than short run curves.

The *supply function* is the relationship between the quantity supplied to any market during a given time-period and its various determinants: the price of the goods or service, factor prices, technology, the profitability of alternative lines of production and so on. Movements along these curves are induced by changes in price.

EXERCISES

8-1 Describe the effects on the supply curve of cereal crops like wheat of the following changes:

(a) the imposition of legal limits on the production of milk;
(b) an increase in the price of pesticides;
(c) a fall in the price of agricultural land;
(d) a tendency for there to be warmer, drier summers;
(e) the development of new, more productive strains of wheat;
(f) an increase in the price of breakfast cereals due to higher demand;
(g) the clearance of hedges and woods from farms growing cereal crops.

Illustrate your answers diagrammatically.

8-2 Using the *Monthly Digest of Statistics* collect data on the annual amount of wheat harvested in the United Kingdom for the last 20 years. Which of the factors in Exercise 8-1 do you think explains the trends in wheat harvests over this period?

8-3 The following information relates to sales of socks:

Week	Sales (thousand)	Price (pence)
1	10	40
2	20	50
3	30	65
4	40	90
5	60	40
6	70	50
7	80	65
8	90	90

Plot the data on a graph. How would you interpret these figures? What has happened to the supply curve? And what has happened to the demand curve?

8-4 Detail the factors that might govern the supply of the following items in both the short and the long run:

(a) steel
(b) whale meat
(c) computer software.

8-5 Formulate a hypothesis—a conditional prediction with an 'if ... then ...' format—about the relationship between coalminers' pay and the supply curve for coal from British pits.

(a) Draw up a checklist of the data that you would require to test your hypothesis.
(b) Find out which of the data items on your checklist are available from published sources and which are not. How does the availability of data affect your testing the hypothesis?

9

EQUILIBRIUM

9-1 INTRODUCTION

The purpose of this chapter is to introduce and examine the concept of *market equilibrium.* This concept is of fundamental importance in economics at both the micro- and macro-economic levels. In neo-classical economics equilibrium is important because this school of thought takes markets to be in a state of equilibrium as a general rule. Austrian economists, who argue that markets are in a state of constant change and thus not generally in equilibrium, nevertheless see equilibrium as the goal towards which the process of economic change normally moves. Our analysis of equilibrium and the process by which it is achieved draws extensively on the theories of supply and demand developed earlier.

9-2 MARKET EQUILIBRIUM

Equilibrium may be defined as *the position in which supply and demand are in balance.* At equilibrium, the volume of sales equals the volume of production and the market is said to *clear.* Conversely, a market is in disequilibrium if supply and demand fail to balance. A market in this position is likely to be characterized by mounting stocks of unsold goods (if there is excess supply) or by queues of unsatisfied customers (if there is excess demand).

Table 9-1 shows the supply and demand levels for a hypothetical market. The supply data relate to the short run. It is clear that supply and demand are in balance when price equals £5, for this price induces both suppliers to produce 80 units per week and consumers to buy 80 units per week. £5 and 80 units are said to be the *equilibrium price* and *equilibrium quantity* respectively.

Table 9.1 Supply of and demand for cans of motor oil

Price (£)	Quantity demanded	Quantity supplied
1	120	–
2	110	20
3	100	40
4	90	60
5	80	80
6	70	100
7	60	120
8	50	140
9	40	160
10	30	180

The equilibrium price in an individual market is the outcome of the interaction between the forces of supply and demand (or *market forces* as they are sometimes called). This may be shown diagrammatically by putting the supply and demand curves on the same graph, as in Fig. 9.1. It is now clear why, in our discussion of demand, the focus of attention fell on the relationship between price and quantity rather than on any other relationship: this is the only one which can be related directly to supply by means of a price–quantity graph. (This type of diagram is known as the *Marshallian cross* after its progenitor, Alfred Marshall, who was professor of economics at Cambridge at the turn of the century.)

9-3 DERIVING EQUILIBRIUM

It is clearly important to be able to establish the price at which a market will attain equilibrium. This can often be achieved using a graph as in Fig. 9-1. While such graphical

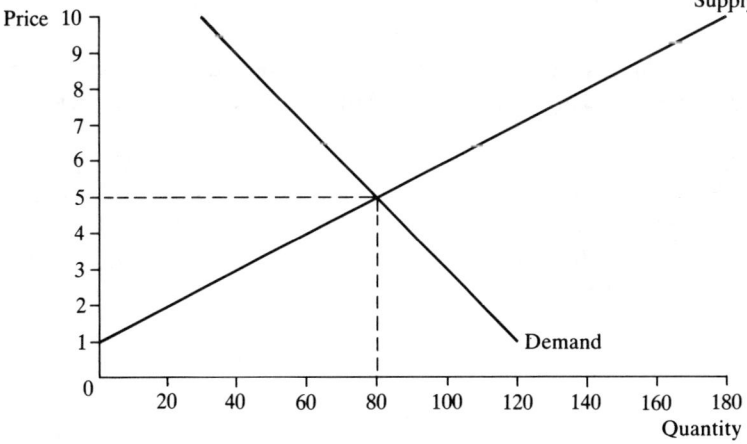

Figure 9-1 Supply and demand curves

analysis is frequently useful, it can be both cumbersome and inaccurate (given that we are reading equilibrium values from the scales on the graph). A more convenient method is provided using *simultaneous equations.*

The supply and demand situation shown in Table 9-1 and Fig. 9-1 can also be expressed in equation form.

$$Q_d = 130 - 10P \qquad (9\text{-}1)$$

$$Q_s = -20 + 20P \qquad (9\text{-}2)$$

In terms of economic analysis we are looking for a price that will 'clear' the market, that is, will balance Q_d and Q_s. In mathematical terms, we are searching for a solution such that we have values for P and Q which will satisfy both the two equations *at the same time.* There are obviously solutions (values of P and Q) which will satisfy Eq. (9-1) *or* Eq. (9-2), but there is in fact generally only *one* unique combination of values for P and Q which satisfies *both* equations simultaneously.

Given that the definition of market equilibrium is that $Q_d = Q_s$ we can use the two equations to give:

$$Q_d = Q_s$$
$$130 - 10P = -20 + 20P$$

Rearranging gives:

$$130 + 20 = 20P + 10P$$
$$150 = 30P$$
$$P = 5$$

thus confirming the graphical equilibrium price. To find equilibrium quantity we can substitute $P = 5$ into *either* Eq. (9-1) or Eq. (9-2) (as they are both equal at equilibrium). This gives $Q = 80$.

However, such an approach is not always possible with more complex formulations and it is necessary to provide a general method of solution that can be applied to all such problems. There are a number of different solution methods possible, but, arguably, the easiest to follow is the one detailed here. The method initially may look complex but it is based on the simple concept that, in any equation, if we change one side of the expression the basic relationship will be unaltered as long as we make the *same* change to the other side of the equation.

As a simple example, suppose we have the equation $10Y = 100$. Obviously, $Y = 10$ here. But to illustrate the basic point suppose we make a change to the left hand side (LHS) of the equation by multiplying by 5, giving $50Y$. The basic relationship, with Y still equal to 10, will remain as long as we make the *same* change to the right hand side (RHS) of the original equation, giving $50Y = 500$. So, we can make any arithmetic change to the LHS of an equation as long as exactly the same change is undertaken on the RHS.

How does this help? Assume that we had been given Eqs (9-1) and (9-2) in a different (but common) form:

$$2Q + 20P = 260 \qquad (9\text{-}3)$$

$$3Q - 60P = -60 \qquad (9\text{-}4)$$

(You should confirm for yourself that these equations are identical to the original.) A general solution can now be adopted. Let us multiply the LHS to Eq. (9-3) by 3 (you will see why we use this number shortly). To enable the equation to stay the same we must also multiply the RHS by 3 to give:

$$6Q + 60P = 780 \tag{9-5}$$

Now, let us look at Eq. 9-4 and multiply this through by 2 to give:

$$6Q - 120P = -120 \tag{9-6}$$

Now we will subtract the same number from both sides of Eq. (9-6). The number we will subtract is 780. However, this number, as we can see from Eq. 9-5, is mathematically equal to $(6Q + 60P)$. So, we can subtract $(6Q + 60P)$ from the LHS of equation 9-6 and subtract 780 from the RHS and we shall still be changing both sides in exactly the same way. This will give:

$$6Q - 120P - (6Q + 60P) = -120 - (780)$$

$$-180P = -900 \tag{9-7}$$

So the result of this manipulation has been to transform one of our equations into a form where we have removed one of the two unknowns (Q) from the expression. It must be emphasized that Eq. (9-7) has been derived from the original equations and conveys exactly the same mathematical information but in a different form. Eq. (9-7) can now easily be solved to give $P = -900/-180 = 5$. Returning to either of our two original equations we can now substitute $P = 5$ into either (or both) of the equations to find the value that Q must take. From Eq. (9-3), substituting $P = 5$, we can confirm that $Q = 80$.

The logic of using 3 and 2 to multiply our original equations should now be apparent. The method used has eliminated the variable Q from the resulting Eq. (9-7). This is achieved by multiplying the first equation (9-3) through by the coefficient associated with Q in Eq. (9-4) (which is 3) and then doing the same for Eq. (9-4) (that is, multiplying through by 2, the coefficient associated with Q in the first equation).

Although in this simple example the method may seem overcomplicated it must be emphasized that the solution process identified can now be used to solve any set of linear simultaneous equations. In our example we had a system of 2 equations and 2 unknowns (P, Q). The general principles can be applied to any system of n equations with n unknowns to find the set of values for the unknowns that satisfies all the equations in the system simultaneously.

9-4 MOVING TOWARDS EQUILIBRIUM

In the previous section we established a means whereby we can quantify the equilibrium position in a market. The *process* whereby the market attains such an equilibrium position, however, still remains to be discussed.

A distinction must now be drawn between the *market price* which may be observed in a market and the underlying *equilibrium* price. The market price is the price which currently prevails between buyer and seller and the equilibrium price is the price that will allow the market to clear. In an equilibrium situation the two will necessarily be equal. If, however, there is a shift in either, or both, of the supply and demand curves a *new* equilibrium price would be established and the existing market price (equal to the *old* equilibrium price) would no longer coincide with it.

To analyse the process by which the market price moves back towards the equilibrium price let us assume that the market had previously been in equilibrium at point *A* in Fig. 9-2—that is, where the two curves intersect. Let us further assume that there is some change in the conditions of demand causing the demand curve to move to a new position as in Fig. 9-2. The new equilibrium price is £5 whilst the prevailing market price is £9.

Readers will recall that schedules like those in Table 9-1 describe the *plans* of producers and buyers: they describe the actions which will be set in motion under certain conditions. One of the 'conditions' is the price of the good. At £9, producers will offer 160 units a week for sale, but consumers will only buy at the rate of 40 per week. Producers' plans will thus be frustrated for the most part, and will naturally have to be revised. Production will be cut and the unsold stocks will be offered for sale at discount prices. The average price will therefore drift down, say to £7. News of lower prices will then cause consumers to revise their buying plans in turn, and sales will rise to a rate of 60 units a week. At a price of £7, however, output is still running ahead of sales, unsold stocks will still be piling up (although at a slower rate). Plans will be revised again: there will be a further round of cuts in production, falls in price and increases in sales. This process will only come to an end when the rate of production and the rate of consumption have fallen into step and any unsold stocks disposed of.

Had the starting point been a price below equilibrium, the reverse of this process would

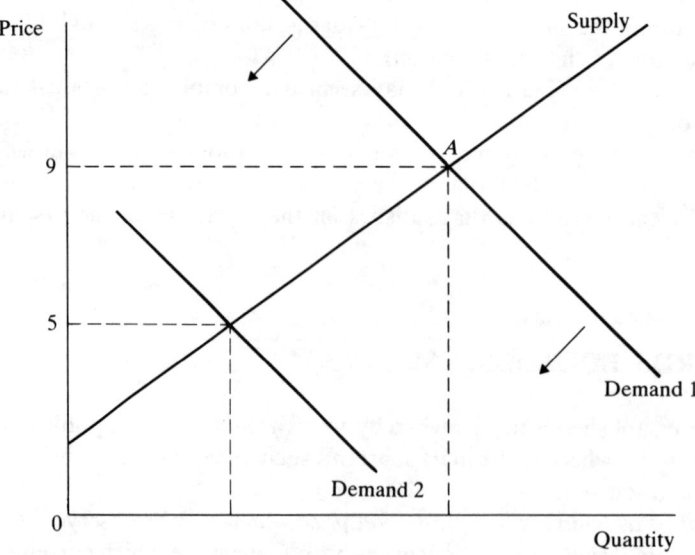

Figure 9-2 Change in demand

have occurred. Production would have been low and demand would have exceeded it. Prices would have drifted up, prompting producers to raise production and eliminating excess demand. As a result the market would have moved again toward equilibrium.

It is important to note that price and output will usually move back towards their equilibrium values when disturbed. The market economy is thus thought to resemble a self-righting lifeboat which quickly returns to an upright position after being capsized.

There is, however, one force which can thwart this natural movement towards equilibrium and that is intervention by the public authorities. Governments may occasionally dictate prices for political reasons, and if these differ from equilibrium levels, then markets will be prevented from attaining equilibrium. For example, the prices of agricultural goods in the European Community (EC) are currently determined not by market forces but by the Common Agricultural Policy (CAP). The CAP's prices are far above equilibrium levels because the policy-makers' intention is to bolster the incomes of farmers. The result of this artificial price-setting has been that farmers have expanded production while consumption has to some degree been discouraged. Predictably, farm products are in excess supply and the EC authorities find themselves obliged to buy up the extra supplies to prevent their prices from falling. These surplus stocks have then to be put into store: there are 'mountains' of butter, powdered milk, grain and meat and 'lakes' of wine in storage depots in every country in the Community. The position is illustrated in Fig. 9-3 which shows an ordinary supply curve and a demand curve which is shaped to reflect the EC's commitment to buy unlimited quantities of output at the appointed price.

Government intervention more usually takes the form of stipulating that a good shall not be sold at all. While such regulations may be successful in reducing the purchase and sale of the goods in question, it is often the case that 'black markets' develop as people try to obtain them despite the law. One of the best-known examples of this was the trade in

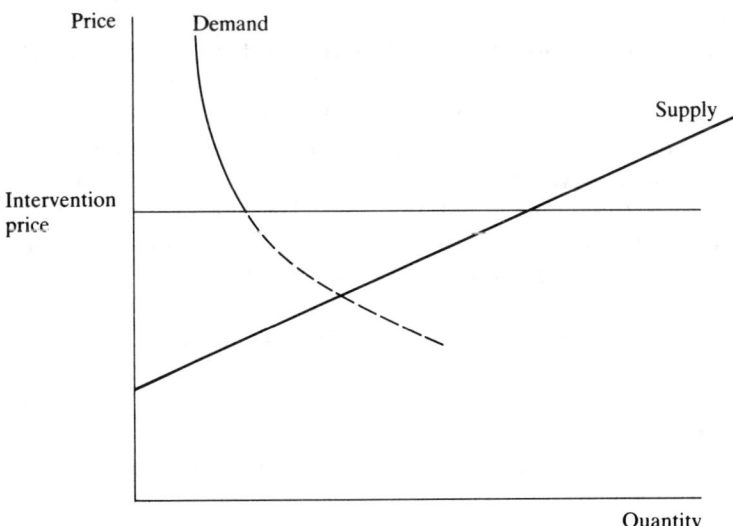

Figure 9-3 Government intervention

'bootleg' liquor in the United States in the 1920s when the sale of alcohol was forbidden. The law became so difficult to enforce that it was eventually repealed. In cases like narcotics, however, the black market may have less public sympathy and governments may have more success in preventing the use of such drugs.

9-5 AUSTRIAN ECONOMICS, EQUILIBRIUM AND THE ROLE OF INFORMATION

The second comment on the process of equilibration is that Austrian economists believe it to reinforce the importance of enterprise. They argue that the business of moving a market towards equilibrium is the work of the entrepreneur. If a market has excess demand, it is the entrepreneur who identifies this—it may not always be obvious—and marshals the resources to meet it. In the case of a market with excess supply, it will fall to entrepreneurs not merely to reduce production but to find new products for their factories to make and to find buyers for the unsold stocks. Equilibration, as Austrians see it, is not an automatic process but one which needs to be consciously organized by entrepreneurs.

Austrians also believe that this activity never really ceases. They argue that no sooner is some progress made towards equilibrium than fashions change or some new product is invented and the process has to start all over again. Because of this, economists of the Austrian school hold the view that the process of equilibration—rather than the equilibrium position—should hold the attention of economic analysts.

The process of economic adjustment, according to Austrian economists, is rendered problematic by the fact that these changes are, to a degree, uncertain. Entrepreneurs can never be sure, for example, that new products will find buyers or that new technology will work. The process of searching for equilibrium is, for Austrian economists, a series of experiments as entrepreneurs try to discover which products will sell and the prices that consumers are willing to pay.

Neo-classical economists, by contrast, are content to assume that markets go quickly and smoothly to their equilibrium points and are therefore quite happy to base their analyses on the idea that most markets are in equilibrium for most of the time. They are prepared to uphold this idea because they are willing to make one assumption of critical importance: that economic agents have perfect information. That is not to say that neo-classical economists believe that everyone is endowed with superhuman powers. Rather they hold that people have sufficient relevant information and that more information can be found with reasonable ease. The assumption of perfect information is, they argue, a fair approximation.

When the assumption of perfect information is built into economic models, it has the effect of making it easier for them to attain equilibrium. To see this, let us return to the example used earlier in Fig. 9-2 and imagine that price stands at £10—above equilibrium. There would be, as was argued above, excess supply and a build-up of stocks. If it is now assumed that everyone was aware of this, producers would instantly realize that there was no point in maintaining production at its current rate and they would swiftly begin the process of cutting output and prices. Equilibrium would rapidly be established. Without the assumption of perfect information, the course of events might be slower and more problematic. Each producer might believe that his own failure to sell all his output was purely temporary and he might carry on producing in the expectation that things would improve. Disequilibrium would therefore continue and stocks would build up to an even greater extent. Price cuts, when they came, would have to be all greater and the market might lurch from one disequilibrium to another before settling down. In other words the assumption of *perfect information* is an integral part of the neo-classical view that markets are either in, or close to, equilibrium.

9-6 GENERAL EQUILIBRIUM

Thus far, we have focused our attention on the process of equilibrium only in one market. *General equilibrium* analysis is the name of a branch of neo-classical economics which attempts to examine the economic system in its entirety. The economy is composed of innumerable markets for products, services, factors of production and so on. General equilibrium theory seeks to establish whether *every* market could come into equilibrium *simultaneously*, and if so, whether that situation would be stable. It is thus to be distinguished from *partial equilibrium* analysis which is concerned with individual markets.

The two forms of analysis differ in their treatment of the relationship between markets. This arises because the supply and demand for every good depends upon the price of other goods: the demand curve for porridge is constructed on the assumption that the price of muesli is constant and if the latter changes, the demand curve for porridge will shift, so altering the price of porridge. This would alter the demand for salt (a complementary good) and so on *ad infinitum*. In partial equilibrium, these interconnections between markets are ignored by means of the assumption of *ceteris paribus* but general equilibrium analysis tries to take them into account.

The complexities of this task can be reduced when it is stated in a more abstract way. Let us imagine that there are n goods in the economy. Each will have a supply curve and a demand curve each of which can be described by an equation. There will therefore be n demand equations and n supply equations: $2n$ equations in all. What is required is a price and a quantity for all n products. That is to say, there are $2n$ unknowns. Our previous discussion of simultaneous equations established that it is possible to calculate the values of each of n unknowns given n equations (remember that we had two unknowns, P and Q, and two equations). The implication seems to be that it should be possible to find an equilibrium price and quantity for every product, that is, that a general equilibrium ought to be attainable.

One problem for general equilibrium analysts is that this conclusion only holds if it assumed that everyone has perfect information. If this assumption is relaxed and it is assumed, say, that buyers are unaware of the full range of goods that could be produced, then it cannot be guaranteed that the economy will arrive at a general equilibrium position. General equilibrium theorists have therefore been trying to provide an explanation of how information may be communicated across the economy. How successful they have been is not a question that can be addressed here. It is nevertheless of interest to note that different assumptions about information have quite different implications for the ease with which an economy or a market can be thought to attain equilibrium.

9-7 SUMMARY

Equilibrium is, *ceteris paribus*, a stable position where supply and demand are in balance. The process of equilibration is the mechanism by which a market moves towards equilibrium.

The *equilibrium price* is the price for the good or service which will *clear* the market. The *market price* is the prevailing price for the good or service. In a state of market disequilibrium it will differ from the equilibrium price.

General equilibrium refers to the simultaneous attainment of equilibrium in all markets. *Partial equilibrium* refers to the attainment of equilibrium in an individual market.

Simultaneous equations are a method of finding a unique solution to a set of n linear equations with n unknowns.

EXERCISES

9-1 The demand and supply equations for a particular market are:

$$Q_d = 80 - 5P$$

$$Q_s = -10 + 4P$$

(a) Draw both curves on the same graph and determine equilibrium.
(b) Using simultaneous equations confirm the graphical solution.
(c) The demand curve now changes to:

$$Q_d = 120 - 5P.$$

(i) Find the new equilibrium position.
(ii) What factors can you suggest that would cause such a shift?
(d) The supply curve now also changes to:

$$Q_s = -10 + 3P$$

(i) Find the new equilibrium position.
(ii) What factors can you suggest that would cause such a shift?
(e) Use a computer spreadsheet to quantify the differences between Q_d and Q_s in (a) and (d).

9-2 Contrast the neo-classical and Austrian views of the process by which markets move towards equilibrium. Which do you consider to be:

(a) more realistic?
(b) more useful?

9-3 If the market for a Giffen good moved away from equilibrium would it tend to return to an equilibrium position?

9-4
(a) What are the signs of:
(i) excess supply?
(ii) excess demand?
(b) Identify a product or market that currently falls into each of the two categories in (a) and suggest reasons for the excess.
(c) What is the outlook for the price of a product in each of these two sets of circumstances?

EXPLAINING AND PREDICTING

10-1 INTRODUCTION

The previous chapter showed how the forces of supply and demand operated to produce a position of equilibrium—in terms of price and quantity—in a market. The purpose of this chapter is to take this framework of supply, demand and equilibrium and set it to work to perform two vital roles. The first is to explain past changes in prices and outputs in markets: to provide hypotheses about the causes of past changes. Such hypotheses can then be tested against the available data. The second role of this economic framework is to produce predictions about future changes in prices and quantities based on the historical analysis. Information like this is, after all, one of the principal results expected from economic theory.

Such an application of economic theory, and the supporting quantitative techniques and data sources, will be illustrated by examining recent developments in the gas industry. Readers will recall that, since the mid 1970s, sales of gas to domestic customers have risen considerably. It is not the intention of this chapter to undertake a rigorous analysis of the gas market but rather to show how economic principles can be applied to a real data set to explain (and predict) economic behaviour. There will be areas of analysis where we will be unable to reach definite conclusions based on the available data, but we may still be able to suggest future areas for research and investigation.

10-2 DOMESTIC GAS CONSUMPTION—PAST TRENDS

Figure 10-1 shows the total level of consumption of gas by the domestic sector in the United Kingdom since 1975. It is apparent that there has been a steady and consistent increase in domestic gas consumption over this period. As economists we need to try and determine

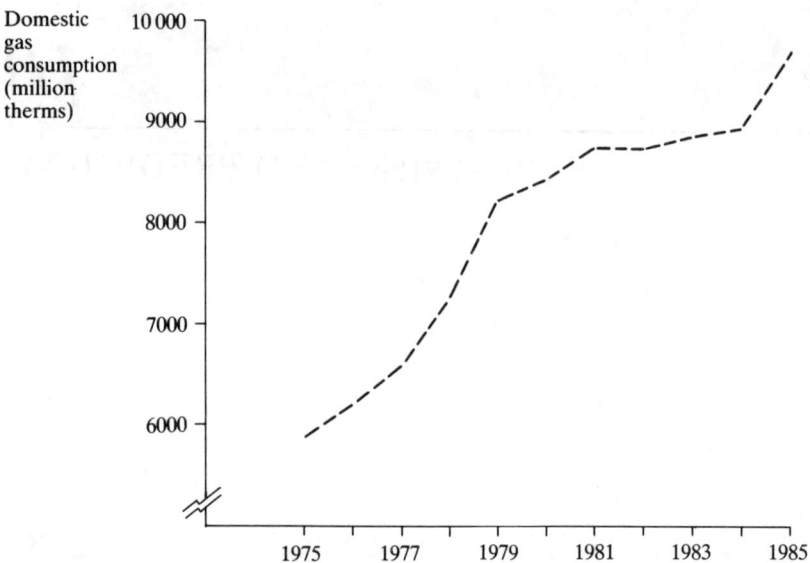

Figure 10-1 Domestic gas consumption by final users on a heat-supplied basis, 1975–85 (*Source: Digest of UK Energy Statistics*)

why. From the aspects of micro-economics that we have previously discussed we are able to detail a number of factors which, potentially, lie behind such a trend. Demand-side factors will include the price of gas to the domestic customer; the price of alternative fuels; income factors; changes in consumers' tastes; and gas as a complementary good. Supply-side factors, on the other hand, will include costs; productivity; and market changes. These factors are by no means all that we may want to consider at this stage. And they remain, in the terminology we have introduced, no more than hypotheses at this stage. In order to try and determine which of these factors (if any) allow us to explain such economic behaviour (and to form the basis for predictions of future changes) we now need to try and disprove the effects of each of them if possible. The data used in this Chapter cover the period to 1985 and are taken from a number of published sources including *Economic Trends Annual Supplement*; the *Digest of UK Energy Statistics*; British Gas Annual Reports; *General Household Survey*; and the *Family Expenditure Survey*. In the analysis that follows some of the data used are in their original form from the appropriate source. In other cases the data have been compiled by the authors using the techniques introduced earlier in the text.

10-3 PRICE AND EQUILIBRIUM

The immediate difficulty we face is that supply and demand curves cannot be observed directly. Available data relate to actual sales and actual prices rather than to entire supply and demand schedules. For example, we know that in 1985 domestic consumers used a total of 9600 million therms at an average price of 42p per therm. But how is this information to be interpreted? The answer is quite simply that it is taken to represent an equilibrium point which, by definition, lies on *both* the supply and demand curves.

By extension, the price–quantity combinations for each year must also be taken to represent an equilibrium point. The cause of any change in equilibrium price and quantity must, of course, be a change in either the supply or demand curves (or perhaps a change in both). Thus, the ultimate causes of any price and quantity movements are to be found in the causes of those shifts—that is, in the causes of changes in the conditions of supply and demand. In other words, the statistics for any period only reveal one point on each curve. The work of the economic analyst is, therefore, to gather data from which past shifts in the curves can be reasonably inferred. This illustrates the general way in which economists explain past trends: changes in prices and/or quantities are interpreted as being a reflection of changes in equilibrium, and the ultimate cause of those changes is sought in the factors which made one or both curves shift.

Thus the data in Fig. 10-1 can be interpreted being a series of cross-over points between a combination of three possible situations: a more or less constant demand curve and a number of shifting supply curves; a number of shifting demand curves and a more or less constant supply curve; and a changing set of both demand and supply curves. These alternatives are illustrated in Fig. 10-2.

Special note should be taken of the role played by price. It is the link between producer and consumer. As we have already seen in Chapter 8, there was a rapid expansion of gas sales caused primarily by the new availability of North Sea gas. In the gas industry the improved conditions of supply were communicated to consumers by the gas industry's lowering its tariffs, and the consumers then reacted to the lower charges by using more gas. The chain of causation at that time was therefore: improved conditions of supply leading to a lower price leading to higher consumption.

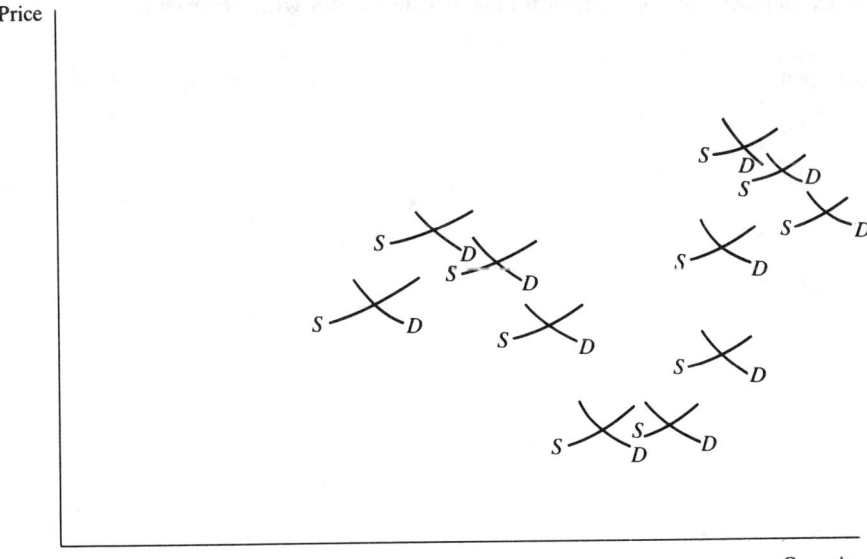

Figure 10-2 Supply and demand equilibria

10-4 DEMAND-SIDE FACTORS

The difficulty of establishing whether changes are originating on the demand side or on the supply side is amply illustrated in Fig. 10-3 which shows annual domestic gas demand and the average revenue. Before looking at Fig. 10-3 in detail we must digress to explain why we use average revenue in preference to a *price* variable. The difficulty arises in that the price charged to the domestic customer per therm may well change within a particular year and part of the payment for gas consumed is represented in a fixed element in the form of a quarterly standing charge. If

$$AR = \frac{TR}{Q}$$

where AR is average revenue, TR total revenue and Q demand, and

$$TR = P \times Q$$

where P is price, then

$$AR = \frac{P \times Q}{Q}.$$

Given this expression, it does not seem unreasonable to use average revenue as a proxy for price.

Note also that, as with all the data used in this chapter measured in monetary units, all values have been deflated using the Retail Price Index to express such series in 1975 prices.

Returning to Fig. 10-3, we might expect to see a typical downward-sloping demand curve linking average revenue to demand. As is apparent, however, there is no clear pattern over the period under examination. In some years increases in average revenue are associated with increases in consumption and at other times with decreases.

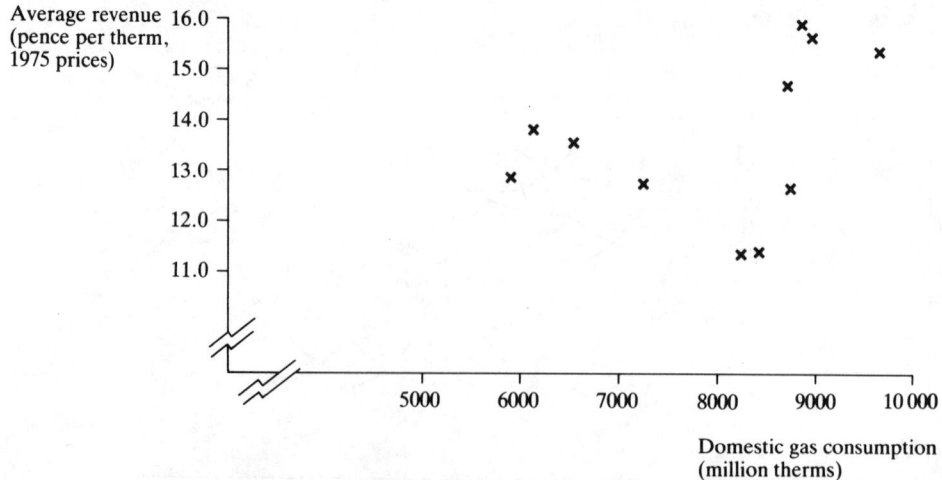

Figure 10-3 Scatter diagram of real average revenue per therm and domestic gas consumption (*Source: Digest of UK Energy Statistics; Economic Trends Annual Supplement*)

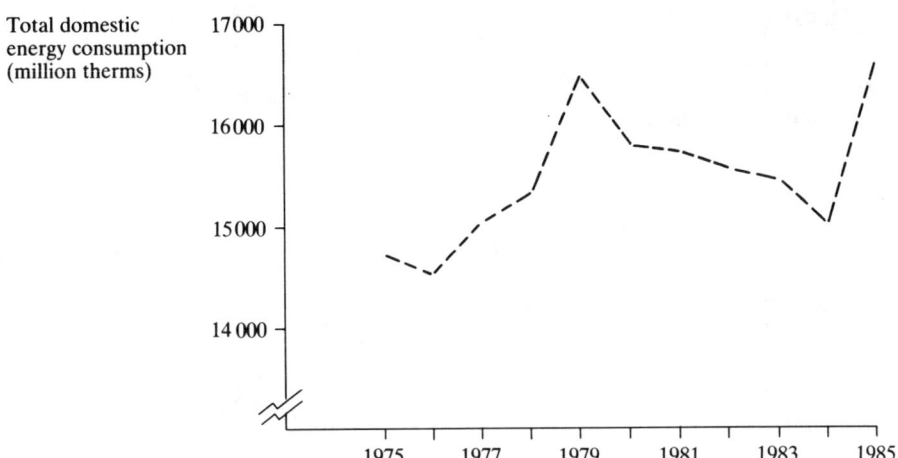

Total domestic energy consumption (million therms)

Figure 10-4 Total domestic energy consumption by final users on a heat-supplied basis (*Source:* as Fig. 10-1)

The data in Fig. 10-3 show a series of points of equilibria between demand and supply over this period. It is impossible to determine, at this stage, which curve is shifting and which staying constant.

It is apparent that we have no evidence to support our hypothesis that the increase in demand is attributable directly to changes in the price of gas. The pattern of gas-price changes evokes no consistent response in demand. Although the real price of gas to the domestic consumer fell during the middle part of this period while demand increased, demand did not stop increasing when the real price again began to rise. Indeed gas demand started to increase rapidly at the start of the period even before the real price fell. We have no evidence, therefore, to show that price was the major responsible factor.

Let us now turn to the second of our possible factors, that of the *relative price* of gas. Before doing so, it may be worth putting the domestic demand for gas into the context of the whole energy industry. After all, we have yet to examine the other sectors of the domestic energy market. It may make a considerable difference to our analysis if we find, say, that demand for all types of fuel has shown similar rapid increases.

Figure 10-4 shows the level of total domestic energy consumption over the same period. Again, no clear pattern emerges. Until 1979 demand showed a steady increase but then decreased to 1984. Again in 1985 there was a sharp rise in total demand but whether this marks a new period of increasing demand remains to be seen.

A clearer picture emerges, however, if we show the market penetration of gas. Figure 10-5 shows the share of the total domestic consumption going to gas and the share going to other sources of domestic energy (electricity, oil and solid fuel). It is clear that, over this period, gas was establishing an increasingly dominant position in the domestic market, until by 1985 gas was supplying around 57 per cent of the total market. Given that the price of gas itself does not appear to be a major factor behind this trend perhaps the prices of competing fuels are a factor. Figure 10-6 shows the relevant trends. The data show the average revenue in real terms for gas and other fuels as an index, base 1975. (The index for other fuels is an average weighted by the percentage share of the domestic market.)

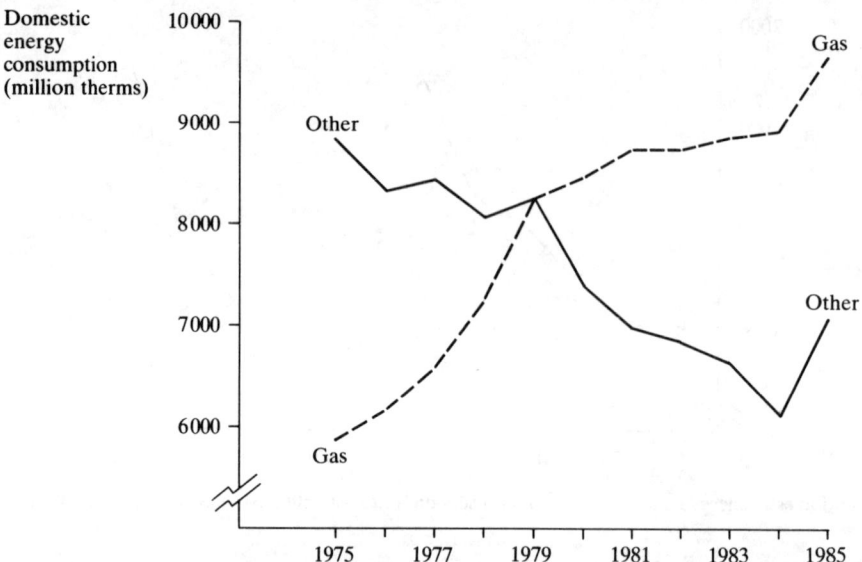

Figure 10-5 Domestic energy consumption by fuel type (*Source*: as Fig. 10-1)

It is apparent that from 1976 there was an increasing price differential between gas and the alternative domestic fuels. This gap was at its widest in the period between 1978 and 1981 when, in real terms, the price of gas was actually falling. Referring back to Fig. 10-5, this also coincides with the period of a rapid increase in the market penetration of gas. So the hypothesis that the relative price of gas is, at least in part, responsible for the increase in domestic gas consumption cannot be rejected.

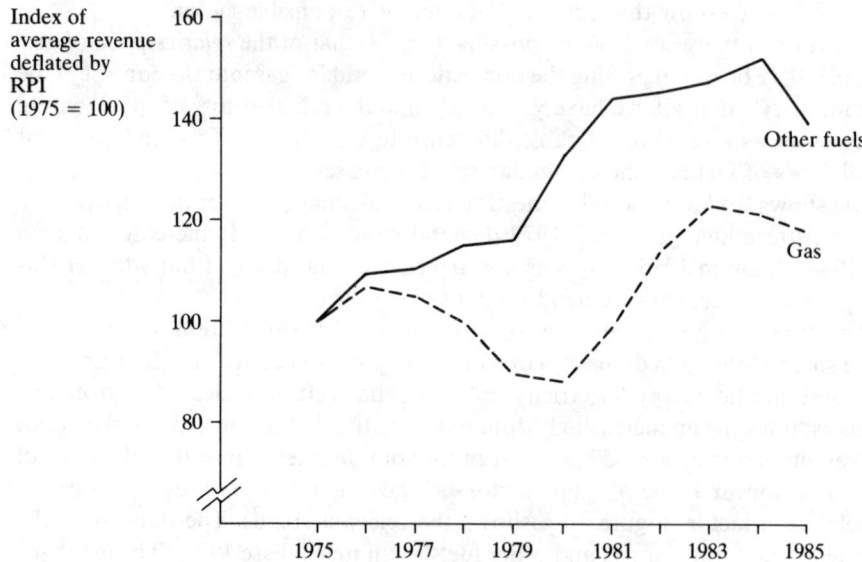

Figure 10-6 Index of real average revenue by fuel type (*Source*: as Fig. 10-3)

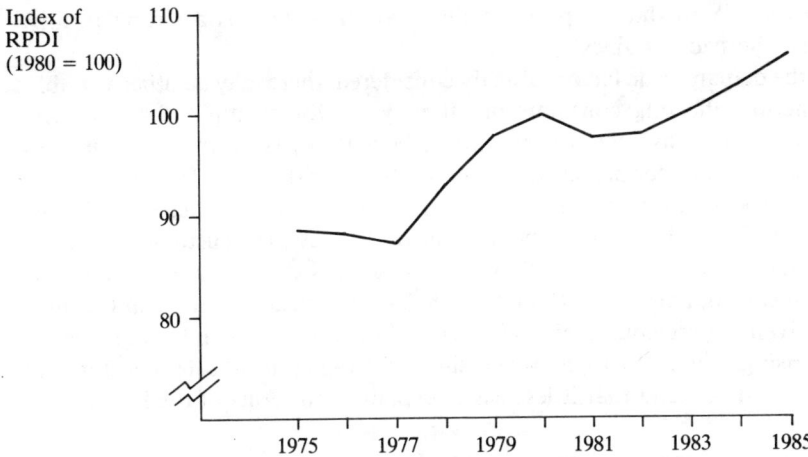

Figure 10-7 Index of Real Personal Disposable Income (*Source: Economic Trends Annual Supplement*)

The third potential factor on the demand side was *income. Ceteris paribus,* we would anticipate that changes in income will lead to changes in demand. Unless the product is regarded as inferior, an increase in income, for example, will lead to an increase in demand. In terms of energy as a whole, it seems plausible to suppose that consumers do not regard energy as an inferior good. It would be reasonable to argue that as incomes increase demand will increase as consumers' extra income allows them to install central heating or to use more energy to maintain higher house temperatures and so on.

Figure 10-7 shows the trend in personal disposable income (in real terms, shown as an index with base 1980). The apparent pattern is a general increase in real personal disposable income (RPDI) over this period. Figure 10-8 shows RPDI against total domestic energy consumption and appears to confirm the view that as income rises, *ceteris paribus,* so does

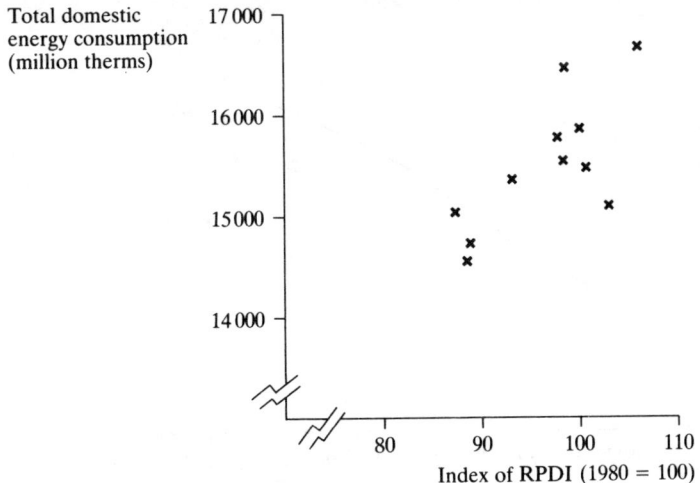

Figure 10-8 Scatter plot of total domestic energy consumption and personal disposable income (*Source:* as Fig. 10-3)

the demand for energy. With the exception of the 1984 data there is a strong positive relationship between the two variables.

In addition to the demand-side factors already considered, there may be other variables in the demand function affecting consumption. It may be, for example, that changing attitudes and tastes among consumers worked to the benefit of gas. In this area there are potentially a considerable number of factors that could be at work. Apart from the relative price, demand may have been influenced by factors such as consumers' tastes, marketing, advertising and so on. Figure 10-9 shows the number of domestic gas customers over this period. (Note that data taken from the published British Gas Annual Reports relate to financial rather than calendar years.) In total, there has been a steady increase in the number of customers. Given the previous analysis in terms of relative prices and rising incomes this is not too surprising. Figure 10-10, however, shows average (mean) sales per domestic customer and this reveals a trend that it less easily explained in terms of the factors considered thus far.

Until 1979 average sales increased quite sharply. It is easy to see why total sales might increase (given the factors discussed earlier) but less easy to see why, on average, customers should be using more gas. We must seek possible reasons for this.

One possible factor, which is connected to rising incomes, is the demand for domestic central heating, in which gas features as a *complementary good*. Given that both incomes and expectations about living standards have changed it is not too surprising to find from the *General Household Survey* that the number of households with central heating has increased: in 1972 37 per cent of households had some form of central heating, and by 1984 this had risen to 66 per cent. Unfortunately, we have no information on the market share of gas central heating but given the data on the comparative cost of gas it seems reasonable to hypothesize that the demand for gas central heating over this period is likely to have risen considerably. Given that central heating systems in general use more energy it also seems a reasonable hypothesis to suggest that this trend may be one of the causes of the trend in average gas consumption.

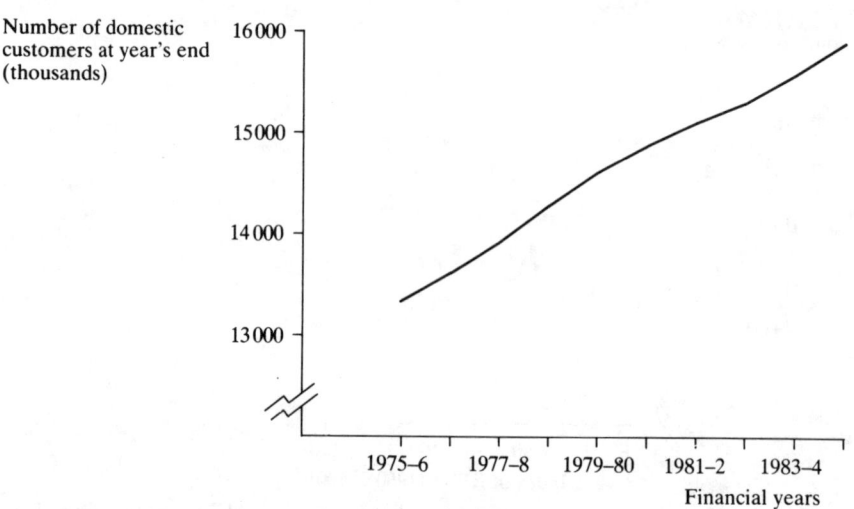

Figure 10-9 Number of domestic gas customers at year's end (*Source* as Fig. 10-9)

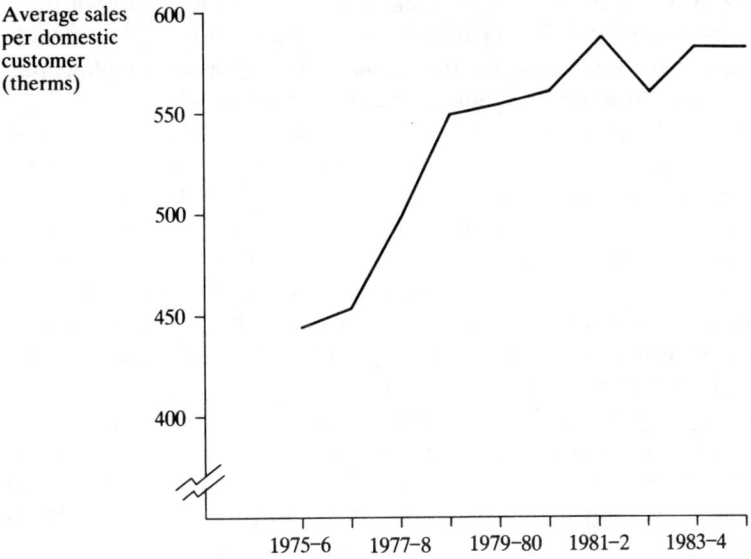

Figure 10-10 Average sales per domestic customer (*Source*: as Fig. 10-9)

Figure 10-11 shows the number of central heating installations undertaken by British Gas (who do not have a monopoly in this area). It can be seen that the period of a high level of installations coincides with the period of rapid growth in average sales per customer.

A second possible factor relates to other gas appliances such as cookers and fires which have had an unexciting public image. Over the last decade or so, however, there has been a dramatic change in the style of these appliances and presumably a change in consumers'

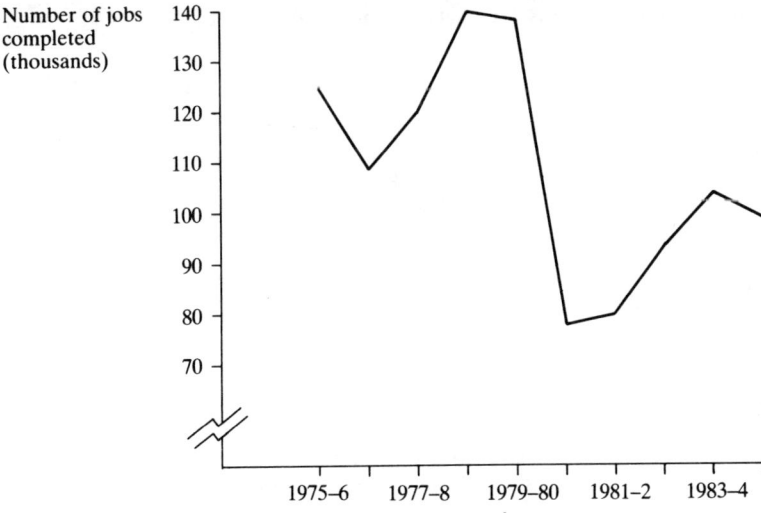

Figure 10-11 Installation of central heating units (*Source*: as Fig. 10-9)

attitudes to them. Cookers, for example, have become much more 'hi-tech' in appearance and the advent of split-level cookers (with separate hobs and ovens) may well have had a considerable stimulus on sales and hence on the demand for gas as a complimentary good. Advertising, of course, has played a major role in this image-building.

In both these instances, however, we have an illustration of the practical difficulties facing the economist in trying to corroborate theory with evidence. Appropriate data to allow us to test these hypotheses are simply not available (except to British Gas). It is apparent, however, that there is considerable scope for data collection and analysis using the methods of market research. Surveys into consumer behaviour would obviously play an important role in assessing the impact of such factors and it will come as no surprise to realize that organizations such as British Gas are frequently undertaking or commissioning such research to support their economic analysis. (Chapters 11–13 will introduce methods appropriate for analysing such market research information.)

We have, then, three hypotheses on the demand side—that comparative prices, income and changes in consumer tastes are responsible for the increase in domestic gas consumption—that cannot be rejected after examining the data as possible factors explaining the change in domestic gas demand: The supply side, however, may also be contributing to such changes.

10-5 SUPPLY-SIDE FACTORS

On the supply side the first factor to consider is *costs* of factors of production. Changes in costs may, *ceteris paribus*, lead to a shift in the supply curve and hence to a shift in the position of equilibrium between supply and demand. Figure 10-12 shows the total costs in real terms as an index with base 1975. It can be seen that there has been a steady increase in real costs and hence we would hypothesize a continuous change in supply curves as British Gas reacts to changing real costs with changes in the amount it is willing to supply at particular price levels. One important point that further adds to our difficulties is that in 1980–1 the government introduced a gas levy which added to these costs. In 1984–5, for

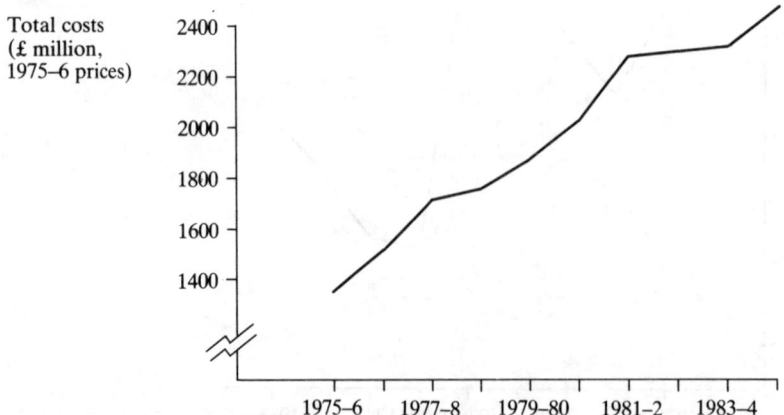

Total costs
(£ million,
1975–6 prices)

Figure 10-12 British Gas: total costs, at constant prices (*Source*: as Fig. 10-9)

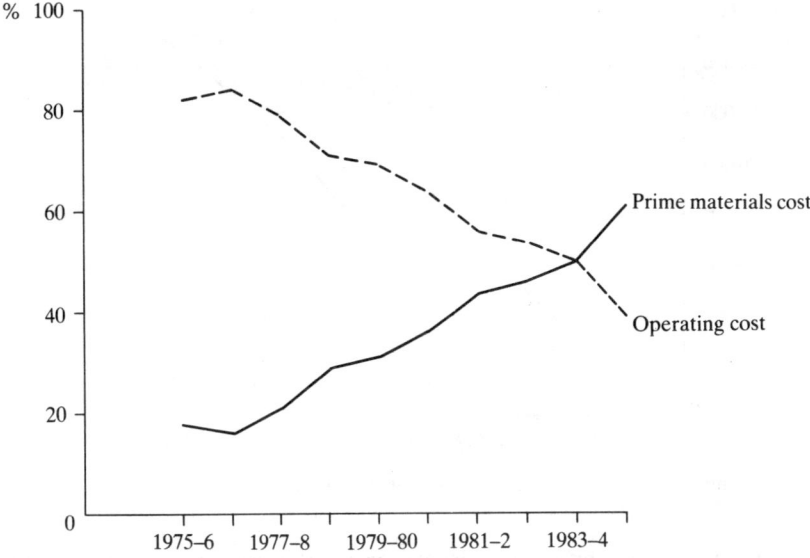

Figure 10-13 Operating cost and prime materials cost as a percentage of total costs (*Source*: as Fig. 10-9)

example, this levy added approximately £500 million (in current price terms) to the cost structure.

More revealing, however, and potentially more important for predicting future changes, is Fig. 10-13, which shows total costs broken into two elements. *Operating costs* relate to the costs associated with running the organization, while *prime costs* refer to the purchase costs of gas (and the gas levy). The distinction is an important one. Operating costs are, to a large extent, controllable by British Gas. Prime costs are largely determined outside the organization and will be influenced by a number of external factors such as the supply of oil from the Middle East, world demand for oil and gas and so on. Figure 10-13 reveals a fundamental change that has taken place in the overall cost structure that is likely to have major implications for the future. Gradually, it is prime costs that have become increasingly important as a part of total costs as British Gas has moved from being a producer of town gas to a supplier of natural gas. British Gas has been extremely successful at controlling operating costs—the data available show that, in real terms, operating costs are more or less the same in 1984–5 as they were in 1975–6. This is supported by the data on turnover per employee (which is a measure of *productivity*) shown in Fig. 10-14.

Prime costs, on the other hand, have become an increasingly larger part of total costs. Given their uncontrollability, from the viewpoint of British Gas, they represent an area of considerable future uncertainty.

The final aspect that we shall examine is that of *market changes*. British Gas's willingness to supply gas to the domestic market at a particular price level could well have been influenced by changes in other parts of the energy market. If the relative profitability of selling gas to different parts of the energy market had changed we could, *ceteris paribus*, hypothesize that this would have repercussions for the domestic market. It is evident that over this period there have been major changes in the industrial structure of the economy

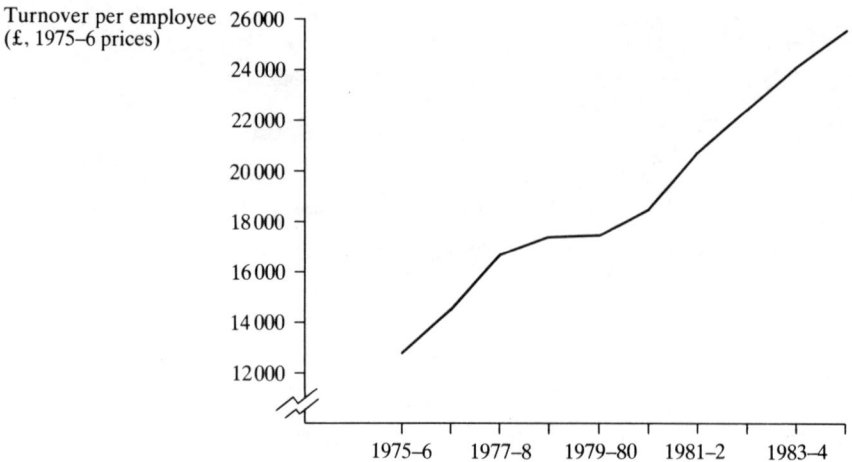

Figure 10-14 Turnover per employee, at constant prices (*Source*: as Fig. 10-9)

(manifested most obviously in unemployment levels) and if the demand for gas in other markets has been severely affected this may be expected to have a 'knock-on' effect in the domestic sector. The supply curve of gas to domestic consumers can be expected to shift in response to the profitability of gas sold to other types of customer.

Figure 10-15 shows non-domestic gas sales over this period. It is apparent that sales of this type have been adversely affected since 1979 (and further analysis would reveal that it was demand from industry in particular that was worst affected). Since gas is bought by British Gas under contracts which last for several years, total supplies of gas are effectively fixed in the medium term and we might hypothesize that marketing efforts would be made in the domestic market. We have no information available to suggest whether such a strategy actually took place but, returning to Fig. 10-1, we can see that this was the period when the relatively rapid growth in domestic demand flattened out. It would appear that

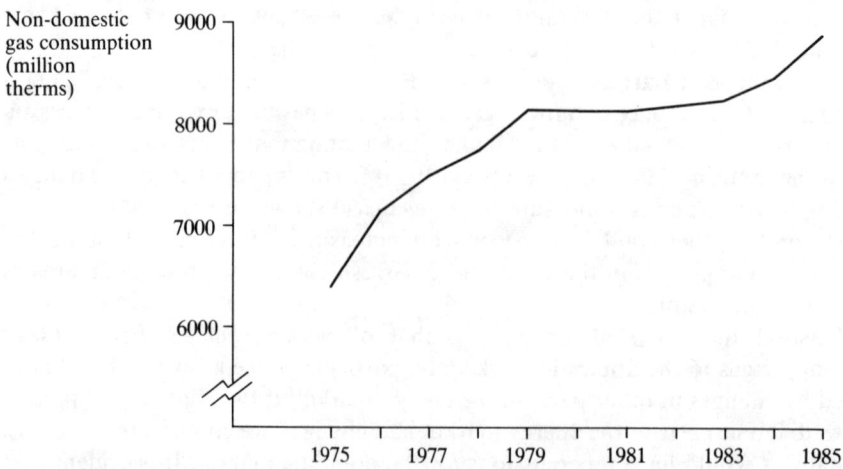

Figure 10-15 Non-domestic gas sales on a heat-supplied basis (*Source*: as Fig. 10-1)

there is no support for the hypothesis that the slump in non-domestic gas sales had a knock-on increase effect on the supply to the domestic market.

10-6 PREDICTION

Our brief analysis of the domestic gas market has revealed, therefore, that there are a number of factors which may explain past economic behaviour in this area: the relative gas price; income levels; changes in consumer tastes and attitudes; and changes in costs. Combinations of factors on both the demand and supply side can, therefore, be used to support our attempts to use economic theory to explain such behaviour. Predicting the future follows logically from this analysis. Having determined a number of key factors behind past changes in gas consumption we would now need to form a view of the future movements in terms of these factors to predict how domestic gas sales are likely to be affected in the future.

The basic process of predicting changes in price and output in any market consists of estimating the size of any likely changes in the conditions of supply and demand and assessing their probable effects. Management at British Gas would need to determine the probable relative gas price, for example, in the future, given that this is one of the factors linked to past sales. Similarly, given that prime costs have become increasingly important the industry will need to determine likely future movements in international oil prices. It is clear that a knowledge of the relationships between the various factors can only come from an adequate understanding of past market changes (which explains why British Gas employs a considerable number of economists). Although accurate predictions of future changes can be made by pure luck the rational decision-maker will wish to base such predictions on something more substantial.

The formation of a view of the future requires a combination of both analytical and subjective skills on the part of the decision-maker. Predicting how the price of gas will change relative to prices of competing fuels is obviously necessary but fraught with difficulty and uncertainty. The degree of uncertainty can often be reduced and occasionally assessed using the techniques introduced in this text. But there are aspects to the problem which often cannot be quantified and some irreducible role for personal judgement remains.

EXERCISES

10-1 Following the analysis undertaken in this chapter update the various data series that have been presented.

(*a*) What evidence is there of any recent changes in the trends discussed in this chapter? What reasons can you suggest for such changes?

(*b*) British Gas was privatized in 1986. Summarize the key reasons for this.

(*c*) What evidence (in terms of the performance of British Gas) is there to show whether the reasons in (*b*) for privatization were justified?

10-2 You have been asked by a national car manufacturer to write a report on the future trends in car sales in the United Kingdom.

(*a*) Draw up a checklist of the data you think would be useful for such analysis.

(*b*) Find out which of the data items on the checklist are available from published sources.

(*c*) Using the principles outlined in this chapter determine the major trends evident from your data.

(*d*) Suggest possible reasons behind such trends.

11

PROBABILITY

11-1 INTRODUCTION

Business decisions are rarely made in the full knowledge of their consequences. More usually, a choice has to be made between alternative decisions under conditions of uncertainty. British Gas, for example, have to agree to purchase quantities of North Sea gas without knowing how much they will be able to sell. Similarly, they set their prices for domestic consumers without knowing what prices their competitors—among them British Coal and the CEGB—will be charging. Equally, economists may have to produce forecasts about, say, the outlook of the price of a particular commodity without having full and certain knowledge of how the relevant shift factors will change.

Both business organizations and economists, therefore, find it necessary to assess the likelihood of specific events occurring in the future. The analysis and quantification of such assessments is known as *probability theory* and forms the basis for this chapter which will also introduce the normal probability distribution. In Chapters 12 and 13 we shall introduce the principles of probability by which we can make inferences about a statistical population based only on the limited data available from a sample from that population.

11-2 BASIC VOCABULARY

As with most areas of statistics, the topic has its own vocabulary with which you must become familiar. Fortunately, many of the concepts will already be familiar because, whether you are aware of it or not, we all use probability on a daily basis. What are my chances of passing the exam? What are my chances of getting the job? What chance have United got of winning Saturday's match? and so on.

Conventionally, probability is expressed as a value between 0 and 1, either in fractions or as a decimal. A probability of 0 implies that the event has, literally, no chance of occurring, while a probability of 1 indicates a guaranteed outcome.

Experiments and events

In statistical terms probabilities revolve around *events*, which are possible outcomes from doing something. So tossing a coin has two events associated with it—the coin showing heads or showing tails. The activity that produces an event is known as an *experiment*.

Independent and conditional events

Some events are classed as *independent* events while others are *conditional*. Independent events are those whose probability is unaffected by the occurrence (or non-occurrence) of other events. Some events, however, will be dependent, or conditional, on other events. For example, let us consider the experiment of tossing a coin twice. We may define event 1 as the coin showing heads on the first toss and event 2 as the coin showing heads on the second toss. It should be apparent that the probability of event 2 is totally unaffected by event 1. In other words, it does not matter whether the first toss showed heads or not, the probability of the second toss showing heads remains the same. However, a different experiment may have events which are not independent. Assume we have an experiment to draw two cards from a pack of 52. We draw the first card and note whether we have drawn an Ace. Without replacing this card we draw a second and wish to know the probability that we will choose an Ace again. Obviously, the probability of the second event will depend on what happened with the first event as there is one less card to choose from and there may also be one less Ace to select. In this case the second event is said to be conditional on the first.

Mutually exclusive events

If two events are *mutually exclusive* they cannot both occur simultaneously. The previous example of tossing a coin related to two mutually exclusive events, in that the coin could show either heads or tails but not both. Some events, however, may happen simultaneously. Consider the example of drawing a card from a pack of 52. Suppose we define the first event as the card being an Ace and the second event as the card being a heart. It is obviously possible for *both* events to occur with the same card.

11-3 MEASURING PROBABILITY

The probability of an event occurring can be expressed as:

$$P(\text{Event}) = \frac{\text{Number of ways the event could occur}}{\text{Total number of outcomes}}$$

Thus if we were to roll a six-sided die and calculate the probability of the die showing an even number we would have:

$$P(\text{Even number}) = \frac{\text{Die shows 2, 4 or 6}}{\text{Total outcomes}} = \frac{3}{6} = 0.5$$

This assumes, of course, that the die is not weighted!

Similarly, if we were to choose one card from a normal pack of 52 and we wished to calculate the probability that the card is a heart:

$$P(\text{heart}) = \frac{13}{52} = 0.25$$

It is important to understand what the probability value represents, and what it does not. In the last example it does not mean that if we were to repeat the experiment 52 times then exactly 13 hearts would be chosen. Rather, it is an indication of the average or long-run outcome. If we were to repeat the experiment a *large number* of times, we would expect an *average* of 25 per cent of cards to show hearts. The correct interpretation of a probability calculation is of considerable importance in decision-making.

11-4 RULES OF PROBABILITY

Typically in economics and business we are analysing situations where a combination or a sequence of events may take place. Probability can be applied in such situations through two basic rules.

The multiplication rule

The multiplication rule is concerned with situations where we are interested in a sequence of events occurring. For example, we toss two coins and we wish to calculate the probability that both coins show heads.

However, to apply the multiplication rule correctly we need to distinguish those experiments where events are independent and those where they are conditional. If the events are independent, as with the coin-tossing above, the probability is calculated by multiplying (hence the name) the probabilities of the two events together. If event A is the event that the first coin tossed comes up heads, then the probability that event A occurs, which we denote $P(A)$, is equal to 0.5. If event B is the event that the second coin tossed comes up heads, then $P(B)$ also equals 0.5. Since A and B are independent,

$$P(\text{both coins show heads}) = P(A \text{ and } B) = P(A) \times P(B)$$
$$= 0.5 \times 0.5 = 0.25$$

That is, there is a probability of 0.25 of both coins showing heads. Simple logic confirms the rule: in tossing two coins there are a total of four possible outcomes (heads/tails, heads/heads, tail/heads, tails/tails) but only one of these is the defined event.

The basic rule is easily extended to cover more than two events. The probability of three coins showing heads would be $0.5 \times 0.5 \times 0.5 = 0.125$.

For events which are conditional the basic multiplication rule must be amended. Assume we have an experiment to draw two cards from a pack of 52 and we wish to know the probability of drawing two Aces. We draw the first card and note whether we have drawn an Ace. Without replacing this card we draw a second and wish to know the probability that this card is also an Ace. In this example the events are conditional, as the probability of the second event is affected by the outcome of the first event.

Let event A be the event that the first card drawn is an Ace. Then $P(A) = 4/52 = 0.077$. *Let* B be the event that the second card is also an Ace. To calculate the probability of event B is straightforward. Both events can only occur providing the first event is 'successful', that is, an Ace was chosen. Given that there are now only 51 cards left and only three of them are Aces, $P(B)$ will be $3/51 = 0.059$. Now, using the multiplication rule we have:

$$P(\text{both cards are Aces}) = P(A \text{ and } B)$$

$$= \frac{4}{52} \times \frac{3}{51}$$

$$= 0.077 \times 0.059$$

$$= 0.0045$$

Using standard probability notation we would express such a probability as:

$$P(\text{both cards are Aces}) = P(A) \times P(B \mid A)$$

where $P(B \mid A)$ refers to the probability of event B *given that* event A has occurred. Note that for independent events $P(B \mid A) = P(B)$.

The addition rule

The addition rule is concerned with experiments where we are interested in at least one of two or more events occurring simultaneously. For example, we choose a card from a pack of 52 and we wish to calculate the probability that the card is *either* an Ace *or* a King.

The addition rule is easily applied to such events but again we must distinguish between two types of situation—those where events are mutually exclusive and those where they are not. With the example above, where the events are mutually exclusive, the probability is calculated by adding the probabilities together. If A is the event that the card chosen is an Ace, then $P(A)$ is equal to $4/52$; if B is the event that the card is a King, then $P(B)$ is also equal to $4/52$. Thus

$$P(\text{card is either an Ace or a King}) = P(A \text{ or } B)$$

$$= P(A) + P(B)$$

$$= \frac{4}{52} + \frac{4}{52} = \frac{8}{52}$$

$$= 0.154$$

Obviously, the addition rule simply reflects that, in our example, eight different cards from the pack are either Aces or Kings.

For events which are not mutually exclusive, however, the rule as given will not work. Let us amend, the problem so that we now wish to know the probability of choosing either an Ace or a heart. If we apply the rule we have:

$$P(\text{card is either an Ace or a heart}) = \frac{4}{52} + \frac{13}{52} = \frac{17}{52}$$

which, on reflection, is incorrect. (If you can't see why take a pack of cards and select all the hearts and Aces and count how many cards you have. It will *not* be 17). It is apparent that using the above rule we have double-counted one card which is *both* an Ace and a Heart. To resolve this we can amend the addition rule:

$$P(A \text{ or } B) = P(A) + P(B) - P(A \text{ and } B)$$

giving:

$$P(\text{Ace or heart}) = P(\text{Ace}) + P(\text{heart}) - P(\text{Ace and heart})$$

$$= \frac{4}{52} + \frac{13}{52} - \frac{1}{52} = \frac{16}{52}$$

$$= 0.308$$

The probability of 1/52 was obtained using the multiplication rule developed earlier.

These two simple rules dealing with probability situations form the basis for complex problem-solving.

11-5 EXPECTED VALUE

Probability theory is of considerable importance in decision-making in business because decisions must be made, and resources allocated, on the basis of an assessment of their probable effects. In economics and business the basic rules of probability are frequently used to calculate what is known as the *expected value*. We can illustrate the concept with a simple example which illustrates the potential for using probability in decision-making.

A firm involved in motor vehicle accessories is considering marketing a new product in time for the Christmas market when a considerable volume of sales occurs, though the exact level of sales is uncertain. The product consists of a small DIY emergency toolkit and sells for £5.99, generating a profit of £1 per unit sold, and the manufacturer has exclusive production rights ensuring that there is no other company with a directly competing product. Market research has indicated that sales will fall into one of two categories: there is a probability of 0.3 that sales will average 100 000 units and a probability of 0.7 that sales will average 50 000 units. The manufacturer wants to know what profit is likely to be achieved.

Knowledge of these probabilities allows us to apply simple logic to the problem of quantifying the likely profit and we can introduce the idea of averaging the possible profits. Obviously, it would not be appropriate simply to add the two profits together and divide by two as this would indicate they were both equally likely. Instead, we must *weight* each possible profit with the probability of its being achieved:

$$0.3 \times £100\,000 = £30\,000$$

$$0.7 \times \quad £50\,000 = £35\,000$$

$$\text{Average} = £65\,000$$

It is this average, calculated by weighting outcomes by their respective probabilities, which is known as the expected value. What does it represent? It does *not* represent the actual profit earned (which will be either £100 000 or £50 000). It is an indication of likely profits in the sense that, if we were to repeat this problem with a large number of firms or over a long period of time profits would average out at £65 000. As such, this information could be used by the manager to decide whether the likely profit from the new product is adequate for the firm, given other aspects such as costs, interest rates and so on.

11-6 PROBABILITY DISTRIBUTIONS

So far we have looked at the probability of individual events. Equally useful is the concept of a *probability distribution*. A probability distribution shows the probability of all outcomes occurring from a particular experiment. At this stage, the easiest way to visualize such a distribution is as a type of histogram where, rather than measuring frequencies on the vertical axis, we measure probability instead. Figure 11-1 shows the probability distribution for the outcomes of rolling a six-sided die.

Normally, such probability distributions can be derived in one of two ways: *theoretically*, that is, they are calculated using the basic probability rules, as in Fig. 11-1; and *empirically*, that is, they can be constructed from a frequency table or histogram.

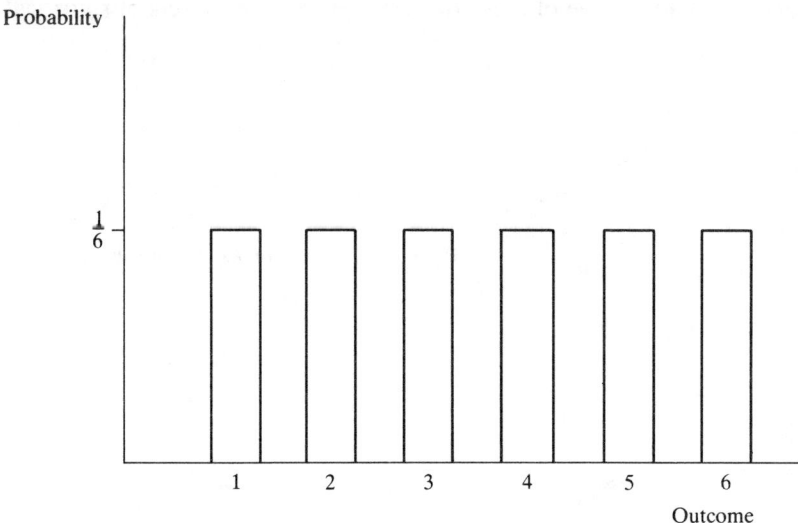

Figure 11-1 Probability distribution for rolling a die

The importance of probability distributions is that they provide a means of finding the probability of an event without having to resort to the probability rules, which for complex problems may be difficult to calculate. We can use a probability distribution to find probabilities in the same way as we would use a histogram or ogive to find frequencies.

11-7 THE NORMAL DISTRIBUTION

One of the most important probability distributions you will encounter is the normal distribution. This takes the general shape illustrated in Fig. 11-2: a symmetrical distribution often referred to as 'bell-shaped'. It is important, first, because it typifies many observed distributions such as intelligence, height and weight; and second, because it can be used to make statistical inferences about a population based on a sample set of information (we shall be developing this aspect of the normal distribution in Chapter 12).

Unlike many other types of distribution the normal distribution has two particularly useful features. One is that any variable which is normally distributed will differ from any other normally distributed variable only in its average value and the dispersion around the average. For the normal distribution we generally use the arithmetic mean as the average statistic. You will remember from Chapter 3 that the mean has the advantage of using all the data items and a symmetrical distribution will not, of course, be distorted by extreme values. Accordingly, the measure of dispersion is the standard deviation. Figure 11-3 illustrates two normal distributions which have the same mean but different standard deviations; while Fig. 11-4 shows two which have different means but the same standard deviation.

The second useful feature of the normal distribution is that for *any* normally distributed variable the same *proportion* of observations will occur in the same part of the distribution. For example, as we shall see later, for any normally distributed variable approximately 68 per cent of observations will lie within one standard deviation of the mean for that variable.

Statisticians have taken advantage of these two features to produce sets of statistical

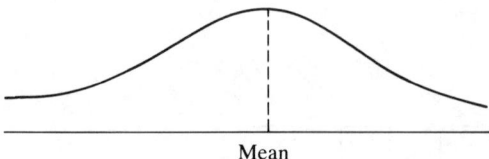

Mean

Figure 11-2 Normal probability distribution

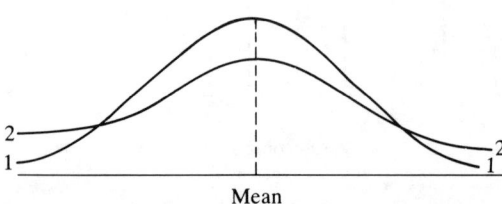

Mean

Figure 11-3 Normal distributions with the same mean and different standard deviations

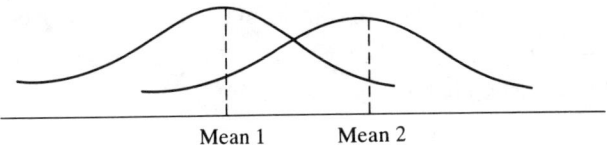

Figure 11-4 Normal distributions with different means and the same standard deviation

tables that show, for any normally distributed variable, the proportion of items that will occur within a certain distance (measured in standard deviations) of the mean. Such a table is shown in Appendix B. In order to use it we must first *standardize* the distribution we are dealing with. Such standardization is straightforward. We define a statistic, known as the Z statistic, as:

$$Z = \frac{X - \mu}{\sigma}$$

where μ (the Greek letter 'mu') is the arithmetic mean of the normal distribution, σ ('sigma') is the standard deviation of the normal distribution, and X is the value of the variable for which we are trying to find a probability.

The Z statistic expresses the difference between the X value and the mean in multiples of the standard deviation of the distribution. The probability corresponding to this Z statistic can then be read directly from the table.

Let us illustrate with a simple example. A producer of canned foods operates two production lines for one of his products. On one line the product is packed into tins weighing, on average, 100 grams. Because the packing and weighing equipment is not perfect there is some variation in the weights of individual tins and the standard deviation has been calculated as 10 grams. On the second production line the product is packed into tins with an average weight of 500 gms and a standard deviation of 50 gms. In both cases, the distribution of tin weights around the average is normal. The producer picks a tin from the first line at random and wants to know the probability of the tin weighing less than 90 grams (perhaps because of trading standards legislation). Similarly a tin is selected from the second production line and we wish to know the probability that this will weigh less than 450 grams.

The probability distribution for the first production line is shown in Fig. 11-5. If we define the total area under the curve as equal to 1 (this is the sum of the probabilities of all possible weights) then we are trying to find the area shaded, which shows those tins weighing less than 90 grams. A similar process is apparently needed for the second production line. But, in fact, we know that the two distributions are identical except for the

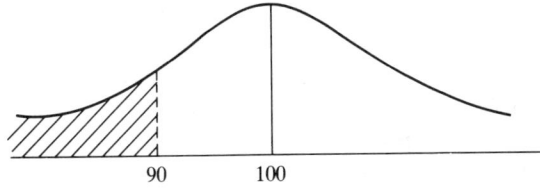

90	100

Figure 11-5 Critical area

mean and standard deviation. Using the Z statistic we can transform the data from *absolute* to *relative* values. For Production Line 1:

$$Z = \frac{X - \mu}{\sigma} = \frac{90 - 100}{10} = -1$$

Similarly for Production Line 2:

$$Z = \frac{X - \mu}{\sigma} = \frac{450 - 500}{50} = -1$$

We can see that both distributions have the same Z statistic. How can this be interpreted? In both cases the value we are interested in (90 grams and 450 grams respectively) has a Z score of -1. That is, in both cases, the X value is one standard deviation *below* the mean of the distribution.

Effectively, what the Z score formula does is to calculate relative values for a normal distribution, in terms of the number of standard deviations above and below the mean. Table 11-1 illustrates this for our example.

Table 11-1 Calculation of standard scores

Production Line 1 weight (grams)	60	70	80	90	100	110	120	130	140
Production Line 2 weight (grams)	300	350	400	450	500	550	600	650	700
Z score	-4	-3	-2	-1	0	$+1$	$+2$	$+3$	$+4$

Table 11-1 shows weights of tins on the two production lines that are comparable in the sense that they are the same number of standard deviations away from their respective means.

This means that, as in both cases the Z score is the same, the same *proportion* of items lie below 90 grams and 450 grams respectively. In effect the probability is the same for each of our selections. The availability of a table (see Appendix B) showing the standardized Z scores means that such probabilities do not have to be calculated but can be read directly from the table. The first column in the table relates to the Z score calculated. Note that only *positive* Z scores are shown. Given that the normal distribution is symmetrical both halves of the distribution (around the mean) are identical. If the table shows the probability associated with a value a certain number of standard deviations *above* the mean, the value an equivalent number of standard deviations *below* the mean must have the same probability.

Thus, with our Z score of $(-)1$ we can follow this column down until we get to the appropriate row. We now read off a value opposite this Z score of 0.1587. This indicates that 15.87 per cent of observations will occur to the *left* of a value 1 standard deviation below the mean. In the context of our problem, there is a probability of 0.1587 of selecting a tin at random that weighs less than the amount defined (90 and 450 grams respectively).

Note that if our Z score calculation had given a value which included up to two decimal places we would have used the rest of this row in the table. Thus, a Z score of 1.01 has an associated probability of 0.1563, a Z score of 1.02 a probability of 0.1539 and so on. Note also that if you are using your own set of statistical tables the same information may be presented in a different format, sometimes showing the area to the *left* of the specified value, not the right.

The important principle in this example is that this probability will apply to *all* normal distributions. 15.87 per cent of observations in any such distributions will occur in the area to the left of 1 standard deviations below the mean. What differs from problem to problem, of course, is not the probability but the mean and standard deviation values.

11-8 PROBABILITY AND ECONOMICS

While probability theory is useful in business decision-making the idea of probability does not square easily with either neo-classical economics or with Austrian economics. A key assumption of the former school holds information to be perfect, implying that economic agents are endowed with perfect foresight. Were this true, there would clearly be no need to assess probabilities. At the other extreme, Austrian economists might argue that the most important decisions in business are related to wholly new products, to the adoption of new technologies and so on. In such cases, of course, no meaningful estimates of probability can be made.

In practice, however, economists of all schools are, like business, forced to use probability theory. For example, when forecasting trends in, say, the number of passengers a bus company might have to carry, an economist might conclude that the number of passengers had a probability of 0.5 of remaining at its current level, a probability of 0.3 of rising by 5 per cent per annum and a probability of falling by 10 per cent per annum of 0.2. As with the company in the motor-vehicle accessory market these probabilities could be compounded by the different actions which competing bus companies might take. Appropriate application of the multiplication and addition rules could be applied when the forecast values are influenced by a number of factors, each with its own probability of occurring. In practice many economic predictions are couched in probability terms.

11-9 SUMMARY

Conditional events are events which in some way affect each other's likelihood.

An *event* is a defined outcome of an experiment.

An *experiment* is a process which generates specified outcomes.

Independent events are events which have no influence on each other.

Mutually exclusive events are events which cannot occur together.

The *normal distribution* is a symmetrical, bell-shaped distribution.

Probability indicates the likelihood that an event will occur.

Expected value is the sum of probabilities multiplied by their respective outcome. It represents the average outcome, in the sense that probabilities have been taken into account.

EXERCISES

11-1 You have been asked to conduct a survey into the saving habits of different groups of the population: who saves with banks, who saves with building societies and so on. As a preliminary stage you are assessing the probabilities of certain types of person being included in the survey. The survey interviewers have been given instructions to include in the survey only those individuals who form part of the 'working population'. This is defined as those who are in paid employment, those unemployed but seeking work, those in the armed forces and the self-employed. The following data are available:

Distribution of the working population, United Kingdom, 1985 (thousands)

	Total	Male	Female
Paid employees, of which	21 466	11 950	9 516
in manufacturing industries	5 532		
in service industries	14 011		
in agriculture	339		
Self-employed	2 623	1 987	636
Armed forces	325	309	16
Unemployed	3 179	2 197	982
Total working population	27 593	16 442	11 150

Source: Annual Abstract of Statistics

On the assumption that the survey only includes those in the working population, determine the probabilities of the following types of individual being included in the survey:

(*a*) a female;

(*b*) an unemployed person;

(*c*) a member of the armed forces who is not female;

(*d*) someone in paid employment in manufacturing;

(*e*) someone who is both self-employed and male;

(*f*) someone who is either unemployed or employed in agriculture;

(*g*) someone who is male or unemployed.

11-2 On a particular production line, all the items produced are examined by two inspectors. If the first inspector spots a faulty item it is removed from the production line, so the second inspector only examines those items the first inspector thinks are not faulty. The first inspector has a record of spotting only 70 per cent of all faulty items that pass before him. The second inspector does slightly better, spotting 90 per cent of all faulty items that pass before him.

(*a*) During one day's production there are a total of 100 faulty items produced. How many will not be spotted by either inspector?

(*b*) Would it be better if the two inspectors changed places, with the second inspector now being the first to check the items?

The firm's output is such that an estimated 1000 items per week are faulty. Any faulty items not spotted by the two inspectors are sold to customers but, inevitably, incur costs of £10 each to repair. The firm is considering adding a third inspector to the line to try and improve the detection rate. This inspector will spot 60 per cent of faulty items that pass before him. How much should he be paid?

11-3 The company engaged in the motor-vehicle accessories market is now considering two alternative products for the Christmas market. Given the company's current situation (in terms of available capital, manpower and so on) the director knows he can only produce and sell one of the two products.

Product A sells for £5.99 and the manufacturer has exclusive production rights, ensuring that there is no other company with a directly competing product. Some basic market research has indicated that sales will fall into one of 3 basic groups: sales may be high (100 000 units sold), medium (50 000) or low (10 000). For Product A he has decided that there is a 30 per cent chance of achieving high sales, and a 60 per cent chance of medium sales. Product B is slightly more uncertain because of the possibility of a competitor product being sold by another firm. He feels that if he decides to manufacture Product B there is a 70 per cent chance that a competing product will appear on the market, thus reducing his sales levels. If such a competing product does appear a high sales figure will certainly not be achieved, although there is still a 40 per cent chance of medium sales and a 60 per cent chance of low sales. If he produces Product B and no competing product appears the probabilities of achieving different sales figures are the same as Product A. Product B sells for £9.99. Assuming the manufacturer wishes to optimize revenue which product should he produce?

11-4 A firm has recently introduced a new domestic gas central heating system on to the market and is keen to collect and analyse information relating to the efficiency of the system in terms of gas used. The firm has contacted 500 customers and monitored their energy consumption:

Therms used	No. of customers
970 <975	4
975 <980	7
980 <985	22
985 <990	46
990 <995	75
995 <1000	96
1000 <1005	95
1005 <1010	76
1010 <1015	45
1015 <1020	22
1020 <1025	9
1025 <1030	3

(a) Calculate the mean, median, standard deviation and coefficient of skewness.
(b) Obtain the probability distribution for the data.
(c) From the frequency table calculate the probability that a customer chosen at random will use:

   (i) more than 1020 therms;
   (ii) less than 985 therms;
   (iii) between 980 and 1000 therms;
   (iv) between 995 and 1010 therms.

(d) Using normal probability tables determine the probabilities in (c) above.
(e) Why are your answers in (c) and (d) different? Which method of finding the probabilities would you prefer to use?

11-5 A firm packaging cornflakes has equipment which packs an average of 760 grams per box, with a standard deviation of 5 grams. The firm advertises that its boxes contain at least 750 grams.

(a) Find the proportion of boxes that will be:

   (i) below this advertised weight;
   (ii) between 769.8 and 750.2 grams;
   (iii) between 772.9 and 747.1 grams.

(b) To reduce the incidence of underweight boxes to one in a thousand or less what should the average contents packed per box be?

11-6 A firm is currently setting up in business to manufacture small micro-computers. The firm anticipates that it will sell 1250 units per month. The firm has to take a decision on the guarantee period which it will offer on every computer sold. The guarantee periods of its competitors vary, with some offering a three-month guarantee, others six or twelve months. The firm feels that its decision is particularly important. If the period is too short, potential customers may be attracted to other competing models. If it is too long, the firm may find that it is incurring high costs of repairing faulty units. The repair department has estimated that it will cost an average of £7.50 to repair a unit returned within the guarantee period. Exhaustive tests have also been carried out on the reliability of the firm's product. The firm has found on average that the product will last for 424 days, with a standard deviation of 37 days, before developing a fault which requires repair. The distribution around this average has been found to be normal.

(a) Calculate the repair costs the firm can expect to incur from a month's sales if it offers a 12-month (365-day) guarantee.
(b) Calculate the guarantee period (in days) the firm should offer if it wishes to keep repair costs for a month's sales to no more than £375.

12

STATISTICAL INFERENCE

12-1 INTRODUCTION

Earlier in the text we were using data to describe and test hypotheses about economic behaviour. One of the data sets used related to incomes for a hypothetical 100 households in an inner-city area. These data were *sample* data in that they represented only part of the data set that could have been collected—the statistical population. Clearly, however, it is the *population* in which we are interested. Typically it is only the *sample* for which we have data. We know the average income—£122.50—for the sample. The question arises: what does the sample tell us about the population from which it is taken and which is our real area of interest? More precisely, we wish to know how close the sample mean is to the population mean. If it is close—and if we can quantify how close—then we can use the sample data as a proxy for the population in the process of hypothesizing about economic behaviour.

To answer these questions we must return to probability and the normal distribution.

12-2 THE SAMPLING DISTRIBUTION

In the case of the example of inner-city incomes we have a sample of 100 households. No matter how correctly we have drawn this sample from the population—in terms of its being fair, representative, unbiased and so on—it would be unreasonable to expect the sample mean to be arithmetically equal to the (unknown) population mean. After all, the sample mean is based on only 100 observations from a population which may contain hundreds of thousands. It is reasonable, however, to expect the sample mean to be fairly close to the population mean (always assuming our sampling methods were appropriate).

Additionally, our sample is but one of the many different samples of 100 households we could have chosen from the population. If we had chosen a different sample the same logic would have applied. We would not necessarily expect this second sample mean to be equal to the population mean but rather to lie somewhere close to it. Nor would we expect this second sample mean necessarily to equal that of the first sample chosen. We would expect, not unreasonably, some variation between the different sample means *and* between the sample means and the population mean.

Assume that we continue this process of selecting different samples from the same population, and that for each sample we calculate the mean until we have taken every possible and different sample. Naturally, we would not in practice be able to do this except for populations which were extremely small as the number of different samples is likely to run into billions. (Remember that only one item out of 100 needs to be different to make the second sample different from the first.) Let us now assume that, for the inner-city data set, we have calculated the mean of every sample taken, and that we have constructed a histogram of all these sample means. That is, we find the number of samples giving the same mean and show their relative frequencies. This histogram is known as the sampling distribution of sample means. Can we suggest what the histogram will look like? At first this might seem impossible unless we know what the population distribution looks like.

In fact—assuming that the number of items in each sample is reasonably large—the sampling distribution will take the shape of the normal distribution *no matter what the shape of the original population distribution.* This is a concept of fundamental importance to economics and to business and deserves further explanation.

12-3 THE CENTRAL LIMIT THEOREM

This concept is supported by an appropriate mathematical theorem known as the *Central Limit Theorem* which we shall simply state. *If we take random samples of size n from a population the distribution of sample means is approximately normal. This approximation becomes more accurate the larger is* n. The logic of the theorem can be seen intuitively. Let us assume, for purposes of illustration, that our data set of 100 household incomes in fact represents a *population*. We know from Chapter 3 that this data set is not normally distributed but positively skewed. Assume that we now take repeated samples of 30 observations from this population. We could show that even from a population of only 100 items there are over 29 372 339 800 000 000 000 000 000 *different* samples of 30 items that could be taken. Each of these samples will have a mean. Some of these means will be the same as the population mean, others will be close to this value, yet others less so. Logic suggests that most of the sample means will lie relatively close to the population mean. On reflection, only one sample (out of over 29 372 339 800 000 000 000 000 000) can include the lowest 30 items in the population. This is the sample mean which will be the furthest below the population mean. Similarly only one sample will include the 30 highest values in the population, giving the sample mean furthest above the population mean. Most samples, however, will include items dispersed across the population distribution, that is around the population mean. Remember that we are looking at sample averages so that even if a sample includes one extreme item from the population the bulk of items in the sample will counterbalance this. Accordingly, it is logical to argue that the distribution of sample means will be normal.

Figure 12-1 illustrates a simulation of this process. A large number of samples was drawn, at random, from this population (which you will remember from Fig. 2-2 is positively skewed), each sample mean calculated and the histogram of sample means plotted. This was done for different sample sizes with n at 30, 50 and 90. As can be seen, even though the population is not normally distributed, the histograms of the sample means (which simulate the sampling distribution) are, as the theorem predicts. It can be seen also that the histograms approximate more and more closely to a normal distribution as the sample size increases. Even for n at 30, however, the distribution is still reasonably normal, bearing in mind that the simulation does not include all the sample means.

In addition to predicting the shape of the sampling distribution, the theorem states that:

the mean of this sampling distribution will be the same as the population mean, and the standard deviation of the sampling distribution will be given by $s/\sqrt{n}$, *where* s *denotes the standard deviation of the sample and* n *is the sample size.* (This is frequently referred to as 'the standard error').

The first statement is straightforward. The mean of the sampling distribution will simply be the average of all the items in the distribution. These items are the sample means so the average of *all* the sample means (which will cover *all* the population data) must be the same as the population mean.

The second point requires more thought. The standard deviation of the sampling distribution measures dispersion in *this* distribution, which is the distribution of sample means dispersed around the population mean. In other words, the standard deviation of the sampling distribution indicates the dispersion of sample averages around the population average. We shall see shortly how important this is.

At this stage it will be useful to distinguish between the different sets of data with which we are dealing. We have the population, the sample and the sampling distribution each of which will have a mean and a standard deviation. To avoid confusion, different symbols are used for the different groups. Table 12-1 summarizes the notation used. To try and avoid confusion the standard deviation of the sample distribution is often referred to as the *standard error*. Students are sometimes confused over which set of data is being dealt with. The important point is that, generally, the only data we actually have relates to the sample, for which we can calculate the sample mean and sample standard deviation. The population and sampling distribution are, in general, unmeasurable. We can, however, speculate about their mean and standard deviation using the sample information.

Table 12-1 Features of the population, sample and sampling distribution

	Mean	Standard deviation
Population	μ	σ
Sample	$\bar{X}$	s
Distribution	μ	$s/\sqrt{n}$

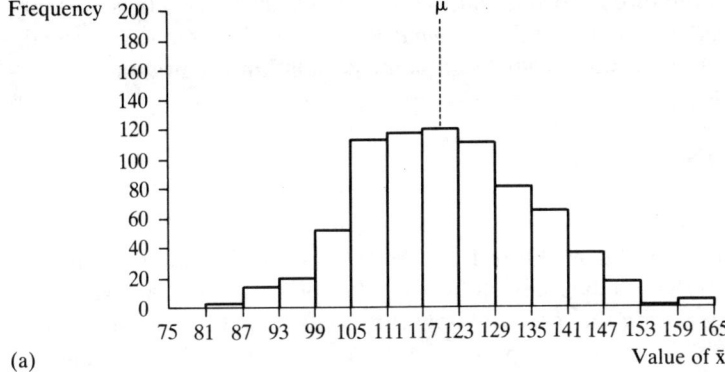

(a)

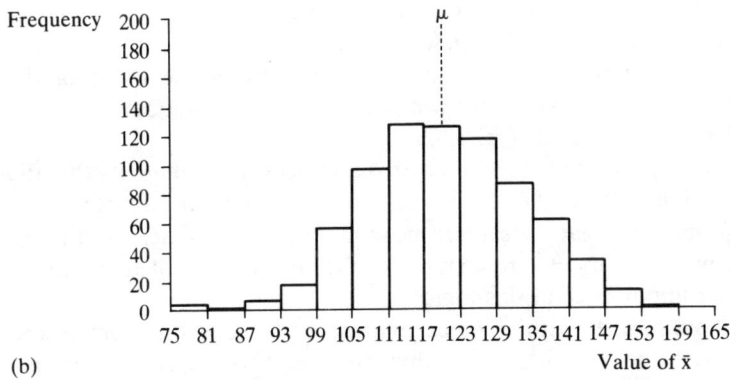

(b)

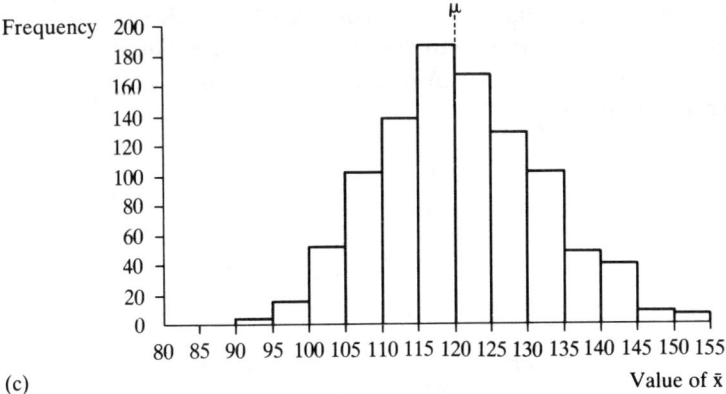

(c)

Figure 12-1 Simulation of sampling distribution: (a) $n = 30$; (b) $n = 50$; (c) $n = 90$

A further point worth reinforcing at this stage relates to which set of data is normally distributed. The theorem predicts that it is the *sampling distribution* that is always normally distributed. It is immaterial as to whether the sample or population are normal.

12-4 CONFIDENCE INTERVALS

The potential importance of the Central Limit Theorem is easily demonstrated. Let us return to the inner-city sample data. We know from the calculations in Chapter 3 that the sample mean is £122.50 and the standard deviation £77.97 for the sample of 100 households. We started this chapter by posing the question: how can we deduce the population mean when we only have sample data? We can now use the Central Limit Theorem, and the normal distribution probabilities, to resolve this.

We now know that our sample with a mean of £122.50 forms part of the sampling distribution for this population, and that the sampling distribution will be normal. We also know that we now have a method (using normal probabilities) of relating the sample mean to the mean of the sampling distribution (which is the same as the population mean). From our previous use of normal probabilities we know, for example, that 95 per cent of items in *any* normal distribution will fall within 1.96 standard deviations of the mean of the distribution. That is, 95 per cent of sample means will occur within 1.96 standard errors of the population mean. This is illustrated in Fig. 12-2.

We can express this in a slightly different way. There is a 95 per cent probability that the sample mean (at £122.50) will lie within 1.96 standard errors of the population mean—that is, there is a 95 per cent probability that the sample mean and population mean will be no further apart than 1.96 standard errors. Before we move to the appropriate calculations it is worth while reinforcing the importance of this logic.

What we have just found is a method of calculating how close the sample and population means are likely to be. This is exactly what we set out to achieve. We started with the sample result and we wanted to identify a likely value for the population mean. Note that we are not in a position to guarantee what the population mean is, because we cannot guarantee where the sample mean actually lies in the sampling distribution. Instead we use probability to indicate a likely relationship between the two averages. The key implication is that a distance of no more than 1.96 standard errors is, with a 95 per cent probability, likely to separate the sample mean from the population mean. The appropriate calculations are straightforward. Our sample mean is £122.50. The sample standard deviation is £77.97. Hence the standard error is

$$\frac{s}{\sqrt{n}} = \frac{£77.97}{\sqrt{100}} = £7.80$$

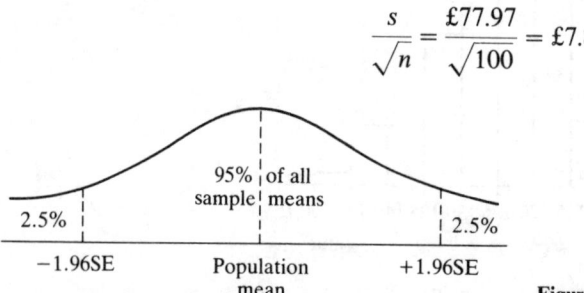

−1.96SE Population mean +1.96SE

95% of all sample means

2.5%   2.5%

Figure 12-2 Sampling distribution

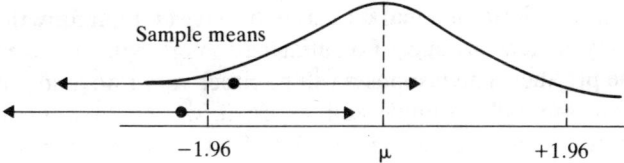

Figure 12-3 95% confidence interval

and 1.96 times the standard error is 1.96 × £7.80, or £15.29. That is, the sample mean and population mean are likely, with a probability of 0.95, to be no more than £15.29 apart.

We have been able, based on only a sample of 100 items, to calculate a range of likely values for the population mean income. This range of values is known as a *confidence interval* and is frequently used in assessing sample results. A 95% confidence interval (a range that had a probability 0.95 of including the population mean) would range from 1.96 standard errors less than the sample mean to 1.96 standard errors more than the sample mean. In this example, the 95% confidence interval would be £107.21 to £137.79. Similarly a 99 per cent confidence interval would range from 2.58 standard errors below the sample mean to 2.58 standard errors above the sample mean.

The interpretation and use of confidence intervals is of particular importance. A confidence interval, at a particular probability level, indicates a range around the sample result which is likely to include the (unknown) population mean value. The reason why we cannot guarantee (that is, attach a probability of 1) that the interval will include the population mean is that we do not know for certain where the sample mean lies within the sampling distribution. Figure 12-3 shows this. The two points marked (at −1.96 and +1.96 standard errors) indicate where, with a probability of 0.95, the sample mean will fall in the sampling distribution. As long as the sample mean does lie in this part of the sampling distribution the confidence interval *must* include the population mean value. But there is a slight probability (of 0.05) that the sample mean will fall into one of the two tails of the sampling distribution and, therefore, the interval calculated will *not* include the population mean value. Given that we have no way of actually seeing the sampling distribution we can only speculate about the value of the population mean, not provide a guaranteed prediction.

Even so this is likely to be of tremendous benefit to the economist and decision-maker. Using only limited sample information we can, first, identify a probable mean value for the statistical population in which we are actually interested and, second, quantify the likelihood associated with this value.

One point to remember throughout any confidence interval calculation is that we are assuming the sample is properly representative of the population from which it is taken. That is, that all the appropriate methods have been adopted to try and obtain a fair, representative and unbiased sample. If the sample is in any way unrepresentative then any confidence interval calculation will be inaccurate.

12-5 SAMPLE PROPORTIONS

Thus far we have been concerned with sample means. There are frequently occasions when we have collected sample data in attribute form—that is, data which have no numerical value. Consider the situation of a firm undertaking market research to try and quantify the number of customers likely to buy a new product. Potential customers will be asked whether or not they would buy the product. The responses will be either yes or no, and not in number form. As such, our data are still a sample and, as usual, we would want to speculate about the population response based on the sample data. That is, we would want to calculate an appropriate confidence interval. It is usual to express results like these in percentage or proportion form, to say things like '68 per cent of the sample responded "Yes"'. But how can we calculate the corresponding standard error and the appropriate confidence interval? For this, we would need the standard deviation of the sample, which is patently impossible, for how can we calculate dispersion around 'Yes/No'? In such cases, a different formula is used to calculate the standard error:

$$\text{Standard error} = \sqrt{\frac{p(100 - p)}{n}}$$

where n is the sample size, and p is the sample percentage response. This can then be used to calculate the appropriate confidence interval.

If, for example, 68 per cent of a sample of 500 potential customers had said they would buy a particular product and we wanted to calculate a 95 per cent confidence interval for this figure, we would proceed as follows. We first calculate the standard error, which is $\sqrt{68(100 - 68)/500}$, which equals $\sqrt{4.352} = 2.086$. Our confidence interval ranges from 1.96 standard errors below the sample proportion to 1.96 standard errors above the sample proportion, that is from $68 - (1.96 \times 2.086)$, which equals 63.91, to $68 + (1.96 \times 2.086)$, which equals 72.09. That is, there is a probability of 0.95 that between 63.9 per cent and 72.09 per cent of *all* potential customers (the statistical population) would buy the new product.

12-6 HYPOTHESIS TESTS

Confidence intervals are useful as general indicators of where the population value is likely to be, in relation to the sample value. Frequently in economics and business, however, we have a particular belief about what the population value is. In this section we introduce the concept of *hypothesis testing* which can be used to determine whether observed sample data are compatible with a specific assumed value for the population.

Let us assume that a car dealer network is considering establishing a car showroom in the suburban area, for which we have sample data. Market research previously undertaken by the company indicates that, to ensure success (in terms of sales and profits), the showroom should be located in an area where the average income level is more than £250 per week. A simple, but critical, question the company wishes to resolve is whether the suburban area satisfies this criterion.

We could use confidence intervals to try and answer the question but, instead, we shall undertake a formal hypothesis test. There are five basic stages to such a test. We need to establish: a *null hypothesis*; an *alternative hypothesis*; a *rejection region*; a *test statistic*; and a *calculated statistic*. The correct formulation of the null and alternative hypotheses is fundamental to the test. The formulation of the null hypothesis is the complete opposite of everyday logic. The alternative hypothesis is generally set out to relate to that which we wish to prove (or disprove), whilst the null hypothesis encapsulates the very opposite of what we are trying to prove.

A useful analogy is to compare a hypothesis test to a court of law. Should you ever have the misfortune to be charged with some offence, you will be asked to register a plea—guilty or not guilty. The wording is very specific. You are not asked whether you are *innocent*, but whether you are *not guilty*. The distinction may seem to be nothing more than semantic quibbling but is of fundamental importance to the accused. The accused does not have to prove his or her innocence but rather the prosecution must prove guilt. In other words, the null hypothesis ('not guilty') is accepted unless and until the alternative hypothesis ('guilty') is proved to the court's satisfaction. If you are found 'not guilty' this does not mean that you have proved your innocence but rather the prosecution has failed to prove your guilt. The onus of providing the proof is placed upon the prosecution.

In a hypothesis test the same principle applies. Until sufficient statistical evidence is provided the null hypothesis stands. If we fail to accept the alternative hypothesis this does not imply the null hypothesis is necessarily true, but rather we have failed to provide satisfactory evidence to accept the specified alternative.

In our example, the alternative hypothesis will be that the population average income is more than £250 per week, and the null hypothesis will be that the population average income is *not* more than £250. Using the standard notation of hypothesis tests we would express this as:

$$H_0: \mu \leqslant £250$$

$$H_1: \mu > £250$$

where H_0 stands for the null hypothesis and H_1 for the alternative hypothesis. Until we prove otherwise the null hypothesis stands, that is that average income is no more than £250 per week. But how can we determine whether there is sufficient proof to accept the alternative hypothesis?

The answer is that we must use our knowledge of the sampling distribution (of which the observed sample mean forms part) to calculate a *rejection region*, that is, a criterion by which we can determine whether to reject the null hypothesis. This rejection region is determined using the principles we have outlined in the previous section. We know that, arithmetically, the sample mean, at £300.50, is higher than the figure of £250. But we also know that the sample mean may be different from the population mean simply because it is a sample. That is, it is possible that we have selected a representative sample from a statistical population with a mean no more than £250 and the sample simply happens to include a disproportionate number of high income values. The question that arises, therefore, is: could this sample (with a mean of £300.50 and standard deviation of £77.69) have been drawn from a population with a mean of more than £250?

We cannot answer such a question with certainty but we can use probability to determine the likelihood. Assuming that the population mean (the mean of the sampling distribution) is no more than £250 (as specified in the null hypothesis) we can use probability to determine where the mean of a sample drawn from such a population is *likely* to occur. As before, with confidence intervals, it is conventional to use one of two probability levels: 95 per cent or 99 per cent. Let us use 95 per cent. It is conventional to define the area representing the rejection region as α which is expressed as $(1 -$ the confidence level chosen). Here α would be $(1 - 0.95) = 0.05$.

We can now exploit our knowledge of probability and the sampling distribution. If the null hypothesis is true then we can determine where the mean of a sample drawn from such a population is likely to occur, at a particular level of probability. Here, the null hypothesis states that the population mean is no more than £250. If this is the case then, using probability tables, we can determine that any sample drawn from such a population will, with 0.95 probability, lie no more than 1.6449 standard errors *above* the population mean of £250. This is illustrated in Fig. 12-4. This represents the sampling distribution on the assumption that the null hypothesis is true, that is, that the population mean is no more than £250. The value of 1.6449 standard errors indicates the upper limit within which we would expect the mean of a sample to occur, if such a sample were taken from the specified population. It is important to understand what this critical value represents. We are saying that, if the null hypothesis is true we can predict, with a 0.95 probability, where the mean of any sample taken from this (assumed) population will occur. Here, if the null hypothesis is true, the mean of any sample taken from the population specified in the null hypothesis ought to occur *no higher than* 1.6449 standard errors above the assumed population mean.

This critical value of 1.6449 standard errors defines the rejection area for the null hypothesis and obviously the acceptance area for the alternative hypothesis. If we find that the sample mean does actually occur below this critical value we have no reason for rejecting the null hypothesis as such a value for the sample mean would be consistent with the null hypothesis. If, on the other hand, the sample mean lies above this critical value (in the rejection area) then we must reject the null hypothesis and accept the alternative hypothesis. The logic behind such a decision is that, at the chosen level of probability of 0.95, we would not have expected the sample mean to lie in the rejection area *if* the null hypothesis is true.

The last part of the test is, therefore, to calculate whether the observed sample mean actually occurs, in the rejection area or not. We need to calculate how many standard errors above the assumed population mean the sample mean lies. In general this will be calculated from the expression:

$$\text{Test statistic} = \frac{\bar{X} - \mu}{SE}$$

where $\bar{X}$ is the observed sample mean, μ is the assumed population mean and SE is the standard error. In our example this would be:

$$\text{Test statistic} = \frac{300.5 - 250}{77.69/\sqrt{100}} = 6.5$$

That is, the sample mean lies 6.5 standard errors above the assumed population mean of £250. The interpretation of this is straightforward. The test statistic is higher than the

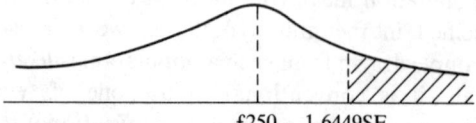

£250   1.6449SE   **Figure 12-4** Rejection area: one-tailed test (95% level)

critical statistic. We cannot accept, at the 0.95 probability level, that such a sample (with a mean of £300.50) was in fact taken from a population with a mean no more than £250. It is more probable that the sample was taken from a population with a mean above £250, that is from a population as defined in the alternative hypothesis. We must, therefore, reject H_0 and accept H_1, the alternative hypothesis, which states that the population average income is more than £250 per week. Accordingly, we would recommend that the company establishes a showroom in the suburban area as it meets the defined criterion in terms of average income.

Note also that we ought to point out to the company that we cannot offer a guarantee that we have made the right decision. There remains the probability (at 0.05 or less) that the sample mean was in fact indicative of a population mean as defined in the null hypothesis.

The procedure for a formal hypothesis test may, at this stage, seem unduly complex and, to some extent, unnecessary. It is, however, an essential technique when evaluating sample information. We are often in the position of wishing to compare a sample result against a specific and clearly defined population value. The use of a formal hypothesis test is essential if we are to make the comparison on an objective and scientific basis, rather than on a subjective one.

To summarize, the process of undertaking a hypothesis test comprises the following steps:

1. Define the specific value for the population parameter (here £250).
2. Formulate the two hypotheses (null and alternative). Ensure that the alternative hypothesis formulates what you are trying to prove or disprove.
3. Choose an appropriate probability level at which to undertake the test (normally 0.95 or 0.99).
4. Find an appropriate critical value (from statistical tables) which defines the boundary between the rejection and acceptance areas.
5. Calculate a test statistic for the sample result.
6. Compare the test statistic with the critical value and determine which hypothesis is most probable.

12-7 OTHER FORMS OF HYPOTHESIS TEST

The test detailed above is but one of a whole variety of tests that can be undertaken on sample data.

One-tailed versus two-tailed tests

The test above is technically known as a *one-tailed test*, because the rejection area is clearly focused on only one tail of the sampling distribution. Obviously, in some cases this critical region may lie on the right hand side or on the left hand side depending on the problem.

In other cases, however, the rejection area may include both tails of the distribution. This occurs when we formulate a hypothesis of the form that the population mean is equal to, or is not equal to, a specified value. In such a case, we would reject the null hypothesis if the test statistic fell into *either* of the two tails. This is illustrated in Fig. 12-5.

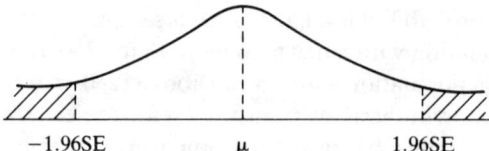

−1.96SE μ 1.96SE   **Figure 12-5** Rejection area: two-tailed test (95% level)

The important point is that we must define the rejection area value in a slightly different way. If we are carrying out a two-tail test with, again, a probability of 0.95 then the total area of the rejection regions must sum to 0.05. This means that each tail (given the symmetrical distribution) will encompass 0.025 and the appropriate critical statistic from the probability tables will now be ± 1.96.

Test involving proportions or percentages

We saw in an earlier section that we could calculate a suitable confidence interval for sample data expressed as a percentage of the total. We can also undertake an equivalent statistical test. There will be, however, a number of differences. First, in terms of notation the population parameter is now indicated not by μ (the population mean) but by π (the population percentage). Similarly the sample result is not $\bar{X}$ but p. Second, the standard error is calculated using the formula defined earlier, but which in a hypothesis test uses the assumed π value not the observed p value. Thus the standard error will be:

$$\text{Standard error} = \sqrt{\frac{\pi(100 - \pi)}{n}}$$

The remaining stages are exactly as before.

12-8 CONCLUSION

This chapter has covered the key areas of statistical inference. Arguably, this is the technique of most importance in your study of economics and business decision-making. It is of fundamental importance to your studies that you understand the concepts discussed in this chapter. The calculation of a confidence interval and the process of a hypothesis text are, technically, not difficult. Students rarely have trouble in performing the calculations. What is equally, if not more, important is that you understand the concepts of statistical inference. Failing to develop an appropriate understanding of the key concepts will inevitably cause you to misinterpret or misunderstand the results of your calculations.

As with most of the techniques in this text the only way such understanding can be achieved is through practice, and the exercises at the end of this chapter are designed to help the reader in this respect.

12-9 SUMMARY

The *Central Limit Theorem* predicts that the sampling distribution will approximate to the normal provided sample sizes are sufficiently large.

A *confidence interval* is a range of values around the sample average that will, at a specified level of probability, include the population average.

A *hypothesis test* is a formal test of a sample result against some specific assumed population value.

The *sampling distribution* is the theoretical probability distribution of all sample averages taken from some population.

The *standard error* is the standard deviation of the sampling distribution.

EXERCISES

12-1 Determine the major reasons why an organization will normally collect sample data rather than data relating to the population.

12-2 Using the *Family Expenditure Survey* (or an equivalent) determine how the sample is selected and what efforts are made to ensure the sample is representative of the population.

12-3 Since the introduction of legislation relating to the compulsory wearing of seatbelts by motorists a number of surveys have been carried out to identify the proportion of motorists who do use their belts. One such survey was carried out on 500 motorists and it was found that 85 per cent stated that they usually use their seatbelts as required by law. Calculate 95 per cent and 99 per cent confidence intervals for this result and explain what your interval measures.

12-4 A large retail store is trying to forecast sales and revenue. A sample of 100 customers is taken and the amount of money they spent in the store analysed. On average, people in the sample spent £25.68, with a standard deviation of £5.42.

(*a*) Calculate a 95 per cent confidence interval and discuss how this might be useful to the store.
(*b*) The store also estimates that it has 1200 customers per day. Estimate average daily revenue.

12-5 A manufacturer of electronic equipment buys microchips from a supplier in packs of 14. On average two out of the 14 are damaged in transit and accordingly the price paid reflects this, with the manufacturer only paying for 12 chips per pack supplied. The manufacturer, however, decides to check that he does in fact get 12 chips per pack. A sample of 400 packs is taken and it is found that on average 2.25 chips are damaged per pack, with a standard deviation of 1.8. Should the manufacturer renegotiate the price he pays per pack supplied?

13

FURTHER HYPOTHESIS TESTING PROCEDURES

13-1 INTRODUCTION

In the previous chapter the concept of a hypothesis test was developed. The test detailed is but one of a large number of tests that are used to help economists and decision-makers make inferences about a population with only sample information available. In this chapter we shall introduce some of the more common tests available. These are all based on the same principles as the test introduced in Chapter 12.

13-2 SMALL-SAMPLE TESTS

Thus far, in our attempts to make statistical inferences about population parameters based solely on sample data, we have focused on samples which are described as 'large'. The definition of a 'large' sample is somewhat imprecise but is often taken to be a sample size of 30 or more. Very often, however, we may be making statistical inferences on samples with fewer observations than this. Remember that the whole basis of statistical inference so far has rested on the Central Limit Theorem, which states that the sampling distribution is approximately normal, *provided* that sample sizes are sufficiently large.

If sample sizes are not large then the Central Limit Theorem can no longer be applied, and the whole basis of our statistical inference techniques (confidence intervals and hypothesis tests) becomes suspect. Fortunately, all is not lost. An employee of Guinness Breweries at the turn of the century, W. S. Gossett, determined that the sampling distribution for small samples would also be approximately normal, *provided* that the distribution from which the samples were taken was symmetrical. (Remember that for the Central Limit Theorem we did not need to specify the shape of the population distribution to know that the sampling distribution would be normal.) Further, he discovered that the size of the sample would influence how normal the sampling distribution would be. The smaller the sample size the 'flatter' the sampling distribution would become, that is, the greater its dispersion.

Indeed, it was shown that for small samples there would be not one sampling distribution, but a whole family—one for each sample size—with each differing slightly from the others. Accordingly it follows that if we are dealing with small samples, we cannot use the probabilities for statistical inference obtained from the Z score tables. Instead, we must use tables which refer to the *Student's* t *statistics*. Such a table is shown in Appendix C. The table shows t values for two parameters: the significance level, α; and the number degrees of freedom, written as v (Greek 'nu') and defined as $n - 1$, that is one less than the sample size. Notice in particular that as the degrees of freedom gets larger (as the sample size increases) the t statistic values get closer and closer to the values that would be obtained from the large-sample tables used previously.

For the purpose of constructing a confidence interval or undertaking a hypothesis test the only difference from the previous method would involve replacing the critical statistic taken from the Z score table with that taken from the t statistic table. In all other respects calculation and interpretation remain exactly as before. The only further point that must be stressed is that in using small samples for statistical inference we are making the assumption that the population from which the small sample is taken has a symmetrical distribution. This is easy to forget but is a crucial assumption underpinning any hypothesis test on a small sample.

We can easily illustrate a hypothesis test using the t distribution. Let us assume that an economist has been monitoring the wage increases negotiated by trade unions for their members. Over the past 12 months she has collected information on 20 trade unions and calculated that, on average, these unions have negotiated an increase of 6.2 per cent in basic pay rates, with a standard deviation of 1.4 per cent. Information for the previous year shows that, for all unions, pay increases achieved averaged 4.8 per cent. Can we conclude, based on the sample, that unions are achieving higher wage settlements this year compared with last? Following the procedure detailed in the Chapter 12 we have:

$$H_0: \mu \leqslant 4.8$$

$$H_1: \mu > 4.8$$

$$\alpha = 0.05$$

$$n = 20$$

$$v = n - 1 = 19$$

Critical t (from Appendix C) $= 1.729$

$$\text{Calculated } t = \frac{6.2 - 4.8}{1.4/\sqrt{20}} = 4.47$$

At the 0.95 probability level we are, therefore, forced to reject the null hypothesis and accept the alternative hypothesis. Based on a sample of 20, the evidence suggests that trade unions are achieving higher wage settlements this year than last year. Again, we must reinforce the point that such a conclusion is based on the assumption that the sample is fair and that the population represented by the sample is symmetrically distributed.

A question asked by students at this stage is: when do I use the Z table and when the t table? Our suggestion is to use the t table exclusively. If the sample is large the test statistic is the same as that from the Z tables in any case. If the sample is small you are still using the correct table.

13-3 COMPARING TWO SAMPLES

Thus far, our interest has been focused on comparing the result of one sample with an assumed value for the population. Frequently, however, we wish to compare a sample result not against an assumed population value but rather against another sample result, in order to identify their differences or similarities. In the terminology of hypothesis testing, we wish to test whether the two samples are from the same population. Such comparisons are frequent in economics: we wish to compare samples from different regions or countries, samples taken at different times, samples before and after some change has been introduced and so on.

Test on two sample means

We actually started this text with such a comparison. Remember that we had two samples for data on weekly household income—one sample for an inner-city area, the second for a suburban housing development. The key sample results are summarized in Table 13-1.

Although there is a large arithmetic difference between the two average income values can we be sure that the difference is, in fact, a real one and does not simply reflect the fact that we have sample data? In other words, are the samples taken from the same statistical population or from different populations (with different mean values)? A hypothesis test on the *difference* between the two samples is obviously called for. Such a test follows the same process as our previous tests but with variations in some of the calculations. Our test is now based on the difference between the two results so we can define the statistic in which we are interested as $(\bar{X}_1 - \bar{X}_2)$, that is, the difference between the two means. The Central Limit Theorem indicates that the sampling distribution of this statistic will be normally distributed (as long as sample sizes are reasonably large) and will have a standard error:

$$SE = \sqrt{\frac{s_1^2}{n_1} + \frac{s_2^2}{n_2}}$$

Table 13-1 Key sample results, inner-city area group and suburban housing development group

	Inner-city area	Housing development
Sample size	100	100
Mean	£122.50	£300.50
Standard deviation	£77.97	£77.69

where s_1 and s_2 are the standard deviations of the two samples, respectively, of size n_1 and n_2. The appropriate calculations for this example would be:

$$SE = \sqrt{\frac{77.97^2}{100} + \frac{77.69^2}{100}} = \sqrt{60.79 + 60.36} = 11.01$$

As with our previous tests we could carry out either a one-tailed or two-tailed test. The content of the problem will determine which is most appropriate. In some cases we will be satisfied to determine whether there is a difference or not (a two-tailed test) in other cases whether the difference is positive or negative (a one-tailed test). In our example it would be appropriate to undertake a one-tailed test given that we wish to know whether the suburban population has a higher average income than the inner-city area population. Thus the test becomes:

$$H_0: (\mu_1 - \mu_2) \geqslant 0$$

$$H_1: (\mu_1 - \mu_2) < 0$$

If we set α at 0.05 the appropriate critical statistic is 1.6449. The test statistic is:

$$Z = \frac{(\bar{X}_1 - \bar{X}_2) - (u_1 - u_2)}{SE}$$

where standard error is as defined earlier. The calculation therefore, is:

$$Z = \frac{(122.5 - 300.5) - 0}{11.01} = 16.2$$

Accordingly, as the test statistic is greater than the critical statistic we must reject H_0 and accept the alternative hypothesis that the mean for the suburban area is greater than that for the inner-city area. In statistical terminology we would conclude that the two samples were taken from populations with different means.

Test on two sample proportions or percentages

An equivalent test can be undertaken when the sample results are expressed as percentages. The differences between this test and that for two sample means are, first, that the null hypothesis is specified as the difference between the two population percentages, that is as $(\pi_1 - \pi_2)$, and second, that the standard error for the sampling distribution of the percentage differences is:

$$SE = \sqrt{\frac{p_1 n_1 + p_2 n_2}{n_1 + n_2}}$$

where p_1 and p_2 are the sample percentage/proportion results. The rest of the test procedure, however, is identical to that for two sample means.

Comparing two samples—small sample test

Again, it is common to want to undertake a formal hypothesis test when the two sample sizes are small. For reasons connected with the size of the calculated standard error, such a small sample size test is almost invariably undertaken on sample means and not on sample percentages. When compared with the two-mean test on large samples there are two key differences: the critical statistic will be a t statistic with $(n_1 + n_2 - 2)$ degrees of freedom, and the standard error will be calculated using the formula:

$$SE = \sqrt{\frac{(n_1 - 1)s_1^2 + (n_2 - 1)s_2^2}{n_1 + n_2 - 2}}$$

Additionally, the t test is based on two critical assumptions: that both populations from which the samples are taken are normally distributed, and that the variances (the square of the standard deviation) of the two populations are equal.

Statistical independence

It must be pointed out that all the above tests are undertaken on the assumption that the two samples which are being compared are statistically independent. The tests detailed here cannot be used where the two samples represent what is known as a *paired sample* test. That is, where the same items are used in both samples. An example of this (frequently seen in TV advertisements) would be where we ask the same group of people to test two alternative products so as to compare the difference in responses. The appropriate test would not be one of those detailed here as the two samples are not statistically independent. The development of appropriate tests in such a situation is beyond the scope of this test.

13-4 CHI-SQUARE TESTS

The final hypothesis test that we shall consider is known as the χ^2 (pronounced 'ki square') test. This test is one of the simplest of a variety of non-parametric tests. All the tests thus far have focused on a particular parameter (the mean) of the data. In cases where we wish to test not just one feature of the sample but all the data χ^2 tests are appropriate.

The χ^2 test has two general areas of application. The first is in testing *goodness of fit*. This is to compare a sample distribution with some specified population distribution. The second is in testing *contingency tables*. Contingency tables can be constructed where each item in a sample can be categorized in at least two different ways. In both cases the χ^2 test is virtually identical, with observed values from the sample compared with expected values generated from the null hypothesis to determine whether there is a statistically significant difference between the two sets.

Goodness of fit tests

We shall illustrate this type of test with a simple example. Table 13-2 shows the number of workers in each household for the UK as a whole and for the North. It shows the number of workers per household for the UK as a percentage. For the North the actual (observed) frequencies are shown. Thus, in the sample there are 1383 households classed as having no workers. We may wish to determine whether there is a different pattern for households in the North compared with the UK as a whole. Such a distinction may, for example, be the first stage in determining whether income patterns and hence car-ownership patterns are different in the two regions.

Using tests previously developed we could calculate the mean number of workers in the

Table 13-2 Number of workers in each household

No. workers	UK (%)	North observed (O)	North expected (E)	$O - E$	$(O - E)^2$	$(O - E)^2/E$
		Frequencies				
0	31.8	1 383	1 202	181	32 761	27.255
1	30.5	1 059	1 152	−93	8 649	7.508
2	29.0	1 031	1 096	−65	4 225	3.855
3	6.2	223	234	−11	121	0.517
4	2.2	72	83	−11	121	1.458
5 or more	0.3	10	11	−1	1	0.091
	100.0	3 778	3 778	0	45 878	40.684

Source: Compiled from the 1984 *FES*, Table 27, p. 74.

sample for the North and carry out a formal hypothesis test to determine whether this sample mean was different from that in the UK. The problem with such a test is that it only compares the *average* number of workers per household and not the whole distribution. Not infrequently (particularly if the average is not unduly representative of the distribution) we may find no difference between two means although the distributions themselves may differ considerably.

The χ^2 test compares the observed frequencies for the North with a set of expected frequencies. These are calculated on the assumption that the distribution is the same as that for the UK as a whole. Thus, the percentages in the UK column are applied to the total frequencies for the North (at 3778) to calculate what the North's distribution would be if it were the same as that for the UK. The logic of the test is then straightforward. If the observed and expected distributions are the same we would expect the difference ($O - E$) to be small. As with the standard deviation calculation we square these differences and then divide through by the expected value for each part of the distribution.

This gives a result of 40.684. This is the calculated χ^2 statistic, obtained on the null hypothesis that there are no significant differences between the observed and expected distributions. Technically, if this were true we would expect a χ^2 statistic of zero, but, given that we are dealing with sample data we must expect some sampling variation. This is done by using appropriate statistical tables (Appendix D) which show the critical statistic values for differing combinations of α and the number of degrees of freedom. For the goodness-of-fit test degrees of freedom is one less than the number of classes or intervals in the distribution. Here, there are six classes so we have five degrees of freedom and, from the Appendix a critical χ^2 statistic of 11.07 at the 0.95 probability level.

The decision rule applied to all the other tests is equally applicable here. The critical statistic, 11.07, indicates the maximum value the calculated statistic can take if we are not to reject the null hypothesis. Given that the calculated statistic at 40.684 is above the critical we have no option but to reject the null hypothesis (that the two distributions are the same) and accept the alternative hypothesis (that the two distributions are different). Note that the test does not indicate in what ways the two distributions differ, it simply indicates that they do. We are 95 per cent confident, therefore, that the distribution of workers per household in the North is different from that for the UK as a whole.

Contingency tables

The second standard application of the χ^2 test relates to contingency tables. Such a table is shown in Table 13-3. The table shows the employment status of the head of household on a regional basis. Our interest in the table lies in the distribution of the data between regions. We might raise the question as to whether there were different employment patterns in different regions. That is, is employment status dependent (or contingent) on region? To answer this question from the data in Table 13-3 we can work out what the distributions for each region would be if employment status and region were not dependent upon each other. In probability terms, we are assuming the two characteristics are statistically independent. These frequencies will then form the *expected* frequencies for the χ^2 test. But how can we derive them? The answer is to apply the basic rule for dealing with events which are (or in our case are assumed to be) statistically independent. This is the multiplication rule developed earlier. The logic applied is simple. We can identify the probability of an individual, selected at random, coming from a particular region. We can also calculate the probability of an individual selected at random falling into a particular employment group. Given that we are assuming independence, multiplying the two probabilities will give us the probability of an individual coming from a particular region *and* falling into a particular employment group.

For example, the probability of choosing an individual who comes from the North is 3778/11 759 or 0.3213. Similarly the probability of choosing an individual being employed is 6530/11759 or 0.5553. So the probability of an individual coming from the North *and* being an employee is 0.3213 × 0.5553 which equals 0.1784. Given that there are a total of 11 759 in the sample we would expect 2098 (0.1784 × 11 759) people to fall into this particular category. This is the frequency we would expect in this cell of the table *if* there is no dependence between the two characteristics. Likewise we can calculate expected values for each cell in the Table, shown in Table 13-4.

So we now have a set of observed and expected frequencies and can calculate a χ^2 statistic in the same way as before. The calculated value (obtained from Table 13-3 and Table 13-4) is 140.463. To find the critical statistic from tables we need to know the degrees of freedom. For a contingency-table test this is: $(c - 1) \times (r - 1)$ where c is the number of columns of data (excluding totals) and r the number of rows (excluding totals). Here, we have 12 degrees of freedom ($5 - 1 \times 4 - 1$) and, at the 95 per cent level, a critical statistic of 21.03. Accordingly, we conclude that there is a statistical difference between the observed and expected frequencies. Given that the expected frequencies were based on the assumption of independence between the two attributes (the null hypothesis) we are effectively concluding that the two attributes are *not* independent but are, in some unspecified way, connected. There is, in other words, a link between region and employment status.

Statistically, the χ^2 test is particularly powerful and useful. You must use it with care, however, and the following points should be noted:

1. The test must be carried out on frequencies (not percentages) and frequencies take integer values.
2. For statistical reasons the test becomes invalid if any cell contains a zero frequency or more than 20 per cent of cells have frequencies less than 5. Often, this problem can be overcome by regrouping the data.

Table 13-3 Contingency table: employment status of head of household, by region

	Employed	Self-employed	Retired	Unoccupied	Total
North	1905	265	1057	551	3 778
Midlands	1384	162	544	308	2 398
East Anglia	272	50	140	55	517
South East	2412	356	921	351	4 040
South West	557	94	268	107	1 026
Total	6530	927	2930	1372	11 759

Source: Compiled from *FES*, 1984.

Table 13-4 Expected frequencies

2 098	298	941	441	3 778
1 332	189	597	280	2 398
287	41	129	60	517
2 243	318	1 008	471	4 040
570	81	255	120	1 026
6 530	927	2 930	1 372	11 759

3. The test indicates dependence or independence. It does not indicate cause and effect nor the particular pattern of dependence, should it exist. In our example, we conclude there is some connection between the two attributes but we do not know what form this connection takes.

13-5 SUMMARY

The hypotheses tests introduced in this chapter are based on the principles of statistical inference that have been developed over the last few chapters. All are concerned with testing specific hypotheses about a statistical population based only on sample information.

Given the importance of being able to formulate *and* test hypotheses in economics and business the potential importance of these techniques cannot be overemphasized.

EXERCISES

13-1 A small engineering firm uses computer-controlled machine lathes on its production line. In order to ensure efficient operation of the lathes a key component needs to be replaced at frequent and regular intervals. At present the firm purchases the replacement components from a German supplier. These components have been found to have an average life of seven months.

The firm has recently been approached by a British supplier claiming to be able to supply a comparable replacement part at a lower price. You have been asked to investigate and recommend whether or not the engineering firm should switch suppliers. The British supplier has provided six parts for testing and you have found the life of these six test items to be (in months):

6.5   7.6   6.1   6.3   7.4   6.2

Draft a report recommending whether or not the engineering firm should switch from the German to the British supplier. Your report should include the following areas:

(a) The basic principles of hypothesis tests and statistical inference.
(b) Why it is necessary to use the t distribution when making inferences about a population mean from a small sample.
(c) Other factors you might wish to consider in making a recommendation.

13-2 Following deregulation of local passenger transport a local bus company has been experimenting with different fare structures to assess the impact on passenger demand. For a trial period a cheap off-peak bus ticket was introduced on a number of routes to try and attract additional passengers and increase revenue. Before the trial a random sample of 75 weekdays was taken to determine the number of passengers normally travelling on these routes. The average daily number of passengers was found to be 1748 (with a standard deviation of 246).

A similar sample was taken after the introduction of the cheap ticket. From a random sample of 120 weekdays the average number of passengers was found to be 1945 (standard deviation 242).

Draft a report concluding whether the new ticket has been successful in attracting more passengers. Include in your report a discussion of the elasticity concept and its relevance to the company in this context.

13-3 Your company operates in a large central office employing several hundred people. Around the office are a number of automatic drink-vending machines for use by staff. The machines are leased from the vending company and cost your organization £23 each per month in rental and maintenance. Under the leasing agreement drinks cost 15p each and the revenue is kept by your company. It is company policy that the vending machines are required to be self-financing.

The vending-machine firm has approached your company to see if it wishes to replace the existing machines with a newer model which offers the latest technology, has a built-in voice response and offers a wider variety of drinks of better quality.

The price charged per drink will remain the same but the hire charges will increase by £3 per machine per day. The vending firm argues, however, that this extra cost will easily be recouped through increased sales. To allow your company to assess the potential the vending firm has loaned your company a new model and you have closely monitored the results. For a trial period of 20 working days one of the old models sold an average of 170 drinks per day (with a standard deviation of 33). The new model, over the same period, sold on average 220 drinks per day (with a standard deviation of 40).

Draft a report to management recommending whether the new model should be installed permanently. Your report should include details of the appropriate test and an explanation of the methods used in reaching a conclusion.

13-4 The data shown below relate to the 1985 *FES* and shows the percentage of households owning a particular type of durable good. The data relates to the United Kingdom as a whole and to the South East.

Durable good	Percentage of households	
	South East	UK
Car/van	67.7	62.1
Central heating	72.4	67.7
TV	97.3	97.4
Telephone	86.5	79.4
Home computer	14.6	12.6
Video recorder	34.9	30.1

The number of households in the South East in the survey was 3982. Carry out an appropriate test to determine whether the pattern of ownership of these durable goods in the South East is different from the United Kingdom as a whole.

14

COST

14-1 INTRODUCTION

One factor underlies all supply curves: cost. Quite simply, the cost of producing an item determines how much of it entrepreneurs will wish to produce, and later chapters will examine in some detail the relationship between cost, output and profit. By influencing supply, of course, cost also bears upon price and output because, as we have seen, supply and demand act in conjunction to determine the equilibrium position for the market. Cost is thus fundamental to economics, and this chapter is accordingly devoted to its analysis.

The costs of business organizations are often set out in their 'profit and loss' accounts. These relate, of course, to the past—they are retrospective. What is of interest to economists and decision-makers, however, is the expected cost of future actions. Thus cost must often be calculated *ex ante*, that is, before production is undertaken. This forms a link between cost-estimation and probability and hypothesis testing. This is because costs calculated for the purpose of making decisions are *estimates*, whose reliability may vary according to circumstances. For example, a petrol company which already runs 100 service stations will have more information upon which to draw when estimating the cost of a new station than a company with only five existing stations. Decision-makers who estimate costs find themselves—implicitly or explicitly—using probability and the rules of inference.

14-2 OPPORTUNITY COST AND PAYMENTS TO FACTORS OF PRODUCTION

The economist's definition of cost may be easily stated. The cost of consuming a good is the enjoyment of the alternative goods that have been forgone in order to consume that good.

Choosing to spend money in one way means that it cannot be spent in another, and the pleasure of consuming the rejected items is necessarily forgone. These forgone pleasures are the ultimate cost of the choice: they are its *opportunity cost*.

Similar considerations apply to the spending of time. A student who joins the hockey team would not, for example, be able to spend Wednesday afternoons studying. Thus the opportunity cost of playing hockey would be the forgone pleasure of good essay marks. Indeed, the principle of opportunity cost can be applied to every situation which requires a choice between different courses of action.

One area of choice relates to *employment*. In a market economy, people are not forced to work in a particular job but can choose from a variety of occupations or indeed can decline to be employed at all. Selecting one option means forgoing the benefits of the other possibilities: taking any job at all means that some of the pleasures of whippet-racing and allotment gardening must be given up; working long hours on an oil rig means that family life must be forgone for long periods, and becoming a teacher may mean longer holidays but the higher living standards enjoyed by people with similar qualifications in other professions must be forgone. In short, taking employment imposes an opportunity cost on the worker. In this context, wages and salaries can be seen as compensation for this cost.

The opportunity cost of *enterprise* may be thought of in a similar fashion. To become a full-time entrepreneur, a person would give up his or her job and thus suffer the opportunity cost of the lost income (or rather, the pleasure of spending that income).

Capital likewise has an opportunity cost. Capital goods have to be paid for out of savings: the money which firms borrow from banks to buy new equipment is money which people have saved in their bank accounts. In making these savings, people have faced choices and thus incurred opportunity costs. The choice over savings is whether to spend money straight away or to go without those consumer goods until some time in the future. Thus the opportunity cost of saving is the *deferral* of consumption, and interest payments are made to savers to compensate them for this sacrifice.

The opportunity costs associated with *land* are the forgone benefits of the rejected alternative uses. For instance, the opportunity cost to a landowner of leasing his property to a developer is the rent, now forgone, that was formerly paid by the dairy farmer. The rent paid by the developer will serve to compensate him for this cost.

14-3 OPPORTUNITY COST IN THE MACRO-ECONOMY

The principle of opportunity cost also affects the government. If a government has committed itself to a certain level of expenditure, then the inclusion of a new scheme will necessarily mean the exclusion of another. More money spent on, say, building motorways will mean less for, say, scientific research and thus the opportunity cost of the motorway programme is the forgone research.

If the government does not regard itself as being restricted to a given budget, extra projects can be included in its expenditure plans without any having to be discarded. The principle of opportunity cost nevertheless continues to apply, because the additional spending has to be met, ultimately, by higher tax payments. The opportunity cost of greater public programmes is, therefore, the consumer goods which people now find themselves unable to buy.

This may be illustrated constructing a model. Let us assume that an economy can produce only two goods: cars and food. If all the economy's resources were committed to vehicle production, then we may suppose that 1,000 cars could be made every month (and no food). If, on the other hand, all resources were to be devoted to agriculture, then food production would run at, say, 2,000 tons per month (but there would be no cars). If resources were allocated to the two industries simultaneously, the economy would produce both cars and food. Naturally the balance between the two goods would reflect the way resources had been allocated. Figure 14-1 shows this diagrammatically. The Production Possibility Frontier (PPF), that is, the curve *AE*, shows the productive capacity of the economy. It indicates the various combinations of cars and food that our hypothetical economy could produce when all resources are employed. At point *A*, only cars are manufactured, at point *E*, only food, while at points *B*, *C* and *D*, different combinations of both are made. If the economy were to be found inside the PPF at, say, point *F*, then it would be possible to raise the production of cars, food or both. The implication must be that at *F* the economy has a measure of excess capacity, that is, that resources are not fully employed. Point *G*, on the other hand, is unattainable in that the economy lacks the necessary resources. Should more resources become available through a rising population, a programme of investment or through advancing technology, the PPF will shift outward and point *G* might well become attainable.

Movements along the PPF like that from *D* to *C* illustrate the principle of opportunity cost. At *D*, the economy produces 1600 tons of food and 600 cars per month. A decision to raise car production to, say 800 cars (moving to *C*) would imply a fall in food production to 1400 tons a month, a reduction of 200 tons. Thus the opportunity cost of the extra 200 cars

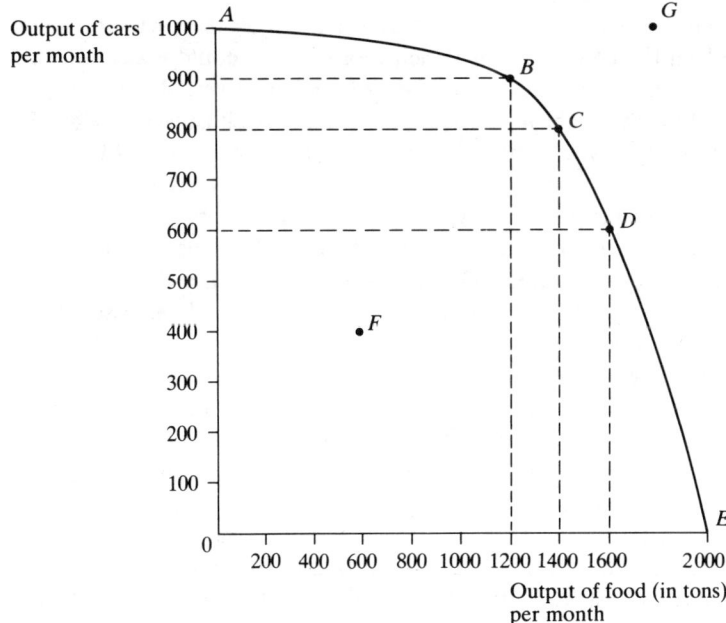

Figure 14-1 The production possibility frontier

is 200 tons of food. (Had the economy been in a state of unemployment at F, car production could have advanced without a cut in food output, that is, there would have been no opportunity cost.)

A further increase in car production by a move from C to B would, interestingly, incur a different opportunity cost. Although going from C to B trims food production by a further 200 tons, the gain in terms of extra cars is this time only 100, as against 200 cars for the loss of the first 200 tons of food. The motor-car production programme, in other words, is running into increasing difficulties because of rising opportunity cost.

Graphically, rising opportunity cost comes from the fact that the PPF is non-linear. This is because different resources have different aptitudes. Some workers are natural foundry-men or assembly workers who would find farming difficult, while others might be born agriculturalists. If, however, the economy were at point E, all the workers would be making food. A process of transferring resources from agriculture into vehicles would begin by moving those who were not good at their jobs in food production but very good at making cars. The loss of output of food would therefore be small, but the gain in car output would be large (E to D). As more and more workers were transferred, however, those with less aptitude for car-making would be recruited into the car industry and opportunity costs would rise.

14-4 THE FIRM AND OPPORTUNITY COST

The principle of opportunity cost affects firms in a number of ways. In the first place, it usually dictates the price that a firm has to pay for the services of the factors of production that it uses. These payments reflect the factors' opportunity cost: their owners are forgoing opportunities to earn income elsewhere in the economy (or to enjoy their leisure). Their forgone incomes are based on the contributions which those factors could make to other industries. For example, if a worker has the skill to earn £14,000 in advertising this would indicate that she could add £14,000 a year to the economy's output of business services. By recruiting her, her new employer—say, a textile firm—is depriving the economy of £14,000's worth of business services. The salary which the textile company pays to the worker thus reflects the opportunity cost which it is imposing on the economy at large.

In the second place, opportunity cost affects the way in which firms assess the cost to themselves of the work which they undertake. This assessment is the basis on which firms set their prices. It is clearly important that it be realistic, for if costs are underassessed, firms will find themselves doing work which is not profitable, while if they are overassessed they will fail to perceive profitable lines of business.

In assessing the cost of work done (or rather, the cost of work to be done, since the assessment must be made at the very outset), firms should take account of their own opportunity costs. Firms usually operate in several markets and offer different services to a range of customers. Let us take the example of an oil company with interests in many parts of the world. It may be considering whether or not to explore a new oilfield in, say, Malaysia. Such a venture would entail transferring exploration teams and their equipment from existing fields in the Middle East where they were finding oil at a satisfactory rate. Let us assume that the Middle East exploration work was earning a profit of 20 per cent per year on average. Naturally, the figure of 20 per cent would have been calculated using the rules for expected values set out in Chapter 11. Having assessed the profits to be forgone in the Middle East, the company would arrive at the conclusion that the opportunity cost of exploring the Malaysian oilfield was the payments that would have to be made for labour, materials and so on *plus* those forgone profits. This amount would indicate what the company was giving up to explore the Malaysian oilfield. (It would also indicate to the world economy that if this particular oil company were to explore the Malaysian oilfield, the international market would be deprived of a certain amount of Middle Eastern oil.)

The level of profit which a firm generally manages to earn over the whole range of its business is termed *normal profit*. This level of profit serves as a threshold: if there is no prospect of earning normal profit in a particular market, then a firm will withdraw from that line of business and concentrate its resources elsewhere. Thus the formal definition of normal profit is the level of profit necessary to keep a firm in its present industry. Because normal profits reflect the opportunity costs of firms, it is conventional for economists to take average costs as including normal profits.

The task of assessing cost is, moreover, sometimes complicated by three factors: imputed costs, depreciation costs and external costs.

14-5 COSTING FOR DECISION-MAKING

Imputed costs

Let us assume that the oil company, besides exploring and developing oilfields, also transports and refines oil before selling the products. Let us focus upon the operations of the division of the company responsible for transporting the oil from the Middle East to the refineries in Europe. This division, let us assume, has its own tankers. The only payments made by this division are therefore the cost of running the tankers (crews' salaries and so on). These may come, let us assume, to £20 million per year. The question is: is £20 million the true cost of transporting the oil?

The answer is that £20 million is an understatement of the cost. This arises because, tankers, like most other items of capital equipment, can be chartered or hired on the open market. By using its own tankers, the company is forgoing any rental income which the tanker fleet could command. If this were £40 million, then the true cost of transporting the company's oil would be £60 million. In other words, the ownership of a resource may mean no financial outgoings but it does not mean there are no opportunity costs.

One way to include opportunity cost in profit and loss accounts is to divide the business up into its separate elements and then to use the device of *imputed costs*. The oil company could thus be divided into several separate divisions, one of which would have the role of simply owning all the company's fixed assets like the tanker fleet. The transport section would also be counted as a separate division which hired tankers (and any other company assets) from the asset-owning division. The transport division would then be charged an *imputed* cost for these assets. The word 'imputed' is used because, as before, no money would change hands. The charge would nevertheless appear in the accounts and would show the true position of the transport division. (This principle could clearly be extended by making the transport division 'buy' oil from the oilfield division and 'sell' it to the refinery divisions at imputed prices which reflected the market prices of oil in the two locations. The transport division would thus have both costs and revenues and could produce its own profit and loss accounts.)

Accounts drawn up in this way plainly facilitate decision-making. If every division were to produce profit and loss accounts, the company would be able to see whether its profits were arising from exploration, transport, refining or operating service stations. It could therefore decide which divisions to expand or close down. It could also decide which assets to hold. Suppose, for example, that for some reason a large number of surplus tankers were offered for hire, driving charter rates down dramatically. This would reduce the imputed costs of the transport division, so that it would show a larger profit. The imputed income from owning tankers would, however, fall and the company could decide to dispense with its fleet and simply use the charter market in future.

Depreciation

The task of assessing the cost of work to be done is complicated by another factor. It relates to the cost of long-lived capital equipment, and it gives rise to a special kind of imputed cost called a *depreciation* charge.

Capital equipment is usually classed as fixed in the short run, and is thus available to the firm at all times. Although the firm may well have to pay for the equipment over a number of years (having bought it on credit, perhaps) these payments do not reflect the cost to the firm of continuing to use it and, indeed, would have to be made regardless of whether the equipment were used or not. Capital equipment only has a cost to the firm when the decision to purchase is made: at that moment, the directors must choose between the equipment and their money. Once the contract to buy the machinery has been signed, however, the firm is committed to paying for it and no *extra* sacrifices have to be made. 'Bygones are forever bygones', in the words of one of the founders of neo-classical economics, Stanley Jevons.

As was argued earlier, the cost of using a resource or asset which is owned by the company are the earnings which could have been secured by hiring it out to another user. In some cases, there is a regular market in which similar assets are hired out, and the forgone earnings can be ascertained easily by looking at the rates paid in that market. For example, the forgone earnings of the oil company's tanker fleet can be established by looking at the charter rates charged for similar vessels. In other cases, however, there is no regular market for the hire of assets, particularly equipment which is highly specialized. For example, few businesses besides British Rail would want to buy or hire locomotives. In such circumstances, the only value which the asset has is its scrap value, as this is the only money which the firm forgoes by keeping it. It follows that the opportunity cost of keeping specialist equipment is minimal.

Let us suppose that some of the oil company's equipment, say a seismographic recorder, is in the second category—specialized equipment for which there is no hire market. These machines cost, we may assume, £300,000 and have a useful life of five years. The question which now arises is how the company is to decide upon the cost of using the recorder on different pieces of work. To answer this question, let us suppose that the company is about to start work on a new oilfield. Clearly the decision will turn upon the relationship between the value of the oil to be found and the costs of the exploration work. Let us assume that the former figure has already been established. What then of the costs? If the oilfield were to require the use of a recorder for five years, then clearly the company would be justified in including a sum of £300,000 in its estimates. Let us now suppose, however, that the firm's assessment of the oilfield suggests that the recorder could only be used there for three years. How should the costs be estimated then? The practice of business accountants in such a situation would be to include a proportion of the cost of the equipment used. This is the depreciation charge. In the example of the recorder used for three years, it would amount to £180,000 (£300,000 × 3/5).

From the point of view of an economist, this practice may seem altogether too simple. The logic of this chapter suggests that no such charge ought to be included since the use of the equipment entails no opportunity costs. What justification is there, then, for such a charge, and what are its consequences?

From the point of view of the firm, the depreciation charge is clearly a means of accumulating funds which can eventually be used to replace the equipment when it has to be scrapped. Provided that oil prices reflected the exploration costs, the firm would have, at the end of three years, a fund of $180,000 in the bank. Another two years' work on another oilfield would, presumably, produce another £120,000 so that the company would have the necessary £300,000 to buy a replacement for the recorder which would be now worn out. (If prices were going up, of course, the firm's accountants would base the charge not on the past purchase price of the equipment but upon the price that the firm would expect to pay when the time for replacement arrived.)

The economist would stress that depreciation charges could, in principle, be ignored by firms' decision-makers. The oil company could, if it desired, decide to go ahead and explore an oilfield even though the value of the oil was not expected to cover the depreciation charge for the seismographic equipment. Conversely, the company could explore a field which was expected to be extremely rich in oil so that the depreciation charge was more than covered by sales revenues. In other words, there is no necessity in practice for depreciation charges to be covered by sales receipts. Indeed, for the economist, the critical question is whether or not the company earns enough money to cover its depreciation charges. While the accountant asks 'how much are the depreciation charges for this piece of work?', the economist asks 'will these charges be covered by sales revenue?'.

Clearly, three cases are possible. First, the revenue from the oilfield could coincide with the accountants' cost estimates. The firm would then earn the funds to replace the asset. Such a price would also indicate to the consumers of oil the costs of the resources used in bringing oil to market.

Second, the price may be below the cost estimates. The firm would then be counted as making a loss. Being unable to replace its assets as they wore out, in the long run it would be forced to leave the industry.

Third, the price may exceed the cost estimates. The firm would then be able, if it so desired, to expand its stock of capital equipment. Indeed, the high revenues would indicate that above normal profits were being earned, and the directors may take this as a signal to expand operations.

External costs

Firms' operations may sometimes impose costs upon other members of society. For example, an oil tanker which spills oil can despoil beaches and so ruin a locality's tourist industry. This is an instance of an *external cost* and is analysed further in Chapter 23.

14-6 OPPORTUNITY COSTS: THE AUSTRIAN VIEW

While accepting the general principle that the true cost of any course of action is the benefits which have to be forgone, Austrian economists would tend to stress that costs are *estimated ex ante*. For them, financial accounts can only have a limited use in decision-making because they are retrospective. Profit and loss accounts can state how money was earned and spent in the past, but they can be no more than a guide to the costs and profits of future business operations, because these are inevitably matters of judgement.

Austrian economists would also argue that opportunity costs differ from one firm to another. This is because their opportunities for profit elsewhere are different. Returning to the example of the oil company, it was argued that the cost to the firm of exploring the Malaysian oilfield ought to include any profits forgone on work elsewhere. Other firms considering applying for permission to look for oil in Malaysia would, however, have their own profit opportunities which would have to be forgone. They would therefore have different opportunity costs. Quite apart from factors like technical skills and productivity, there will thus be good reason to expect firms to have different costs for the same work.

The above argument could be developed to suggest that firms' opportunity costs are subject to constant change because of the constant discovery of new opportunities. For instance, if the oil company were to find that it could earn good profits from a new oilfield in say, Peru, this would have to be taken into account in assessing the costs of other potential fields.

14-7 SUMMARY

The *opportunity cost* of any decision is the value of the best alternative that is forgone. Opportunity cost arises only at a decision point. If there are no alternatives, there can be no opportunity cost.

The *production possibility frontier* illustrates the trade-off that has to be made to secure an increase in the output of one industry in terms of the loss of output from another.

Normal profits are the level of profits required to keep a firm in an industry. They reflect the profits which it could earn elsewhere.

Imputed costs are costs which firms 'charge' themselves for the use of assets which they own. These imputed costs reflect the money which those assets could have earned had they been hired out.

Depreciation charges indicate the cost of using fixed assets. In reality, these assets may have low or zero opportunity cost, and the depreciation charges must be thought of as indicating not the (past) cost of their purchase but rather the (future) cost of their replacement.

External costs are costs which are imposed on society but which are not paid for. Pollution is an example.

EXERCISES

14-1 Describe the opportunity costs of:

(*a*) your attendance at college

(*b*) mounting a campaign of public information to counter the spread of a contagious disease

(c) failing to mount such a campaign

(d) building a motorway through a national park.

14-2 An amateur cricket club has £320 in the bank but the pavilion needs a new roof. A professional builder would charge £800 for the job, while the materials would cost £300. Rather than paying a builder, the members decide to do the job themselves. It will take them 100 man-hours. Ought they instead to consider paying the builder, raising the rest of the money through jumble sales and barbecues? How should they decide?

14-3 A civil engineering firm, CE Contractors, currently repairs sewers in the United Kingdom, where they generally make a profit on each contract equal to 10 per cent of the agreed price. They are considering tendering for a contract to build a bridge in the Third World. The work would take two years. This will entail transferring senior personnel to that country, so restricting work in the United Kingdom, and buying earth-moving equipment with a useful life of 10 years. You are a consultant hired by the firm to assist them make a decision.

(a) Write a report suggesting ways in which the company ought to draw up a tender for the work.

(b) Add an appendix with recommendations on how the company's organization or accounting procedures should be amended to facilitate future decisions.

14-5 An oil company has recently undertaken exploratory drilling tests near the Shetland Islands. The exploratory tests have cost £10 million and appear to indicate that oil worth £500 million is present. Previous analysis reveals that such exploratory tests prove correct in 90 per cent of cases. The company is now faced with the key decision as to whether or not to develop the site. The money spent will naturally be lost should the tests prove incorrect. The company faces the problem that development and operating costs are not known with certainty because it has never operated in such deep, northerly waters before. The company estimates that there is a 60 per cent chance that these costs will come to a total of £490 million and a 40 per cent chance that they will amount to £350 million.

(a) Calculate the appropriate expected values.

(b) Assume you are a consultant hired by the firm to advise on the decision. Write a report to the managing director setting out your advice.

14-6 A company runs a number of stores throughout the country. Its weekly costs at 30 of the stores are as follows:

1502 1930 2367 2211 1669 1867 1108 1830 1960 1533 1836 1834 1803 1596 1402 1276 1498 2214 2778 1831 2343 1029 1606 1123 2013 2688 2316 2127 1374 1107

The company is considering opening another store. Estimate the weekly costs at the 95% confidence level. Draft a report to management outlining the meaning and potential use of your results.

15

COST AND OUTPUT

15-1 INTRODUCTION

Chapter 14 showed that financial costs derive from the principle of opportunity costs. The discussion in that chapter suggested that business organizations might find that financial payments alone were not an accurate reflection of total cost. Such payments might well require amendment to take account of the need to impute costs for factors of production owned by the firm, of depreciation charges and so on. Assuming that such adjustments have been made—so that financial payments and opportunity costs are in line with each other—it becomes possible to analyse the way in which costs change.

To most business organizations costs can be linked directly to production or output or, if the organization is not directly involved in production, to workloads. This analysis is important because costs determine prices, sales and profits and thus the level of supply. In this chapter, therefore, we shall be analysing the relationship between costs and output.

We shall begin the analysis of the cost–output relationship by looking at the short-run situation.

15-2 SHORT-RUN COST CURVES

Total costs

The first cost curve we shall focus on is that of total costs. As the name suggests this represents all the costs incurred by the firm at different levels of output. Not surprisingly, if the firm were to change its level of output we would anticipate that total costs would also change. However, not all of the cost elements which make up total costs would alter. In general, an organization will distinguish between two broad types of costs in the short run.

The first of these is *fixed costs*, which refer to the cost of those resources whose supply is fixed in the short run such as land, equipment and skilled labour. By their very nature we would not expect such costs to change as output levels changed. The second is *variable costs*, which are the costs of resources which can be varied in the short run such as raw materials and components, energy and possibly unskilled labour. In general, as output increases, we shall require more of these variable resources and hence variable costs will increase.

Let us return to the example from Chapter 14 of an oil company. Assume that the company has carefully monitored its cost and output levels with regard to the production of one of its products, say five-litre cans of engine oil for the private motorist. The relationship between total, fixed and variable costs is shown in Table 15-1 and Fig. 15-1.

We can see that total costs rise as output rises. Fixed costs remain unchanged no matter what the level of output and variable costs mirror total costs but with a difference representing the fixed-cost element.

While the actual cost figures will obviously differ from organization to organization, the general shape of both the total cost curve and the variable cost curve will tend to follow the general pattern of those in Fig. 15-1. The reasons for this lead us to an important concept in micro-economics—that of *returns to scale*.

In the case of both total and variable costs it is clear that costs increase with output but at different rates at different points of the curve. At low levels of output the increase in costs

Table 15-1 Total costs, fixed costs and variable costs at different levels of output

Units produced (thousands)	Total costs (£ thousands)	Fixed costs (£ thousands)	Variable costs (£ thousands)
1	590	500	90
2	665	500	165
3	725	500	225
4	775	500	275
5	815	500	315
6	850	500	350
7	880	500	380
8	915	500	415
9	955	500	455
10	1000	500	500
11	1055	500	555
12	1125	500	625
13	1210	500	710
14	1315	500	815
15	1440	500	940
16	1590	500	1090
17	1765	500	1265
18	1975	500	1475
19	2220	500	1720
20	2500	500	2000

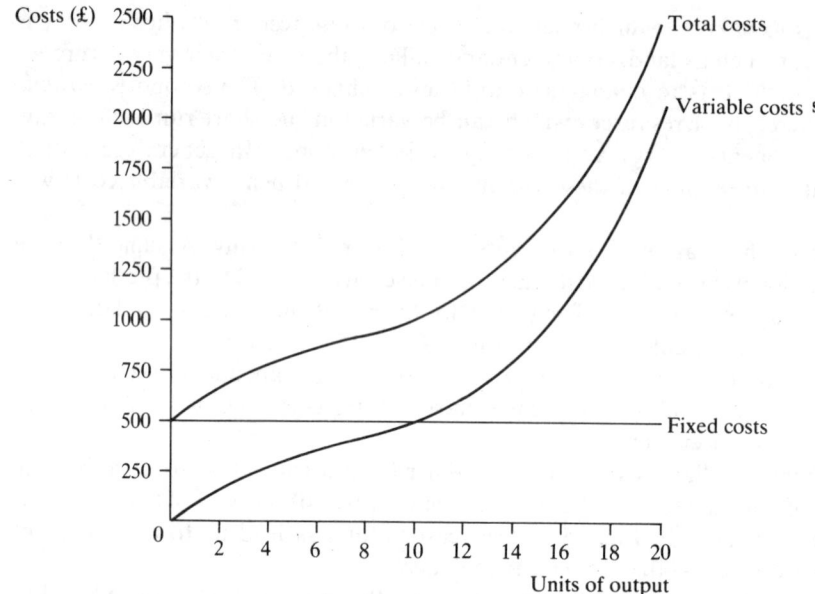

Figure 15-1 Costs

is quite high as it is also for high levels of output. In the middle of the output range, however, while costs are increasing they do so at a less rapid rate. In mathematical terms the slope of the cost curve changes according to output levels.

The major principle behind such a pattern is that there will be some optimum level for the combination of variable and fixed resources at which efficiency will be maximized. A simple example will illustrate this. Let us assume that the firm has a fixed number of machines which fill the empty cans with oil. Let us further assume that labour is variable in the short run. It is logical to assume that there will be some optimum allocation of labour to each machine. If the firm allocates too few workers then output is likely to suffer as it will not be able to make best use of the fixed supply of machinery. Similarly, if the firm employs too much labour for the fixed supply of equipment some workers will be underemployed even though they contribute to the firm's costs. At some stage, however, there will be just the right combination of labour to each machine to allow all the resources to operate at maximum efficiency with respect to costs. Thus, given the fixed supply of machines, there is some size of work-force which will maximize efficiency.

From Fig. 15-1 we can see that, as the firm increases the supply of variable resources, costs rise relatively rapidly until we get to an output level of five units. We then enter a period of *increasing returns to scale* as further supplies of variable resources lead to increased efficiency: output increases at a faster rate than costs. At an output level of around 10 units however, costs begin to escalate as we enter a period of *diminishing returns to scale* where costs are rising at a faster rate than output.

Obviously, this principle will apply not only to labour and machines but to all the resources that may be required by the organization. This change in total costs can be related to an important concept: *marginal product*. The concept will be developed in detail in a later chapter but it is sufficient for our purposes at this stage to outline the broad principle. Marginal product is defined as the change in total output brought about by the use of one extra unit of the variable factor.

In the example above, after a certain point each extra worker employed adds to production, but at a *decreasing* rate. This phenomenon occurs because of the fixed supply of other factors of production. This extra output is referred to as the marginal product or, more accurately, as *marginal physical product*.

Naturally, exactly the same principle will apply to other factors of production. If we held the labour supply constant and varied the supply of capital (or land) then the marginal physical product would follow the pattern established.

Average and marginal costs

Another way of analysing the relationship between costs and output is to look at average cost curves. These are illustrated in Table 15-2, which shows the average total cost, which is total cost divided by output; average fixed cost, which is fixed cost divided by output; average variable cost, which is total variable cost divided by output; and marginal cost, the extra cost of producing an additional unit of output measured by the difference between two total cost figures. These costs are shown in Fig. 15-2. Let us examine each in turn.

It is evident that *average fixed cost* (AFC) must fall as output rises because this constant cost is spread over larger and larger output levels.

Table 15-2 Average costs, average fixed costs, average variable costs and marginal costs at different levels of output

Units produced (thousands)	Average total costs (£ thousands)	Average fixed costs (£ thousands)	Average variable costs (£ thousands)	Marginal costs (£ thousands)
1	590	500	90	90
2	332.5	250	82.5	75
3	241.7	166.7	75	60
4	193.75	125	68.75	50
5	163	100	63	40
6	141.7	83.3	58.3	35
7	125.7	71.5	54.3	30
8	114.4	62.5	51.9	35
9	106.1	55.6	50.6	40
10	100	50	50	45
11	95.9	45.5	50.5	55
12	93.75	41.7	52.1	70
13	93.1	38.5	54.6	85
14	93.9	35.7	58.2	105
15	96	33.3	62.7	125
16	99.4	31.25	68.125	150
17	103.8	29.4	74.4	175
18	109.7	27.8	81.9	210
19	116.8	26.3	90.5	245
20	125	25	100	280

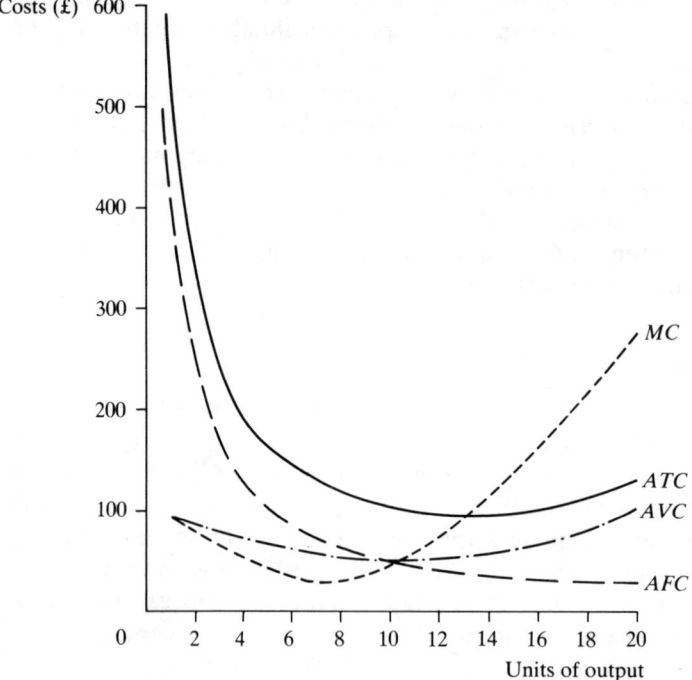

Costs (£)

Figure 15-2 Average and marginal costs

The *average variable cost* (AVC) curve is usually *U*-shaped, and the shape relates directly to the effects of increasing and diminishing returns to scale. The reason why the AVC curve does not fall as sharply as the average total cost curve in its early stages is that the AVC curve does not include the fixed costs element.

The usual shape of the *average total cost* (ATC) curve (note that average total cost is the sum of the average fixed and average variable costs) is often described as being *U*-shaped. The reasons for such a shape are twofold: first, over the early stages of production the ATC curve will fall sharply as total fixed costs are spread over larger levels of output. Second, at higher levels of output the ATC curve starts to rise as diminishing returns comes into play: that is, total variable costs are increasing at a faster rate than output. When we have reached an optimum allocation of variable resources to those which are fixed, average costs will be at their minimum position.

Marginal cost (MC) is the change in total costs resulting from a change in output of one unit. Thus, as we increase output from one unit to two, total costs increase from £590 to £665—a marginal (or extra) cost of £75. Again, the MC curve is generally *U*-shaped and takes its shape directly from the total costs (TC) curve.

From Fig. 15-2 it can be seen that the MC curve crosses the ATC curve at the latter's lowest point. This is not coincidence but follows from the nature of the two curves. It is important to understand why. Both curves are derived from the TC curve and it can be seen that while the ATC curve is falling, marginal cost is below average total cost. Since MC is the addition to costs of an extra unit of output it follows that if the marginal cost of a unit is below the average, then that unit's cost must bring the average cost down. Similarly, when MC is above the ATC curve the ATC curve is climbing upwards. Again, if the extra cost of an additional unit is above average then that unit must be pulling average costs upwards. It follows that MC and ATC must be equal at the lowest point on the ATC curve.

This point also represents the optimum short-run rate of output. That is, the rate of output at which, given the supply of fixed resources, the firm can operate with maximum efficiency and minimum cost. Note that we cannot necessarily equate 'most efficient' with 'most profitable'. Profit will obviously depend on price and revenue as well as on costs and will be examined in detail later.

15-3 LONG-RUN COST CURVES

In the short run, supplies of at least some of the factors of production are strictly fixed. In the long run, by definition, all factors of production are variable. If, in the short run, the firm has a fixed supply of machinery then, in the long run, it can acquire more machinery as it wishes. Similarly in the long run the firm could decrease the amount of fixed resources. To establish the nature of the long-run cost curves it is best to view the long run as a series of potential short-run situations. Effectively in the long run the firm decides upon its mix of factors of production which is then fixed for the short run.

For simplicity, let us assume that the firm faces only four alternative sets of fixed costs—say four alternative sizes for its factory. These are represented in Fig. 15-3. Thus, the firm faces four possible short-run situations each with its short-run ATC curve. SAC_1 represents the short-run ATC curve for a relatively small factory and SAC_2, SAC_3 and SAC_4 represent increasingly larger factories. Each SAC represents a short-run situation but together they also represent the firm's *long-run* ATC curve.

If the firm were planning to produce up to output level X_1 the firm would construct a factory size to correspond to SAC_1. If output were between X_1 and X_2 the firm would move to a short run position equivalent to SAC_2. Similarly, with output between X_2 and X_3 the appropriate short run curve would be SAC_3 and if output were above X_3 SAC_4 would represent the relevant short-run cost situation. Aggregating the appropriate parts of these four short-run curves would therefore generate a long-run ATC curve as illustrated in Fig. 15-4.

In practice, of course, the firm would not face four short-run positions but an infinite choice of combinations of factors of production and for each short-run situation there would be a corresponding ATC curve. The long-run ATC curve would, therefore, develop

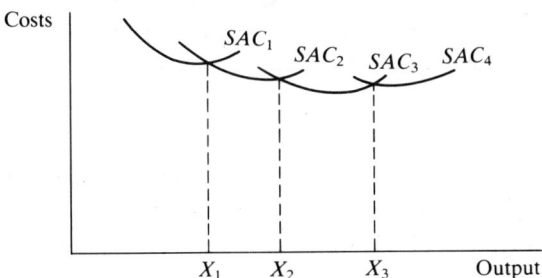

Figure 15-3 Long-run average costs

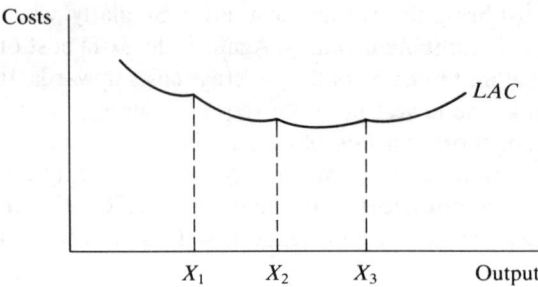

Figure 15-4 Long-run average cost curve

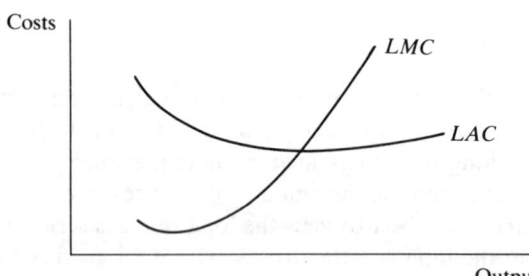

Figure 15-5 Long-run average and marginal costs

into a smooth curve comprising parts of each short run curve (mathematically, it would comprise one point from each short run curve). This is illustrated in Fig. 15-5.

Similarly, the long-run marginal cost curve could be constructed from the series of short-run MC curves and will have the same relationship to ATC in the long run as it did in the short run. The long-run MC is also shown in Fig. 15-5. Again, the long-run MC curve will intersect the long-run ATC curve at the minimum point and this level of output will represent the 'optimum' in the sense of maximum efficiency of resources (but not necessarily of profit).

15-4 ECONOMIES OF SCALE

Economies of scale arise from the existence of high fixed costs. These may have a number of causes: marketing costs; research and development costs; distribution costs; and risk sharing. While the ATC curve may develop into the U-shaped curve firms operating under particular market conditions may be faced by the type of ATC curve shown in Fig. 15-6, caused by high fixed costs—particularly in the long run. Such a curve is referred to as an 'L'-shaped curve and can be explained by reference to economies of scale factors. For a variety of reasons a firm may be able to reduce its ATC in the long run almost indefinitely. Such reasons would include:

1. *Marketing.* A large organization will be able to undertake an extensive company-wide advertising campaign spreading the high cost across all its product lines.
2. *Research and development.* Firms need to reach some critical size to support their own research and development programme for new products.

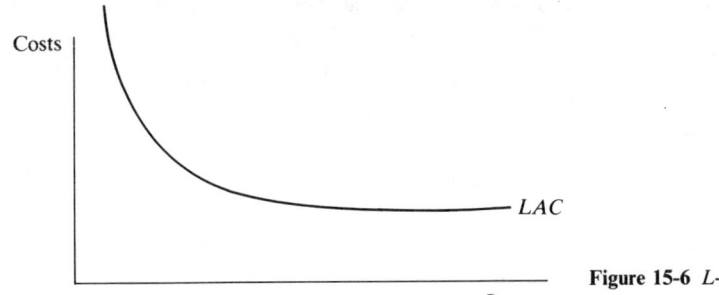

Costs

LAC

Output

Figure 15-6 *L*-shaped long-run average cost curve

3. *Technology*. Maximum cost reductions resulting from new technology may only be achieved through high output levels which, in turn, can only be supported by large firms.
4. *Distribution and communication*. Distribution or communication costs may be prohibitive for any level of output below a certain limit. The cost of constructing a distribution network for North Sea gas, for example, effectively prohibits direct competition. The enormous fixed costs must be shared over high levels of output.
5. *Risk sharing*. The risks attached to the production of a single product may be prohibitively high. A large organization with a number of different products will be able to spread these risks and their associated costs.

15-5 SUMMARY

Fixed costs represent the costs of those resources whose supply is fixed in the short run.
  Marginal cost is the additional cost associated with additional output.
  Variable cost represents the cost of those resources whose supply is not fixed.
  Total cost comprises fixed cost and variable cost.

EXERCISES

15-1 Determine the major fixed costs and the major variable costs for the following firms:

(*a*) a brewery
(*b*) a road haulage firm
(*c*) a computer software company
(*d*) your university or polytechnic
(*e*) a coalmine.

15-2 Compare the potential for economies of scale for the following types of firm:

(*a*) a local milkround
(*b*) a national dairy
(*c*) a holiday travel company
(*d*) a pharmaceutical company

15-3 From the latest British Gas Annual Report try and determine the level of fixed costs and of variable costs, and the major categories of costs incurred.

15-4 The following data relate to daily output levels and associated total costs for a small firm.

Output (units per day)	Total costs (£)
0	200
1	252
2	292
3	326
4	360
5	400
6	452
7	522
8	616
9	740
10	900

(a) Using a computer spreadsheet derive the following costs:
  (i) total fixed cost;
  (ii) total variable cost;
  (iii) average total cost;
  (iv) average fixed cost;
  (v) average variable cost;
  (vi) marginal cost.
(b) Plot these costs curves on two graphs, one for the total costs and one for average and marginal costs.
(c) Do the data relate to the firm in the short run or long run?
(d) At what level of output does the firm minimize:
  (i) marginal cost?
  (ii) average total cost?
(e) Explain why the total cost curve takes the shape it does.

QUADRATIC FUNCTIONS AND DIFFERENTIAL CALCULUS

16-1 INTRODUCTION

In Chapter 15 we examined typical cost patterns for a firm and saw that, particularly for average and marginal costs, such patterns may well follow a U-shaped curve. As with other aspects of economic analysis we need to be able to express such information not only in verbal and graphical terms but also in terms of mathematics. For example, we have seen that the optimum level of output, expressed in terms of efficiency of use of resources, is found at the minimum point of the average cost curve, where the marginal cost curve intersects it. Apart from drawing a graph—which can be both tedious and inaccurate—how can we determine what this output level will be?

The mathematics introduced so far—that related to linear relationships—is inadequate for our needs here since the relationships dealt with in Chapter 15 are patently *non-linear*. We must develop new techniques to analyse such relationships.

16-2 QUADRATIC FUNCTIONS

The *U*-shaped curve that typifies average and marginal cost relationships can conveniently be modelled using a specific type of non-linear mathematical equation of the form:

$$Y = a + bX + cX^2 \tag{16-1}$$

where X and Y are the two variables (in our example Y would represent average cost and X would represent output) and a, b and c are the relevant constants or parameters. An equation taking such a form is referred to as a *quadratic* equation and, in general, can be expected to take one of two forms as illustrated in Figure 16-1. That is, a quadratic function will tend to follow a U-shape, with the Y value decreasing as X increases, reaching some minimum level and then increasing again (Fig. 16-1a). Alternatively, the function may follow an inverted U-shape, with the Y value climbing to a maximum then decreasing as X increases (Fig. 16-1b).

Let us return to the example of the oil company in the last chapter that had analysed its cost patterns with reference to the production of one of its products: five-litre cans of engine oil. The firm's average total costs can be represented by the quadratic function:

$$ATC = 560 - 65Q + 2.5Q^2 \tag{16-2}$$

where Q is output up to a level of 20 (remember we expressed Q in thousands of units). Recognizing that the function is quadratic we know that it will follow one of the two patterns in Figure 16-1. But which one? We could, of course, resort to drawing a graph of this function (and readers are required to draw a graph of this function as an exercise). It

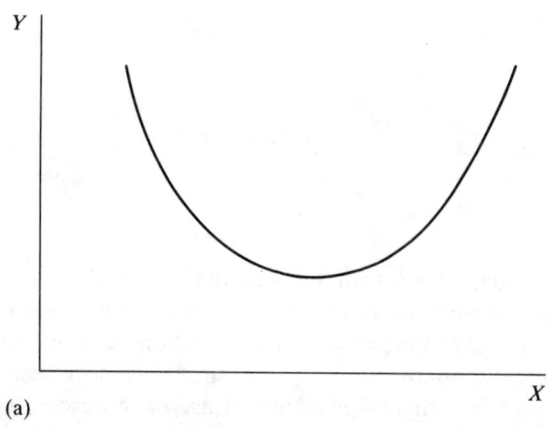

(a)

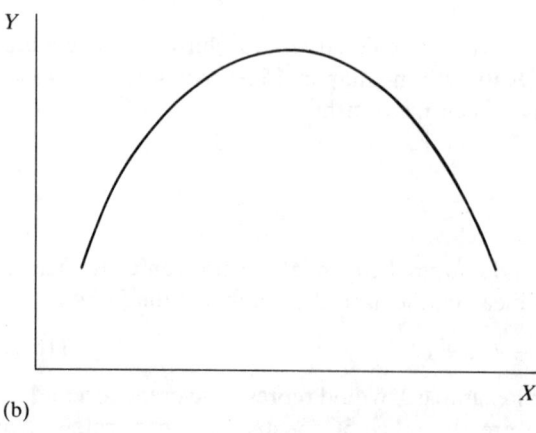

(b)

Figure 16-1 Quadratic functions, general form

may be worth doing this now in order better to follow the rest of the text.) The alternative is to examine the c term in the quadratic expression which determines which of the two forms the quadratic function follows. If the c term is positive the function will take the standard U-shape whilst if it is negative the function will follow the inverted U-shape pattern.

As with linear functions the a term of the quadratic also indicates the Y axis intercept, that is, where the function will cross the Y axis when X takes a zero value. So, by looking at the a term and the c term of a quadratic function we can, without any calculation, sketch its general shape. This is frequently useful in more complex problems. It is also useful, however, to determine the 'turning point' of a quadratic function, that is, the point at which the slope changes from positive to negative or vice versa. Such a turning point would represent the *minimum* Y value for a U-shaped function and the *maximum* Y value for the inverted U-shaped function. There are a number of alternative ways of finding such a value but we shall concentrate on two: using the roots of the quadratic equation and using differential calculus.

In our example, such a turning point would represent a minimum average cost level of output. From our understanding of cost patterns we know also that such a point would be where the marginal cost curve (also U-shaped, hence also a quadratic) intersects the average cost curve. Let us assume that the same firm's marginal cost function is expressed as:

$$MC = 176.5 - 42Q + 3Q^2 \qquad (16\text{-}3)$$

We know from our knowledge of economics that ATC and MC are equal at the point of minimum ATC. That is $ATC = MC$, hence $ATC - MC = 0$. We have an equation for each of the two costs, so substituting gives us:

$$(560 - 65Q + 2.5Q^2) - (176.5 - 42Q + 3Q^2) = 0$$

and collecting terms together we end up with:

$$383.5 - 23Q - 0.5Q^2 = 0 \qquad (16\text{-}4)$$

The result is not an equation that relates to costs *per se* but rather an equation that measures the difference between the two equations. We are now looking for the level of output at which the difference between ATC and MC (as expressed by the last equation) is zero. Graphically, of course, this is where the two curves cross.

16-3 ROOTS OF A QUADRATIC FUNCTION

One feature of quadratics that is not always apparent is that when we have two quadratic functions that intersect they will do so not at one point but at two. This arises from the symmetrical shape of a quadratic function and is not always apparent in the quadrant of the graph we are examining. The graph relating to these two equations—(16-2) and (16-3)—has an X axis scale from 0 to 20. If we were to continue the scale in the other direction (that is with X taking negative values) we would see that the two curves cross again in this quadrant of the graph. Naturally, in the context of our economic analysis there is little point considering this part of the graph as it does not represent 'real' levels of output as such. However, in other business contexts the second point of intersection may also have a meaningful interpretation.

In mathematical terms, however, these two points—which represent the two X values in a quadratic expression which give Y a zero value—are referred to as the *roots* of the function. This is what we are looking for here: the level of output that will give Y—which measures the difference between ATC and MC—a zero value. There are alternative methods available for finding such roots.

When the general quadratic equation (16-1) is set equal to 0, the two roots of the equation are given by the formula

$$X = \frac{-b \pm \sqrt{b^2 - 4ac}}{2c} \tag{16-5}$$

where a, b, c are the appropriate constants from Eq. (16-1). Thus in order to solve Eq. (16-4) we set $a = 383.5$, $b = -23$, and $c = -0.5$. Substituting into the formula gives

$$Q = \frac{-(-23) \pm \sqrt{-23^2 - (4 \times 383.5 \times (-0.5))}}{2 \times (-0.5)}.$$

$$= \frac{23 \pm \sqrt{529 + 767}}{-1}$$

$$= \frac{23 \pm 36}{-1}$$

Denoting the two Q values by Q_1 and Q_2, we evaluate this expression by using the $+$ and $-$ signs in turn (it does not matter in what order). This gives:

$$Q_1 = \frac{23 + 36}{-1} = \frac{59}{-1} = -59$$

$$Q_2 = \frac{23 - 36}{-1} = \frac{-13}{-1} = 13$$

That is, Eqs (16-2) and (16-3) intersect (the difference between them is zero) when Q is -59 and when Q is 13. From an economic viewpoint negative quantities have no meaning so we are left with the solution that when Q is 13 MC and ATC are equal. This is the output level which minimizes average total costs. If the firm wishes to produce a level of output which minimizes average cost then it must produce 13 (000) units.

This method of finding the roots of a quadratic function can be used in a number of areas of economic analysis and there are exercises at the end of the chapter to illustrate the potential uses.

16-4 DIFFERENTIAL CALCULUS

The second method we can use to find the turning point of a quadratic function is to use *differential calculus*. To understand the general approach we must return to a concept introduced much earlier in this text: that of the *slope* of a function. When we were using a linear function we saw that its slope (which relates changes in Y to changes in X) was constant and could be obtained directly from the b parameter of the linear equation. It is evident that for the cost functions we have been examining, which are quadratic rather than linear, the slope of the curve is not a constant but changes with X. More than that, if we look at the ATC function introduced earlier and you refer to the graph that you have drawn you will see that to begin with the slope of the function is steeply negative, gradually becomes less so as Q increases and then becomes increasingly positive as Q increases further.

One useful, and important, feature of any quadratic function is that there is a *single* point when the slope changes from negative to positive (in the case of a U-shaped function) or from positive to negative (in the case of an inverted U-shaped function). At this turning point the slope will be neither positive nor negative—it will be zero; and this zero slope can only occur at the turning point.

If, therefore, we wanted to find the output level which gave minimum average total cost we could find the point on the ATC curve which had a zero slope. Differential calculus provides us with a mechanism for achieving this since the technique is concerned with measuring the slope of an equation. In practice, calculus can be used to provide such an expression (referred to as the *derivative*) for any mathematical function. For our purposes, however, we shall limit our attention to linear and quadratic functions.

The general approach is as follows. From our original mathematical equation (related here to ATC) we shall be obtaining a second equation (the derivative) which will allow us easily to calculate the slope of the ATC function. The need for this is to allow us to find the point on the ATC function which has a zero slope—in our case the level of output which will give the minimum ATC.

If the original function takes the form:

$$Y = kX^n \tag{16-6}$$

then the derivative of the function can be expressed as:

$$\frac{dY}{dX} = nkX^{n-1} \tag{16-7}$$

We shall illustrate with a simple example. Suppose we have a linear function such that $Y = 10X$. Because it is a linear function we know that its slope will be 10 ($=b$). But we shall also use the derivative method. The linear function corresponds to the function form:

$$Y = kX^n = 10X^1$$

where $k = 10$ and $n = 1$. Using the derivative rule we have:

$$\frac{dY}{dX} = nkX^{n-1} = 1(10)X^{(1-1)} = 10X^0 = 10.$$

(Observe that any variable raised to the power zero equals 1.) The derivative expression shows the slope of the original (linear) function. That is, the derivative indicates that the slope of $Y = 10X$ is 10.

If we have a quadratic function rather than a linear one the derivative rule is just as straightforward. Suppose we had: $Y = X^2$. Here, $k = 1$ and $n = 2$ so the derivative would be:

$$\frac{dY}{dX} = 2(1)X^{(2-1)} = 2X^1 = 2X$$

What does this mean? Since the original expression was quadratic we know that its slope is not constant. The derivative we have obtained is an equation which measures the slope of the original equation anywhere along its length. If we wanted to know the slope of $Y = X^2$ at the point when $X = 10$ we would substitute $X = 10$ into the derivative expression:

$$\frac{dY}{dX} = 2X = 2(10) = 20$$

When $X = 10$ the slope of the original equation is 20. That is, at this point if X were to change by some small amount Y would change by 20 times that amount. If we now wanted the slope when $X = 4$ we would again use the derivative expression and find the slope to be 8. That is, at this point on the original function there is a eightfold change in Y for a given small change in X.

Let us now return to the ATC function given by Eq. (16-2). To find the derivative of this equation we simply consider each term on the right-hand side in turn. Suppose first of all that $Y = 560$. In our standard format, this is the same as saying $Y = 560Q^0$. Therefore

$$\frac{dY}{dQ} = 0(560)Q^{-1} = 0.$$

In other words, since $Y = 560$ is the equation of a line parallel to the Q axis, it has zero slope, and the derivative confirms this.

From the foregoing you should be able to confirm that if $Y = -65Q$ then $\frac{dY}{dQ} = -65$, and that if $Y = 2.5Q^2$ then $\frac{dY}{dQ} = 5Q$. We can now assemble together these separate pieces of information to form the derivative of our ATC equation:

$$\frac{dATC}{dQ} = -65 + 5Q. \tag{16-8}$$

This equation, which you should be able to see is linear, allows us to calculate the slope of the ATC function at any level of output. The relationship between ATC and the derivative is shown in Fig. 16-2. The line representing the derivative clearly shows that the slope of the ATC function is negative (but gradually less so) from low levels of output up to 13 units. After 13 units the derivative line is positive (and increasingly so). At 13 units of output the line crosses the X axis, indicating the slope is zero for this level of output.

Confirming this algebraically is straightforward. We wish to find the level of output when the slope of the ATC function (that is the value of the derivative) is zero. Setting the derivative to zero and solving give:

$$\frac{dATC}{dQ} = -65 + 5Q = 0$$

$$5Q = 65$$

$$Q = 13$$

When Q is 13 units, therefore, we have reached a point on the ATC function with a zero slope and this must represent the minimum point for this quadratic function.

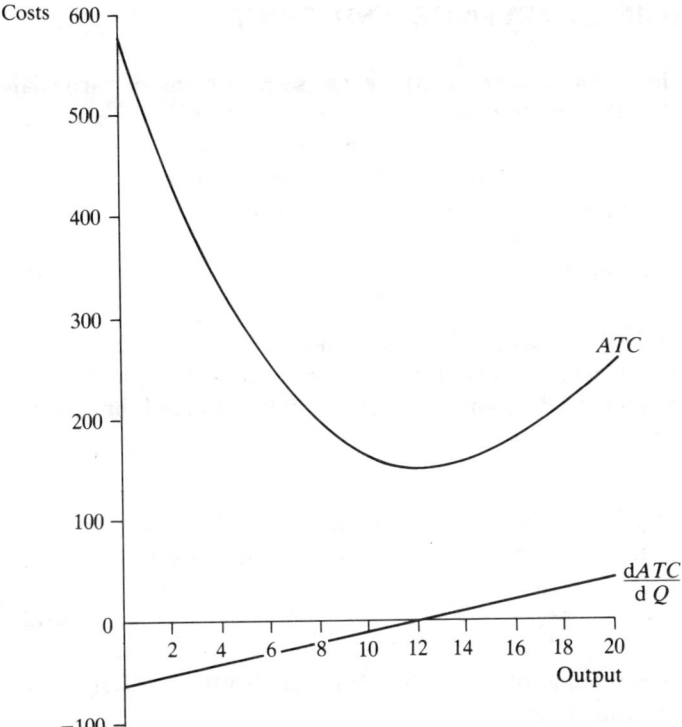

Figure 16-2 Average costs and its derivative

The second derivative

In the example above we recognized that the turning point derived using calculus represented a minimum. In other situations, however, particularly if we develop models using expressions involving higher powers, it is necessary to be able to check whether the turning point represents a maximum or a minimum position. This is achieved through the use of the *second derivative*.

A simple rule applies. Having determined the first derivative, we can decide whether this is a maximum or minimum value by taking *its* derivative in turn. If this second derivative is *negative* the zero-slope point found is a *maximum*. If the second derivative is *positive* we have a *minimum* point.

In the case of the ATC function, the first derivative was given by Eq. (16-8). Applying the same rule of differentiation we can find the second derivative of this expression:

$$\frac{d^2 ATC}{dQ^2} = 5 \tag{16-9}$$

(Note the way the second derivative is written: in general, if Y is a function of X then the second derivative is given by $\frac{d^2 Y}{dX^2}$.) Here, the second derivative takes a positive value, indicating that the turning point found using the first derivative related to a minimum point on the curve.

16-5 ELASTICITY, MARGINAL REVENUE AND PRICE

In the earlier analysis of the theory of demand, elasticity was seen as being of particular importance. Readers will recollect that, up to now, we have been able to measure elasticity only as an average across some part of the demand curve (see Section 5-4). Differential calculus provides a suitable method of quantifying elasticity of demand at any *point* on the demand curve. Using calculus, the formula for calculating point elasticity is:

$$\text{Point elasticity} = \frac{dQ}{dP} \times \frac{P}{Q} \qquad (16\text{-}10)$$

where dQ/dP is the derivative of the demand equation and P and Q are the specific price and quantity values at that point on the demand curve for which we require an elasticity value.

Assume our oil company has undertaken some market research and found that it faces a demand curve given by:

$$Q = 100 - 8P \qquad (16\text{-}11)$$

The firm is currently charging a price of £10 and wishes to determine elasticity in order to assess the impact of a price change. The derivative of the demand equation is:

$$\frac{dQ}{dP} = -8 \qquad (16\text{-}12)$$

and at the current price Q takes a value of $100 - (8 \times 10) = 20$. Thus, the elasticity of demand at this point on the demand curve is:

$$\frac{dQ}{dP} \times \frac{P}{Q} = -8 \times \frac{10}{20} = -4$$

Elasticity is high, at this point, therefore, indicating that a policy of reducing the price charged will, *ceteris paribus*, increase the firm's total revenue while a policy of price increase will have a detrimental effect on revenue.

The ability to quantify elasticity at any point on the demand curve leads us to an important relationship in the theory of demand: that between price, elasticity and marginal revenue.

We saw earlier in this chapter that the derivative of a function provides an expression for the slope of that function anywhere along its length. More importantly, from the viewpoint of economic analysis, the derivative shows the change in one variable associated with a change in another. When discussing cost we saw that the derivative provided an expression for marginal cost. Equally, from the revenue side we can examine the total revenue function and its derivative.

An expression for total revenue is easily obtained from the demand equation. Given that total revenue will simply be the units sold multiplied by the price charged, then

$$TR = P \times Q$$

It is conventional, as with total cost, to express TR solely in terms of Q, so we must eliminate P from the total revenue equation. Since the demand equation provides an expression relating price and quantity, we can rearrange this to express P in terms of Q and substitute this expression back into the total revenue equation.

For example, our oil company has found itself facing a demand curve given by Eq. (16-11). Rearranging this gives

$$P = 12.5 - 0.125Q$$

Substituting into the total revenue equation gives:

$$TR = (12.5 - 0.125Q) \times Q$$

$$= 12.5Q - 0.125Q^2 \qquad (16\text{-}13)$$

It will be observed that the total revenue equation (16-13) is a quadratic. It is apparent that this will always be the case, given a linear demand curve. The derivative of the total revenue function is readily obtained. In the case of our oil company it is

$$\frac{dTR}{dQ} = 12.5 - 0.25Q \qquad (16\text{-}14)$$

This shows the change in TR as Q changes. In economic analysis this expression is known as *marginal revenue*—the change in total revenue as output changes by one unit. As we shall see in the next chapter it is, together with marginal cost, a concept of crucial importance in

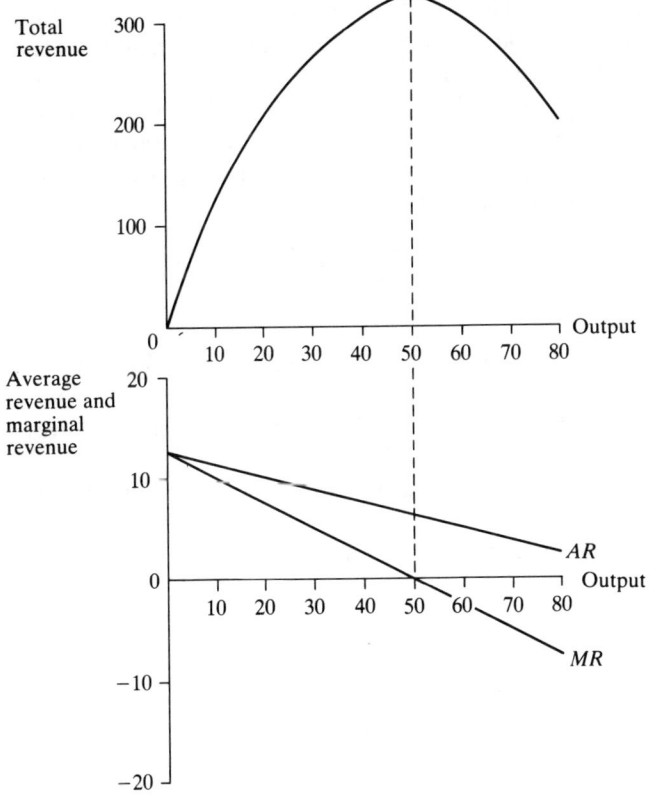

Figure 16-3 Total, average and marginal revenue

micro-economics. Note also that, from the total revenue equation, we can derive an expression for *average* revenue. Again, in the case of our oil company:

$$AR = \frac{TR}{Q} = \frac{12.5Q - 0.125Q^2}{Q} = 12.5 - 0.125Q$$

which, it will be observed, is the same as demand curve. All three curves are shown in Fig. 16-3.

A number of important points arise from the relationship between these three (interrelated) curves. First, the marginal revenue curve will always lie *below* the average revenue curve, and will have a steeper slope. It is easy to see why. Given a downward-sloping average revenue (demand) curve the only way the firm can increase its sales is by cutting the price it charges on *all* units sold. Marginal revenue is the change in revenue from the *last* unit sold. Inevitably, given that the price must be reduced to sell this extra unit, the *extra* revenue must be less than the *average*.

Second, the marginal revenue curve moves from taking positive values to negative values. That is, after a certain level of sales (in our example, 50 units) total revenue will start to decline with each extra unit sold. Given an understanding of elasticity this comes as no surprise. We have already determined that there will be circumstances such that with a highly inelastic demand total revenue will be affected in this way.

In fact, the connection between total revenue, marginal revenue and elasticity is evident from Fig. 16-3. While marginal revenue is above zero (in our example, up to an output level of 50 units) total revenue is increasing, albeit at a decreasing rate. Along this part of the average revenue curve, therefore, demand is highly elastic. Beyond this output level marginal revenue is negative and total revenue gradually declines. Here, demand is inelastic. At the turning point on the (quadratic) total revenue curve we encounter a position between the two: of unit elasticity. This is where marginal revenue is zero.

16-6 SUMMARY

The *derivative* of an equation $Y = f(X)$ is an expression showing the slope of that equation for any X value.

A *quadratic function* $Y = f(X)$ normally has a U- or inverted U-shape and involves a term in X^2.

The *roots* of a quadratic equation $Y = f(X)$ are the two values that X takes when $Y = 0$.

A *turning point* is the point where the gradient of a curve is zero.

EXERCISES

16-1 Differentiate the following functions and find their roots:

(*a*) $Y = 2X^2$
(*b*) $Y = 2X - 0.2X^2$
(*c*) $Y = 0.6X^3 - 2X^2 + X$

Calculate the slope for equations when $X = 0, 1, 3$. Sketch the equations.

16-2 A firm manufactures microcomputers and the firm's cost function has been estimated as:

$$TC = 1000 - 500X + 25X^2$$

where X is the number of items produced.

(a) What is the level of the firm's fixed costs?
(b) Using the cost function given, determine total cost when X is:
  (i) 9 units
  (ii) 10 units
  (iii) 11 units

(c) From your answer to (b) what conclusion do you reach about an output level of 10 units?
(d) Derive an expression for marginal cost and, using this, calculate the marginal cost of the 10th item.

16-3 A firm's demand function is given as:

$$Q_d = 200 - 20P$$

(a) Derive an equation for total revenue and for marginal revenue.
(b) Calculate total revenue if the firm charges a price of 8, and a price of 9. Calculate the percentage change in price and revenue.
(c) Calculate elasticity of demand when $P = 8$.
(d) What does your result tell you about this item at this price level? How can the firm use this information?
(e) Repeat (a), (b) and (c) using a price of 2 and 3.

16-4 A firm has collected information on both costs and revenue over the past few years and has obtained a profit (Y) function given by:

$$Y = -32 + X - 0.005X^2$$

where X represents the number of units of the firm's product (measured in thousands) and profit is measured in thousands of pounds.

(a) Plot the firm's profit function up to a production level of 200 000.
(b) From the graph determine at what production level the firm first makes a profit.
(c) Given that 'breakeven' is defined as the point where profit equals zero find the two breakeven points algebraically.
(d) At which production level does the firm make most profit? What profit does it make at this level of production?

16-4 A firm faces a demand curve given by

$$Q_d = 1200 - 20P$$

and a cost function given by

$$TC = 12\,500 + 7.5Q$$

(a) Determine an equation for total revenue, expressed as a function of quantity.
(b) Determine the price the firm should charge to maximize revenue.
(c) Given that profit is the difference between TR and TC, derive a profit equation.
(d) Find the two breakeven levels of output.

17

PROFIT MAXIMIZATION

In previous chapters both demand and costs have been analysed (and the appropriate mathematical techniques provided to support such analysis) and in this chapter these two important areas of micro-economics will be brought together. The analysis will begin with the assumption that the objective of all business organizations is to maximize profit. Like all such simplifying assumptions this can be criticized on a number of grounds—some firms may seek to expand and dominate the market, for example—but it serves as a reasonable basis for the analysis that follows.

17-1 TOTAL REVENUE AND TOTAL COST

On such a basis the individual firm will be trying to reach decisions on its output levels (and hence on related decisions such as investment, raw materials, labour requirements and so on) by comparing its costs at different levels of output with its likely revenue. The firm will rationally choose the output level where the difference between total revenue and total cost is largest. Using the analytical techniques available to us we can represent this situation both graphically and mathematically.

Let us assume that our oil firm faces a total cost function represented by:

$$TC = 500 + 0.5Q^2$$

where TC is total costs and Q is output. In addition, the firm faces a demand curve given by:

$$P = 120 - Q$$

where P is price. Using the techniques of Chapter 16 we can derive the total revenue equation as follows:

$$TR = P \times Q = (120 - Q) \times Q = 120Q - Q^2$$

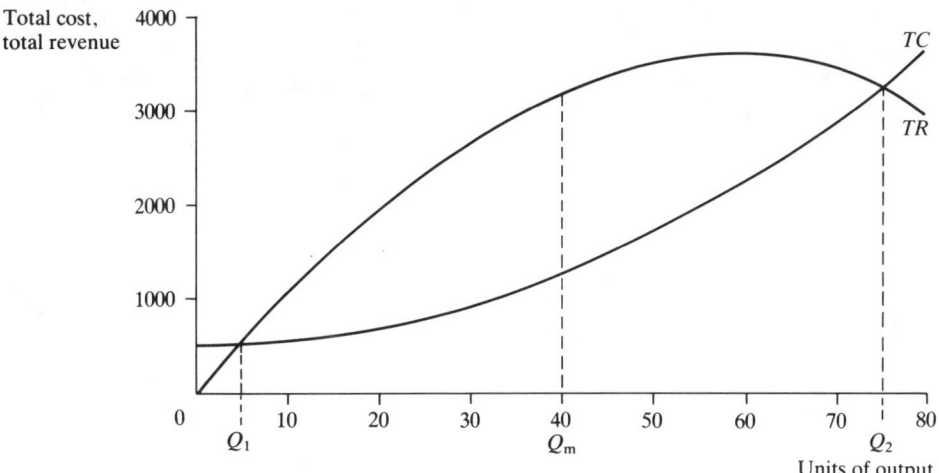

Total cost, total revenue

4000

3000

2000

1000

0   10   20   30   40   50   60   70   80

Q_1 Q_m Q_2

Units of output

Figure 17-1 Total cost and total revenue

Both the total cost and total revenue functions are shown in Fig. 17-1. It will be observed that, up to an output level of Q_1, total costs exceed total revenue (in other words the firm is operating at a loss). For output of between Q_1 and Q_m total revenue exceeds total costs and beyond Q_m costs again exceed revenue. Maximum profit—the greatest difference between total revenue and total costs—will be achieved at output level X_m where the gap between the venue curve and cost curve is widest. From Fig. 17-1 we can see that this equates to a level of output of 40 units.

But how can we find this solution mathematically? There are two alternative methods that can be used. We shall illustrate both as they reveal different aspects of the same problem.

17-2 THE PROFIT FUNCTION

The first method is to use the total cost and total revenue functions to obtain a third function, that for profit. In the case of our oil company:

$$\text{Profit} = TR - TC$$
$$= (120Q - Q^2) - (500 + 0.5Q^2)$$
$$= -500 + 120Q - 1.5Q^2$$

This function is shown in Fig. 17-2, together with the total cost and total revenue functions. The relationship between the three functions is clear. The profit function intercepts the vertical axis at -500. That is, at zero output the firm makes a loss of £500 which is identical to the fixed cost element of the total cost equation. At output level Q_1, where the total revenue and total cost curves intersect, profit is zero. Likewise, profit is zero at Q_3. (It is

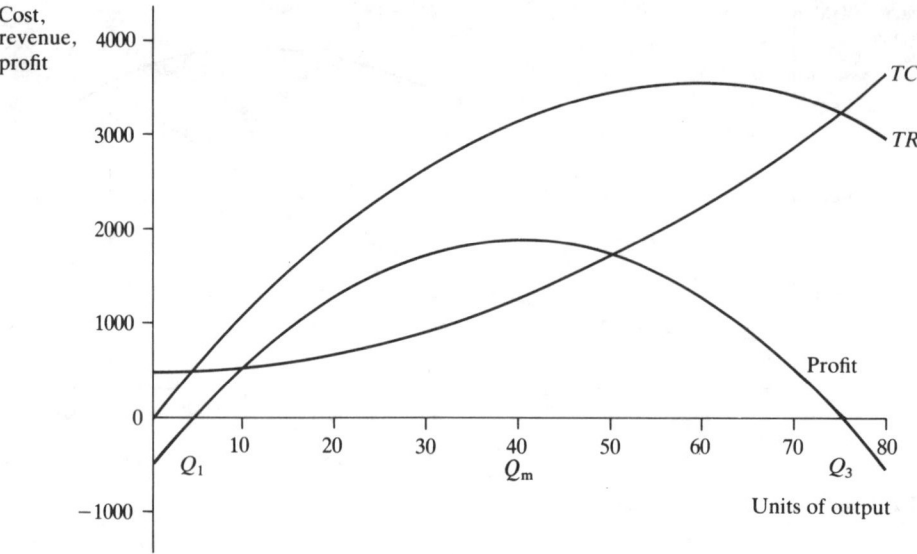

Figure 17-2 Total cost, total revenue and the profit function

apparent that, by finding the roots of the quadratic profit function, we can find points Q_1 and Q_3, which will give the output levels such that profit is zero.)

At output level Q_m the profit function reaches its highest value, corresponding to the widest gap between total revenue and total cost. We can readily calculate what this optimum output level would be. The slope of the profit function at this output level will be zero (that is, this level of output represents the turning point). Using calculus, we can find the derivative of the profit function:

$$\frac{d\,\text{Profit}}{dQ} = 120 - 3Q$$

Setting this derivative to zero and solving for Q we obtain a value for Q of 40 units. That is, when Q is 40 the slope of the profit function is zero which, for the quadratic function shown, is its maximum point.

We can readily confirm that this is indeed the maximum profit. Substituting $Q = 40$ back into the profit function we obtain a profit of £1900. If the firm produced 39 units then profit would be £1898.50. Similarly, if the firm produced 41 units, then profit would also be £1898.50. Looking at the profit function in Fig. 17.2 we can see that this pattern of taking three successive values for Q and finding that the profit level rises then falls only occurs at one point. This point must be the turning point of the function. Alternatively, we could simply have used the second derivative of the profit function:

$$\frac{d^2\,\text{Profit}}{dQ^2} = -3$$

Since this is negative, the turning point must be a maximum.

17-3 MARGINAL COST AND MARGINAL REVENUE

The second method of finding the profit-maximizing level of output also uses the concepts of slope and calculus. Returning to Fig. 17-1, we see that the slopes of the total revenue and total cost functions differ at the same level of output. The total cost function starts with a low positive slope which gradually increases. The total revenue curve, on the other hand, starts with a high, positive slope which gradually becomes less and less positive (and then negative). At one point, however, the slopes of the two functions will be identical as Fig. 17-3 illustrates. At output level Q_1 we can see that the slopes of the two functions (as measured by the tangents to the curves at that point) are different, as they are at output level Q_3. At output level Q_m, the profit-maximizing level of output, however, the slopes of the two curves are identical. We can make use of this to determine the point of profit maximization.

The derivative of the total revenue function is:

$$\frac{dTR}{dQ} = 120 - 2Q$$

and for total cost:

$$\frac{dTC}{dQ} = Q$$

profit will thus be at a maximum when the two derivatives (that is, the two slopes) are equal. To find this point we can set the two derivative equations equal:

$$120 - 2Q = Q$$

giving

$$120 = 3Q$$

$$Q = 40$$

confirming the profit-maximizing solution.

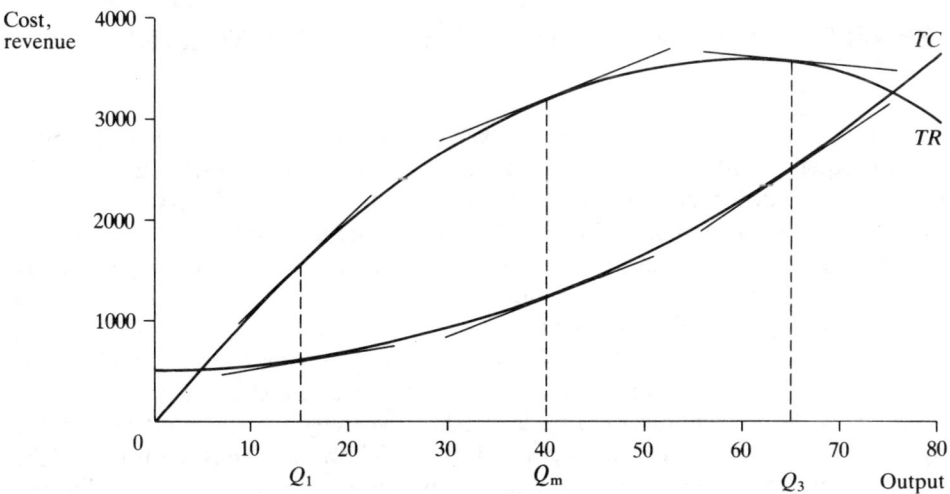

Figure 17-3 Marginal cost and marginal revenue

Either of the methods outlined in this and the previous section can be used to determine the optimum output level. Using the derivatives of the total cost and total revenue functions, however, leads to an important aspect of economic analysis, namely the identification of marginal cost and marginal revenue. Let us return to the derivative of the total cost function. We have previously explained that the derivative of any function $Y = f(X)$ measures the slope or gradient of that function. The slope of a function, in turn, measures the rate of change in the Y variable as the X variable changes. For example, the slope of the total cost function shows how total costs change as output changes. Readers will recollect that marginal cost was defined as the change in total cost as output changes by one unit. In other words the derivative of the total cost function is, quite simply, marginal cost.

Similarly, the derivative of the total revenue function will equate with marginal revenue, showing the change in total revenue as output changes by one unit.

When we determined the profit-maximizing level of output by equating the two derivatives, we also, therefore, found the point where marginal cost and marginal revenue were equal. This, in fact, is the most common way of defining the profit-maximizing level of output. Apart from the mathematics, why should this be so?

Marginal cost indicates the increase in cost as we increase output, while marginal revenue shows the increase in revenue. If, at a particular level of output, marginal cost is less than marginal revenue then it makes sense for the business (given the assumption of trying to maximize profit) to increase output further. Since such an increase in output will add more to revenue than to cost, profit will increase. On the other hand, if marginal cost is greater than marginal revenue the last unit of output produced adds more to cost than it does to revenue, hence is adversely affecting profit. In such a case this unit of output should not be produced by the firm. Equilibrium will obviously be reached when marginal cost and marginal revenue are equal as the firm will have no incentive either to increase or decrease output levels further. Thus profits are maximized by looking at the cost and revenue condition *at the margin*.

17-4 PROFIT MAXIMIZATION UNDER DIFFERENT MARKET STRUCTURES

This general conclusion—that profits are maximized when marginal cost and marginal revenue are equal—holds true for all profit-maximizing business organizations. The implications of the rule for the profits made by firms in different types of market conditions are different, however. Economists distinguish market structures largely by the degree of competition faced by the firms in the industry. At one extreme an industry may consist of only very large firm—a monopoly. At the other extreme, the industry may be made up of a large number of very small firms—a market structure referred to as *perfect competition*. Ranging between these two extremes are various degrees of 'imperfect competition' such as duopoly (two large firms) or oligopoly (a small number of large firms). Often in markets like this, firms follow the conventions of 'price leadership', whereby one company, usually the largest, takes the initiative in setting prices and others follow suit. Thus the prices of the different companies tend to move in step. While companies may compete by advertising and by offering higher-quality goods, it is unusual for them to compete by undercutting each other's prices. While all firms in any type of market structure will maximize profits by equating marginal revenue and marginal costs, the degree of resource efficiency and the *levels* of profit will differ markedly.

With one exception, the market structures detailed above share one feature in common. This is that the demand curve facing firms in these markets slopes *downwards* from left to right. These demand curves resemble those discussed earlier in the text and carry the implication that, under these market conditions, firms can only raise the quantity of sales by cutting prices. The important exception to this is the market structure described as *perfect competition*, which is examined in detail in Chapter 18.

17-5 PROFIT MAXIMIZATION UNDER MONOPOLY

Let us examine further the profit-maximizing position of a firm in a monopoly situation. A monopoly arises when a single firm is the sole supplier of a good or service. In such a situation the firm *is* the entire industry. Such a situation arises largely through the existence of *barriers to entry*, which may take a number of forms. The first of these are *legal* barriers, when the government establishes a monopoly by law, such as that relating to British Gas or the Post Office. The second of these barriers is the *availability of resources*, as when a firm has full control over the only available supply of some specific factor of production, such as a raw material, or owns the patent on some invention. The third barrier to entry is the *availability of capital*. The initial amount of capital needed to set up in competition with an existing firm may be prohibitive as, for example, in the oil industry. Equally, an existing producer can artificially increase this capital requirement by running an extensive advertising campaign for his product which any potential newcomer would have to match from the outset. The fourth barrier to entry is *restrictions imposed by existing firms*. Firms already in the industry may collude to prevent entry by new firms, for example by having an agreement between themselves to undertake a price-cutting campaign against newcomers. Existing firms may also establish a *cartel* by agreeing to set identical prices for their product. Such a cartel was established by the member nations of OPEC in an attempt to fix the price of oil on the international market.

The monopoly model

Economists have established a formal model for analysing monopoly. Its initial assumptions are as follows:

1. There are many buyers.
2. They seek maximum satisfaction.
3. There is only one seller.
4. The seller seeks maximum profit.
5. There are barriers to entry into the industry.
6. The participants have all the relevant information.

The way in which a monopolist maximizes profit can be deduced by examining the firm's costs and revenues. Figure 17-4 shows average and marginal cost curves (taking the form discussed in Chapter 15). It should be noted that the ATC curve includes what is

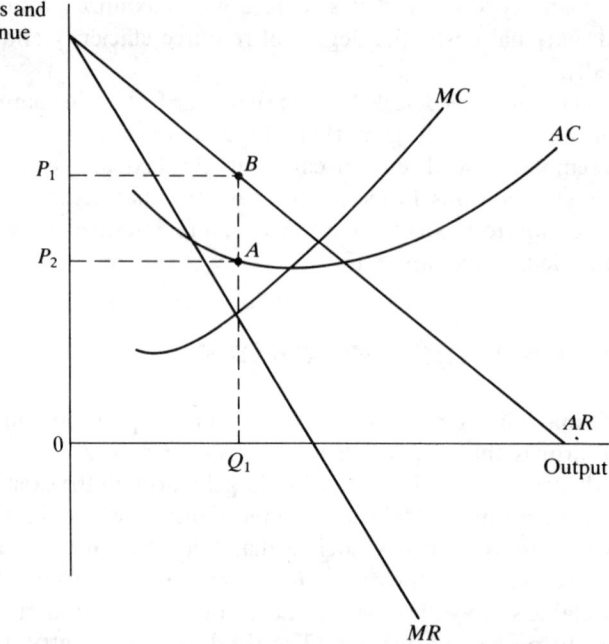

Figure 17-4 Profit maximization under monopoly

referred to as 'normal' profit. That is, a profit element is included in costs as the normal reward to enterprise. The corresponding average and marginal revenue curves are also shown.

The equilibrium level of output is determined, as predicted, by equating marginal cost and marginal revenue. This occurs at output level Q_1 and price p_1. The profit the firm will achieve can also be derived. We can see that the total cost associated any level of output will be given by multiplying average cost by output. So the area Q_1OP_2A will represent total costs.

Similarly, total revenue can be derived from the demand curve (which is also the AR curve) so the area Q_1OP_1B will represent total revenue. In a monopoly market structure the difference between total revenue and total cost (given by the area AP_2P_1B) is referred to as *supernormal* profits.

The adjustment process under monopoly

Figure 17-4 may also be used to undertake the usual comparative static analysis for a monopoly firm. Let us examine a number of possible changes.

First, let us assume that the monopoly's fixed costs increase. The AC curve will shift upwards but the marginal cost curve will remain unchanged (remember that fixed costs are not part of marginal costs). The equilibrium point, where marginal cost and marginal revenue are equal, will remain unchanged but the level of supernormal profits enjoyed by the monopoly firm will be reduced. This has an important implication for policy towards monopoly firms. If the government imposed some sort of special tax or levy on the monopoly as part of fixed costs then the burden of this would fall on the monopoly not the consumer. (Readers may remember from Chapter 10 that in certain years central government imposed a special gas levy on British Gas.)

Second, let us assume there there is some increase in the firm's variable costs—through higher factor prices, for example. The average cost and marginal cost curves will now shift upwards. The marginal cost curve will now intersect the marginal revenue curve at a lower level of output. The new equilibrium, therefore, will cause the monopoly firm to reduce output and increase price.

Finally, if there were some change in the underlying conditions of demand then the average revenue and marginal revenue curves would shift. If the demand curve shifts outwards for some reason then the marginal revenue curve will now intersect the marginal cost curve at a higher level of output. The monopoly will, therefore, produce more but at a higher price, *ceteris paribus*.

It is important to realize, however, that these adjustments will usually still leave the monopoly earning supernormal profits. As Chapter 18 shows, this phenomenon differentiates monopoly firms quite sharply from firms operating under conditions of perfect competition in which supernormal profits cannot persist indefinitely.

17-6 MARGINAL COSTS AND MARGINAL REVENUE IN THE REAL WORLD

Discussion of profit maximization so far has established that profits are maximized when marginal cost and marginal revenue are equal. This is not, of course, the same as saying that, in the real world, firms actually calculate marginal costs and revenues. Indeed, most businesses are unlikely to have come across the terms. Although the economic analysis of profit maximization is entirely logical, it is hardly a description of the process whereby firms make decisions on how to make the most profits. Does this imply that economic theories are so unrealistic as to be unusable?

Several arguments can be put forward to defend economic theory. The first—associated with the neo-classical school—is the point that economic theory is not intended to be descriptively realistic. The value of a theory is to be judged ultimately by the accuracy of its conditional predictions. Thus if price and quantity change in accordance with the adjustment process suggested by the theory then the model is to be accepted. This argument thus suggests that although businesses may be unaware of marginal cost and marginal revenue, in practice they still act as if they are aware.

The Austrian attitude is that the important feature of profit is its role as an incentive. What matters is not whether profits are in fact maximized—indeed, this can never be established—but the fact that business decisions are taken with a view to making maximum profits. From this perspective, businessmen's alleged ignorance of marginal costs and marginal revenues would simply not be important. What matters are that businesses believe that a particular course of action will maximize profits and that they act in accordance with their expectations.

17-7 SUMMARY

Profit maximization will occur at the level of output where maginal cost equals marginal revenue.

The *slope* of the profit equation will be zero at the optimum output level, and the slopes of the total revenue and total cost curves will be equal.

Market structures are distinguished primarily by the degree of competition. At one extreme is *perfect competition*; at the other is *monopoly*. Monopoly is usually brought about through the existence of a number of *barriers to entry*. Under monopoly conditions a firm will earn *supernormal* profits. Such profits will not normally be eroded through the market adjustment process but, in the absence of external change, will persist indefinitely.

EXERCISES

17-1 A firm has collected data on its demand function and found that:

$$P = 120 - 1.5Q$$

where P is price and Q is quantity demanded. The firm has also calculated its total cost function as:

$$TC = 1000 + 20Q + 0.5Q^2$$

(*a*) Derive an equation for total revenue.
(*b*) Derive an equation for profit.
(*c*) Plot all three equations on a graph (for values of Q from 0 to 50).
(*d*) Explain why the total revenue equation starts at the origin.
(*e*) Using algebra, find the range of output over which the firm at least breaks even (that is, does not make a loss). Find the corresponding area on your graph.
(*f*) Using differentiation, find the profit-maximizing level of output.
(*g*) Calculate the profit the firm earns at this level of output and the price it must charge.
(*h*) Calculate the marginal cost and marginal revenue at this level of output and for the levels of output which are one unit less and one unit more than the optimum. What pattern do you observe? How do you explain this?
(*i*) Calculate the elasticity of demand at the optimum level of output. What implications does this have for the firm?

17-2 A firm has noted the following quantities sold at particular prices:

Price	205.8	190.4	173.6	214.2
Quantity	106	128	152	94

The firm's accountant has reported that fixed costs at £7500 and calculated an average cost equation:

$$AC = \frac{7500}{Q} - 60 + 0.3Q$$

(*a*) Derive a demand equation in the form $P = f(Q)$.
(*b*) Derive a total revenue equation.
(*c*) Derive a total cost equation and, hence, a profit equation.
(*d*) Find the following levels of output:
　(*i*) minimum cost
　(*ii*) maximum revenue
　(*iii*) maximum profit.
　Explain why these levels of output are not the same.
(*e*) Calculate the profit the firm will earn at each of the levels in (*d*).
(*f*) Calculate eleasticity of demand at the profit-maximizing level of output. What implications does this have for the firm?

PRICES AND PROFITS UNDER COMPETITION AND MONOPOLY

18-1 INTRODUCTION

Chapter 17 examined the way that firms in general, and monopolies in particular, might maximize profit. This chapter will show that profit, prices and output are rather different when firms face the pressures of competition. Indeed, so great are the differences that the promotion of competition is one of the major responsibilities of government, and this chapter will accordingly go on to discuss the principal features of policy in the area.

To undertake these tasks, it is be necessary to develop a full-scale model of competition to complement that of monopoly set out in Chapter 17. We follow the normal procedure of setting out the assumptions, making deductions, changing some of the initial conditions and seeing how our deductions affect the model. We shall see that the models carry the direct implication that governments should maintain competitive conditions in the economy. To act on this finding it is, of course, necessary to be able to distinguish between competition and monopoly in the real world and this, as we shall also see, is not as easy as it might appear.

18-2 THE ASSUMPTIONS OF THE MODEL OF PERFECT COMPETITION

The model of perfect competition starts from the following assumptions:

1. Everyone in the market has all the relevant information.
2. There are many buyers.
3. Buyers seek maximum satisfaction.

4. The sellers (firms) seek to maximize profits.
5. There are many sellers.
6. There are no barriers to entry into the industry.
7. The product is homogeneous.

The first four assumptions are, of course, common to this model and that of monopoly. The difference between the two models arises in the fifth assumption, which states that there are many firms, rather than just one, in the industry, and in the sixth assumption, which states that the number of firms may expand. Entry can be hindered by a number of factors like patents which make it illegal to copy a firm's invention. The existence and extent of entry barriers account for much the difference between a competitive industry and a monopoly, and they are something to which we shall return later in our analysis.

The seventh assumption states that the product is assumed to be homogeneous, that is, that no difference between the products of different companies can be found. Although there are many suppliers, there is effectively only one product. Crude oil, for example, is crude oil, regardless of which company supplies it. It follows that it must sell for one single price, for no firm would be able to charge a price greater than the market price without losing all its customers. This prevailing price, of course, is the industry's equilibrium price which is set by the interaction of supply and demand. Since each firm is assumed to be small in relation to the market, the equilibrium price is beyond its control. It must take this as given, that is, as part of the environment within which it has to work. At the prevailing price, however, its goods are perfectly saleable. Indeed, because the firm is relatively small, demand at that price is virtually without limit. Unlike firms in other kinds of market structures, the individual firm in a competitive market faces a demand curve (an average revenue curve) which is *infinitely elastic*. Graphically this is represented by a line horizontal to the quantity axis. Mathematically, the demand equation is of the form:

$$P = a$$

where a is the equilibrium price. Average revenue curves of this nature have one exceptional property: marginal revenue and average revenue are identical.

Other assumptions specifying external conditions like wage rates in the industry or the level of interest rates could be added to the list, so that later we could explore the effects of altering them. At this early stage, however, such details would be an encumbrance and it is better to regard them as being implicit.

18-3 EQUILIBRIUM IN THE SHORT RUN

The situation of the typical firm in a competitive industry can now be deduced from the above assumptions. Our attention will initially be confined to the short run: the period over which some element of the firm's capacity is fixed. The firm thus faces the short-run cost curves described in Chapter 15, together with the infinitely elastic demand curve outlined above. The situation is illustrated in Fig. 18.1, where P_1 is the pre-existing equilibrium price.

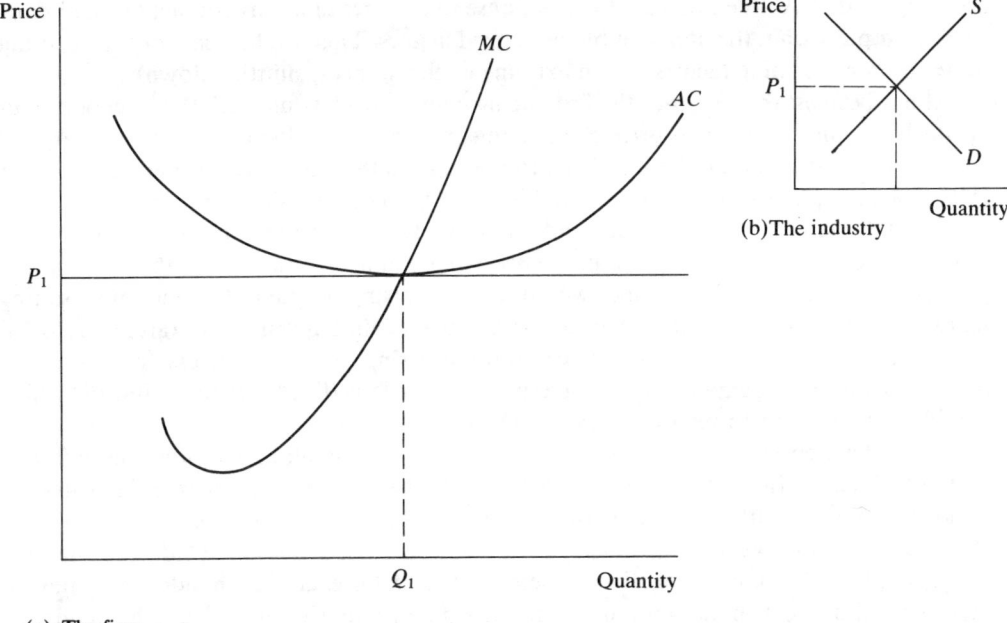

(a) The firm

Figure 18-1 Perfect competition: (a) The firm; (b) The industry

The firm will proceed to maximize profits according to the principles set out in Chapter 17: it will select that level of output at which marginal cost equals marginal revenue. Since marginal revenue and price are the same, profits are maximized when marginal cost equals price. In the diagram, this occurs at Q_1.

Selling one more unit simply adds that unit's proceeds—its price—to total revenue. Thus for a firm under perfect competition, price – $AR = MR$. Showing this mathematically is straightforward:

$$P = a$$

$$TR = P \times Q = aQ$$

$$MR = \frac{dTR}{dQ} = a$$

18-4 ADJUSTMENT IN THE SHORT RUN: THE SHORT-RUN SUPPLY CURVE

We can now explore the reactions of the typical firm to changes in its situation. Since some element(s) of the production process are fixed in the short run, the options open to the firm are fairly limited. All the firm can do in response to changes in its environment is to alter its level of output within the limits set by those fixed factors. This would mean, of course, using more or fewer variable factors (or, in extreme circumstances, shutting down).

It has been established that the firm facing competition would seek the level of output at which marginal cost equals price. Should outside conditions alter either price or marginal cost, theory predicts that the firm will act to re-establish their equality by altering its output level. For example, a firm might find itself in short-run equilibrium with price at P_1 and its output at Q_1 (Fig. 18.2). If the demand curve for the whole industry were then to shift upwards because, perhaps, of a fall in the price of a complementary good, then the market price would rise to, say, P_2. The firm would react by raising output to Q_2, once more setting marginal cost equal to marginal revenue. Were a further shift in demand to raise price to P_3, a similar adjustment would occur with output rising to Q_3. Conversely, downward displacements in the demand curve would induce price falls (like those to P_4 and P_5) which would cause the firm to restrict output to Q_4 and Q_5.

It can be seen that the firm ajusts its output by moving along its short-run marginal cost (SMC) curve. In other words, the SMC acts as the firm's supply curve: it indicates the various amounts of output that the firm will offer for sale at different prices. To establish the short-run supply curve for the whole industry, all that is necessary is to 'add together' the supply curves (SMC curves) of all the different firms. If, for example, an industry contained 100 identical firms, then its short-run supply schedule would simply be found by taking the quantities offered by a single firm at different prices and multiplying them by 100.

Changes on the cost side would also affect the profit-maximizing output of the firm

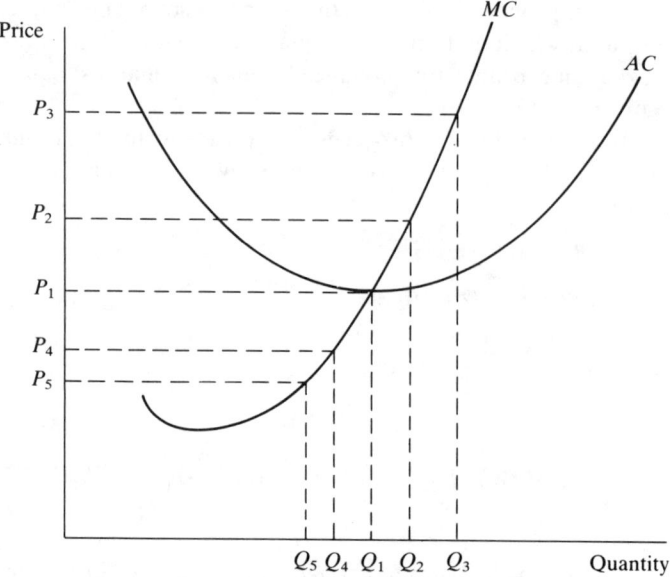

Figure 18-2 Short-run adjustment under perfect competition

(and thus of the industry). For example, if labour were a variable resource, a rise in pay for the industry's workers might cause the marginal cost curve to shift upwards. Firms would then equalize marginal cost and price by reducing output. The effect of other changes on output would depend on the particular form they took. Naturally, such changes would constitute *shifts* in the industry's short-run supply curve.

18-5 ADJUSTMENT IN THE LONG RUN

In the long run, by definition, all factors can be varied and there are therefore no limits on the output levels that firms can select. They have the option of expanding or contracting capacity, of entering the industry or leaving it. Which course they follow is determined by the level of profit which they expect to attain.

It is important to realize that maximum profits are not the same as high profits. A firm may indeed maximize profits and still earn profits which are low or even negative. (Readers will recall that it is conventional to include normal profits within average costs. Thus a loss is any level of profit below normal profit.)

The absolute level of profit can be found on a price–quantity graph such as Fig. 18-3. Total cost, for instance, is average cost per unit multiplied by the number of units. In Fig. 18.3, when price is at P_1, total cost is shown by the rectangle $OABQ_1$. Total revenue can similarly be found by multiplying average revenue (that is, price) by output. Again for price P_1, total revenue is OP_1DQ_1, making total profit the rectangle AP_1DB. At a lower price like

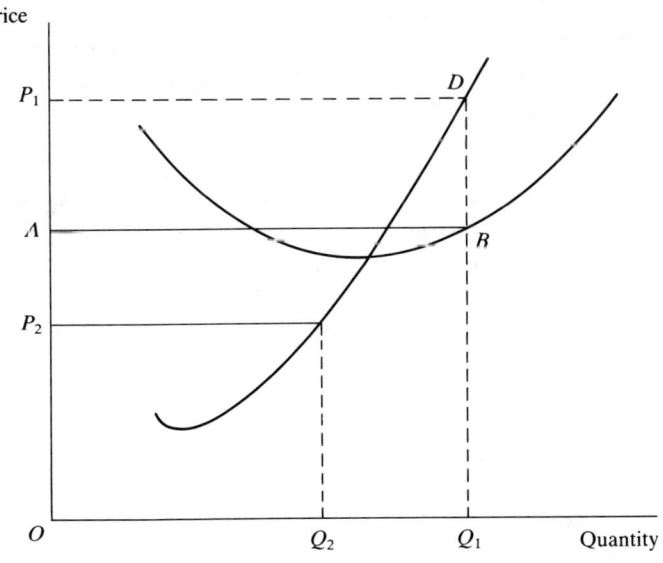

Figure 18-3 Revenue, costs and profits

P_2, total cost would exceed total revenue and the firm would sustain a loss. (Q_2 is nevertheless the best level of production as it keeps the loss to a minimum: marginal cost equals marginal revenue is the rule both for profit maximization and for loss minimization.)

There are clearly three possible categories of profit level: supernormal profits, normal profits and losses. Let us take these in turn. If firms in a competitive industry are earning supernormal profits, two consequences will follow. First, those firms will begin to invest in extra capacity so as to earn supernormal profits on an even greater volume of output. Second, by the assumption of perfect information, other members of the business community will hear of the industry's high profitability and will therefore try to enter. Since there are no barriers to entry, their only obstacle will be the time that it takes to marshall the necessary resources. Because some elements of the production process are fixed over the short run, both processes—expansion by existing firms and entry by new firms—can only be effected over the long run.

The result of the quest for supernormal profits is, paradoxically, the elimination of those very profits. As the new capacity comes into operation, a greater volume of goods will be offered for sale and, *ceteris paribus*, prices will fall. The gap between *AC* and *AR* accordingly narrows and ultimately disappears. At this point, naturally enough, new firms cease to enter the industry.

The converse process occurs when losses are recorded, that is, firms will leave the industry by closing capacity or converting it to other uses. Like the work of augmenting capacity, these changes can only be made over the long run. Their result is likewise the elimination of the initial cause: as capacity contracts, the volume of production falls and this causes prices to increase. This in turn reduces the losses that the remaining firms are making. Eventually, losses are eliminated altogether and the process of exit from the industry comes to an end.

The position in which firms are earning normal profits is clearly unique. Only in this case are firms breaking even. They are thus under no inducement to alter capacity and the industry and its constituent firms are thus in long-run equilibrium.

Figure 18-4 shows the processes of change graphically. This particular example traces the effects of an increase in demand. It commences at X, a point of long-run equilibrium at which firms just earn normal profits. Equilibrium price and quantity stand at P_1 and Q_1 respectively. Point X lies, let us assume, on demand curve D_1, and the change is initiated by an upward shift in the demand curve to D_2. Prices immediately begin to rise. In response, firms step up their production by using more variable factors and so moving along their SMCs to point Y. The line XY, therefore, traces out the shot-run supply curve. At Y, firms maximize their profits and are thus in shoft-run equilibrium. They are, however, receiving supernormal profits, and entry into the industry begins. Output therefore expands even more, prices weaken, supernormal profits are whittled away and the industry moves to a new long-run equilibrium at Z.

The line XZ traces out the long-run supply curve of the industry. It shows the volume of output offered at different prices after long-run adjustments to capacity have been taken into account. The long-run supply curve (LSC) is more elastic than the short-run supply curve because factors of production are more mobile over the long run. The gradient of the LSC will depend on the underlying conditions of production. A positive slope would indicate that the industry could only deliver larger volumes of output if it were sold for higher prices. Since it is equilibrium positions which are being compared, the higher prices cannot

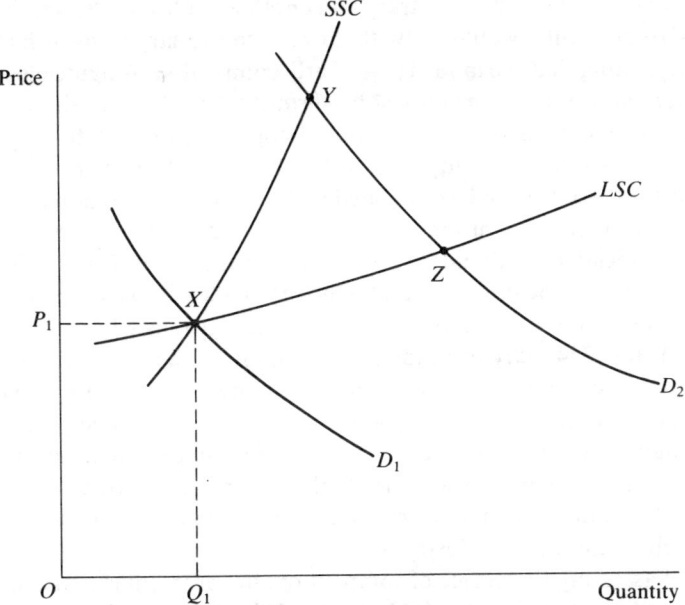

Figure 18-4 Long-run adjustment under perfect competition

be producing supernormal profits: by definition, there are only normal profits in long-run equilibria. The cause of higher prices must lie, therefore, in higher costs. The industry must, in other words, be facing diminishing returns. As readers will recall from Chapter 15, a horizontal LSC would indicate constant returns and a negative slope increasing returns.

Following through the preceding example of a change initiated by a shift in demand, the analyst might expect to find evidence of the following developments: an increase both in the relative price and in the output of the good (the short-run adjustment); and a continued increase in output accompanied by a reversal of the price rise (the long-run adjustment). Other developments which had the effect of altering the profits of an industry would set similar adjustments in motion. Examples might include changes in taxation, changes in legal regulations or movements in interest rates. These effects could clearly be incorporated into testable hypotheses.

18-6 MEASURING COMPETITION

If the foregoing theory of perfect competition is to be used as a basis for the formulation of predictions about the world, it is plainly necessary to be able to classify industries as competitive, monopolistic, oligopolistic and so on. In other words, economists should be able to assess the degree of competition in an industry. The conventional approach is to compute an industry's *concentration ratio* (CR). This is found by dividing the aggregate sales of the largest five firms in an industry by the industry's total sales, and is designed to measure the dominance exercised by these firms. The resulting concentration ratio is called the industry's '5CR'. (The number 5 is, however, arbitrary and another could equally well be used.) A low 5CR—perhaps 10 per cent—would show that even the five largest firms had a small share of total sales, suggesting that the industry was fairly competitive. A figure close to 100 per cent, however, would indicate that the biggest five firms had a dominant share of the market. Such an industry would be described as being oligopolistic or sometimes as 'highly concentrated'. Monopoly is thus a limiting case with a 1CR of 100 per cent.

It is clear that concentration ratios cannot be calculated without a clear definition of an 'industry'. The problem is that such a definition is often lacking. No fewer than four definitions are offered by the official 1980 Standard Industrial Classification (SIC). This contains 10 divisions (denoted by a single digit), each of which is divided into classes (two digits) of which there are a total of 60. Classes are divided into 222 groups (three digits) which are themselves divided into 334 activity headings (four digits). The classifications thus go down into finer and finer levels of detail, each category being included in the one above. To illustrate, a company making offshore oil platforms could be accounted part of division 3 (Metal Goods, Engineering and Vehicles), class 32 (Mechanical Engineering), group 320 (Industrial Plant and Steelwork) or activity 3205 (Boilers and Process Plant Fabrications). Thus the task of deciding which industry the platform-maker is in reduces to the question of deciding which definition of industry to use.

From the point of view of assessing the degree of competition, the problem is that each definition of an 'industry' would produce its own 5CR. As the definitions grow narrower, industries appear to be more highly concentrated. Ultimately, any firm could be made to appear a monopoly firm if the industry were defined sufficiently narrowly.

Economists approach the problem of deciding which definition to use by looking at barriers to entry, that is, the four factors described in Chapter 17: legal barriers, availability of resources, the amount of capital required, and restrictions imposed by existing firms. If there were no barriers to entry, an industry could not be considered a distinct industry in any true sense of the term. In other words, it is entry barriers, not administrative divisions like the SIC, which determine the boundaries of industries.

A corollary of this line of argument is that an activity or group with a high 5CR would, in the absence of entry barriers, have to be deemed to be competitive. This is because any monopolistic behaviour would simply attract entry. Industries like this are sometimes described as being 'workably' competitive or as having 'contestable' markets.

Within this broad approach, the stances taken by neo-classical and Austrian economists differ. Neo-classical economists approach the question by assessing the *degree* of difficulty facing firms from other industries wishing to enter an industry. When entry barriers of perceptible size are found—like those stemming from heavy advertising, perhaps—attention is directed to assessing their affects in terms of the intensity of competition in the industry.

For Austrians, by contrast, there are only two categories of entry barrier: those which an entrepreneur could surmount by using sufficient capital and ingenuity, and those which are utterly insurmountable. The latter category are those which are created by the government, and for Austrians, they are the only barriers which count. All the others can ultimately be circumvented.

One of the better-known versions of this approach was developed by Joseph Schumpeter (an economist at Harvard from 1932 to 1950). His argument was that monopolies would, in the long run, be overturned by the development of new industries. He called this process the 'gale of creative destruction', in which the central role is played by the innovating entrepreneur. An example is provided by the fate of the American railway industry. In the later nineteenth century this industry was largely run by cartels and local monopolies who were able to charge high fares. Eventually, however, their power was eroded by competition. That competition did not come from new railway companies, but from the entrepreneurs who built up the motor industry. In other words it was the advent of a wholly new mode of transport which undermined the position of the railways, and it was their monopoly profits which constituted the incentive for the new car-makers. Schumpeter concluded that monopolies were transitory and there was therefore no need for a competition policy. Indeed, he argued that such a policy would in fact be harmful as it would remove the incentives for innovation.

18-7 EFFICIENCY, COMPETITION AND MONOPOLY

The foregoing models have been used to support the argument that monopolies misallocate resources. This argument is developed by comparing the two models' long-run equilibria. If an industry is characterized by competition, then price (as Chapter 17 demonstrates), marginal cost and average cost will all be equal at this point. Under monopoly, however, price exceeds both marginal cost and average cost. The effect of these differences is twofold. First, the difference between average cost and price produces the monopoly's supernormal profits. Second, economists argue that the divergence between marginal cost and price indicates that consumers are being deprived of goods which they are willing to buy. The cost to society of supplying goods is shown by their marginal cost, and if consumers are willing to pay those costs, then the goods ought to be supplied. In terms of Fig. 18-5, this output is OQ_2. The monopoly's level of output, however, is only OQ_1. In effect, consumers are losing Q_1Q_2 units of the good. Because it is a monopoly, the industry is smaller than it 'ought' to be. In effect, a monopoly is able to contrive an artificial shortage of the product, permitting it to charge a price in excess of cost and thus to read monopoly profits. In the eyes of economists, however, the fundamental flaw of monopoly is that such an industry operates on too small a scale. This failing is described as an 'allocative inefficiency' because it pertains to the allocation of resources.

The argument that monopoly results in a misallocation of resources has also been extended to suggest that monopolists might simply allow costs to rise. Controlling costs, as every businessman knows, is hard work and the managers of a monopoly may well be tempted to take the benefits of their sheltered position in the form of reduced effort rather than as profit. The result would be the toleration of inefficient work practices or overmanning. This is sometimes termed *X-inefficiency* to distinguish it from allocative inefficiency.

Monopolies have, however, been defended on the grounds that they may permit large-scale production which could lead to reduced costs. It would, for example, make little sense to have two gas companies competing by laying their own pipe systems down every street. In these cases of 'natural monopolies', the lower costs of large-scale production might well be sufficient to allow the consumer cheaper prices *and* to give the monopoly a supernormal rate of profit.

The second defence of monopoly (or, more precisely, of oligopoly) is that supernormal profits can be used to finance research and development (R&D). Since the result of this

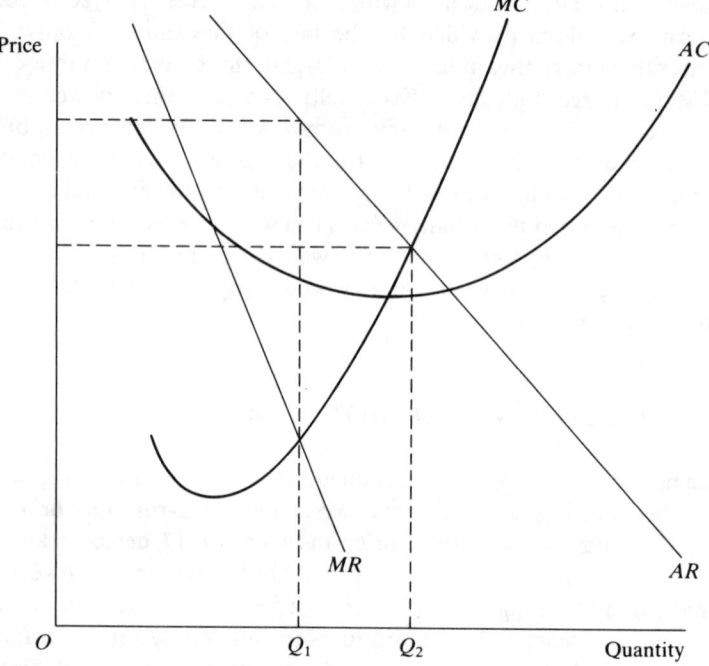

Figure 18-5 The allocative inefficiency of monopoly

activity is the creation of new products and advanced technology, some economists argue that a little allocative inefficiency is but a small price to pay for benefits of this kind. There is clearly common ground between this argument and the ideas of Joseph Schumpeter.

18-8 COMPETITION POLICY

The implication of the foregoing discussion is that, in general, the economy would be better served by competitive industries than by monopolies. Governments throughout the world have found this argument to be so persuasive that they have attempted to follow its prescription. In particular, they have sought to promote competition in the following ways: by pursuing a policy of free trade which upholds the right of overseas suppliers to compete in the domestic market; by prohibiting collusion between firms; by taking the power to control or to break up monopolies; and by taking the power to stop mergers which could result in the formation of new monopolies. While the first element of policy, free trade, relates to a country's international economic affairs, the other three require the establishment of a *competition policy* in relation to the home economy. In the United Kingdom, such a policy dates from 1948 and is administered by several different organs of the state. It has three main aspects. First, most forms of collusion have been declared illegal and a Restrictive Practices Court has been established to try groups of firms accused of running cartels. Second, the Director General of Fair Trading monitors competition policy and reports infringements to the Secretary of State for Trade and Industry who has the responsibility for implementing the policy by perhaps using his powers to forbid a proposed merger and to force a company to sell a subsidiary. He can seek the advice of a special body, the Monopolies and Mergers Commission (MMC), which reviews cases referred to it by the Secretary of State. The MMC thus examines the conduct of any existing monopolies to see if there are any abuses such as overcharging customers. It can also scrutinize mergers to ensure that no new monopoly will result.

Austrian economists, as was noted above, tend to lay more stress on the possibility of entry than do neo-classical economists. For Austrians, the vital question is not 'how many firms are there in the industry?' but 'is it possible for entrepreneurs to enter it?' Since entry usually *is* feasible, Austrians conclude that the bulk of the economy is characterized by competition (despite high 5CRs) and thus see competition policy as being largely unnecessary. Austrian economists feel particular concern over monopolies created by the state, such as the nationalized industries' monopolies or the public sector's practice of using its own employees, rather than private contractors, for work like cleaning. The distinguishing feature of these sorts of monopoly is that they cannot be overcome by commercial ingenuity or by spending money on R&D or advertising. Barriers like these are absolute and their removal, so the argument runs, is the proper responsibility of any government that is concerned to promote competition. Their views have been particularly influential in the recent policy of *privatization*.

18-9 PRIVATIZATION

This refers to a number of distinct policies that have been pursued towards public sector organizations. The first has been to sell publicly owned companies to private investors. Some (like Amersham International in 1981) were sold to financial institutions in the City, some (like the National Freight Corporation in 1982) to their own managers and some to the public at large (like British Gas in 1986). The justification for this policy has been that owners with a direct interest in the company's financial performance would run it with greater efficiency than a government ministry with no such interest.

The second policy in this approach has been to open up to competition markets which had hitherto been restricted. One example—which did not involve publicly owned companies—was the abandonment of route licences for coach operators. These licences had reserved routes for certain operators, and the scrapping of the system inaugurated a spate of competition. Another aspect of this approach was the policy of putting out to tender services which had been performed by public authorities' own departments, such as refuse collection, laundry services and office cleaning. While the existing departments were usually allowed to submit tenders, they were placed in direct competition with outside firms. This policy of opening markets to competition has been termed *liberalization*.

The distinction between liberalization and privatization is important for economists. While competitive (liberalized) markets (normally) contribute toward the attainment of the optimum allocation of resources, privatized companies will be positively detrimental if they are monopolies. There is, indeed, scope for conflict between the two arms of the policy. For example, when British Telecom (BT) was sold to the private sector it was the sole supplier of telecommunication services in the UK. The government had the option of liberalizing the telecommunications market by breaking the company up into different units—perhaps one to maintain the network while others were allowed to compete in the provision of different services in local areas. This would, however, have made it rather more difficult to sell BT to private investors, who naturally preferred the steady profits of a guaranteed market. In the event, the government allowed one new company, Mercury, to enter into competition with BT. Because it was starting from scratch, Mercury was not able to offer effective competition to BT for several years. Thus the government can be seen as having obtained the best of both worlds: BT was sold as an effective monopoly and thus found ready buyers, yet by permitting Mercury to begin operations the government sowed the seeds of future competition.

18-10 SUMMARY

Perfect competition is a model of a market structure which lies at the opposite end of the spectrum from the model of monopoly in that it assumes both that many firms are in the industry and that others may enter. Its characteristic feature is that individual firms, because they sell identical products, face demand curves which are infinitely elastic.

Short-run equilibrium is reached when, as with monopolies, marginal cost and marginal revenue or price are equal. When price increases, firms adjust by increasing output: a movement along their marginal cost curves. For each firm, therefore, the marginal cost curve is the supply curve.

Long-run adjustment involves entry into or exit from the industry in response to the levels of profit earned—supernormal profits attracting entry, losses causing exit. Entry and exit serve to restore profits to normal levels. In long-run equilibrium, therefore, firms only earn normal profit.

The *efficiency* of competition is urged on the grounds that firms produce at the lowest points on their average cost curves and consumers are allowed to buy the goods they wish at prices which reflect their cost. Monopolies, by contrast are argued to give rise to *allocative inefficiency* by failing to operate on a sufficiently large scale. It is also argued that monopolies promote *X-inefficiency* by allowing costs to drift up. Defenders of monopoly (like Schumpeter) point to economies of scale and to the R&D efforts of many large oligopolies.

Competition policy attempts to maintain competitive conditions by restricting mergers. Liberalization has meant the opening of markets formerly closed by regulation, while privatization has meant the selling of public companies to private investors.

EXERCISES

18-1 Compare and contrast the models of monopoly and perfect competition in terms of:
(*a*) firms objectives;
(*b*) their other assumptions;
(*c*) long-run equilibria;
(*d*) the long-run adjustment process.

18-2 The models of competition and monopoly suggest that liberalizing coach services would be expected to increase both services and efficiency. How could such a hypothesis be tested?

18-3 Assume you are working in the planning department of a large multi-divisional firm. Write a report for your section head evaluating the barriers the firm might face in trying to enter the following industries:

(*a*) brewing;
(*b*) washing-powder manufacturing;
(*c*) garden tools;
(*d*) local radio broadcasting;
(*e*) pharmaceuticals.

18-4 A Bill is before Parliament to end patent protection. Your employer, the head of a chemical company, opposes the move and decides to hold a press conference to publicize his views. Write notes for him to refer to during the briefing.

18-5 Describe the role of supernormal profits in perfect competition.

18-6 Describe the process by which a perfectly competitive industry would adjust to a fall in demand in both the short and the long runs.

19

DISTRIBUTION AND FACTORS OF PRODUCTION

19-1 INTRODUCTION

Having looked in the previous chapters at the supply and demand for goods and services, our attention now turns to factors of production and the incomes they receive. Income, of course, is a matter of interest both to individuals and to businesses. In economic terms, incomes are rewards paid to factors of production, and in consequence they are an indispensable element in the mechanism for allocating productive resources between different industries and occupations. This chapter accordingly examines both the theory and the practice of factor markets.

Figure 19-1 is a histogram which shows the distribution of pre-tax incomes in the United Kingdom in 1985 (a full statistical analysis of the data set was the basis of one of the exercises for Chapter 2). It can be seen that the pre-tax income distribution is positively skewed, reflecting an uneven distribution among individuals in the economy. Economists distinguish between the *personal* distribution and the *functional* distribution of income. The former refers to the way income is distributed among individuals (as in Fig. 19-1) while the latter relates to the rewards paid to (the owners of) capital, labour, land and enterprise—the four factors of production. To economists, the income of any individual is simply the sum of the rewards paid to the factors which he or she owns.

The starting point for the analysis of the functional distribution of income is the fact that factors of production are traded in factor markets: the labour markets, the capital market and the land market. This chapter will therefore begin by examining the supply of factors to the economy as a whole, and will then turn to factor markets in individual industries.

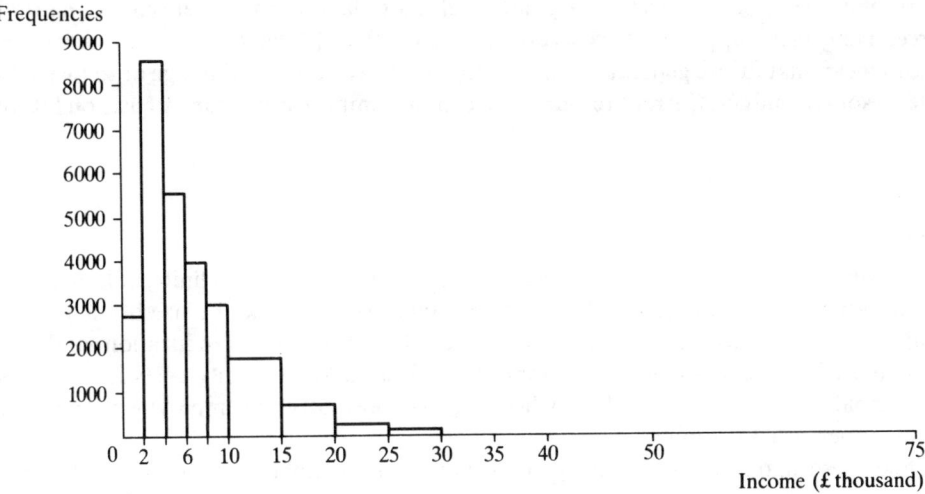

Figure 19-1 Pre-tax income distribution 1985

19-2 OPPORTUNITY COST AND THE SUPPLY OF FACTORS OF PRODUCTION TO THE WHOLE ECONOMY

The various factors and their rewards were defined in Chapter 8. The forces which influence the supply of each to the national economy will be looked at in turn.

Land

The amount of land available to an economy is determined, fundamentally, by its area, while climatic, topographical and geological factors will dictate its usefulness in terms of fertility, mineral deposits and so on. Factors which like this are supplied by nature are called *endowments*.

David Ricardo, an economist of the early nineteenth century, put forward the argument that land was, in terms of opportunity cost, a free resource. His logic was that landowners did not forgo anything by putting their land into economic use. Nor, of course, were any resources needed to produce land, since it was a gift of nature. He drew the conclusion that the payment of *rent* arose purely from land's scarcity, and was thus a pure surplus. As we shall see later, this use of the word 'rent' to denote surplus payments to factors has passed into the terminology of economics.

In terms of land, there are two major exceptions to Ricardo's argument. The first is land *at the margin*, where opportunity costs are unavoidable. In a mature economy like the British, the supply of usable land can only be extended by drainage or by reclaiming derelict sites. These activities absorb resources, and would naturally be undertaken on a larger scale if the price of land were to rise. Although there is therefore a limit to the supply of land to any economy, the supply of land for productive use can be taken to respond positively to increases in its price, that is, it has a supply curve which slopes upwards to the right.

A second exception to Ricardo's argument relates to land in the wider sense of natural resources. Here again, opportunity costs are involved in that the depletion of these resources today can mean that future generations have either to make good the damage or to live with a tighter resource budget. Current resource use can thus impose opportunity costs on future generations.

Labour

Labour is similar to land in that ultimately its supply to the economy is finite, at least in the short run. Within these limits, social conventions tend to determine the size of the groups seeking employment by setting retirement ages, the duration of education and the acceptability of mothers' going out to work. As with land, opportunity costs for workers arise principally *at the margin* for those who have to choose between employment and their domestic duties or education.

While these marginal opportunity costs suggest that higher salaries will call forth greater supplies of labour over the short run, it must be borne in mind that the historical trend over the last hundred years has been for higher incomes to be associated with shorter working weeks and longer holidays. Whereas people worked 60 and even 80 hours a week in the early factories, the typical working week is now less than 40 hours, and annual holidays are longer. The long-run supply curve of labour in a mature, industrial society seems, therefore, to *bend backwards*.

The explanation offered by economists is that, at low levels of income, offers of work at higher pay will be eagerly accepted because they will allow living standards to rise. There is, in other words, a *substitution effect* at work as consumers give up leisure to obtain the highly-valued wages. Later, when many material aspirations have been met people's priorities will switch from gaining extra income to securing more leisure. This is, of course, an instance of an *income effect* with leisure acting as a superior 'good'.

Capital

Although the word 'capital' normally refers to man-made aids to production, these can only be purchased by diverting income from its usual purpose of consumption, that is, by saving. Thus the opportunity cost of capital arises from the decision to save. This may be undertaken both by individuals and by firms who may retain profits rather than paying them all out to shareholders in the form of dividends. In reality, of course, consumption is not so much diminished by the act of saving as simply deferred: the saver being able to retrieve (and spend) his or her savings at a later date. Most consumers, of course, prefer consumption in the present to consumption in the future, and the deferral of consumption must clearly be counted as reducing their welfare, that is, as involving an opportunity cost. The compensation for this reduction in welfare is the payment of interest, and it is usual to assume that higher rates of interest will induce people to undertake greater levels of saving.

Savers also run the risk of losing the money which they lend, and will accordingly suffer more displeasure when undertaking more risky investments. Often risks increase with the length of a loan—shorter loans being safer than long ones. For this reason, short-term loans usually bear lower interest payments than longer-term investments.

Enterprise

The supply of enterprise to an economy will depend upon three basic factors. The first is social attitudes to the taking of risks and the starting of new businesses. A society where these practices are entirely normal may be said to have an 'enterprise culture', and will clearly have more entrepreneurs than a more conservative, 'risk-averse' society. The second factor is the rewards which entrepreneurs can gain, which will be influenced to some degree by the level of tax which they are compelled to pay. Third, since entrepreneurs generally need to borrow funds for their business ventures, high rates will, *ceteris paribus*, tend to diminish the supply of enterprise.

Needless to say, Austrian economists regard enterprise as the locomotive force behind all economic change, and believe that its importance has been understated by other schools of economic thought.

19-3 THE SUPPLY OF FACTORS OF PRODUCTION TO INDUSTRIES AND FIRMS

Given the aggregate supplies of factors to the economy at large, what are the elements which determine their supply to any particular industry? The answer is that supply at the micro level is determined primarily by factors' opportunity costs. For an employee, working for any one employer necessarily means that other jobs cannot be taken, and the salaries which accompany them must be forgone. By joining the research department of a securities broker, for instance, an economist would be passing up the opportunity to work as a college lecturer. The opportunity cost of working in the broker's office is, therefore, the forgone salary from lecturing. Likewise, the opportunity cost to a landlord of renting land to a supermarket is the rent which he or she forgoes from its alternative use in, say, agriculture. Thus the opportunity costs of the factors which an industry uses are the rewards which other industries are paying.

The opportunity costs and indeed the benefits of any occupation cannot be considered solely in monetary (after-tax) terms, of course. While the broker can offer a high salary, he is unlikely to match the college in terms of vacations. Nor are the pension arrangements, the staff canteen and all the other conditions of service likely to be the same. What the worker has to evaluate is the 'net advantages' of the two posts. (It remains, however, the general rule that jobs with the lowest financial remuneration also have worse working conditions.)

Because of the above opportunity costs, the supply of factors to a particular *industry* will have a positive gradient: to secure more productive resources, an industry would have to pay higher rates of interest, rent and pay. These higher rewards will make the industry attractive to larger groups of resource-owners, thus increasing the pool of resources available to the industry. It is, however, necessary to note that this supply curve has to be constructed on the assumption that the opportunity costs of factors—the rewards available in other industries—remain constant.

The supply of factors to an individual *firm* will, under most circumstances, not be an upward-sloping function but a horizontal line. Since firms are typically very small in relation to the total supply of any factor, it will normally be the case that infinite amounts will be available at the going rate of pay. When, however, factor supplies are scarce, even small firms may have to outbid their rivals to obtain factor supplies.

19-4 TRANSFER PAYMENTS AND ECONOMIC RENT

The opportunity costs of factors give rise to the important distinction which economists make between total earnings and *transfer* earnings. Transfer earnings are defined as the earnings which a factor could secure in another line of work, and they are clearly opportunity costs under another name. The term derives from the idea that these are the rewards which have to be offered to induce the worker to transfer from one job to another.

Any surplus income above transfer earnings is described as *economic rent* (following David Ricardo). It is a payment which reflects not the opportunity cost suffered by the worker in switching jobs but rather the strength of the employer's desire to secure the services of the person in question. This may be because the person possesses some special talent which is in short supply. Economic rent is to labour as supernormal profits are to enterprise.

19-5 FACTOR MARKETS IN PRACTICE

A number of special conditions apply to the markets for factors of production. These are taken in turn after a discussion of one force whose influence pervades all factor markets: technology.

Technological change

For the purposes of economics, technology is the quantitative relationship between inputs and outputs: how much is produced from a given volume of resources. Earlier we have called the ratio of output per unit input *productivity*, and it may be more useful to consider technology as the technical knowledge which underlies productivity. Technological change (or innovation) produces changes in productivity—an increase in output from given resources.

Although innovations save resources, they typically involve an alteration in the mix of factors used in the production process. Many technical changes, like the use of robots to assemble cars, involve the substitution of capital for labour. In practice, innovations usually come 'embodied' in the form of new capital equipment. Technology, that is to say, cannot be purchased independently of capital. It is therefore often difficult to distinguish the purchase of *more* items of capital from the purchase of *better*.

Though most innovations from the spinning jenny to the diesel locomotive have been labour-saving, innovations which save capital are not unknown. Modern computers, for example, are both more productive and cheaper than older ones. Innovations which save on the use of land (other than changes in agriculture) are few—the main instance being the development of high-rise blocks. Nevertheless, developments in transport and communications have the effect of making more land accessible from any given place, and thus enhance its supply in an economic sense.

To examine the effects of technological change, let us focus upon one factor, labour. A labour-saving innovation would have two effects on the demand for labour. The first effect would be to allow the shedding of labour as firms installed machines to replace their workers—the substitution effect. Second, by raising efficiency, the innovation would allow the firm to cut prices and sell more goods. This, known as the *output effect*, would boost the demand for all the resources used by the firm, including labour. The net outcome upon the number of workers employed would depend upon the relative strengths of the two effects. At the same time, of course, by raising productivity, technical advance usually means higher pay for those workers who remain in the industry.

The labour market

Of all factor markets, this is perhaps the most imperfect. Labour is notably immobile, both in geographical terms (people moving from one region to another) and in industrial terms (workers changing from one industry or occupation to another). Moreover, the relative pay of different occupations is heavily influenced by social conventions. Indeed, Guy Routh who examined pay in Britain in the twentieth century concluded that 'if supply and demand were at work, their influence is but dimly discerned'.[1] His argument was that the relative positions of different groups had remained, with one or two exceptions, constant during the entire period rather than fluctuating in response to changes in market forces. This is not, of course, to suggest that no changes occurred in the allocation of labour among industries. Rather, labour markets responded to changes in supply and demand primarily by means of quantity adjustments: if demand for a certain category of labour fell, its pay rates did not fall but rather it stopped recruiting new members. Conversely, an expanding profession would not see its pay rise but would meet demand mainly by recruiting people who had just entered the labour market. Routh also noted that the wide variations in pay *within* occupations made it difficult to speak of an 'average rate' for any particular occupation, a fact which hindered empirical work on the topic.

Another element is, of course, trade unions who seek to advance the pay and conditions of their members by negotiating agreements with employers and, in some cases, by regulating the recruitment of new members to the occupation. In economic terms, these practices may be thought of as moving the supply curve for labour upwards to the left.

In pursuing these objectives, trade unions face a major problem. As we will see in Chapter 20, there are demand curves for factors just as there are supply curves. This means that any attempt to raise the price of labour will lead, *ceteris paribus*, to a fall in the quantity demanded: better pay will mean fewer jobs. In many industries one way unions can defend jobs and at the same time improve pay is by cooperating in technological change, and many unions have adopted this policy.

Capital market

The capital market *per se* should not be confused with the market for new capital goods like machines. The latter is analogous to any other product market, with buyers weighing the usefulness of the item (measured by its expected contribution to revenues) against the price charged by the manufacturer. The phrase 'capital market' is reserved for the activity of raising business finance and the capital in question is 'liquid capital', that is, money. It is primarily associated in the United Kingdom with the City of London. On the Stock Exchange, for example, companies can raise cash (for the purchase of capital goods) by selling 'new issues' of their shares. These shares entitle the holder to receive a dividend from the company, and firms with better prospects find it easier to raise money. In this way, funds are allocated between competing ends like any other resource.

Dealings in shares is by no means restricted to the issue of new securities. Shares may, of course, be sold by one holder to another, and most share deals are of this nature—transactions in second-hand securities—rather than new issues. Good profits and dividends, coupled of course with the prospect of more to come, will naturally boost the demand for, and therefore the price of, a firm's shares. Conversely, a poor outlook for a company's profits will produce a low share price, which will render the firm vulnerable to being taken over. It could then either be placed under new management or closed down and the assets sold off. In either event the old management would find itself out of work. Thus the threat of takeover acts as an incentive to managers to raise efficiency.

The general level of share prices on the Stock Exchange indicates the prospects for the profits and dividends of industrial and commercial companies. Shares will rise when investors expect the economy to expand and companies to make good profits. A stock market boom, therefore, is often a harbinger of expansion in the 'real' economy of manufacturing and commerce. Conversely, a stock market slump may herald a downtown in the 'real' economy. Low share prices, moreover, can depress the economy directly in so far as they reduce demand for capital goods. There is, after all, little purpose in spending a lot of money on, say, new lorries when an entire haulage company, complete with lorries, can be bought cheaply on the Stock Exchange.

Land

The major economic issues relating to land stem arise from conservation. In some areas, privately owned land either provides important habitats for wildlife or contributes to the landscape in some other way. There are thus restraints upon the owner's rights to build on land or disrupt those habitats in other ways. In the United Kingdom, for example, land can be designated a Site of Special Scientific Interest or be included in the Green Belt. Sometimes, of course, there can be conflicts of interest over these matters. A further issue relates to the natural resources which are associated with land: minerals, fresh water, forests, the seabed and indeed the sea itself. The depletion or despoliation of these environmental resources—like the erosion of topsoil in many parts of Africa, China, the Soviet Union and indeed parts of the United Kingdom—clearly often carries grave implications for the future. Many have concluded that governments have a responsibility to ensure that decisions taken today have proper regard for the consequences.

19-6 SUMMARY

The *personal distribution of income* is the distribution of income among individuals, while the *functional distribution of income* refers to the returns earned by the four factors of production: land, labour, capital and enterprise.

Supply and demand in *factor markets* determines the level of reward which different factors receive.

Endowments of factors are the stocks of those factors which are provided, free, by nature.

Transfer earnings are the rewards which factors could earn in an alternative occupation; *economic rent* refers to any payment that is made in excess of this level.

EXERCISES

19-1 Collect data on the pre-tax income distribution for 10 years ago and contrast it with the latest data available. What trends are apparent? How would you try and relate these trends to the factor markets?

19-2 Compare the trends in the following series:

(*a*) the index of average earnings for all employees;
(*b*) the Minimum Lending Rate.

Both should be expressed in real terms and on an annual basis. What inferences can you make, based on these trends, about payments to the factors of production concerned?

19-3 Obtain the annual reports and accounts for a number of publically quoted companies in the UK. From each company's consolidated balance sheet find the total 'capital and reserves'. From the corresponding profit and loss account find the profit for the last financial year. Divide the second figure by the first to give the Rate on Capital Employed (ROCE) and express this as a percentage.

(*a*) For all the companies determine the mean ROCE, and the corresponding standard deviation.
(*b*) Determine the weighted average ROCE using capital as the weight.
(*c*) Comment on the different ROCEs achieved by the various companies.
(*d*) Remembering the sample size, construct a suitable confidence interval around the mean (unweighted) ROCE.
(*e*) Comment on the interpretation of the confidence interval.

REFERENCE

1. Routh, G., *Occupation and Pay in Great Britain, 1906–79*, 2nd edn, Macmillan, London, 1980, p. 208.

20

THE DEMAND FOR FACTORS OF PRODUCTION

20-1 INTRODUCTION: DERIVED DEMAND

This chapter builds directly upon the previous one on the supply of factors of production by looking at the demand for factors. As with all markets, supply and demand interact to produce equilibrium prices (that is, rates of pay, rents and so on) and quantities (that is, levels of employment, stocks of capital equipment and land use). The analysis focuses on the demand of a single firm, on the grounds that the demand of a whole industry for a particular factor of production can be found simply by aggregating the demand curves of the industry's constituent firms.

The fundamental point to note about the demand for factors of production is that employers only use their services as a means to an end, namely, the earning of profits. The demand for a factor is therefore described as a *derived demand*. This demand has the same general characteristics as the demand for consumer goods, that is, it can be shown as a curve with a positive intercept and a negative gradient. This is because, as a factor becomes more expensive to employ, entrepreneurs find it more difficult to make profits by hiring it. They thus tend to curtail their use of it, either by reducing the scale of their operations or by using other factors in its place.

To demonstrate this point requires, of course, a model. Its assumptions are:

1. Firms seek to maximize profits.
2. The following items are constant: the demand for the firm's product; the firm's stocks of other factors; the price of those factors; and technology.

The discussion below takes labour as an example but the principles apply equally to capital and land.

The concept which economists use to analyse the elasticity of demand for a factor is that factor's *marginal revenue product* (MRP). This may be defined as the change in total

Table 20-1 Marginal revenue product of labour

Labour	Weekly production saving (hrs of production)	Marginal physical product (hrs of production)	Sales revenue from extra oil (£)	MRP of labour (£)
9	27	–	5400	–
10	30	3	6000	600
11	32	2	6400	400
12	33	1	6600	200

revenue which is attributable to the employment of another unit of a factor. The importance of a factor's MRP is that it indicates the value to an employer of successive units of the factor, that is, the extra revenue that will be gained by increasing the work-force. Table 20-1 above illustrates the position of a maintenance team looking after an oil refinery and its associated network of pipelines. The team has a certain stock of equipment for detecting faults and repairing them, and this we shall take as fixed. The table shows that extra workers means that faults are located and repaired more rapidly so that less production time is lost and the company can sell more oil. When working normally, the refinery makes 100 tonnes of oil products per hour. (We may assume that each faults are of the same size and that the price of oil is unchanged at £20 per tonne.)

The second column shows labour's marginal physical product—the effect on physical output of increasing the work-force by one worker. It can be seen that additional workers make a declining contribution to the work of the team. This is clearly an instance of diminishing returns discussed in Chapter 15. The fourth column shows the value of the output obtained by teams of different sizes. The fifth column, however, is the most important: it shows the MRP of successive workers. Quite simply, this shows the value of successive workers to the company—it therefore shows the company's demand for maintenance labour. In other words, a factor's MRP curve *is* the firm's demand curve for that factor. The demand curve for a factor naturally has both a gradient and an intercept. We will take these in turn.

20-2 THE ELASTICITY OF DEMAND FOR A FACTOR

As with a consumer good, the gradient of the demand curve for a factor indicates the elasticity of the entrepreneur's demand for it. This will be determined by the forces which set the slope of the MRP function. These are, first, the marginal physical productivity of the factor; second, the elasticity of demand for the firm's product; and third, the factor's share in total costs.

The marginal physical product of successive recruits to the refinery maintenance team is shown in the second column of Table 20-1. The rate at which this falls will depend on the nature of the work process and the other factors being used. For example, if maintenance requires men physically to inspect pipework and repair it with welding guns, then more workers would mean that faults would be repaired more rapidly. On the other hand, the team might use automatic equipment (such a robot which moves along a section of pipe, cleaning it and at the same time lining the inside of the pipe). Under such circumstances, an extra worker would not be able to make much contribution to the team's work. In other words, the MPP curve is determined basically by technological considerations.

In the short run, of course, the technology (and the capital stock in which it is embodied) are, by definition, fixed. There are thus few possibilities for bringing in different factors of production. In the long run, however, decisions could be taken to switch between human welders and robots. Clearly the ease with which the employer can substitute between different factors in the production process is an important influence upon the elasticity of demand for labour. Since the installation of new equipment (like robots) is classed as a long-run decision, it follows that the elasticity of demand for labour must be more elastic in the long run, when an employer can substitute one factor for another, than in the short run, when he is committed to a certain capital stock and thus a certain work process.

The elasticity of demand for a factor is also influenced by the elasticity of demand for the product. In Table 20-1, the price of oil was assumed to be constant, implying that demand for oil was infinitely elastic. To demonstrate the effect of demand elasticity, it will be necessary to change our assumptions and imagine that the refinery is located in a country in which the company has a monopoly of oil products. As a result, it faces a downward-sloping demand curve. For the maintenance team, the implication is that if it helps to refine more oil, the price will tend to fall. This leads to the situation shown in Table 20-2.

The difference between Tables 20-1 and 20-2 lies in the last two columns. Because the price of oil falls as more reaches the market, the sales revenue from the additional pumping is depressed below its former level. The result is that extra men on the maintenance team produce less value for the company: their usefulness is reduced both by diminishing returns in physical terms and by the falling price of the final product. As a result, the demand for labour under these circumstances is rather less elastic than before.

Finally, the elasticity of a firm's demand for a factor is also influenced by the factor's share in the firm's total costs. This can be seen by imagining two identical refinery maintenance teams: the first uses outdated equipment so that labour accounts for 70 per cent of total costs, while the other uses new capital-intensive methods with the result that labour only absorbs 30 per cent of costs. A 50 per cent rise in salaries would clearly affect the two teams differently, raising the cost of the first by 35 per cent and those of the second by only 15 per cent. In both refineries, maintenance operations would be cut back and workers would be laid off. The scale of the reduction would, *ceteris paribus*, be greater for the labour-intensive team than it would for the more capital-intensive one.

Table 20-2 Marginal revenue product of labour

Labour	Weekly production (hrs of production)	Marginal physical product (hrs of production)	Sales revenue from extra oil (£)	MRP of labour (£)
9	27	–	5400	–
10	30	3	5900	500
11	32	2	6250	350
12	33	1	6350	100

20-3 THE POSITION OF THE FACTOR DEMAND CURVE

Like other demand curves, factor demand curves are constructed on the assumption that a number of things are held constant: the demand for the product, the firm's stock of other factors, the price of other factors and technology. Again as with the demand for consumer goods, changes in these items will displace the entire factor demand curve.

Shifts in the demand for the final product will clearly cause the demand for the factors which make it to shift also. For example, the fall in the price of oil in 1985–6 reduced the demand for coal. This in turn led to a fall in the NCB's demand for factors of production: pits were shut and miners were laid off.

The demand for a factor would shift in response to changes in the stocks of other resources which the firm uses. More capital will, *ceteris paribus*, make labour more productive and thus raise a firm's demand for it.

The demand for a factor will also be influenced by the price of other factors. The oil company's demand for maintenance workers would clearly be influenced by the relative costs of labour and robots.

Finally, technical innovations generally allow firms to produce more output with fewer resources. For those factors which remain, productivity will rise. For example, should the maintenance team be provided with new equipment, the data in Table 20-1 would have to be entirely recompiled. Although technical change generally makes labour more productive, it often enhances the productivity of capital to an even greater extent, and thus leads firms to substitute capital for labour. The net effect on the number of workers employed would be determined by the balance between the output and the substitution effects described in Chapter 19.

20-4 EQUILIBRIUM AND ADJUSTMENT IN THE MARKET FOR A FACTOR

The model we have constructed of a factor market resembles those of other markets in that there is a supply curve, a demand curve and an equilibrium price (the factor's reward) and quantity. One characteristic of equilibrium is that employers will be seeking maximum value from their expenditure on factors of production. This gives rise to the rule that maximum profits will be earned when the last (say) £100 spent on one factor yields as much marginal revenue as the last £100 spent on another.

This can be seen by imagining a situation in which £9000 would allow the maintenance team to hire, for a year, either an extra worker or a robot. An extra worker might mean 30 more hours' output saved, while a robot might mean 45. Clearly the robot would be the wiser option: it saves pumping time at a cost of £200 per hour, while a man costs £300 per hour's output saved. However, if the hire of a robot were to rise to £14 000 the balance of advantage would lie with hiring a man. If the hire price were £13 500, the extra productiveness of the robot would be exactly balanced by the extra expense. More generally, the rule is that of equiproportional marginal returns, and states that *the ratio of the marginal revenue productivities of any two factors should, when profits are maximized, be equal to the ratio of their prices.* Algebraically:

$$\frac{MRP_L}{MRP_K} = \frac{P_L}{P_K}$$

The implications of the rule can be illustrated by varying the original assumptions with which we have been working and deducing the implications. Let us return to the maintenance team which, we will assume, is in equilibrium and thus following the rule. Let us also assume that the team employs 10 workers for £9000 per year each. It also rents 4 robots for £13 500 per year. The MPP of the last worker is 30 hours of output saved per week while that of a robot is 45. Now let the price of labour rise by, say, 10 per cent. The rule has now been violated. To restore the rule the team would have to find some way of raising the MPP of labour. Since marginal product generally falls as the labour force rises, this can best be done by reducing the number of people employed. To make good the lost output, it might well hire more electronic robots. In other words, just as consumers will substitute against goods which become relatively more expensive, so will employers substitute against factors which become relatively more expensive.

It may be objected that the model is unrealistic since businessmen may be unaware of the MRPs of their factors. This is, of course, similar to the arguments we have encountered about consumers being unaware of their marginal utilities and firms being unaware of their marginal revenues. The rebuttal is also similar: that the model is simply an extension or implication of the idea that firms maximize their profits. *If* profits are being maximized, *then* $MRP_L/MRP_K = P_L/P_K$. Whether one accepts the rule depends, therefore, on whether one accepts the notion that firms maximize profits. The reader is referred to the discussion of the point in Chapter 17.

20-5 USING THE MODEL TO FORMULATE HYPOTHESES

As with other markets, equilibrium in factor markets will vary in response to shifts in the supply and demand curves. Prices and quantities will, in other words, change when the items in the *ceteris paribus* pound undergo alteration. The foregoing discussion identified these shift items as, on the demand side, the demand for the final product, the stocks of other factors used, the prices of those factors and technology and, on the supply side, tastes (the subjective estimation of the displeasure of working, saving and so on) and changes in the rewards offered by other industries.

On this foundation it ought to be possible to construct and test hypotheses about the causes and consequences of changes in factor prices. They would take the form of supposed relationships between the shift items on the one hand and factor prices and quantities on the other. For example, one of the shift items in the demand curve for any one factor are the prices of other factors. Hypotheses might therefore be constructed around the process of substitution between factors as firms adjust to changes in factor prices.

An item to appreciate in the process of construction of hypotheses is the interconnection between factor markets and product markets. We have noted that a shift in the *demand* for a product will cause a shift in the demand for the factors which make it. Analogous links, moreover, run in the other direction: a shift in the *supply* of a factor will be transmitted to the market for the final product. For example, an outbreak of armed hostilities in oil-producing areas would induce a leftward shift in the supply curve. The costs of all oil-using industries would clearly rise, that is, their supply curves would in turn shift left. As a result, the prices charged for their product would rise and the quantity consumed would fall. Thus it ought to be possible to put forward hypotheses which relate to both factor and product markets simultaneously.

20-6 SUMMARY

The *marginal revenue product* of a factor indicates the value to a firm that is derived from the employment of successive units of the factor. It thus shows how much the firm could, at the limit, pay for that factor—it is the firm's demand curve for it.

The *law of equiproportional returns* states that, in profit-maximizing equilibrium, factor payments should be proportional to their marginal productivities.

EXERCISES

20-1
(a) According to the *Annual Abstract of Statistics*, 1987, female workers employed full-time in the manufacturing sector earn around 61 per cent of the earnings of males employed full-time in manufacturing. Why should this be?
(b) Collect data for a spread of dates over the past 20 years on male and female earnings in manufacturing. Plot the trends in the earnings differential. What patterns are observed? How do you explain this?

20-2 Imagine that a Russian nuclear reactor has caught fire and contaminated sugar beet and sheep over a wide area. Assuming that the Russian government would then attempt to make up the shortfall in domestic output by entering international markets:

(a) trace the effects in as many markets (for products and for factors of production) as you can;
(b) imagining that you are a stockbroker, write a 500-word circular advising clients which assets (including company shares) to buy in order to take advantage of the situation.

20-3 Tables 31 and 37 in the Department of Employment's *New Earnings Survey* give details of earnings of samples of workers, including standard error statistics, broken into manual and non-manual workers. Select a group of workers from each category—manual and non-manual (for example, dustmen and brain surgeons). Using an appropriate hypothesis test determine whether the average earnings of each of your groups is different from the overall average of the manual or non-manual group from which it was taken. Comment upon why you think such earnings differentials exist.

21

LINEAR PROGRAMMING

21-1 INTRODUCTION

Throughout the text so far, considerable emphasis has been placed on the concept of *optimization*. Both firms and individuals will seek to optimize their situation: firms will wish to maximize profits, minimize costs, determine the optimum combination of resources and so on. Similarly, individuals will wish to maximize their income or earnings, gain the maximum satisfaction from using their income and so on. We have already introduced differential calculus as a means of establishing such an optimum point under certain conditions. This chapter introduces a technique which is similarly concerned with optimization—Linear Programming (LP). The technique is largely concerned with resource allocation and it should be apparent that much of economics is also concerned with this task.

As the name suggests, LP is concerned with linear relationships and seeks to establish an optimum solution to a problem, given that, typically, there will be a number of restrictions or constraints to the options available. The technique itself can be applied to a considerable array of economic problems. As we have seen, much of economic and business analysis is concerned with decision-making, where the decisions to be taken relate to finding the best possible use of limited resources. Such decisions bring problems because decision-makers normally have available only a limited amount of most, if not all, resources and must decide on some rational basis how these resources can be utilized most effectively.

In the real world, Linear Programming is carried out via computer-based analysis. The basic ideas underpinning the technique, however, can best be illustrated and understood using a graphical approach. Our example will be centred around a typical production decision.

21-2 FORMULATION OF THE PROBLEM

Let us return to the example used in Chapter 20—that of an oil company. Let us suppose that the company has produced a certain quantity of oil and is now considering refining it. For simplicity we shall assume that the firm faces two alternatives: the oil can be refined either into petrol or into diesel fuel for sale to the motorist through the company's chain of petrol stations. We shall assume that under existing market conditions the current profits for the two products are £20 for each unit of petrol and £25 for each unit of diesel. Let us further assume that the following conditions prevail:

1. There are three factors of production required for the production of either item: land, labour and capital.
2. The supply of these factors is fixed in the short term at: 1200 units of capital; 2400 units of labour; and 250 units of land.
3. Both petrol and diesel production require some combination of all three of the factors: 1 unit of petrol requires 2 units of capital, 6 units of labour and 0.4 units of land; and 1 unit of diesel requires 3 units of capital, 3 units of labour and 0.25 units of land.

The basic question facing the firm is what combination of petrol and diesel it should produce with the given resources of land, labour and capital.

At this stage, even with such a simplified problem, there is no obvious means of determining the decisions that obviously must be taken, in terms of the mix of production. Clearly, before we can attempt to identify a solution to the problem we must identify an objective. Given that this is a problem faced by an individual firm at the micro-economic level we would clearly establish that profit-maximization was the appropriate objective.

21-3 FORMULATING THE OBJECTIVE FUNCTION

Given the prevailing profit figures for the two products the firm's profit will be given as:

$$\text{Profit} = 20P + 25D$$

where P and D represent the number of units of petrol and diesel produced. This expression is known as the *objective function*.

At this stage, it may be tempting to suggest that the firm should specialize in the production of diesel, given that this product contributes more to profit than petrol per unit. However, the objective function that we have identified is only concerned with one part of the problem. We also need to examine the resource requirements of the two outputs as well as their profit contributions. There would be little point in the firm producing a unit of diesel for £25 if we found out later that the same resources could have been used to produce, say, 2 units of petrol for a profit of £40.

21-4 FORMULATING THE CONSTRAINTS

A quick review of the circumstances the firm faces indicates that there are three factors which will restrict the level of production, and hence profit, the firm can achieve, and thus constrain the firm's decisions. These are the available supply of capital, labour and land.

In the same way as we developed a concise mathematical expression for the objective, we can also formulate expressions relating to the three constraints in terms of production of petrol and diesel. Obviously in each case, the constraint the firm faces is that the demand for this resource—generated by producing petrol and diesel—must not exceed the available supply. This is the equivalent of saying, in the case of the capital supply:

$$2P + 3D \leqslant 1200$$

Similarly, in the case of labour and land, respectively:

$$6P + 3D \leqslant 2400$$

$$0.4P + 0.25D \leqslant 250$$

Thus, our problem is to maximize $20P + 25D$ subject to the constraints represented by the three equations above, and remembering that negative values for P and D are not acceptable, implying that we are restricting the analysis to the top right quadrant of the graph.

21-5 GRAPHING THE CONSTRAINTS

To solve the problem we shall develop a graphical method. It is important to realize at this stage that all our constraints—and the objective function—are linear in form. This means that each constraint can be represented by a straight line and, in order to graph these lines, we will require a minimum of two pairs of coordinates.

Our first constraint, relating to the capital supply, $2P + 3D \leqslant 1200$, implies that our limited resource—supply of capital—has two alternative and competing uses. Let us assume, arbitrarily, that we decide to produce zero output of D, and that *all* of our available capital is allocated to petrol production. The number of units of petrol produced, therefore, is obtained by solving $2P = 1200$, giving $P = 600$. Thus our maximum possible production of petrol when all of the available capital is allocated to petrol production is 600 units.

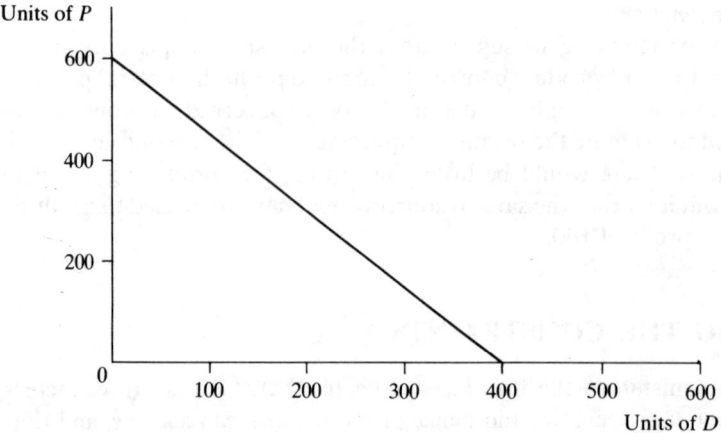

Figure 21-1 Constraint 1

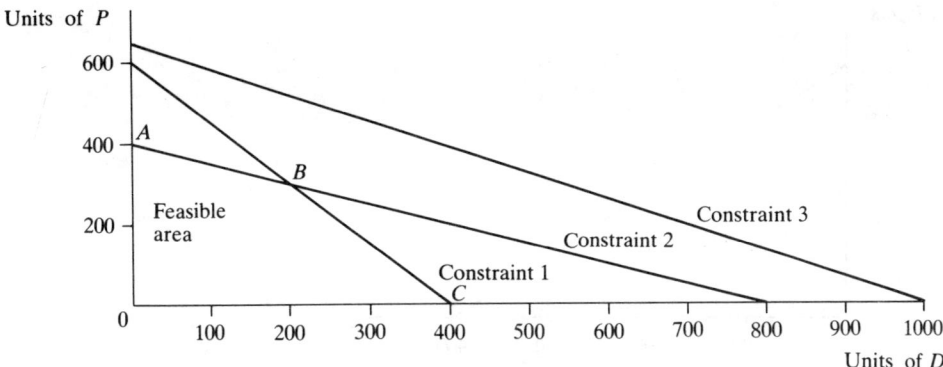

Figure 21-2 The feasible area

Similarly, we can calculate the maximum possible production of D by solving $3D = 1200$, which gives $D = 400$. Accordingly, we have two sets of coordinates for this constraint: (i) $P = 600, D = 0$; and $P = 0, D = 400$. These are all we need to draw the linear constraint, shown in Fig. 21-1.

This line shows the production possibilities and the relationship in terms of competing demand for this particular resource and the tradeoff between production of P and production of D. The graph divides into three distinct areas. The area above the line represents those combinations of the two products that cannot be achieved with the available capital supply. This area represents 'infeasible' combinations. Check this for yourself by calculating the capital requirements of 400 units of petrol and 200 units of diesel. The area below the line represents combinations of the two products which require less than the available capital supply. The line itself represents all combinations of the two products which require exactly the amount of capital available, that is where the demand for the resource is exactly matched by the maximum available supply. The last two areas represent 'feasible' solutions under the existing supply conditions.

The other two constraints can be added to the graph in exactly the same way. The results are shown in Fig. 21-2. The feasible and infeasible areas for each constraint can readily be identified. More importantly, the area which is feasible for all three constraints simultaneously can be identified: this is the area $OABC$. Any combination outside this area may satisfy one or two, but not all three constraints.

21-6 GRAPHING THE OBJECTIVE FUNCTION

Whilst this is an improvement on our original problem we still do not know which of our many feasible combinations of petrol and diesel will achieve our objective—maximization of profit. To resolve this we now need to introduce the objective function into our analysis and onto our graph. Again, the objective function is linear in form, but unlike our constraints, which faced some maximum resource supply, the objective function is not related to a fixed, constant value.

However, let us choose some arbitrary profit figure, say £5000, and calculate the combinations of petrol and diesel which generate this particular profit level. For example, if

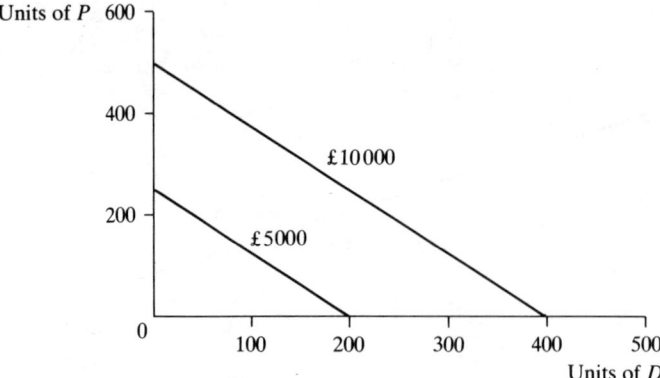

Units of P 600

400

£10 000

200

£5000

0

100   200   300   400   500

Units of D

Figure 21-3 The objective function

D is arbitrarily set to 0 then we must produce 250 units of petrol to attain this profit level, since each unit yields a profit of £20. Similarly, if $P = 0$ then 200 units of diesel will generate the same profit of £5000, since each yields a profit of £25. Figure 21-3 shows the £5000 isoprofit line, that is a line showing equal profit anywhere along its length. Any combination of P and D which occurs on this isoprofit line generates a profit of £5000 and, presumably, the firm will be completely indifferent as to where on a particular profit line it is. Similarly, we could draw the isoprofit line representing £10 000 profit. This is also shown on Fig. 21-3.

Obviously, we could draw any number of such isoprofit lines. The important points to note are, first, that all would be parallel, that is, have the same slope (the slope is given by minus the ratio of the profit from petrol to that from diesel, which obviously stays the same no matter what is produced); second, that the further away the isoprofit line is from the origin the higher the profit represented; and third, that the decision-maker will only be interested in which profit line can be attained, not where on a particular profit line the firm happens to be.

21-7 DETERMINING THE SOLUTION

In terms of the stated objective we are interested in achieving as high a level of profit as possible. Returning to our constraints in Fig. 21-3 it is apparent that some of the isoprofit lines will lie totally outside the feasible area, representing profit levels which are not attainable given our fixed resources. Other isoprofit lines will, however, fall within the feasible area, either in total or in part.

It will be observed that the isoprofit line of £5000 falls entirely within the feasible area. So any combination of P and D which generates a profit of £5000 will be feasible in terms of resources. The isoprofit line for £10 000, which, given our objective, is preferable, only partly falls within the feasible area, so that some production levels of P and D which generate this particular profit are feasible while others are not. We are searching for the highest isoprofit line which also coincides with some part of the feasible area. It is apparent that as our isoprofit line increases—that is, moves upwards and to the right, away from the origin—less and less of the line falls within the feasible area. There will come a point where, in our efforts to reach a higher profit line, we reach Point I on Fig. 21-4. This graph shows both our

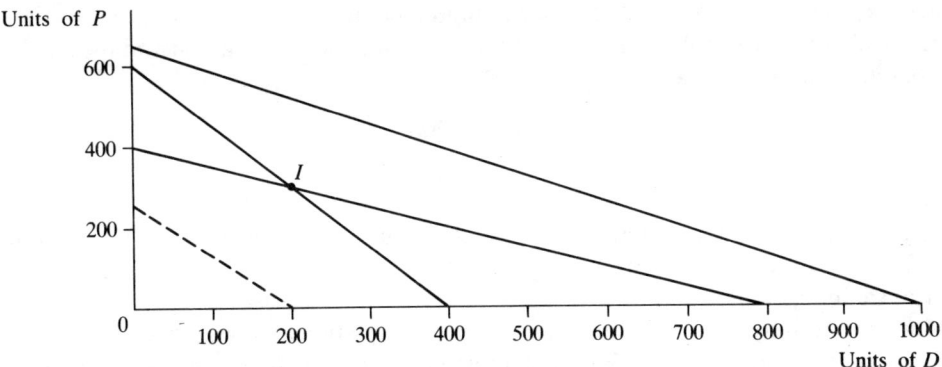

Figure 21-4 The optimum solution

isoprofit line and the feasible area. Although most of the combinations of P and D which generate this particular profit lie outside the feasible area and therefore require more resources than we have available, there remains one point—a single combination of P and D—which occurs on the boundary of our feasible area. From the graph this point can be seen to represent 300 units of petrol and 200 units of diesel, which is our profit-maximizing combination of the two products. Profit using this combination will be 20(300) + 25(200) = £11 000. The next higher isoprofit line, £11 001, is further away from the origin but will be outside the feasible area altogether. Although this profit level is preferable, it represents a combination of production of petrol and diesel that cannot be attained with our current levels of resources. Similarly, other combinations of petrol and diesel which are feasible will generate an isoprofit line lower than our optimum, which obviously would not be consistent with our objective.

21-8 SIMULTANEOUS EQUATIONS SOLUTION

As indicated earlier, one of the problems of using the graphical method of solution is the inaccuracy inherent in a graph. In our problem the solution is (conveniently!) easy to read from the two scales, as the optimum production levels are in terms of whole units. In other situations this is unlikely to be the case, and we may have difficulty reading a precise value from the graph for the two variables in the problem. We can overcome this by verifying the graphical solution using simultaneous equations. This will also have the effect of providing additional information about the solution that may be useful to the decision-maker.

In order to use simultaneous equations we must first distinguish between 'binding' and 'non-binding' constraints. Binding constraints are those which, at the optimum solution, have a directly restrictive effect on the objective function. That is, they prevent the objective function from taking an improved value. In this problem, the two binding constraints will be those relating to the supply of capital and of labour. At the optimum solution the supplies of both these factors are fully utilized. Conversely, land is not fully utilized and the land constraint is non-binding. Land, *ceteris paribus*, is not preventing profit from rising.

Having identified the binding constraints, we can transform the original inequalities into strict equalities, as we know that at our optimum point the two sides of the constraints will be equal (that is, supply will equal demand). Thus, the binding constraints can be expressed in equation form as:

$$2P + 3D = 1200$$

$$6P + 3D = 2400$$

We can now solve for P and D using normal simultaneous equation methods. This confirms the solution previously obtained from the graph and is a useful check on the accuracy of the graphical solution.

More importantly, however, using simultaneous equations allows us to develop an additional part of our analysis. We said previously that binding constraints indicate resources which are fully utilized at the current solution. In other words, binding constraints represent scarce resources. The implication behind such a constraint is that an increase in the supply of one of these resources will lead, *ceteris paribus*, to an increase in production and therefore in profit. Simultaneous equations allow us to quantify these effects precisely.

It is often the case in business and economics that we are trying to assess the effects of changes in resource allocations. We may be considering expanding the work-force, buying additional resources, raising more finance and so on. To illustrate how we can provide information about such decisions let us assume that we can, somehow, acquire one extra unit of capital. We know that this is a binding constraint and therefore is currently fully utilized. The implication, therefore, is that if we acquire an extra unit of this resource it becomes possible to increase production and therefore increase profit.

Our two binding constraints will now be:

$$2P + 3D = 1201$$

$$6P + 3D = 2400$$

Solving gives $P = 299.75$ and $D = 200.5$, and profit £11 007.50, an increase of £7.50. These figures represent marginal changes in our solution, arising from a marginal change in one of our binding resources.

The same marginal analysis can be carried out on the labour constraint:

$$2P + 3D = 1200$$

$$6P + 3D = 2401$$

Solving gives $P = 300.25$, $D = 199.83$, and a profit of £11 000.75.

As well as an optimal solution we now have information on the effect of obtaining more of the two scarce resources. In effect, the two marginal profit changes we have calculated—£7.50 for an additional unit of capital and £0.75 for an additional unit of labour—represent the scarcity value (the opportunity cost) of these resources. Effectively, such opportunity costs measure the value, to the firm, of additional scarce resources.

Obviously, these opportunity costs can also be used to prioritize the acquisition of additional resources. *Ceteris paribus*, additional capital is more valuable than additional labour in terms of increased profit. Equally, such analysis can be used to quantify the effect on profit should there be a reduction in the availability of a particular resource.

21-9 SUMMARY

The *objective function* expresses, in mathematical terms, the objective the decision-maker wishes to attain. The objective function may be expressed in maximization or minimization terms.

A *constraint* is generally an inequality expression which rules out certain combinations of variables. Typically, it represents the availability of some resource.

A *feasible* solution is one which satisfies all the constraints. An *optimum* solution is one which is both feasible and provides the optimum value for the objective function.

The *opportunity cost* (or *scarcity value*) of a constraint is the change in the value of the objective function associated with a change in one constraint.

A *binding* constraint is one which, at the optimum point, has a directly restrictive effect on the value of the objective function. A *non-binding* constraint does not limit the value taken by the objective function at the optimum combination.

EXERCISES

21-1 For the problem detailed in the chapter calculate the opportunity cost for land. Explain your result.

21-2 Assume that the prices of the two products traded change to £30 for petrol and £15 for diesel.

(*a*) Draw the new objective function on the graph and determine the new optimum solution.
(*b*) Confirm the solution using simultaneous equations.
(*c*) Calculate the opportunity costs for the three constraints.

21-3 An investment broker has been asked by a client to invest up to £100 000 in government gilt-edged stock and a variety of shares traded on the Stock Exchange. The gilts are expected to provide a return of 8 per cent. For the shares the return is less certain but has been assessed as follows:

Return (%)	10	12	14
Probability	0.25	0.5	0.25

Gilts currently trade at £100 each whilst the shares the broker is thinking of buying currently trade for £50 on average. The client has stipulated certain conditions to the investment to be made: total investment can be anything up to £100 000; investment in gilts is to be at least £25 000 but no more than £50 000; and investment in shares must be at least £50 000.

(*a*) Determine the number of gilts and the number of shares to be purchased if the client wishes to maximize return on the investment.
(*b*) What return on the amount invested will be earned over a year?
(*c*) What will happen if the price of shares rises, while that of gilts stays the same?
(*d*) What will happen if the return on gilts falls, while that on shares stays the same?

21-4 The students' union cafeteria has recently started offering a vegetarian alternative to the hamburger. The vegetarian burgers—Big Mik—come in two sizes: standard and enormous. Both are made from two basic ingredients—soybean mix and a vegetable/seasoning mix. The difference in the two burgers is their size and the relative quantities of the two ingredients. A standard burger requires 100 grams of soybean mix and 50 grams of the vegetable/seasoning mix. An enormous burger requires 150 grams of soybean mix and 30 grams of vegetable/seasoning mix.

Currently, the burgers sell for £1.00 for the standard and £1.30 for the enormous and cost, respectively £0.50 and £0.60 to produce, cook and sell. The cafeteria manager is trying to determine the optimum quantity of the two burgers to produce on a daily basis. Additional information is as follows:

(*i*) a total of 10 kilos of soybean mix is available daily;
(*ii*) a total of 4 kilos of vegetable/seasoning mix is available daily;

(*iii*) a total of 100 bread buns have been ordered each day;

(*iv*) the manager knows from past experience that at least 50 standard and 10 enormous burgers will be sold each day.

(*a*) Determine the quantity of the two products to be produced if the manager wishes to minimize costs.

(*b*) Determine the quantity if the manager wishes to maximize profit.

(*c*) In both cases identify the binding constraints and comment upon their interpretation in the context of the problem.

(*d*) In both cases determine the cost, profit, quantities of soybean mix, vegetable/seasoning mix and bread buns required.

22

ECONOMIC WELFARE AND ECONOMIC SYSTEMS

22-1 INTRODUCTION

This chapter, in a sense, takes stock of the theoretical work we have accomplished to date by taking an overall view of the mechanisms of resource allocation. It also examines the efficiency of these mechanisms by using the branch of economics known as *welfare economics*. This chapter, therefore, shows the ways in which the market system can, theoretically, contribute to the attainment of human objectives, before moving on to look at the degree to which the British economy and other economic systems conform to that theoretical ideal.

22-2 EVALUATION AND EXPLANATION IN ECONOMICS

Economic theory has frequently been used as the basis for promoting economic policies of one sort or another. Adam Smith's *Wealth of Nations* was at once an exposition of economic principles and a plea for a policy of free trade, while Keynes's *General Theory of Interest, Money and Employment* acted both as an analysis of macro-economics and as an argument in favour of spending public money to reduce unemployment. Today, political parties and pressure groups all maintain economic research departments whose role is to ensure that the organization's policies have a plausible foundation in economic theory. Whether this use of economics as a justification for policies can be avoided is a moot point which goes back to the distinction made in Chapter 1 between *positive* (testable) and *normative* (preference-indicating) statements. The position has been forcibly put by, amongst others, Professor Richard Lipsey that economists should concern themselves primarily with the former. Naturally, the present writers would support warmly a close relationship between economic theories and economic data, that is, we approve of a commitment to the testing and falsifying of hypotheses. Such an approach accords a central place to empirical evidence in debates over policy. Nevertheless, it must be recognized that personal judgement has an irreducible role to play in such debates.

The reason for the use of economic theory in such an evaluative way may stem not so much from the political commitments of (some) economists as from the nature of the subject. It does, after all, purport to be a means of understanding the process of producing and distributing goods and services and it is difficult to classify and describe things without evaluating them at the same time. It would be surprising if *economic* descriptions did not suggest that certain ways of arranging economic affairs were 'better' (in some sense) than others. Indeed, deep within the heart of economic theory can be found a concept which is used to do precisely this—to pass judgement on the usefulness of different economic institutions and policies. This concept is the 'optimum allocation of resources', and it acts as an abstract ideal ('optimum' means 'best') against which any actual state of affairs can be judged. Those which conform closely to the optimum can be commended and those which fall short can be criticized.

22-3 SIX ECONOMIC QUESTIONS

To explain the origin of the concept of the optimum, it may be helpful to consider the things which economics claims to explain. These are grouped under six headings as follows:

1. The composition of economic output, that is, the relative levels of output of the various industries in the economy.
2. The allocation of resources among those industries.
3. The techniques of production, capital-intensive or labour-intensive, which are in use.
4. The distribution of income.
5. The economy's capacity to adjust to change.
6. The level of utilization of society's resources.

The sixth item cannot be explained in terms of the analysis that we have undertaken so far, since it relates to macro-economics, and must therefore be left aside for the present. In every other instance, however, readers should be able to offer an explanation for the situation which should show how the decisions of producers and owners of factors of production reflected the opportunities and constraints or costs which they faced. For example, an explanation for the fact that production processes in the United Kingdom are more capital-intensive than those in India would centre on the point that in the United Kingdom capital is relatively abundant while labour is expensive, whereas in India the reverse is generally the case.

These explanations ultimately come to a stopping point or, more, precisely, to two stopping points, for there are two factors which economists do not attempt to explain but accept as given: the endowment of natural resources and the tastes or preferences of consumers. Lying at the beginning and end of the production process, respectively, these two items are accepted as the limits within which the explanations of economics operate. Explanations in economics, therefore, usually relate patterns of production and so on by saying that things are the way they are because consumer preferences and/or resource endowment force so dictate.

In most discussions, resource endowments are usually given secondary emphasis because, as a gift of nature, they are beyond human control. Primary emphasis falls upon the preferences of consumers and resource-owners. Economists perceive all six issues above (arguably, the last might be excepted) as being governed by consumer preferences. Questions of production and allocation are all, in the final analysis, seen as being decided by the consumer. This idea has been dubbed *consumer sovereignty*. Taking resource-endowments and technology as given and provided that markets are competitive and that consumers are well-informed, consumer choice will dictate the pattern of production, the allocation of resources, the supply of factors of production and the rewards of those factors. Consumer choice, in short, will provide the basic explanation for the first five items above as long as the economy is characterized by competition.

Since there is not one consumer but many millions, it might be more accurate to speak of *consumers' sovereignty*. Nevertheless, every consumer plays a part in deciding the general shape of the economy. With every single purchase, each buyer issues an instruction to producers about the way resources should be allocated and about the kinds of pro-ductive activity that should be undertaken, and these instructions are transmitted back to the owners of factors of production. Every consumer thus participates in the process of allocating resources in proportion to the purchases that he or she makes. It is as if economic issues were decided by ballot, except that consumers have different numbers of votes to cast, depending on how large their incomes are.

22-4 THE OPTIMUM ALLOCATION OF RESOURCES

To the extent that competitive conditions obtain, then consumer preferences must govern the allocation of resources. This leads to the concept of the *optimum allocation of resources*, which may be defined as the deployment of the resources of the economy in such a manner as to satisfy consumer preferences as far as possible, given factor endowments and the state of technology.

Three features of this concept merit attention. The first is that this position of maximum satisfaction for consumers comes about not through charity or cooperation but greed—businessmen are assumed to be motivated not by public duty but by the desire to make as much money for themselves as they can. Indeed, one of the more remarkable results of economic theory is precisely this demonstration that the pursuit of private gain can, provided there is competition, lead to the attainment of the public good.

Second, economists do not, at least, not in their professional capacities, question the wisdom of the choices that consumers make. The conventional stance of economists is that people are to be trusted to buy the things which they like best, given their incomes and the price information which is available. The question of criticizing people's choices simply does not arise.

Third, economists can question the extent to which the principle of consumer sovereignty governs the economy. They can, that is, ascertain the degree to which the conditions necessary for consumers to be sovereign hold in the real world. This work amounts, in fact, to comparing the actual allocation of resources with its theoretical optimum.

Austrian economists dispute the importance of the idea of a static optimum allocation of resources. They believe that no optimum can ever be reached because producers never have sufficient information about consumers' tastes and technological developments. They are, in the Austrian view, constantly engaged in a process of discovering these things. No sooner are they discovered, of course, than they alter and the process must begin anew. For Austrians, the key issue is whether the economy is able to *adjust* to changes in technology and tastes, that is, whether it is flexible. The strength of the market system in Austrian eyes is that, by offering profits to the successful, it encourages entrepreneurs to adjust constantly to new possibilities.

22-5 THE ORGANIZATION OF THE BRITISH ECONOMY

The key feature of the economic organization of the United Kingdom is the fact that decisions are made on a *decentralized* basis. That is to say, decisions about the ways in which money is spent and resources are used are made by millions of individuals acting on their own account. To illustrate, there are nearly 100 000 companies whose shares are quoted on the Stock Exchange, while according to the VAT statistics, there were no fewer than 1.47 million independent businesses in the United Kingdom in 1986. It is clear that economic events in such an economy can conform to no central plan.

Economists would emphasize the role of *prices* in coordinating these decisions. Prices are at once a data base to which every business person and consumer has free access and the signals to which all economic agents respond. By responding to price signals, economic agents bring supply and demand into equilibrium in product markets and factor markets alike, and encourage the shifting of resources from oversupplied markets to those facing shortage.

The above analysis is framed in terms of privately owned businesses which seek to make profit. It must, however, be recognized that business—the work of supplying society with the goods and services it needs—includes many other kinds of organization such as the training and education services, the police, the armed forces, and so on, which are financed largely by taxation. The resources deployed by these public sector organizations are not trivial: the public sector's share of total spending in the United Kingdom stands at about 45 per cent, a figure which is fairly typical of Western economies. Chapter 23 will examine the case for the state provision of goods and services. For the purposes of this chapter, the important point to note is that these organizations do not seek to make profit and therefore do not respond directly to price signals. In general, moreover, decision-making in the public services tends to be rather more centralized than in the private sector.

Half-way between privately owned businesses and public services is found a third form of organization: state-owned companies or nationalized corporations. Nationalization is popularly associated with the Labour Party's periods in government. For example, between 1945 and 1951 the Labour government took into public ownership the steel, rail, gas and road transport industries. The Conservatives, however, have also been known to establish public enterprises such as the electricity industry or the telephone service.

The degree to which nationalized concerns can contribute to the attainment of an optimum allocation of resources has long troubled both economists and government ministers. On the one hand, they could be instructed to mimic the behaviour of private sector firms and maximize profits. The problem here is that some state firms (such as the Post Office) are monopolies, who could make profits simply by overcharging their customers rather than by being efficient. The advice from (neo-classical) economic theory, of course, is that the industries ought to act as if they were under conditions of perfect competition and thus to set prices which equal their marginal costs.

In practical terms, government policy has often been dominated by the fact that many nationalized industries (like the railways) have made persistent losses rather than profits. The only questions for ministers to decide were how much subsidy the industries should get from the taxpayer and how much capacity they should close. To escape from this seemingly sterile situation, the Conservative government of Mrs Thatcher adopted a new approach, privatization, which was discussed in Chapter 18.

22-6 CONSUMERS' SOVEREIGNTY IN THE MODERN WESTERN ECONOMY

In assessing the degree to which the principle of consumers' sovereignty is observed in a modern Western economy like the British, the first point to make is that it applies with virtually unobstructed force to large areas of economic activity. Clothes, food, entertainment, cars, holidays—decisions about all these and much more besides are completely at the discretion of the consumer. So, too, are choices concerning jobs, the deployment of investment funds and the use of industrial equipment. Even if jobs are difficult to find in particular regions, economists would stress that there are no *legal* restrains preventing people seeking work in other parts of the country.

There are, however, several ways in which economic behaviour might not conform to the principle of consumers' sovereignty, the four principal ones being legal restrictions, information distortions (including price information), public goods and the distribution of income and wealth. These will be described in turn.

First, the most noticeable departures from consumer sovereignty are the prohibitions on trade in certain goods and services. It is, for example, illegal to traffic in hard drugs or to sell cigarettes to children. Equally prominent are the goods and services which people are forced to consume by law such as car insurance (for all motorists) and education (for all children under 16). While these regulations can clearly be justified in fairly straightforward terms, they are nevertheless limitations on the private consumer's choice.

Second, economists would identify misleading information as a factor which would hinder the operation of the principle of consumers' sovereignty. Prices, according to economists, play a key role in the transmission of economic information because they tell consumers the relative costs of producing the goods and services which are on offer. It is on the basis of this information and their own preferences that consumers decide what to demand for producers. For these demands to reflect costs, it is essential that prices give a true impression of those costs. Our analysis of competitive markets in Chapter 18 showed that, in equilibrium, price would equal marginal cost and consumers would therefore be given correct information. Monopoly prices, on the other hand, as shown in Chapter 17, overstate costs and thus deter consumers from buying the product. Similarly, goods which bear a selective tax like alcoholic drinks sell at prices which overstate costs and will therefore be 'underconsumed'.

At the same time, other prices *understate* the costs of supplying a good or service. As we shall see in Chapter 23, industries which cause pollution underprice their products in terms of the real resources consumed in the production process. Similarly, the true cost of buying a house is obscured by the tax relief which is given on mortgage interest payments. In these cases, people may be tempted to consume rather more than they would if they were aware of (and had to pay for) all the resources involved.

Some economists like Professor J. K. Galbraith and Ralph Nader have gone further and argued that consumer sovereignty can, and has been, subverted by misleading information from advertising about the nature of products on sale. Consumers, the argument runs, are often given information about products that ranges from the partial to the downright inaccurate.

A third factor of note in this context is the fact that the principle of consumer sovereignty does not take account of the demand for *public goods*. An economy run strictly in accordance with the principles of consumer sovereignty would not have street lighting, for instance. Such a position might not strike the observer as being optimum. Again, these matters are analysed in Chapter 23.

A fourth factor which modifies, rather than undermines, the power of the principle of consumers' sovereignty relates to the distribution of income and wealth. The productive power of the economy will naturally be directed toward meeting only those demands which are backed by money rather than those which are not. Clearly, rich consumers, who have more spending power than poorer consumers, will be able to command more resources. To paraphrase George Orwell's *Animal Farm*, all consumers are sovereign, but some are more sovereign than others.

22-7 ALTERNATIVES TO THE MARKET SYSTEM

Although all economies face the same issues as the British—the six items listed in Section 22-3 above—there is no reason why they should operate on the same principles. The best-known alternative to the decentralized decision-making of the market or capitalist system is the *planned economy*. A prime example was the Soviet Union during the Stalin era. Factories were controlled not by local management but by central government ministries, which issued instructions about what to produce, what prices to charge, the inputs to use and so on. Outputs from industries making capital goods were allocated to user industries by administrative instruction. Naturally, there were markets for items such as privately grown farm produce and repair work, but the bulk of the economy followed the targets set for the whole economy in the Five-Year Plans, which were produced by Gosplan, the central planning agency.

The main problem which Western commentators noted with the planned economy was the lack of incentives. There was no requirement for goods to meet consumer preferences or for resources to be used efficiently: a hundred old-fashioned and unreliable tractors, for example, would meet the output quota just as well as a hundred of a new design. There was, moreover, no stimulus at local level to adopt new ideas since responsibility rested firmly with the centre. This produced one of the signal features of the Soviet economy: its persistent failure to match the West in terms of technological innovation and productivity. Partly as a result, the current Soviet leadership have instituted reforms designed to decentralize the Russian economic system and provide more incentives.

All economic systems face the same problems, even though they may face them on different scales. All have to allocate resources to competing ends, all need some way of distributing incomes and all need some procedures for responding to altered circumstances. All, in other words, are obliged to find answers to the six questions posed in Section 22-3. Economies differ in the way in which the questions are answered. The role of economists is to try to explain the consequences of different approaches to those questions. As this chapter has shown, economists' central criterion for judging the effectiveness of an economic system is the degree to which it provides goods and services which match—as far as costs will allow—the preferences of consumers.

22-8 SUMMARY

Common issues face all economies in that all must arrive at some structure of output, allocate resources between industries, decide on the appropriate technology for production, distribute income and adjust to change.

Consumer sovereignty obtains when consumers are able to dictate the allocation of resources in the economy within the constraints of resource endowments and technology. Obstacles to this include monopolies, misleading advertising and the regulations issued by governments.

The *optimum allocation of resources* is consistent with the pattern of output which most closely conforms to the preferences of consumers (although account must also be taken of demands for public goods, merit goods and the abatement of pollution).

A *decentralized economy* follows no plan, being under the control of independent producers and consumers.

EXERCISES

22-1 To what extent do you agree with the restriction of consumer choice over the following:

(a) full-time education for 16-year-olds?
(b) house-building in the Green Belt?
(c) the compulsory wearing of seat belts by motorists?

Outline the economic case for and against the above.

22-2 Comment critically on the following: 'As long as markets are competitive, the price mechanism will ensure that resources are allocated so as to produce the goods consumers prefer.'

22-3 A private member's Bill which would prohibit the advertising of sweets, crisps and alcoholic drink is before Parliament. You work for a public relations consultant, and you have been asked to draw up an information sheet for circulation to MPs setting out the case of the industries concerned.

Repeat the exercise, imagining that you have been requested to circulate the argument of the Healthy Living Group which supports the Bill.

22-4

(a) Using UK national accounts (tables of national product by category of expenditure) collect data on consumer spending, government consumption, gross domestic fixed capital formation (investment), imports and exports for the latest year, five years ago and ten years ago. Comment on the changes.

(b) From tables in UK national accounts on value added by industry, collect data on the output trends of three different industries over a similar period. Again, explain the changes.

You may find it useful to perform this analysis using a suitable spreadsheet program.

THE ROLE OF GOVERNMENT IN THE ECONOMY

23-1 INTRODUCTION

Chapter 22 set out the argument that markets, if competitive, can produce the goods that people want at their lowest cost and could thus lead the economy to an optimum position. Yet the unavoidable fact is that governments intervene in the economy in innumerable ways: by levying taxation, running large-scale public services, restricting the location of businesses and the kinds of advertising that is permitted and so on. Because it has both a private and a public sector, the United Kingdom is thus said to have a 'mixed economy'. For economists, the question that arises is whether or not this intervention can be reconciled with economic theory. In other words, given that markets promote economic efficiency, what is the economic rationale for this large-scale reshaping of the economic system by legal and political measures?

23-2 MARKET FAILURE

The principal justification for public intervention in economic affairs is the idea that, under certain circumstances, the market mechanism would not generate the optimum level of output of various goods and services. There are three main cases of this: first, there may be barriers to entry into a market or collusion between existing producers; second, the market for the good in question may not exist; and third, there may be external costs or benefits. These three causes of 'market failure' operate in different ways according to circumstances and the responses of governments will naturally depend upon their political views. Past policies towards entry barriers were outlined in Chapter 17. The non-existence of markets for some goods and external costs or benefits form the subject of this chapter. Typically they oblige governments to intervene in the economic system so as to increase or to restrict the output of different goods and services. Policies in these areas may be grouped under the headings of public goods, merit goods and externalities, and this chapter describes them in turn. These policies also have a substantial impact upon the distribution of income and this is discussed in the final section.

23-3 PUBLIC GOODS

Economists often divide goods into two categories: public goods and private goods. The difference between them relates to the effect on resource use of supplying an extra consumer. In the case of a private good like bread, providing an extra consumer with a loaf will require extra supplies of flour, energy and so on. In the case of public goods, by contrast, an additional consumer can be supplied without any more resources being deployed. For example, a motorway may accommodate 1000 cars per hour. Provided that the design capacity exceeds that figure, the arrival of a 1001st car will not necessitate the provision of any more road space. Thus providing the motorway for even one car costs as much as providing it for all motorists. Similar considerations apply to street lights, mass immunization campaigns, law and order, and defence. In economic terminology, the marginal user of these goods imposes a zero cost.

A typical feature of public goods is that people cannot be excluded from using them and thus they cannot be forced to pay for their use. There is no means, for example, of preventing some people from using street lighting. In technical terms, public goods are often *non-excludable*. This feature clearly prevents private firms from meeting the needs for these goods and services and thus obliges the government to ensure their production. (There are, it may be noted, services which possess some of the features of public goods but which are *excludable*, like some sports facilities. These obviously can be provided by the private sector through clubs, for example.)

A major problem with public goods is that, since they have no market prices, the demand for them is difficult to measure. Although it is plausible to argue that there is a need for, say, lighthouses and police forces, it is not easy to establish the value that ought to be placed upon them. In consequence, it is never easy to decide whether the provision of these goods should be increased, because it is not clear whether the benefits of an extra (say) lighthouse will exceed its costs.

Economists' attempts to solve these problems come under the heading of *cost–benefit analysis*. The broad approach has been to try and determine values for goods and services which do not normally have them. For example, attempts have been made to assess the value of peace and quiet by looking at variations in house prices in different localities. Success in finding satisfactory measures for the value of such 'intangibles' has been mixed, and much work remains to be done. It is rather more common to undertake *cost–effectiveness studies* which balance monetary costs (which are usually known) not against monetary benefits but against physical measures of the effects of public expenditure. For example, although the value of an extra lighthouse may not be quantifiable, it is possible to compare the costs of two lighthouses with the number of ships which each might serve. The resultant cost per ship ratios could then be compared. In practice, of course, economists are but one source of professional advice among several that politicians call upon during the process of making decisions over the provision of public goods. In terms of the stance adopted in this book, the problem of quantifying the demand for public goods is that it is difficult to generate falsifiable predictions on the subject.

23-4 MERIT GOODS

These goods (and services) are a hybrid species lying between public and private goods. Merit goods resemble private goods in that extra consumers can only be supplied by using more resources. The distinguishing feature of merit goods, however, is that the benefits which they generate are not confined to the direct consumer but are shared by others as well. An example is education, which benefits both the consumer (the pupil or student, who is enabled to obtain a better job) and society at large, in that a well-educated work-force is more likely to contribute to prosperity, rising productivity and general living standards. The benefits which merit goods provide for those who are not direct consumers are described in economic terminology as *positive externalities*, and the system whereby these merit goods (or more often, services) are provided free is referred to as the 'welfare state'.

Figure 23-1 illustrates the way in which the market will fail to provide the optimum output of such a good. *CC* is the supply curve for the good and *ABJ* is the demand for direct consumers. Left to themselves, consumers would therefore buy *ON* units of the good or

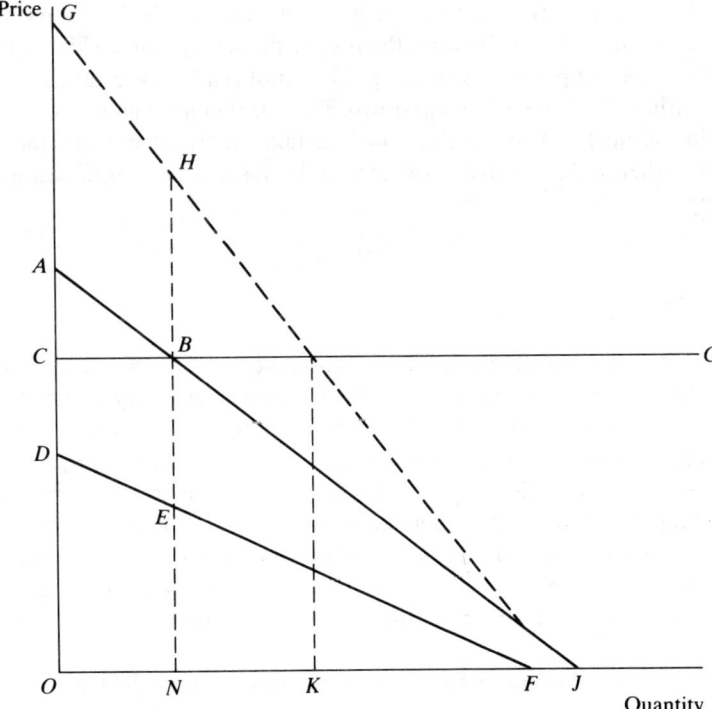

Figure 23-1 A merit good

service at a price OC. The demand curve ABJ, however, ignores the external benefits which the good generates for society at large. These are shown by the curve DEF. Clearly the total benefit of the consumption of a unit of the good or service is the benefit to the direct consumer plus the benefit to everyone else, that is, the sum of the two demand curves ABJ and DEF. This is found by adding the two curves in a vertical manner. For example, the value of the Nth item is the value to the direct consumer ($NB = C$) plus the benefit to everyone else (NE). The benefit to society thus amounts to $NE + NB$, that is, NH. Thus the curve which represents society's demand for the good is GHJ.

This suggests that the optimum scale of consumption should be no ON but OK. In short, the market would undersupply merit goods by some margin. To raise consumption of these goods towards their social optimum, governments have several policies at their disposal. First, they can subsidize the good so that its price is below cost. This should induce direct consumers to move down their demand curves. Should the service be made free—as with most aspects of the National Health Service—consumers will pitch their consumption at point J. Alternatively, governments can force people by law to consume a certain quantity of the good. For example, drivers of cars which are over three years old are bound to submit their vehicles to annual MOT tests (the roadworthiness of a vehicle being, quite obviously, a matter of importance to other motorists as well as to the owner). In the case of education, of course, the state pursues both of the above policies simultaneously, by providing a service free and by insisting that all children under 16 attend school. It should be plain that merit goods can be supplied either by the public sector or by private firms operating on a commercial basis.

The problem with the preceding analysis is the same as that which attends the theory of public goods: it is difficult to quantify. This is because the precise monetary value which one person derives from another's consumption of a merit good cannot readily be established. In terms of Fig. 23-1, the location of curve DEF is unknown. There is therefore no proof that government intervention in the health or education markets takes these services to their optimum—they may still be either under- or overprovided. In the absence of quantification, there is no way of knowing.

23-5 EXTERNAL COSTS

The third instance of market failure relates to external costs (first mentioned in Chapter 14). External costs are to be distinguished from internal costs which are the ordinary payments that an organization has to make in order to acquire the resources it uses. External costs, by contrast, arise when a producer uses resources for which no payment is made. The principal instance of external costs is of course pollution, such as the gaseous wastes which result from the burning of coal and petrol. These are widely believed to produce acid deposition (or 'acid rain') which has caused the death of large areas of forest across northern Europe and eastern Canada. In effect, fuel, equipment, vehicles and human labour are not the only inputs required by electricity production and by motoring. These activities also use the forests.

From an economic point of view, pollution gives rise to the problem that the true costs of a product or service will be understated for the simple reason that some of the resources used have not—like the forests—been paid for. As a result, the goods in question are overproduced. To see this, let us use the example of the oil industry as a whole. Figure 23-2 shows the demand curve, *DD*, which indicates the value which consumers place on the product. The industry's internal costs, upon which decisions are based, underlie the supply curve *CC*. Let us now assume that the industry causes pollution by, for example, spilling oil from leaking tanks. This imposes costs upon other members of society such as hoteliers operating near the beaches which are contaminated with oil. The existence of these external costs means that the costs to society of producing oil exceed the internal costs by some margin. The *social cost* of the good—that is, both internal and external costs taken together—is indicated by the line *SS*. If left to itself, the oil industry would set output at *OF*, with the sales revenue covering the costs of production. The problem, of course, is that the cost of the last unit is not *FE* but rather *FG*. Indeed, when external costs are included, it can be seen that the optimum scale of production—that is, the level at which the value to consumers of the last unit is equal to the total costs of its production—is to be found at point *Z*. In other words, society would be better served by a more restricted output, *OB*, and by a higher price, *OH*, which would more truly reflect the costs of production.

A corollary of this argument is the concept that there can be an optimum level of pollution just as there can be an optimum level of output for any individual good or service. In Fig. 23-2, attaining the optimum level of output of the good does not imply ceasing production altogether for the sake of eliminating pollution, but rather curtailing it and suffering a more limited level of pollution. In that example, moreover, it was implicitly assumed that pollution was inevitable. Often this is not the case—it can be abated by the installation of special equipment like booms to contain oil slicks. Naturally these involve extra costs to producers. Under these circumstances, it may be possible to separate the question of the optimum level of output of the polluting industry from that of the amount of money which ought to be spent on environmental protection.

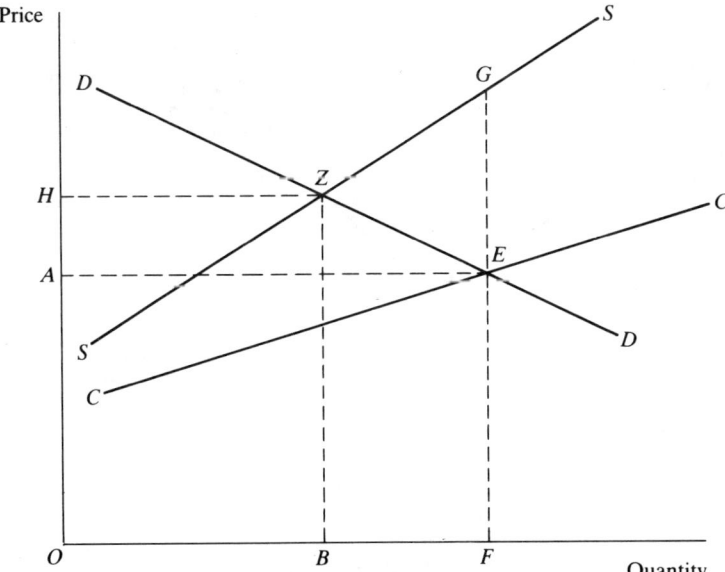

Figure 23-2 Pollution

This question can be analysed by creating a model of the supply and demand for a clean and stable environment, as illustrated in Fig. 23-3. Environmental quality is plotted along the horizontal axis, since this corresponds to a greater output of 'cleaned-up environment'. The graph shows a rising cost of abatement on the assumption that filters and so on will be easier to fit to some sources of effluent than to others. The curve indicating the value of improvements slopes downward to the right showing that consumers place a diminishing importance on successive increments of effluent reduction, as they do with any other good. The intersection of the two curves (point *A*) indicates an optimum level of abatement (*OB*) in so far as abatement beyond that point would involve more expense than was repaid in terms of the value of the improved environment. *OC* indicates the optimum expenditure per unit of environmental improvement. The proposition that pollution should only be reduced to the extent that costs allow, rather than being eliminated altogether at prohibitive expense, is the central conclusion of neo-classical economics on the matter.

The above model may be used to predict the likely consequences of a rise in the general level of pollution. This would make a clean environment more scarce and thus more valuable, and in this context any improvement would yield greater benefits. The demand curve for abatement would therefore shift upwards, resulting in a rightward shift in the optimum level of abatement. This seems to have been the pattern of events over recent decades, in which the rapid but destructive industrial growth of the 1950s and 1960s produced a new awareness of environmental problems in the 1980s.

At the same time it may be noted that the difficulty with this analysis relates, as before, to quantification. Some aspects of the environment are relatively easy to value in money terms, like fishing stocks, commercial forests or agricultural land. By contrast, the recreational, aesthetic and cultural value of landscape have proved to be very difficult to value. Although the general model can be used in broad terms to justify government action

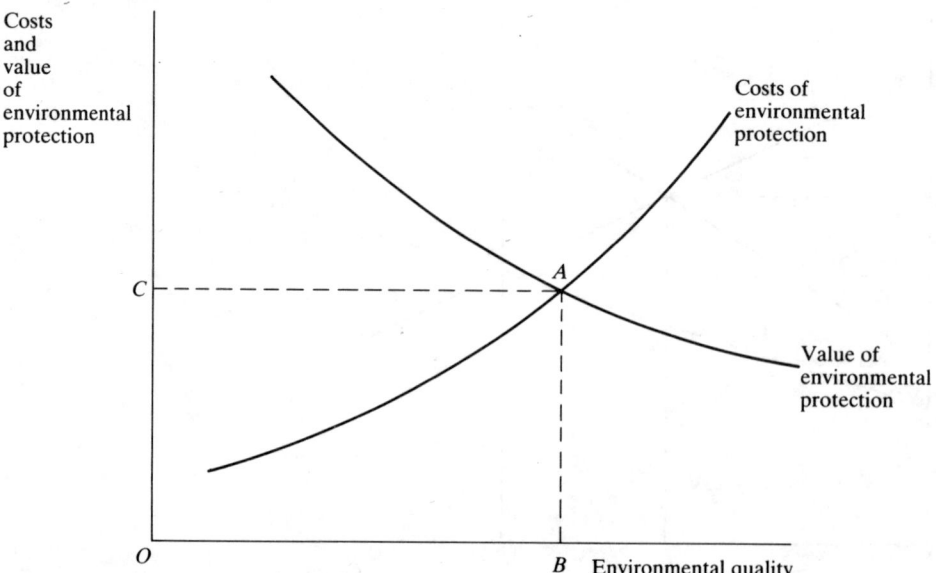

Figure 23-3 The optimum level of environmental protection

to restrict pollution and to promote abatement, it has yet to be used to indicate in precise terms how much pollution should be tolerated and how much should be spent on abatement. In practice, government policy is to limit or even prohibit the disposal of some (but not all) waste products in response to scientific advice and public pressure. There is, of course, no guarantee that these permitted levels bear much relation to the economic notion of the 'optimum'.

A prime cause of the uncertainty over the precise economically optimum level of pollution and abatement is the fact that, unlike other resource inputs, there is often no clear ownership of the resources in question. The result is that the resource can be consistently overexploited by users, while at the same time no one accepts the responsibility (and the associated costs) for its maintenance. Thus the fresh air of northern Europe is not owned by anyone and all are free to use it as a dump for waste products. This state of affairs has been termed 'the tragedy of the commons'. The answer, according to some, is to establish property rights so that resources may be safeguarded and that those who wish to use them can be made to pay, just as, in times past, the common lands of England and the prairies of America were saved from overgrazing by being enclosed. In more recent years, of course, nations have begun to establish rights over large areas of the seabed so as to control both minerals and fisheries.

23-6 EQUITY

The term *equity* relates to the distribution of income or, more accurately, to the fairness of that distribution. Left to itself, the market generates a pattern of income distribution which is notably unequal (readers are referred back to Fig. 19-1). It has long been accepted that inequalities such as these should be reduced, and incomes are accordingly an area in which the effects of government action are extensive: social security payments are the main source of income for perhaps a quarter of all households in the country, while the vast majority of households pay direct taxes such as income tax. (Direct taxes fall upon income or wealth, whereas indirect taxes like VAT fall upon goods and services.) The intended effect of this intervention is to render incomes less unequal, with very high incomes being reduced by taxation and with very poor households having their incomes boosted.

Redistributive policies have three separable elements. First, the free public provision of merit goods (or rather, merit services) like education or health care is clearly of greater benefit to the poor than to the rich, who would be able to pay for any services they required anyway. (At the same time, it must be recognized that certain subsidized services like higher education are used more heavily by the better-off than by the poor.)

Second, the state makes direct financial payments to social security claimants. Here a distinction is to be made between 'universal' and 'means-tested' benefits. With the former, payments do not depend upon the financial position of the recipient. Child allowances, for instance, are paid to all parents with children whether they be millionaires or paupers. By contrast, means-tested benefits, like rate rebates and income support, are only given to people whose incomes fall below certain limits. Plainly the redistributive effects of means-tested benefits are more pronounced than those of universal ones.

The third aspect of redistribution policy is the tax system. Taxation may be categorized as being regressive, proportional or progressive, depending on its relationship with income.

**Table 23-1 Rates of income tax,
1987–8**

Income Band (£)	Tax rate (%)
0–2 425	0
2 426–17 900	27
17 901–23 400	40
23 401–25 400	45
25 401–33 300	50
33 301–41 230	55
41 231 and above	60

Source: Economic Trends.

A regressive tax is one which accounts for a greater share of the incomes of poorer people than of the incomes of the rich. Thus a tax which fell equally on everyone regardless of income (a 'poll tax') would be regressive in that the given sum would represent a greater relative burden for the less well-off. A proportional tax is one which takes a constant proportion of all incomes, higher or low. A progressive tax is one which absorbs a greater proportion of higher incomes than it does of lower ones. For the tax system as a whole to contribute to the equalization of incomes, it is clear that progressive taxes must feature more prominently than others.

The principle progressive tax in the United Kingdom is income tax, which taxes different bands of income at different rates. These bands and their associated tax rates are redefined annually in the Budget, but in 1987–8 they stood as in Table 23-1. The fact that the first £2425 (the 'personal allowance') that a person receives bears no tax allows those on very low incomes to escape income tax altogether. The next £15 474, that is, income from £2426 to £17 900, is assessed at the 'basic rate' of 27 per cent. This is the tax rate which is of interest to most people, since most taxable incomes fall within this range.

Two other progressive taxes are property taxes: capital gains tax (which taxes the increase in the value of assets) and corporation tax (which is levied on company profits). These are progressive not because they have different rates like income tax but simply because the better-off own rather more assets than do those with lower incomes and thus pay more of these taxes.

It would, however, be incorrect to overestimate the progressiveness of the British tax system. First, as has been noted above, very few taxpayers are actually assessed at the higher rates. Those who might become liable for tax at higher rates can often avoid payment by the use of various legal devices. These often arise from governments' desire to encourage different sorts of expenditure for all manner of reasons. For example, the government at present encourages people to invest in small companies through the Business Expansion Scheme (BES). Under this scheme, investments in eligible companies are made allowable against tax—that is, a person's taxable income is calculated after the deduction of both the personal allowance and BES investment payments.

A final factor militating against the progressiveness of the overall tax system is the

Table 23-2 The effect of taxes on household income, 1985

Household average per year, in pounds, with percentage of gross income shown in parentheses

	Group 1*		Group 2*	Group 3*
Gross income	3 454		10 765	28 116
less income tax	−1	(0)	−1 623 (15)	−5 897 (21)
less National Insurance contributions	0	(0)	−517 (5)	−1 381 (5)
plus tax relief at source	+15	(0)	+233 (2)	+510 (2)
Disposable income	3 468		8 832	21 347
less domestic rates	−95	(3)	−340 (4)	−573 (3)
less VAT	−234	(6)	−651 (7)	−1 521 (7)
less tobacco duty	−179	(5)	−193 (2)	−243 (1)
less duty on drink	−48	(1)	−176 (2)	−416 (2)
less other duties and taxes	−105	(3)	−352 (4)	−733 (3)
plus imputed value of benefits in kind†	+1 470	(43)	+1 456 (14)	+1 624 (6)
Final income	4 307 (125)		8 576 (80)	19 485 (69)

* Group 1 consists of households representing the bottom 10% of the gross income scale; Group 2, average households; and Group 3, households representing the top 10% of the gross income scale.

† An imputed value for non-cash benefits received by households such as education, NHS free travel etc.

Source: 'The effects of taxes and benefits on household income', *Economic Trends*, November 1986.

weight of other taxes in household budgets. Value added tax (VAT) is paid by rich and poor alike and is very close to being a proportional tax. Tobacco taxes, local authority rates and the forthcoming community charge (poll tax), on the other hand, tend to be regressive.

The net result, therefore, is that the greatest effect of public intervention through both taxation, social security and the provision of welfare services tends to be felt at the extremes of the income scale: the very rich lose and the very poor gain. The *relative* position of most people remains unchanged although of course their disposable income will be reduced. Table 23-2 shows the effects of such taxes on different categories of household. The table is taken from an article in *Economic Trends* (which regularly undertakes such research). It is apparent that, as expected, different taxes have a different proportionate effect. Income tax affects Group 3 far more whilst VAT affects all three groups' income in more or less the same proportion. The total effect of such taxes (and benefits) can be seen in the final row of the table. Those in Group 1 show an overall 'profit' in that their final income is some 25 per cent higher than their original gross income. Those in Group 3, on the other hand, have effectively 'lost' over 30 per cent of their gross income.

23-7 THE GROWTH OF THE PUBLIC SECTOR

Although economic theory can provide a general explanation for the existence of the welfare state and the other economic interventions of government, there is another feature of the public sector which deserves attention, namely, the way that it has expanded over the decades. Whereas general government expenditure was 17 per cent of total expenditure in 1900, by 1983 this had risen to over 40 per cent. (Measuring the 'public sector share' of the economy is, it ought to be noted, no simple matter. First, the public sector may be defined in several ways depending on which of the nationalized industries and other quasi-autonomous bodies are included. Second, expenditure can be treated in a variety of ways. For instance, tax lost through allowances could be either be ignored or counted as expenditure.)

Two different theories have been advanced to account for the expansion of public expenditure. One is that public goods and merit services are superior goods to which societies devote more resources as they become richer. The implication is obviously that the public sector will continue to expand as incomes grow. The second, rather more complex, theory suggests that the growth of the public sector has been the result of the relative sizes of different voting groups. The interests of the poor, so the argument runs, are served by having a large welfare state financed by taxes on the rich, while the interests of the rich would be best served by minimal public services and light taxation. With the extension of the suffrage late in the nineteenth century, the poor became a majority of the electorate whom politicians of all parties had to appease by raising public spending and taxes. Over time, more and more people were drawn into the tax net. Income tax, once paid only by the well-to-do, eventually fell upon the ordinary worker. As a result, the theory predicts that the number of people favouring the restraint of public spending should grow until a state of balance between the two groups is reached. Thereafter, the public sector share of total expenditure should remain constant. According to this theory, therefore, the growth of public spending will not continue indefinitely but is rather a finite process which will eventually run its course, if it has not already done so.

23-8 EFFICIENCY AND PUBLIC INTERVENTION

The question of whether public money is spent to the best effect is a recurring theme in current affairs. This chapter has already, of course, made mention of the difficulty of establishing the optimum scale of provision of public goods and merit goods, and without such a measure it is impossible to say whether resources are being squandered. In administrative and political terms, the proper use of resources is supposedly ensured by the electorate's right to replace any government considered to be wasting money and by the system of auditing the accounts of public bodies to ensure that funds are not being misappropriated. For economists, however, the main guarantor of efficiency is the pressure of competition. When this is absent, as it is from most of the public sector, then it is difficult to be certain that resources are being used in an optimum fashion.

One issue which is sometimes raised is whether it is better to undertake redistribution through the provision of goods and services like free health care and education than to provide the poor with the equivalent value in cash. It is, after all, fairly easy to show that the recipients would derive more satisfaction from money than they would from provision in kind, since money could be spent in a manner which more suited their tastes. What this argument overlooks, of course, is the fact that the services in question are merit services. The reason for their provision is not that they help to redistribute income but that their consumption by some people provides benefits to others. In other words, the providers of public goods and merit services (the taxpayers) derive satisfaction precisely from seeing that the money is not spent by the poor on just anything but on health, education or whatever.

Another related issue is the appropriate balance between state provision and individual choice. Austrian economists, in particular, favour the minimization of the former and the maximization of the latter for two reasons. The first is that governments can never have sufficient information to know the right scale of provision for merit goods. The second is the argument that while governments may wish to see a certain product consumed by everyone, there is no necessity for that product to be produced by public organizations. Such work can, like car insurance, be left to private companies. Austrian economists would ideally like to see individuals taking financial responsibility for themselves by saving for their old age, finding money for their childrens' education and paying for their own medical care through private insurance schemes. Privately owned schools and hospitals could compete to provide these services and the resultant competitive pressure would raise efficiency in these areas. Relieved of the need to maintain large welfare organizations, the government would be able to reduce tax rates, with the effect that people would find their disposable incomes increasing sufficiently to meet the bills for their own welfare services. Acknowledging society's obligation to provide a 'safety net' of minimum standards, economists of this persuasion argue that the worst-off could be given means-tested grants towards their costs. Overall, this programme has been referred to as the 'privatization of the welfare state'.

A third issue in public finance relates to the 'neutrality' of taxation, that is, the extent to which a tax *distorts* the prices of the goods or services upon which it bears. VAT, for instance, raises the prices of those goods upon which it falls by a uniform 15 per cent (give or take a small margin to reflect their differing elasticities of demand). In other words, VAT leaves the relative prices of these goods more or less unchanged and can therefore be described as being neutral between those goods. By contrast, excise duties (which fall upon alcohol and tobacco) change relative prices substantially. The price of a bottle of whisky, for instance, is quintupled by taxation. Price distortions like this cause problems from an economic point of view in that, like monopoly firms' prices, they give consumers incorrect information about the cost of producing the item and so discourage purchases. As a result, resources are shifted away from their optimum pattern of use.

In some instances, like tobacco or pollution-inducing products, the government may wish to discourage consumption and the distorting effects of selective taxation may be welcomed. In the labour market, however, income tax may produce distortions which are both severe and unintended. These distortions may arise from the way that income tax falls upon earnings *at the margin*. At the extremes of the income scale, marginal rates of income loss can become very much pronounced. At the bottom end of the scale, for example, an unemployed parent who takes a low-paid job would lose unemployment benefit, free school meals for her children, rent and rate rebates, subsidized bus travel, free prescriptions and other means-tested benefits. For some, the loss might exceed the income earned, and the person would be better-off not taking the job. This situation has been termed the 'poverty trap'. Conditions which are some ways analogous can sometimes prevail at the opposite end of the income scale because of the progressive nature of income tax. In the late 1970s, marginal tax rates reached 98 per cent, a figure which induced many of the rich to emigrate to countries with less stringent tax systems. This was clearly to the detriment of the United Kingdom since both revenue and talent were lost.

A group of economists known as the 'supply-side' school, which shares many ideas with

Austrian economics, has gone so far as to argue that lower income-tax rates are the key to increasing the mobility, inventiveness and enterprise of an economy since more effort will be forthcoming if people are allowed to keep more of their earnings. More formally, people may be expected to substitute work for leisure if the rewards of work go up, that is, the substitution effect ought to operate in favour of work. The trouble with this line of argument, of course, is that lower tax rates make people directly better-off and this itself may make them feel that they no longer need to go out of their way to earn more money. The satisfactory testing of supply-side theory, however, remains to be completed.

23-9 SUMMARY

Market failure occurs when the market is unable to generate the optimum level of output of a good or service. This is the primary justification for public intervention.

Public goods may be used by an additional consumer at zero marginal cost. Often they are also non-excludable and can thus not be supplied by the private sector.

Merit goods and services provide benefits both to the direct consumer and to other members of the community at the same time. The market would underprovide such services, and there is therefore a case for free or subsidized provision.

Externalities arise when firms use resources for which they do not pay. Typically the resource in question is the environment, which is used as a dump for waste products.

Equity is the fairness or otherwise of the distribution of income. Redistributing income from the wealthy to the poor necessitates *progressive* taxation, which may reduce the supply of effort to the economy, and *supply-side* economists argue strongly that it should be reduced.

EXERCISES

23-1 What methods could be used to establish the cost and benefits of:
(*a*) a new motorway,
(*b*) a new polytechnic?

23-2 Assume you are a research officer working for an anti-smoking pressure group which supports higher tobacco tax. The chairman of the group is to meet government ministers to argue for these proposals, and your task is to draft notes for the chairman's use. (Good briefing notes will of course include data on recent consumption trends, the state of the industry and so on.)

23-3 Find the equivalent data for Table 23-1 for two years, one five years ago, the other ten years ago. Derive the proportionate effects of the various taxes on the different income groups. What conclusions do you come to about the changing patterns and trends for the different income groups? What reasons can you suggest for such trends?

23-4 Early each year the Treasury publishes a document entitled *The Government's Expenditure Plans*. Find out the details of the government's general income and expenditure for the latest year available. Obtain comparable data for the period five years previously. What changes in government's income and expenditure are apparent? How do you account for these?

23-5 Using either the rates of income tax given in the chapter or more up-to-date ones (see *Inland Revenue Statistics*) work out the income tax to be paid by a single person earning:
(*a*) £5000
(*b*) £18 000
(*c*) £60 000.

For each one, calculate the proportion of income paid in tax. Then imagine each one were to receive a rise of £1000, and calculate the amount of tax which would be paid out of that extra income.

NATIONAL INCOME

24-1 INTRODUCTION

We have seen that, at the micro-economic level, economists are primarily concerned with resource allocation: in using supply and demand for individual firms, industries and markets to explain and predict how resources are allocated among competing uses. Our attention now turns away from micro-economics to look at the macro-economic level, where the economy is viewed as a single integrated system. Here, although we will still be concerned with the allocation process, the analysis is conducted at the level of *aggregate* supply and *aggregate* demand. We shall, accordingly, be developing the analytical tools to explain and predict matters such as the general level of prices, employment and unemployment, interest rates and the balance of trade. We shall begin this process by looking at what is termed *national income*. This is a basic measure of the aggregate production levels of the economy and its allocation between alternative and competing uses. National income data is also used to monitor changes in the macro-economy over time, just as a set of company accounts could be used to monitor the change in activity in an individual firm.

In the United Kingdom national income accounts are compiled by the Central Statistical Office (CSO) and published annually by HMSO as *The UK National Accounts*, the publication generally referred to as 'the Blue Book' (because of the colour of its cover). The national accounts are intended to represent as accurately as possible the money value of the total national output of goods and services in a specific period of time, normally one year. National income is, therefore, a *flow* rather than a *stock*. That is, it is the money value of the flow of goods and services produced in the economy that is measured. It is useful to develop a simple model of such national income flows before looking at the national income accounts in detail.

24-2 CIRCULAR FLOW OF INCOME

Figure 24-1 illustrates a simple model of the circular flow of income at the national level. Like all models, it is a gross oversimplification but serves the purpose of allowing us to identify the salient features of the real world. For simplicity, we assume the economy comprises two groups: households (who own all the factors of production—land, labour, capital and enterprise—and who demand goods and services for consumption), and firms (who demand factors of production in order to produce goods and services to satisfy households' demand). Readers will realize that there are a number of important aspects of the economy omitted from this model—there is no foreign trade, no public sector, or stockbuilding and so on. These elements can easily be introduced into our model, and we shall do so later in the text, but, for our present purposes, they will not affect the conclusions we derive from the model.

Given that households own all the factors of production it is apparent that they will expect some reward (payment) for supplying these factors to firms. Such payments take the form of wages and salaries, rent, interest, dividends and profit. This is shown in the model (Fig. 24-1) by the two flows on the left representing the supply of factors of production and money payments made in return.

With the factors of production thus made available firms will produce goods and services that will be offered for sale to households. With the money payments received from the supply of factors of production, households will be able to purchase the output produced by the firms. Thus, the flows on the right (Fig. 24-1) shows the supply of national output and the payment made by households for this supply.

The model indicates that this flow will continue. With the payments received from households, firms will again demand factors of production (and make the appropriate payments to households), will use these factors to produce national output which will then be offered to households who will again use their income received from supplying factors of production to pay for their consumption demand.

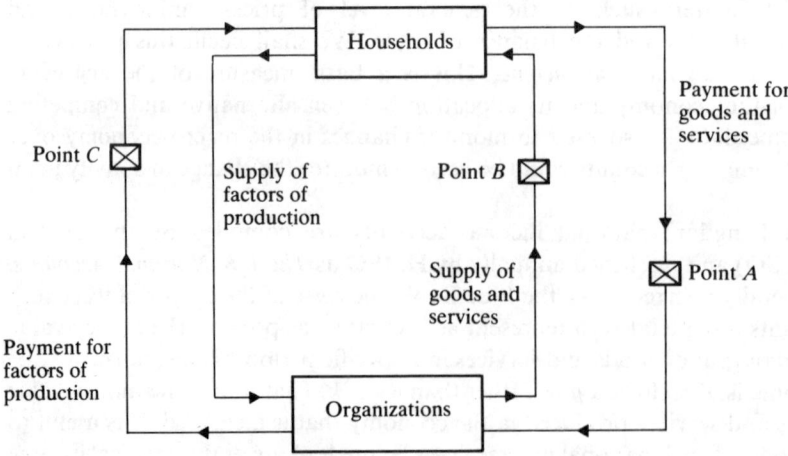

Figure 24-1 The circular flow of income

It is clear from Fig. 24-1 that we could measure the flows that are taking place in the macro-economy at a number of different points. It is evident, however, that no matter where we measure such flows we will arrive at the same figure, given that the flows are circular and self-contained. In terms of national income accounts the flows are measured at three specific points shown on Fig. 24-1: point A, the value of national expenditure, which is the total amount spent in the economy on goods and services provided; point B, the value of national output, which is the total value of the goods and services produced; and point C, the value of national income, which is the total value of the income received from the supply of factors of production. Thus we conclude that

$$national\ expenditure = national\ output = national\ income.$$

In practice, the construction of national income accounts is a statistician's nightmare and we shall examine some of the difficulties later in this chapter. The important conclusion at this stage is that the point at which we measure such flows ought, in principle, to be irrelevant. We shall look at the alternatives in turn.

24-3 NATIONAL EXPENDITURE

Table 24-1 shows the appropriate details of national expenditure for 1985. The first three items are straightforward. We have the three major spending components: those of consumers; those of the public sector; and investment spending, referred to as Gross Domestic Fixed Capital Formation. Note that public sector expenditure refers only to the purchase of goods and services, not to the total spending by this sector. Although it includes civil servants' salaries, it does not include transfer payments like retirement pensions.

Table 24-1 United Kingdom national expenditure (£ million)

(i) Consumers' expenditure	213 208	
(ii) Public authorities' current expenditure on goods and services	74 012	
(iii) Gross Domestic Fixed Capital Formation	60 118	
(iv) Value of physical increase in stocks and work in progress	+ 528	
Total Domestic Expenditure at market prices		347 866
(v) Exports	102 304	
(vi) Imports	− 98 603	
Gross Domestic Product at market prices		351 567
(vii) Taxes on expenditure	− 56 812	
(viii) Subsidies	7 710	
Gross Domestic Product at factor cost		302 465
(ix) Net property income from abroad	3 400	
Gross National Product at factor cost		305 865
(x) Capital consumption	− 41 846	
National Income at factor cost		264 019

Source: National Income Accounts, HMSO, 1985.

Item (*iv*) requires an explanation. In our simple model of the circular flow of income all output produced within a given time period was consumed within that same time period. In practice this will not occur. Given that the accounts are for a discrete period of time it is apparent that, for example, a motor car produced on 31 December will not be sold during that year even though it represents part of national output that year. Similarly, some expenditure in 1985 was on items produced in 1984 and must, therefore, be excluded from the 1985 accounts. Accordingly, a value of output held in stock is estimated.

The sum of these four items is Total Domestic Expenditure. To this we add foreign trade. The value of exports is added and the value of imports deducted from this total. The logic is straightforward. Our objective is to measure the production of the British economy: exports are a part of that production and must be included while imports are not and must be excluded.

This results in Gross Domestic Product (GDP) at market prices. While this represents a flow in terms of money paid by consumers, it will not actually represent the value of the factors of production used. Part of the market price of some products may represent a tax levied by government (such as VAT). Such taxes are deducted from the GDP figure. Similarly, market prices may underrepresent the income received by the producer if the firm is paid some form of subsidy by government. Accordingly such subsidy payments are added to produce GDP at factor cost.

Next we must take account of income payments that may take place to and from other economies—net property income from abroad. This converts our domestic total into a national total—Gross National Product (GNP) at factor cost. Thus, while GDP measures the value of work done within the British economy, GNP measures the value of work done by factors of production owned by British residents regardless of the physical location of those factors.

The final item in the table refers to capital consumption. Each year part of the total (gross) investment that takes place will be to replace obsolete or redundant capital equipment. This part of investment is referred to as depreciation or capital consumption and deducting this from GNP leaves Net National Product (NNP) or, as it is more usually known, National Income.

24-4 NATIONAL OUTPUT

Table 24-2 shows the equivalent process for measuring the flow of national output. It shows the value of output by industrial sector. This is not as straightforward as it might appear and care must be taken in interpreting such data.

Let us look, for example, at the manufacturing sector. Given that we are measuring national output, it is clear that we must be careful to avoid double counting. Output from the steel industry, for example, may be sold to the vehicle industry to produce cars which are then sold to consumers. If, for example, total steel output was £100 million and total vehicle output £250 million it would be tempting, but incorrect, to assume total manufacturing output was £350 million. The error arises because part of the vehicle sector's output is made up of inputs from the steel sector. Thus if the value of such inputs was, say, £25 million the net value of output would be £$(100 + 250 - 25)$ million $= £325$ million. The figures in Table 24-2, therefore, show not the value of total output for each industry but rather the

Table 24-2 United Kingdom national output (£ million)

Agriculture, forestry and fishing	5 485	
Energy and water supply	34 335	
Manufacturing	76 800	
Construction	18 651	
Distribution, hotels and catering	40 384	
Banking, finance and insurance	42 473	
Transport	12 913	
Communications	8 044	
Public administration and defence	21 599	
Ownership of dwellings	17 775	
Health and education	26 187	
Other services	17 987	
Total		322 624
Adjustment for financial services	−16 883	
Residual error	−3 276	
Gross Domestic Product at factor cost		302 465
Net property income from abroad	3 400	
Gross National Product at factor cost		305 865
Capital consumption	−41 846	
National Income at factor cost		264 019

Source: *National Income Accounts*, HMSO, 1985.

value which that industry adds to the inputs it receives from other industries. This figure is often referred to as the industry's *value added*.

Similarly, imports used in the production of output must also be discounted.

From this total value of output is deducted an estimated value for 'financial services'. Again, this is deducted to avoid double counting of interest and loans received by financial institutions which are already included under the financial services sector output.

In theory, this should then result in GDP at factor cost. In practice, however, given the complexities of data collection and preparation and the fact that a number of items are estimates rather than records of flows, adjustment for the differences between the various approaches has to be made. This is achieved via the 'residual error' item. A number of important points must be made about this item. First, by convention, the residual error is applied only to the output table and the income table (which we will examine in Section 24-4). It is not applied to the expenditure table. This does not imply that the expenditure approach is more accurate but rather that the term is used purely as an arithmetical balancing item to ensure all three approaches generate the same totals. Second, the size of the term cannot be interpreted as a measure of reliability of the national accounts data. It is tempting, but again misleading, to assume that a smaller term one year, *ceteris paribus*, means that the accounts are more accurate than for a year when the term is larger. As an illustration, the residual term has varied, over the last 20 years, from 0.03 per cent of GDP to 2.8 per cent.

So, incorporating the residual term, brings us to GDP at factor cost and we can proceed to take account of the remaining items to derive GNP and national income exactly as in Table 24-1.

Table 24-3 United Kingdom national income (£ million)

Income from employment	195 350	
Income from self-employment	29 859	
Gross trading profits of companies	52 977	
Gross trading surpluses of public corporations	7 106	
Gross trading surpluses of general government enterprises	264	
Rent	20 541	
Imputed charge for consumption of non-trading capital	2 681	
Stock appreciation	−3 037	
Residual error	−3 276	
Gross Domestic Product at factor cost		302 465
Net property income from abroad	3 400	
Gross National Product at factor cost		305 865
Capital consumption	−41 846	
National income at factor cost		264 019

Source: *National Income Accounts*, HMSO, 1985.

24-5 NATIONAL INCOME

Our final approach (Table 24-3) measures payments made to the owners of the factors of production used in the production of national output. Again, care must be taken in interpreting such data. This total will not be equal to the sum of all personal incomes for two major reasons. First, some elements of personal incomes are not rewards to the owners of the factors of production. Transfer payments such as unemployment and social security benefits are not rewards as such and are, therefore, excluded. Second, there are some factor payments which are not included in personal incomes, such as undistributed profits or trading surpluses of public enterprises.

Two of the items require further clarification. The item 'imputed charge for consumption of non-trading capital' is an item estimating the effective income of those who are owner-occupiers of property. Although there is no observed flow of income (effectively owner occupiers pay rent to themselves) there is an implied income benefit. The other item, 'stock appreciation', relates to problems arising from inflation. Stocks held at the start of the year are likely to have increased in value by the end of the year, simply because prices have risen. As such, they do not represent a real benefit to the economy as no factor services have been performed. Thus an estimate of this appreciation in the value of stock held is deducted from the total.

Once the residual error is deducted, and GDP at factor cost derived, we can go on to work out national income again exactly as in Table 24-1.

24-6 PERSONAL INCOME

In addition to the provision of data relating to national income, economists are equally interested in data pertaining to personal income. Such data, after all, are likely to be of more

Table 24-4 United Kingdom national income and personal income (£ million)

Income from employment	195 350	
Income from self-employment	29 859	
Rent dividends and net interest	30 582	
National Insurance benefits and other current grants from government	46 127	
Other current transfers	1 630	
Imputed charge for capital consumption of private non-profit making bodies	360	
Total personal income		303 908
UK taxes on income	− 38 205	
National Insurance and other deductions	− 24 048	
Other current transfers	− 1 854	
Personal disposable income		239 781

Source: *National Income Accounts*, HMSO, 1985.

use to the analyst of micro-economics investigating the supply–demand situation in a particular market. Personal income follows logically from the national income total derived earlier (see Table 24-4). The key results are total personal income and personal disposable income, the latter showing the income available directly for consumption.

24-7 INTERPRETING AND USING NATIONAL INCOME ACCOUNTS DATA

Readers should be able to see that all three approaches to national income accounting will provide identical results (allowing for the creative use of the residual term). Given the use that is made of national income data in economic analysis, an awareness of the relationships between the various measures introduced in this chapter is essential. It is also important to appreciate the reliability of such data. Despite considerable efforts by the CSO, inaccuracies are inherent in the accounts data and analysis undertaken using such data must be assessed accordingly.

On a national basis, many analysts monitor the changes taking place in the accounts year by year. In terms of the various totals this may reveal underlying changes in the macro-economy to enable them to assess, for example, whether we are getting 'richer' as an economy. Considerable care must, however, be taken when interpreting national income data in this way.

First, all such data must be adjusted for inflation—that is, expressed in real terms—before annual comparisons can be made. For this reason national income data are available in both current price and constant price terms. Given the complexities of the accounts and the assumptions used in constructing price indices yet another area of uncertainty and inaccuracy is introduced.

Second, an increase in GNP does not, *per se*, mean the economy is 'better-off'. There may be several factors causing such a change. The population may have increased, implying that national income has to be shared among more individuals. Accordingly, analysis is often undertaken in terms of *per capita* national income. Changes in GNP may not reflect changing attitudes on the part of consumers. We may, for example, observe GNP falling and conclude that standards of living are falling. It may well be that consumers are choosing to use more of their time for leisure rather than work. There may be a change in the definitions used in compiling parts of the accounts. For example, with the privatization of a profitable nationalized industry, such as British Gas, the item 'gross trading profits of companies' would rise and that of 'gross trading surpluses of public corporations' fall.

Third, an increase in GNP does not necessarily imply an increase in living standards. To assess the impact of increased national income we would also need to examine the structure of income distribution in the economy. The increase in national income may be benefiting a relatively small proportion of the total population.

Fourth, a large proportion of the data is drawn from samples taken from appropriate groups. As such, despite all attempts at drawing a representative sample, the data can only be regarded as an estimate of the true value.

Fifth, the national income accounts do not include those activities which, for a variety of reasons, are not recorded by the market. Unpaid work done by housewives or by the DIY enthusiast, for example, will not be included. Some estimates put this as high as 80 per cent of GDP. Equally, activities undertaken by the 'black' economy (where paid work is unreported to the Inland Revenue) are unreported and therefore unrecorded in the accounts. Estimates have put this as high as 10 per cent of GNP.

Lastly, some economists argue that such national income figures double-count the effects of 'nuisance' production and thus understate the value of output. For example, the accounts include the output of the electricity industry *and* the costs of restoring forests affected by acid deposits from power station emissions. Many would argue that the net benefit to society would be more accurately shown by deducting the latter figure from the former.

24-8 SUMMARY

Gross Domestic Product (GDP) measures the output produced by factors of production located in the British economy.

Gross National Product (GNP) measures the income earned by British citizens regardless of the location of the factors of production used.

Market prices show national income aggregates at the prevailing market values (including indirect taxes). *Factor cost* shows the same aggregates in terms of the cost of resources used.

National income is also referred to as *Net National Product* and measures GNP at factor cost less depreciation.

Value added is the increase in the value of output as a result of the production process.

EXERCISES

24-1 Collect the data for the latest set of national income accounts to update Tables 24-1, 24-2 and 24-3. You may wish to use a computer spreadsheet to do this as an effective way of ensuring the three tables balance.

24-2 Collect data on the following elements of the accounts for the last 10 years, using constant prices:

(*a*) taxes as a percentage of total personal income

(*b*) Gross Domestic Fixed Capital Formation

(*c*) Gross Domestic Fixed Capital Formation as a percentage of GDP

(*d*) exports and imports as a percentage of GNP.

Comment on the trends observed and formulate testable hypotheses as to the possible causes of these changes.

24-3 Compare the percentage share of national output of the various industrial sectors in the latest set of accounts with the accounts of 10 years ago. Which sectors have expanded most and which contracted? What economic reasons can you suggest for these patterns?

24-4 At the end of your studies you find gainful employment as an economist working for a computer firm. You engage in the following activities:

(*i*) you are paid a salary

(*ii*) you buy a flat

(*iii*) you hire a cleaner to keep the flat tidy

(*iv*) you buy a second-hand car

(*v*) you buy a set of self-assembly kitchen units and install them yourself.

Determine where these activities will appear:

(*a*) in the circular flow of income

(*b*) in the set of national accounts.

25

THEORIES OF THE MACRO-ECONOMY: I
MONETARISM

25-1 INTRODUCTION

Chapter 24 introduced macro-economics by looking at national income accounting. To interpret changes in these data naturally requires a theory (or theories) of the macro-economy. Just as the contrasting approaches of neo-classical and Austrian economics were to be found at micro level, so at macro level we find monetarist and Keynesian schools of economic thought. This chapter looks at monetarism, a theory which relates closely to neo-classical economics and which has grown in importance on the basis of its advertised ability to explain (and thus help to control) one of the major economic problems of recent decades: inflation.

25-2 THE COSTS OF INFLATION

Inflation may be defined as a tendency for the general level of prices to increase. It should not, therefore, be confused either with a one-off increase in prices or with a prolonged increase in the prices of one class of good.

Inflation imposes several costs upon the economy. Some arise from the fact that inflation creates the *possibility* that the allocation of resources will be distorted. For example, retirement pensions which are set in money terms are reduced in real terms as prices rise. Similarly, British goods and services might be priced out of world markets if British costs were to rise more rapidly than those of our competitors. A third danger is that real income and wealth can be inadvertently transferred from one social group to another. For example, if interest rates stay below the rate of inflation, people who place their funds in building societies will find that their deposits have been eroded in real terms, while the people who have borrowed that money to buy houses will have benefited from the low real interest rates and from the way that their houses have risen in value. There will thus have been a transfer of wealth from lenders to borrowers. Wealth can likewise be transferred from the public to the government if there is a progressive tax system. Because inflation reduces the real value of tax allowances, more people become liable to pay tax as money incomes rise. Indeed, one result of the persistent inflation which the United Kingdom has suffered in recent decades has been to turn ordinary manual workers into payers of income tax, whereas in the 1950s this status had been reserved for the better-off.

Because these inadvertent transfers all give rise to some degree of inequity, ways have usually been found to compensate for them: pensions are reviewed annually, tax allowances are automatically raised by the rate of inflation, interest rates have risen and so on. The general practice is known as 'index-linking', because there is often some commitment to adjust payments in line with changes in the Retail Prices Index, which as readers will recall from Chapter 7 is the main indicator of inflation. As a result of widespread indexation, the costs of inflation itemized above have been substantially reduced.

The costs which have not been reduced are those which arise from the nature of the economic system. In a market economy prices indicate the relative costs and values of different products and services. They thus signal to businessmen the ways in which they should alter the running of their businesses: the resources to economize on, the kinds of products to develop, the locations in which to expand and so on. Businessmen are therefore obliged constantly to monitor prices. When there is inflation, price changes in products and factors become more frequent. The problem with inflation is therefore that it makes the task of monitoring price changes very much more arduous simply because there is more information to be sifted. Inflation thus makes running a business rather more difficult, and must therefore discourage investment and expansion.

The costs of very high rates of inflation are as much social and political as economic. The disruption which it causes can even contribute, as in Germany in the 1920s and 1930s, to the destruction of democratic government.

25-3 THE QUANTITY THEORY OF MONEY

Economists who adhere to the monetarist (as opposed to the Keynesian) approach explain inflation by reference to the *quantity theory of money*. This theory was first set out in 1911 by the American economist, Irving Fisher, and has since undergone many modifications. The most important were undertaken by Professor Milton Friedman of Chicago University, whose name will recur several times in our work.

The central ideas of the quantity theory are conveyed in the identity:

$$PY = MV$$

P is in indicator, in the form of an index, of the price(s) of the output of the economy. Inflation would be denoted by an increase in P, and the objective of the quantity theory is therefore to explain (and predict) changes in this variable. Y is the output of the economy, measured in real terms, again in the form of an index. The product of P and Y is an index of the total money value of current output, that is, of GDP measured in terms of current prices. This is sometimes referred to as 'money GDP'.

M is the stock of money in the economy. While this may sound a fairly straightforward idea, in practice it is complicated by the fact that there are (to date) seven competing definitions of the money stock (sometimes called the money supply—the words are here used interchangeably). These are examined later in the chapter.

V is the 'velocity of circulation', and may be thought of as denoting the number of time a unit of money changes hands during the period in question. A low value of V would indicate that units of money changed hands relatively slowly, that is, that people were tending to hold on to their money. This would imply that people had a preference for holding relatively large money balances. On the other hand, a high value of V would suggest that people were content with smaller holdings of money. V may therefore be thought of as indicating people's demand for money—a matter over which there has been much controversy, as our examination will show. In practice, no attempt is made to find an independent measure for V: a value is derived simply by taking money GDP and dividing it by the value of the money stock.

Clearly both sides of the identity pertain to a particular period of time, since both V and T must be expressed as rates per unit of time (in the same way as must supply and demand in micro-economics).

It may be noted that the identity relates only to *current* output. In reality, large sectors of the economy are devoted to buying and selling other things such as products made at some previous time (like houses or second-hand cars) or financial assets (like company shares). Critics of the monetarist approach, particularly Keynesian economists, point to this as a weakness in the theory. Monetarists, however, argue that the use of money in these other markets runs parallel to its use in markets for current output so that the identity as stated is a good approximation to the behaviour of the whole economic system.

To turn the identity into a theory requires the addition of two assumptions. These are that V and Y should be taken as remaining constant from one year to the next. Since Y relates to the real level of economic activity in the economy which is known to change only by a small percentage each year, this may perhaps be accepted. Assuming V to be stable is, of course, tantamount to assuming that the demand for money is stable, and a later section of this chapter looks at monetarist views on this in more detail. If these assumptions are accepted, the implication of the quantity theory for economic management is simple. If the supply of money rises but the demand for it remains constant, people will try to rid themselves of the unwanted money by spending it. If the supply of foods and services which they can buy is constant as well, there will be excess demand and prices will rise. In other words, the central conclusion of the quantity theory is that a rise in the money supply will, *ceteris paribus*, cause an increase in prices, that is, inflation.

25-4 THE FUNCTIONS OF MONEY

To understand the quantity theory of money, it is plainly necessary to examine the nature and properties of money. This section will therefore outline briefly the four functions of money.

First, money is a *medium of exchange*. That is, it is accepted in all transactions and a person may thus sell a product to one person, receive payment in money and then buy goods or services from a third. This procedure is clearly more efficient than the alternative, bartering, whereby someone with a product to sell would have to find someone who both (a) required that particular product and (b) was willing to part with the right consumer goods in exchange.

Second, money is a *store of value* in that it is a form of wealth. This is an attribute which money shares with other assets, both 'real' (like houses and land) and financial (like shares or building society deposits). Indeed, modern theories of money emphasize that it is merely one asset amongst many. If there is inflation, of course, money loses its advantages as a store of wealth.

Third, money acts as a *unit of account*. Money is thus the measuring rod in terms of which everything else is valued. Prices, share values, exchange rates, wages, company balance sheets and national incomes are expressed in monetary units like pounds sterling or, US dollars. A monetary unit can be used as a unit of account even though there is no coin or note of that value: the European Currency Unit (ECU) is one example.

Fourth, money serves as a *standard of deferred payment* in that contracts about future payments are fixed in monetary terms. This is simply a projection of the unit-of-account function into the future. It is, however, notable in that—like money's role as a store of wealth—it is undermined by inflation.

25-5 DEFINITIONS OF MONEY

Having established the functions of money, the task of defining money itself ought, in principle, to present little difficulty. Money is quite simply anything which performs the above functions. More precisely, it is anything which performs the first two—serving as a medium of exchange and a store of value—since these are the more fundamental. Human societies have, at various times, used a number of different commodities in this role: conch shells, cattle, cigarettes and so on. The most widely used currencies, of course, have been metallic coins like copper, gold and silver. Currencies of this type are said to possess *intrinsic* value because the metal in the coins is valuable in its own right. Intrinsic value, however, is not essential, modern currencies having little but still being able to function as money.

The explanation for the use of currencies which are intrinsically valueless is that a currency's ability to function depends, ultimately, upon people's willingness to accept it as payment. Although intrinsic value is one guarantee of acceptability, it is not the only one. For modern paper currencies, acceptability is ensured by the authority of the state which guarantees the value of the currency. As later chapters will show, governments have not infrequently betrayed this trust in so far as inflation has undermined the value of money. When inflation reaches extremely high levels, as in Germany in the 1920s, the national currency can cease to be acceptable: people try to get rid of it as soon as they receive it and resort to the use of surrogates such as cigarettes or the currencies of other countries. Such a decline in the acceptability of a currency would reflect a lack of confidence in its ultimate guarantor, the government.

While the foregoing paragraph referred to 'paper currencies', it would be erroneous to believe that banknotes were the main component of the money supply in modern societies. Notes, together with the metal coinage, are but the small change of the economy. The principal element in the money stock is bank and building society deposits. (While British building societies were for many years restricted by law to the advancing of loans for house

Table 25-1 Components of money stock M1

Item	Amount outstanding at October 1987 (£ million)
Notes and coins in circulation with the public	13 729
UK private sector non-interest-bearing sight bank deposits	31 171
UK private sector interest-bearing sight bank deposits	46 956
Money stock M1	91 856

Source: *Financial Statistics*, December 1987.

purchase, recent changes have lifted many of these restraints. To an increasing extent, building societies will engage in the full range of banking business and the distinction between the two classes of institution will have decreasing significance.) The relative importance of the different items which make up the money supply will vary, of course, with one's choice of definition of money. Earlier it was noted that seven definitions can be used, and Table 25-1 sets out one of them, M1.

As a comprehensive definition of money, M1 is plainly inadequate in that it omits other assets which people are able to use to buy things, like building society deposits. These are included in a broader definition of money, M4, which is given in Table 25-2.

Although M4 includes M1, it also takes in savings accounts. Often it is not possible to write cheques on these accounts while in other cases notice of withdrawal may be required. The latter are thus described as 'time deposits' to distinguish them from 'sight' deposits which may be withdrawn on demand. The money in time accounts, while perfectly good as savings, is not quite as 'spendable' as money in sight deposits. In terms of the functions of money, the difference between M1 and M4 is that the former concentrates on items that are

Table 25-2 Components of money stock M4

Item	Amount outstanding at October 1987 (£ million)
M1	91 856
Private sector sterling time deposits	90 048
M3	181 904
Private sector shares and deposits with building societies	129 078
	310 982
less	
Buildings societies' holdings of M3	13 493
M4	297 489

Source: *Financial Statistics*, December 1987.

Table 25-3 Seven definitions of money stock

M0
Notes and coins with public, *plus*
Notes and coins with banks and building societies, *plus*
Bankers' Balances at Bank of England

M1
Notes and coins with public, *plus*
UK private sector sight bank deposits

M2
M1, *plus*
Private sector shares and deposits with building societies and National Savings Bank

M3 (formerly Sterling M3)
M1, *plus*
Private sector time bank deposits

M3c
M3, *plus*
Private sector holdings of foreign currency bank deposits

M4
M3, *plus*
Private sector holdings of shares and deposits with building societies, *less*
Building societies' holdings of bank deposits

M5
M4, *plus*
Private sector holdings of bank bills, Treasury bills, National Savings instruments and similar securities traded in the money market

Source: Bank of England Quarterly Bulletin, May 1987.

used in everyday transactions, that is, that perform the function of being a medium of exchange, while M4 shifts the emphasis to money's function as a store of value. The technical term for this is *liquidity*: notes, coin and current accounts are highly liquid, while building society savings accounts are rather less so.

The concept of liquidity is the key to the different definitions of money. Table 25-3 shows the definitions and the links between them. As the definitions progress from M1 to M5, assets with less and less liquidity are incorporated. Clearly the actual liquidity of each set of assets will depend on whether building societies offer cheque-book facilities or demand notice of withdrawal. (A major drawback to all the definitions, furthermore, is their omission of one of the most liquid sources of spending power, the credit card.) Nevertheless the general principle remains that the liquidity of the broader definitions is less than that of the narrower ones.

25-6 THE DEMAND FOR MONEY

The modern approach to money (developed by Friedman) is to view money as a commodity like any other for which there is both a supply and a demand. The supply side will be analysed in some detail in Chapter 27 and can therefore be left aside until then. For present purposes, the supply of money will be taken as being determined exogenously by the Bank of England.

The starting point for the analysis of the demand for money is the idea that money is but one form of wealth. Individuals are thought of as holding a bundle or 'portfolio' of different assets, each with its characteristic benefits in terms of yield and/or usefulness. Shares and endowment insurance policies produce financial returns, consumer durables produce satisfaction while houses (often) produce both comfort and a return. The portfolio should, of course, be thought of as including the person's 'human capital', that is, his or her skills and qualifications and their associated earning capacity. The demand for money is therefore constituted by the decision to hold a certain proportion of one's total wealth not in the above forms but as notes, bank balances and so on.

This decision will depend upon the costs and benefits of holding money. The benefits arise from money's functions as a medium of exchange and as a store of value. In its first capacity, money will clearly be required in proportion to one's general rate of expenditure, which in turn will reflect one's income and wealth. Thus those who habitually dine at the Ritz will need to keep more money in their current accounts than those who take sandwiches for lunch. This *transactions demand* for money will also be affected by arrangements for the making of payments—someone paid monthly will tend to have a larger average amounts in his or her bank account than someone who is paid by the week. Economists associated with the Keynesian school also add that people will usually keep money so as to deal with life's contingencies like having to repair the car or taking advantage of special offers. This *precautionary demand* is clearly but an extension of transactions demand to take account of transactions with a rather low probability of occurrence.

As a store of wealth, money will also be in demand. Here, however, its attractiveness is more limited since there is usually a trade-off between the liquidity of an asset and the return which it provides. The most liquid asset of all, a roll of banknotes in one's pocket, produces no financial return whatsoever. To earn a yield of some sort, money has to be put to work as liquid capital in the activity of making and selling goods and services, and this can only happen if it is lent out by, for example, placing it on deposit with a bank or building society. Lending money inevitably means a loss of some degree of liquidity, however slight. To earn higher returns, even greater sacrifices of liquidity generally have to be made. Company shares, property and investment trusts frequently earn higher returns than deposit accounts but they are far less liquid and therefore are not counted as money.

The cost of holding money is the opportunity cost, that is, the interest rate that is forgone by holding wealth in liquid form rather than lending it out. It may be thought that inflation would also affect the demand for money in that rising prices might induce people to reduce their money holdings by spending it before it lost its value. At the same time, however, inflation means that people will need more money for everyday transactions. At low rates, inflation is not deemed to affect the demand for money one way or the other, and the only cost of holding it remains the opportunity cost of forgone interest.

A simple model of the demand for money may be expressed as

$$D_m = f(W, i, T)$$

where D_m is the demand for money, W is the individual's total stock of wealth, i is the interest rate and T is tastes. This formulation clearly embodies the assumptions that

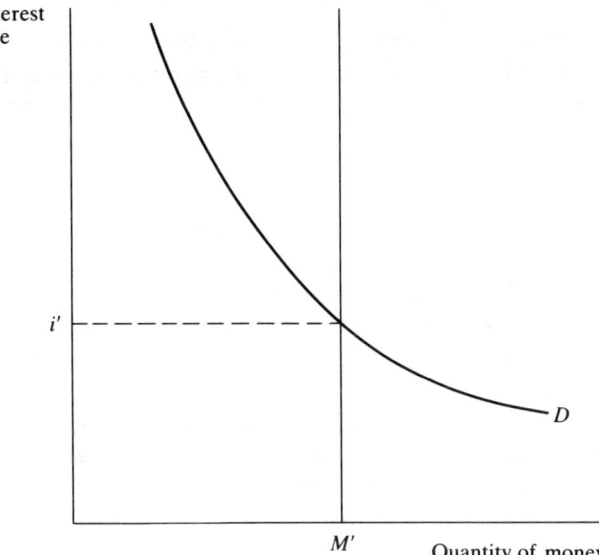

Figure 25-1 The supply of and demand for money

the demand for money by any individual will depend upon his or her total stock of wealth, the opportunity cost of holding money and his or her view of the relative importance of the convenience that money provides. If we were to assume, further, that these three items were given, it could reasonably be inferred that economic agents (individuals and firms) would hold some equilibrium amount of money.

The influence of interest rates can be shown by assuming them to increase. Higher rates will mean better returns from financial securities like deposit accounts, and they will therefore, *ceteris paribus*, encourage people to hold more of their wealth in these forms and correspondingly less as money.

The demand function shown in Eq. (25-2) can be shown graphically. Figure 25-1 shows the quantity of money on the horizontal axis while the cost of money, that is, the rate of interest, is shown on the vertical. (Let us assume that the definition of money that we are using is M4.) M' indicates the fixed stock of money, and i' the equilibrium rate of interest.

25-7 MONEY AND INFLATION

To see how this model can explain inflation, let us look at the consequences of an increase in the stock of money. The mechanisms by which the money supply in a modern economy can increase are complex, and, as noted, are held over for discussion until Chapter 27. For present purposes, the improbable assumption is made that every adult in the country finds a sum of, say, £1000 in notes underneath the floorboards. The question to be explored is how they might react to this.

The broad and unsurprising answer is that the money would be spent. Although £1000 would be a significant addition to most people's holdings of money, it would be a rather smaller change in their total wealth. To restore the ratio between money and total wealth, people would run down their holdings of money, that is, they would do one of two things: they would either spend it or they would invest it in some way by, say, buying securities. These two paths—let us call them the 'spending route' and the 'lending route'—can be examined in turn, starting with the former.

If the economy were to be working at full capacity, the result of an increase in expenditure would be quite simple: prices would rise. This would, of course, be a one-stage jump rather than a continuing process of inflation. It might, of course, take some time, perhaps a year, for the price rises to come through. The effect of higher prices (and incomes) would be to raise the demand for money for transactions and precautionary purposes, since people would have higher incomes which they would be spending on more expensive goods and services. Ultimately, this would raise the demand for money so that people became willing to hold the new, enlarged money stock.

The lending route has much the same effect. By lending the money out, people would tend to drive down the rate of interest. This would stimulate more people to borrow money to spend either on consumer items or one capital goods for their businesses. In either event, demand would rise just as it did when consumers spent their new-found wealth directly, and prices would again rise.

The spending route is seen by monetarist economists as being more important, while Keynesians stress the lending route. Nevertheless, both can have the same result of higher prices. It can be seen that the difference between the two routes is that the former operates directly on prices while the latter goes through the intermediate stage of depressing interest rates. Naturally, if the increase in the money supply, however it came about, were to be repeated, then prices would rise again. Were the money supply to rise continually, inflation would ensue. It is on the basis of the above logic that monetarists come to the conclusions

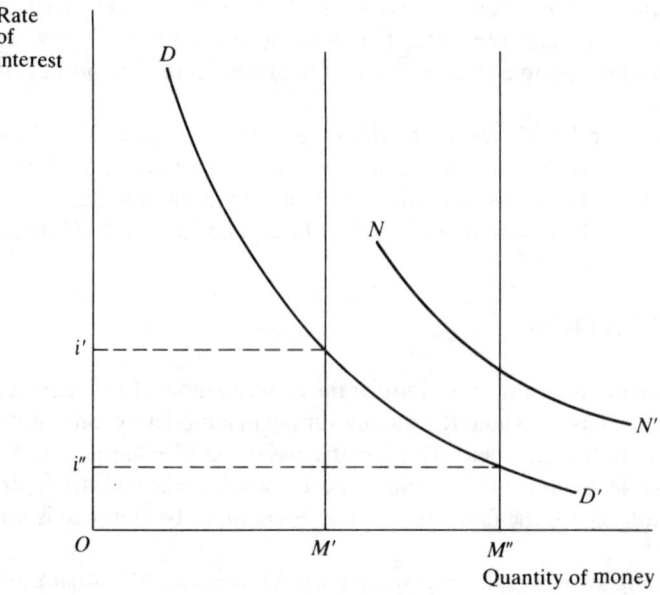

Figure 25-2 Increase in the money supply

that, first, inflation is caused, fundamentally, by expansions in the money supply, and second, that inflation can only be halted by controlling the money supply. These arguments were taken to heart by governments in the United Kingdom, United States and West Germany during the 1980s.

The lending route is illustrated in Fig. 25-2. The discovery of the cash raises the money stock from M' to M''. Given the existing demand-for-money curve, DD', interest rates fall from i' to i''. Lower interest rates will encourage others to borrow, so that the money will eventually be spent on goods and services, thus stimulating demand and raising prices. The effect of higher prices, as explained above, is to raise the demand for money, which pushes interest rates back up again. Figure 25-2 illustrates a theorem which is of some importance from the point of view of policy-makers: it is not possible for the government to control both interest rates and the money supply at the same time.

25-8 MONETARISM VERSUS KEYNESIANISM

The monetarist stress upon the spending route above can be traced back to the work of Jean-Baptiste Say, a French contemporary of David Ricardo. Say argued that every sale was undertaken with a view to the respending of the proceeds. Workers sold their labour so as to be able to spend their wages on consumer goods while businessmen spent their sales revenues either on maintaining their businesses or on themselves by buying consumer goods. Thus total intended sales in any one period must equal total intended purchases. Indeed, monetarism virtually reduces money to a medium of exchange, and virtually ignores its store-of-value function. This assumption then allows monetarists to argue that the demand for money stems primarily from transactions purposes and is therefore quite stable.

By contrast, Keynesians tend to stress the role of money as a store of value as well as a medium of exchange. They take the view that investors may switch, rapidly and on a large scale, between holding money and holding securities. For Keynesians, therefore, the demand for money may be volatile rather than stable. It can, as we shall see when we examine Keynesianism in more detail, act as an independent source of macro-economic instability.

This controversy in macro-economics will occupy our attention for several chapters. Three questions in particular deserve mention. First, what truth is there in the quantity theory: is there indeed a link between changes in the money supply and inflation? If there is, does it run directly from money to prices (as the monetarists would argue) or indirectly through an effect on interest rates (as the Keynesians believe)? Second, if there is indeed a link between an expanding money stock and rising prices, does it involve excess demand? After all, many economies have experienced inflation without showing any marked signs of excess demand. This is addressed in Chapters 31 and 32. If the monetarist view is true, it follows that the money supply must be kept under strict control by the government. Monetarist thinking thus places monetary policy—the control both of money and of interest rates—at the centre of economic policy. (It is, it should be noted, perfectly possible to have a non-monetarist monetary policy.) This leads to the third question, namely, by what means can the money stock increase, or its growth be restrained? This forms the subject of Chapter 27.

Chapter 26 will take up the first of the above questions by introducing techniques that can be used to test such economic relationships as that between money and prices.

25-9 SUMMARY

Inflation is a tendency for the general level of prices to rise persistently. Inflation imposes costs in the form of distortions in prices: export markets may be lost, fixed incomes may fall in value, creditors may lose money to debtors and so on. Businessmen's work of monitoring prices becomes more difficult.

The *quantity theory of money* argues that, as long as the real output of the economy (Y) and the velocity of circulation (V) remain more or less constant, there will be a determinate relationship between the stock of money (M) and the general price level (P). In a phrase, monetarists believe that increases in M lead to increases in P. The velocity of circulation is set by people's demand for money.

The *functions of money* are to act as a *medium of exchange*, a *store of value*, a *unit of account* and a *standard of future contracts*. Money is any asset that performs these functions. Notes and coin are clearly money, but so too are sight deposits, time deposits and foreign currency holdings. These items may be ranged along a spectrum from the most 'liquid' to the least. The definitions of money differ in that some are restricted to the most liquid assets while other take in other, less liquid ones.

Liquidity is the capacity of an asset to be used to make payments.

The *demand for money* is the decision to hold a certain proportion of one's wealth in the form of cash, bank deposits and so on. It is thus determined by one's wealth, one's tastes and the interest which is forgone by holding money.

Monetarists believe that, since the demand for money is stable, a higher money stock must lead to a higher price level, that is, to inflation. Keynesians dispute the stability of the demand for money.

EXERCISES

25-1 Collect data on the following two variables for the last 10 years (available in the latest edition of *Economic Trends Annual Supplement*):

(*a*) Sterling M3 (up to 1986) and M3 (after that date) (amount outstanding, seasonally adjusted).
(*b*) RPI (all items other than seasonal food).

Plot the data on a graph. Which variable do you put on the vertical axis? Why? Is there evidence to support the quantity theory? Repeat the exercise for another measure of the money supply. Comment on the consistency of the picture presented by the different measures you have used.

25-2 Your annual expenditure is £6000. Estimate your demand for money if:

(*a*) you are paid monthly
(*b*) you are paid weekly
(*c*) you run an old car which has one chance in twenty of needing a £100 repair in any week.

25-3 Assume that the money supply is fixed, and the economy is working at full capacity. Assume next that everyone suddenly decides to hold less of their wealth as money. What follows from this decision? Are people successful in running down their money balances?

25-4 The local council is preparing its estimates for next year's expenditure. Clearly some allowance must be made for inflation during the course of the year. You are one of the council's trainee accountants, with an economics degree. Write a one-page report for the chief finance officer estimating the year's inflation and justifying your conclusion.

FORECASTING: SIMPLE LINEAR REGRESSION

26-1 INTRODUCTION

Throughout the text we have seen the necessity of relating variables to each other to try and determine patterns of economic behaviour, linking together such pairs of variables as: price and quantity demanded; price and quantity supplied; income and consumption; costs and output; and profit and output. Essentially in such cases we are trying to identify and quantify connections or correlations between such variables. The purpose of this identification is to seek to predict such economic behaviour and the ability to explain and predict economic events is potentially important for decision-making at every level. The business decision-maker needs to know the precise relationship between price and quantity demanded for a certain product in order to be able to predict what will happen to sales (and therefore to profit, costs, employment and so on) if he or she alters the price of a product. The Chancellor of the Exchequer needs to know the precise relationship between income and consumption levels in order to try and predict what happens if the basic rate of income tax is charged or if the level of govenment spending is altered.

One of the most common methods of quantifying such patterns of economic behaviour between variables, and hence of forecasting such behaviour, is the technique of *regression*. In this chapter we will focus on the basic form of the technique—simple linear regression.

26-2 SIMPLE LINEAR REGRESSION

In the previous chapter we examined the theoretical basis for the link between the rate of inflation and the money supply and concluded, as we have done throughout the text, that it is necessary to test such theory against data. The principles of simple linear regression will be illustrated in this context. It should be noted, however, that the scope for using the technique in economic analysis is wide-ranging and applicable in any situation, at both the macro and micro levels, where we wish to quantify the relationship between two variables. Given that our objective is to explain economic behaviour it is essential that we derive an appropriate and precise mathematical expression for some set of data. The rest of this chapter is concerned with how this is to be done, and how the resulting information can be evaluated and used.

Figure 26.1 shows two variables which formed the basis for one of the exercises at the end of Chapter 25. On the vertical axis we have the RPI for all items other than seasonal food and on the horizontal axis the sterling M3 money supply figures. Both variables are shown on a quarterly basis for the period 1980–5. The diagram, known as a *scatter diagram* because it shows the scatter of points of the two variables, is a common and useful first step in regression analysis. It allows us to see readily whether there is any apparent relationship between the two variables in question. We can see that there is indeed some apparent connection between the two, with the RPI rising as sterling M3 rises, although it is also evident that the relationship between the two variables is not perfectly constant. It should be apparent why RPI has been placed on the vertical axis. In terms of convention the dependent variable is put on this axis and the quantity theory suggests that RPI is dependent on sterling M3. Thus, RPI is denoted as the Y variable (measured as an index) and sterling M3 as the X variable (measured in billions of pounds).

Logically, we are looking for a *linear* equation that best represents the scatter of data that we have in the diagram; in the terminology of regression we are looking for *the line of best fit*. Such an equation will be the precise mathematical relationship that comes closest to

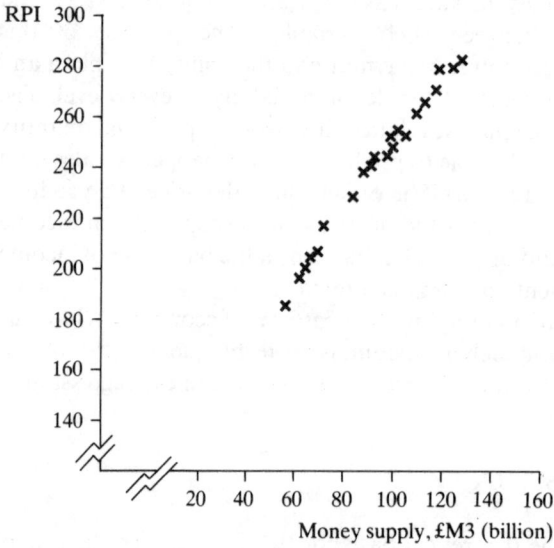

Figure 26-1 Scatter plot of RPI against money supply

the data set. We shall examine later how we can measure this 'goodness of fit' but for now we shall concentrate on the mechanics of finding the parameters of the line.

Readers will remember that the general form of a linear equation is given as:

$$Y = a + bX$$

where a and b are the intercept and slope of the equation. The two parameters of the line of best fit, a and b, can be calculated using the following expressions:

$$b = \frac{n\Sigma X Y - \Sigma X \Sigma Y}{n\Sigma X^2 - (\Sigma X)^2}$$

$$a = \frac{\Sigma Y - b\Sigma X}{n}$$

where n is the number of pairs of data items, ΣX is the sum of the X values, ΣY is the sum of the Y values, $\Sigma X Y$ is the sum of X times Y, and ΣX^2 is the sum of the X^2 values (be careful to distinguish this from the square of the sum of X values, written $(\Sigma X)^2$). The appropriate calculations are shown in Table 26-1, although we assume you will be using an appropriate computer program to perform these calculations.

Table 26-1 Calculations for linear regression

Year/Quarter	Y	X	XY	Y²	X²
1980/1	184.8	58.18	10 751.7	34 151.0	3 384.91
1980/2	195.8	61.48	12 037.8	38 337.6	3 779.79
1980/3	200.4	64.37	12 899.7	40 160.2	4 143.50
1980/4	204.3	67.07	13 702.4	41 738.5	4 498.38
1981/1	209.0	68.58	14 333.2	43 681.0	4 703.22
1981/2	218.9	71.46	15 642.6	47 917.2	5 106.53
1981/3	223.0	74.94	16 711.6	49 729.0	5 616.00
1981/4	228.2	83.96	19 159.7	52 075.2	7 049.28
1982/1	231.2	85.83	19 843.9	53 453.4	7 366.79
1982/2	238.3	87.62	20 879.8	56 786.9	7 677.26
1982/3	240.9	89.56	21 575.0	58 032.8	8 020.99
1982/4	243.1	91.55	22 255.8	59 097.6	8 381.40
1983/1	244.0	95.92	23 404.5	59 536.0	9 200.65
1983/2	248.6	98.09	24 385.3	61 802.0	9 621.65
1983/3	251.6	99.25	24 971.3	63 302.6	9 850.56
1983/4	253.9	101.84	25 857.2	64.465.2	10 371.4
1984/1	255.2	103.81	26 492.3	65 127.0	10 776.5
1984/2	260.0	106.07	27 578.2	67 600.0	11 250.8
1984/3	263.3	109.00	28 699.7	69 326.9	11 881.0
1984/4	267.0	112.14	29 941.4	71 289.0	12 575.4
1985/1	270.0	116.19	31 371.3	72 900.0	13 500.1
1985/2	279.0	118.45	33 047.6	77 841.0	14 030.4
1985/3	280.7	124.14	34 846.1	78 792.5	15 410.7
1985/4	281.9	127.19	35 854.9	79 467.6	16 177.3
Totals	5773.1	2216.69	546 242.8	1 406 610.3	214 374.6

The calculation of the a and b parameters is then straightforward:

$$b = \frac{n\Sigma XY - \Sigma X \Sigma Y}{n\Sigma X^2 - (\Sigma X)^2} = \frac{24(546\ 242.8) - (2216.69)(5773.1)}{24(214\ 374.6) - (2216.69)^2}$$

$$= \frac{13\ 109\ 827.2 - 12\ 797\ 173.04}{5\ 144\ 990.4 - 4\ 913\ 714.56} = \frac{312\ 654.16}{231\ 275.84} = 1.3519$$

$$a = \frac{\Sigma Y - b\Sigma X}{n} = \frac{(5773.1 - 1.3519(2216.69)}{24}$$

$$= \frac{2776.36}{24} = 115.68$$

Thus, the equation representing the line of best fit is:

$$Y = 115.68 + 1.3519X$$

where Y is the RPI and X is sterling M3.

Interpretation of the line of best fit is the same as for any linear equation. The a term denotes the intercept and the b term denotes the slope of the line. In this case, the equation indicates that a unit increase in X will lead to an increase of 1.3519 in Y. Thus, the analysis indicates that an increase in the money supply, as measured by sterling M3, of £1 billion will lead to an increase in the RPI of 1.3519 percentage points.

Forecasting from the equation is straightforward. If we know that sterling M3 is set to be, say, £150 billion than the predicted level for RPI will be:

$$Y = 115.68 + 1.3519(150) = 115.68 + 202.785 = 318.5$$

In Fig. 26-2 the line of best fit has been superimposed on the scatter diagram. This line, as the name suggests, is the line that comes closest to the set of data points. As we can see

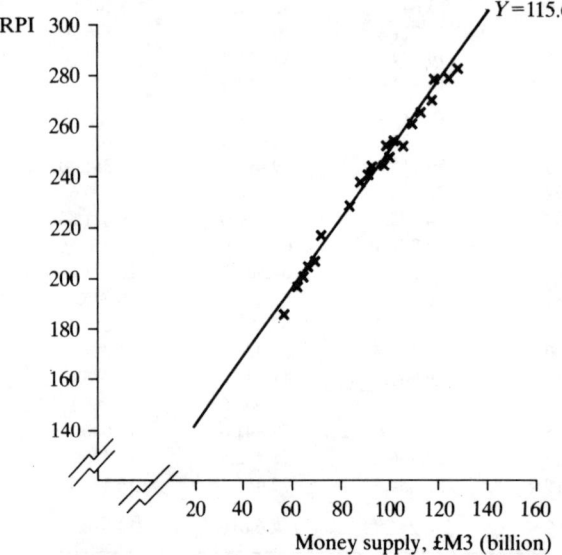

Figure 26-2 RPI and money supply: line of best fit

from the diagram, however, there are discrepancies between the observed points and the best fit line. That is, the line we have calculated is *not* a *perfect* fit to the scatter of data. A conceptual understanding of how the line is derived is important at this stage. Logically, it would be sensible to try and find the line that came closest to the data set. Any line is likely to deviate, to a greater or lesser extent, from the data points themselves. The regression equations used above find the one line where this deviation from the data points is kept to the minimum. As with the standard deviation, the deviations of the line from the data are not measured in absolute terms (given that some will be negative and some positive) but rather by squaring the deviations. The line of best fit is then the line where these squared deviations are minimized. Hence the alternative name for the method we have used: the *method of least squares*.

26-3 CORRELATION COEFFICIENT

Given that we are using regression to measure relationships between economic variables and that we wish to use such equations for predicting economic behaviour it is essential that we have some measure of how accurate and reliable the equation we have obtained is. Obviously, we can obtain a visual assessment by superimposing the line of best fit on the scatter diagram, as we did in Fig. 26.2. Visually, it appears that the regression line is reasonably close to the observed data and hence we would view predictions obtained from the equation with reasonable confidence. Such a visual impression, however, is insufficient. We also require some statistical measure of accuracy.

One such measure is a statistic known as the *correlation coefficient* or, more formally, as *Pearson's product moment correlation coefficient*. The formula is:

$$r = \frac{n\Sigma XY - \Sigma X\Sigma Y}{\sqrt{(n\Sigma X^2 - (\Sigma X)^2)(n\Sigma Y^2 - (\Sigma Y)^2)}}$$

Although the formula looks complex the calculations are straightforward:

$$r = \frac{24(546\ 242.8) - (2216.69)(5773.1)}{\sqrt{(24(214\ 374.6) - (2216.69)^2)(24(1\ 406\ 610.3) - (5773.1)^2)}}$$

$$= \frac{13\ 109\ 827.2 - 12\ 797\ 173.04}{\sqrt{(231\ 275.84)(429\ 963.59)}}$$

$$= \frac{312\ 654.16}{315\ 341.39} = 0.9915$$

But what does the resulting statistic mean? The correlation coefficient measures the strength of the linear relationship between the X and Y variables. Mathematically, the coefficient takes a value between 0 and 1 (which means if you work out a correlation coefficient with a value of 15.6 you've done something wrong!). A value of 0 implies, literally, that there is no correlation or linear connection between the two variables (that they are *independent*). Similarly, a coefficient of 1 implies a perfect linear connection between the two variables.

The coefficient could also take either a positive or negative value. This simply indicates whether the slope of the regression line is positive or negative. So, here, we know from the correlation coefficient that the regression line would have a positive slope. But how do we assess our correlation coefficient of 0.9915? On a scale between 0 and 1 it obviously lies closer to perfect correlation than to zero correlation, confirming the original view from the scatter diagram that the line of best fit is reasonably close to the data and, hence, predictions based on such a regression equation could be viewed as likely to be reasonably accurate.

In fact, we can go one stage further and formally assess the coefficient value through a hypothesis test. As ever, we are dealing with sample data and we wish to determine if there is a *significant* correlation between the two variables. As we have seen previously, conclusions based on sample information are suspect. The null hypothesis will be to assume that the sample data represents a population with zero correlation and the alternative hypothesis that there is some significant degree of correlation. Unless we find sufficient statistical evidence to support H_1, we would have to accept H_0 which states that the two variables are not correlated:

$$H_0: r = 0$$

$$H_1: r \neq 0$$

$$\alpha = 0.05$$

As before we obtain a test statistic from tables and calculate an appropriate statistic. Given the sample size a t-test is appropriate and the number of degrees of freedom is given—for simple linear regression—by $n - 2$ where n is the number of pairs of observations used in the regression. The appropriate calculated statistic is given by:

$$t_{calc} = \frac{r - 0}{SE}$$

where t_{calc} refers to the calculated t value and

$$SE = \sqrt{(1 - r^2)/(n - 2)}$$

From tables the critical value of t is 2.074 and

$$t_{calc} = \frac{0.9915 - 0}{\sqrt{(1 - 0.9915^2)/22}} = \frac{0.9915}{0.0277} = 35.7$$

As the calculated statistic is greater than the critical we must reject the null hypothesis and accept that, at the 95% probability level, the correlation between the two variables is significant. In other words, we are confident that the two variables are correlated with each other. It is important for readers to understand why such a test is necessary. Regression applied to two variables will *always* find the line of best fit and the calculated value for r will tend to be non-zero. Such a non-zero value will occur even when there is no real correlation between the variables. We must have some method, therefore, of distinguishing between those values of r which are statistically significant and those which are not.

It is also important, however, to understand properly the implications of the correlation statistic we have obtained. It is tempting, but incorrect, to assume that we have identified *cause* and *effect* between two variables just because they are significantly correlated. In fact, the correlation coefficient simply indicates whether two variables are connected—it does *not* indicate the *direction* of the connection. Close examination of the equation for calculating the correlation coefficient reveals that it is independent of the X and Y variables. That is, it does not matter which variable we used as X and which we used as Y. In both cases we would obtain the same correlation coefficient value. (If you're not convinced try it and see.)

The choice of X and Y variables and the implied cause–effect structure *must* be based on economic theory and relationships, not on the mathematics and statistics. As with all the techniques we are using in economic analysis, they can be used to disprove the hypotheses we establish based on our knowledge of economic behaviour, but the techniques themselves will not establish what an appropriate hypothesis is. In the context of the data, we have not *proved* that the quantity theory of money is correct but rather have shown that the theory and relevant economic data are consistent.

The value of the correlation coefficient must also be interpreted with care. Remember that the coefficient measures the strength of the *linear* relationship between two variables. If the relationship (like many in economics) is in fact non-linear the correlation coefficient is likely to take a low value. It is tempting to interpret this as evidence that there is no connection between the two variables whereas, in fact, it indicates *the lack of a linear connection*. Suppose, for example, we were trying to obtain a regression equation for an average cost curve for a business. We know that such a curve is likely to be U-shaped rather than linear. If we performed a linear regression we would be likely to obain a low correlation coefficient value. This would indicate, however, not that there was no connection between average costs and output but that the connection was a non-linear one. Obviously, the scatter diagram is very useful here as it would allow us visually to confirm whether we had some non-linear pattern in our data.

26-4 VARIATION AND THE COEFFICIENT OF DETERMINATION

Thus far, we have used the correlation coefficient to indicate the variation between the line of best fit and the datapoints in the analysis. The concept of measuring variation is of such importance in regression analysis that we need to examine it in more detail. One way of looking at regression analysis is in terms of trying to relate movement in the Y variable (variation in Y) to movement in the X variable—(variation in X).

In using regression we are trying to connect the Y variation to the X variation. At one extreme we may find that the Y variation has nothing to do with X variation, while at the other extreme all the variation in Y may be associated with variation in X. In practice, our analysis is likely to result in some position mid-way between the two extremes. In fact, we can distinguish between three (related) types of variation in Y:

> total variation in Y
>
> the Y variation connected to variation in X
>
> the Y variation not connected to variation in X

In the terminology of regression these three types of variation are referred to as:

> total variation in Y
>
> *explained* variation
>
> *unexplained* variation

The words 'explained' and 'unexplained' must be treated with caution as they do not necessarily imply causation as such, but rather form part of the regression terminology.

The measurement of the three aspects of regression variation is illustrated in Fig. 26.3. This shows the line of best fit for some set of data. Also shown is a line representing the average Y value ($\bar{Y}$)—the arithmetic mean—and, for a given value of X, the actual value of Y (denoted as Y) and the predicted value of Y (denoted as $\hat{Y}$). For this single observation we can identify that:

$$\text{total variation in } Y = (Y - \bar{Y})^2$$

$$\text{the part of total variation in } Y \text{ explained by } X = (\hat{Y} - \bar{Y})^2$$

$$\text{the part of total variation in } Y \text{ unexplained by } X = (Y - \hat{Y})^2$$

(remembering, as with the standard deviation, that we must square deviations from the average to measure variation). Thus $(\hat{Y} - \bar{Y})^2$ is the measure of the variation in Y that should occur according to the estimated equation, while $(Y - \hat{Y})^2$ is the measure of the variation in Y that occurred over and above that predicted.

Ideally, we would want all of the variation in Y to be accounted for by the X variable used in the equation. At worst none of the variation will be 'explained'. A ratio therefore of

$$\frac{\text{explained variation}}{\text{total variation}}$$

will indicate the proportion of total variation in Y that can be attributed to the regression equation. At most this ratio will take a value of 1 (where explained is equal to total) and at worst equal to 0 (where none of total variation is explained by the equation). Given that we

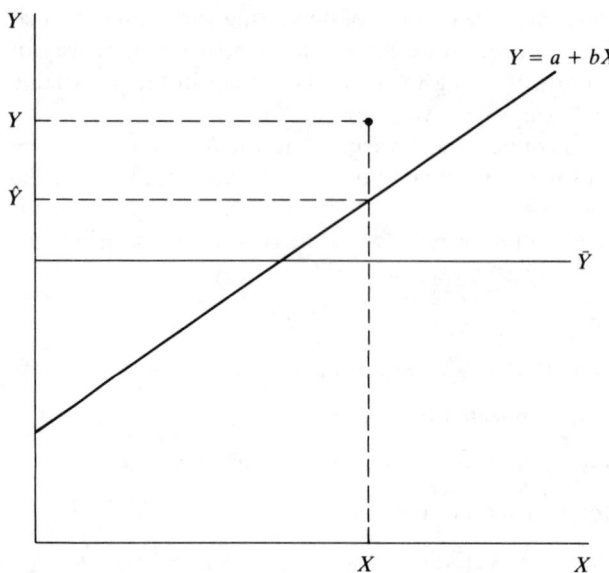

Figure 26-3 Explained and unexplained variation

will be measuring this variation for all observations, not just one, the appropriate calculations will be

$$\text{total variation in } Y = \Sigma(Y - \bar{Y})^2$$

$$\text{explained variation} = \Sigma(\hat{Y} - \bar{Y})^2$$

$$\text{unexplained variation} = \Sigma(Y - \hat{Y})^2$$

Now

$$\frac{\text{explained variation}}{\text{total variation}} = \frac{\Sigma(\hat{Y} - \bar{Y})^2}{\Sigma(Y - \bar{Y})^2}$$

This statistic, denoted R^2, is known as the *coefficient of determination*. It can be calculated using the ratio given above or, more readily, by squaring the correlation coefficient, r (although its meaning and interpretation is far more than is implied by the simple square of the correlation coefficient).

It will be seen from Table 26-2 that the total variation is 17 915.1. The explained variation is 17 611.90. Hence $R^2 = 17\,611.90/17\,915.1 = 0.983$. That is, 98 per cent of the variation in the Y variable is accounted for by variation in X (note that the square root of 0.983 is 0.9915, the value of r). The coefficient of determination is a far more useful statistic

Table 26-2 Calculation of coefficient of determination

Year/Quarter	Y	X	$\hat{Y}$	$(Y - \bar{Y})^2$	$(\hat{Y} - \bar{Y})^2$	$(Y - \hat{Y})^2$
1980/1	184.8	58.18	194.334	3 107.6	2 135.55	90.8972
1980/2	195.8	61.48	198.795	2 002.2	1 743.15	8.9700
1980/3	200.4	64.37	202.702	1 611.7	1 432.17	5.2992
1980/4	204.3	67.07	206.352	1 313.8	1 169.23	4.2107
1981/1	209.0	68.58	208.393	995.1	1 033.82	0.3684
1981/2	218.9	71.46	212.287	468.5	798.57	43.7318
1981/3	223.0	74.94	216.991	307.9	554.84	36.1081
1981/4	228.2	83.96	229.186	152.4	129.05	0.9722
1982/1	231.2	85.83	231.714	87.3	78.00	0.2642
1982/2	238.3	87.62	234.134	5.0	41.11	17.3556
1982/3	240.9	89.56	236.756	0.1	14.36	17.1727
1982/4	243.1	91.55	239.446	6.5	1.21	13.3517
1983/1	244.0	95.92	245.354	11.9	23.12	1.8333
1983/2	248.6	98.09	248.288	64.9	59.94	0.0973
1983/3	251.6	99.25	249.856	122.2	86.68	3.0415
1983/4	253.9	101.84	253.358	178.3	164.15	0.2938
1984/1	255.2	103.81	256.021	214.7	239.48	0.6740
1984/2	260.0	106.07	259.076	378.5	343.36	0.8538
1984/3	263.3	109.0	263.037	517.8	505.80	0.0692
1984/4	267.0	112.14	267.282	699.8	714.81	0.0795
1985/1	270.0	116.19	272.757	867.5	1 037.55	7.6010
1985/2	279.0	118.45	275.813	1 478.7	1 243.76	10.1570
1985/3	280.7	124.14	283.505	1 612.4	1 845.48	7.8680
1985/4	281.9	127.19	287.628	1 710.2	2 216.71	32.8100
Totals	5 773.1	2 216.69	5 773.065	17 915.1	17 611.90	304.0802

in evaluating the reliability of a regression equation and is used extensively in the more advanced applications of the technique. For our purposes, it is sufficient to be able to use and assess the statistic.

26-5 t TEST ON THE EQUATION PARAMETERS

The coefficient of determination and the correlation coefficient can be used to assess the regression equation as a whole. There are frequently occasions in economic analysis, however, when we also wish to test a specific hypothesis relating to part of the estimated equation—that is on either of the two parameters a and b. The reasons for such a test are evident. We may, for example, wish to determine whether, say, the slope of the line predicting the behaviour of one set of data is different from that of another set. We may wish to see if parts of the equation have altered over time and so on. Such tests are carried out through a standard t test on either the a or b parameter of the equation.

t test on a specified b value

To illustrate we shall refer to an equivalent equation relating RPI to sterling M3 for the period between 1970 and 1975. Using the appropriate data the resultant regression equation is:

$$RPI = 32.88 + 1.3973£M3$$

Let us suppose, for example, that we wish to determine whether the b term from the latest regression equation is different from that for the earlier period. The b coefficient we have estimated for 1980–5 is 1.3519. We wish to determine whether this part of the equation has changed over time. In other words, has the responsiveness of the RPI to changes in the money supply altered since 1970–5? If we treat the previous value of 1.3973 as the inferred population value we can set up a standard hypothesis test on the new b term.

$$H_0: b = 1.3973$$

$$H_1: b \neq 1.3973$$

$$\alpha = 0.05$$

(Readers will be aware that we could, equally, undertake a one-tail test to determine whether the b parameter has increased or decreased.) Given the size of the sample this would be a t test with 22 $(n - 2)$ degrees of freedom and, from the appropriate table for the t distribution, the critical statistic will have a value of 2.074. The calculated value can be obtained in the standard way:

$$t_{calc} = \frac{1.3519 - 1.3973}{SE} = \frac{-0.0454}{SE}$$

where the standard error is given by:

$$SE = \sqrt{\frac{\Sigma(Y - \hat{Y})^2/n - 2}{\Sigma X^2 - \frac{(\Sigma X)^2}{n}}}$$

Such calculations are not recommended to be undertaken manually! The necessary calculations have already been undertaken, however, earlier in the chapter.

$$\Sigma(Y - \hat{Y})^2 = 304.0802$$

$$\Sigma X^2 = 214\,374.6$$

$$(\Sigma X)^2 = 2216.69^2 = 4\,913\,714.56$$

Hence:

$$SE = \sqrt{\frac{304.0802/22}{214\,374.6 - \dfrac{4\,913\,714.56}{24}}} = 0.0379$$

So the calculated t statistic becomes:

$$t_{calc} = \frac{1.3519 - 1.3973}{0.0379} = -1.20$$

and, ignoring the negative sign, we conclude at the 95 per cent level that the new estimate of b does not significantly differ from the original, that is, we have no evidence on which to reject the null hypothesis.

Although the mechanics of the calculation are straightforward the principles of the approach are as for every hypothesis test we have encountered. The b term we have estimated (at 1.3519) has to be seen as a piece of sample information. In the text we are trying to infer likely population values for b, based on the sample. The standard error we have calculated shows the expected sampling variation for a set of data this size. We have concluded, at the 95 per cent probability level, that the sample result of 1.3519 is not inconsistent with a population value of 1.397 hence we can infer that the true population value has not changed from its previous value.

The use of such hypothesis tests is of considerable importance when using regression to estimate economic relationships. Such tests allow us to determine both the statistical reliability of the estimated equation and to compare the observed equation against an inferred value.

Equally we could undertake a similar test on the a parameter of the estimated equation. In practice, this is done far less frequently but follows exactly the same approach. The standard error for the a estimate is generally produced as part of the regression program used to perform the analysis.

t test on $b = 0$

As well as testing the b parameter against some assumed population value, as above, it is also common to perform a test with $H_0: b = 0$. In fact, this is simply an alternative to the test detailed on the r value in Section 26.3. By specifying H_0 as $b = 0$ we hypothesize that the slope of the population line of best fit is zero, that is, there is no connection between the X and Y values. Such a test would be undertaken using the approach detailed in the preceding subsection but using $b = 0$ as the inferred population value. A result accepting H_1 would conclude that there was some statistically significant connection (correlation) between the two variables. In practice, it is apparent that the result from this test and the test on r will give identical results and only one needs to be undertaken.

Generally, this test on b will often be a one-tailed test as we will normally have some economic hypothesis about the slope of the line we are trying to estimate.

26-6   ESTIMATING TREND LINES USING REGRESSION

One specialized use of regression is to estimate the trend in some variable over time. Frequently in economics we encounter a situation where we are interested in the movement of a variable over some period of time. For example, we may wish to look at sales of an item over the last few years, or income, or exports of investment. Our interest is often not in trying to find an explanatory variable for the variable in question, but rather simply to find the average change in the variable per unit of time. In such a situation regression is easily applied. The regression equation would be specified as:

$$Y = a + bT$$

where time T is being used as a pseudo-explanatory variable. T would be given arbitrary values in order to perform the calculations. Thus, we might denote the first time period with a value 1, the second with a value 2 then 3, 4 and so on. Calculation of the appropriate parameters (and the array of supporting statistics) is then identical to the methods adopted earlier.

As a brief illustration, suppose we wanted to estimate the trend in the RPI over the period 1980–5. Setting the T values such that 1980/1 = 1 and 1985/4 = 24 we estimate the equation as:

$$RPI = 191.8 + 3.9T$$

That is, RPI increased over this period by 3.9 percentage points each quarter, on average. (Readers may wish to confirm for themselves that for this equation $R^2 = 0.977$ and is statistically significant at the 99% level.) Forecasting the trend line is technically straightforward (although the validity of such forecasting is discussed in the next section). The time period for which we wished to obtain a forecast would take its appropriate value in the time series and this value would then be substituted for T in the above equation. Thus, the forecast for 1987/4 (which would take a T value of 32) would be:

$$RPI = 191.8 + 3.9T = 191.8 + 3.9(32) = 316.6$$

26-7   ASSESSING THE REGRESSION MODEL

Regression analysis is one of the most useful techniques available to the economic analyst and, because of this, one of the easiest to misuse or misinterpret. The logical basis for the application of the technique to an area of economic analysis must be clearly understood as must the statistical and mathematical principles on which the technique is based.

It is necessary to assess the results of a regression model both in terms of the statistical theory and in terms of the economic theory. Not infrequently, the two provide conflicting conclusions regarding the reliability of the results.

To assess the results statistically the following approach can be adopted:

1. Construct the appropriate scatter diagram.
2. Perform the regression calculations.
3. As a quick guide to the results assess the R^2 value.
4. Assess the correlation between the two variables by performing either a test on r, or a test on b where H_0 is set at $b = 0$.
5. If appropriate, test the b (and a) value against the hypothesized value.
6. Compare visually the scatter diagram and the line of best fit to identify any individual observations which are out of pattern with the rest.

The only point which warrants further discussion is the last. Not infrequently, one or two observations may be out of line with the rest of the scatter. (Reasons for this can be varied, including random and unpredictable factors such as strikes, adverse weather, military conflict and so on.) A small number of such occurrences in the data can have severe distorting effects on the results and this may not be apparent from the statistics. Indeed, it is worth stressing that use should be made of the scatter diagram wherever possible, particularly in trying to assess whether the hypothesized relationship is, in fact, a linear one.

Such a statistical evaluation of the model and its results, however, is worthless without a corresponding economic evaluation. Indeed, it is economic theory which must be used *before* regression can be attempted. The choice of which variable is to be dependent and which independent must be made on the basis of economic theory, not statistics. Economics must also be used to determine the probable values of the a and b parameters *before* regression is attempted. It is economic theory, for example, that indicates that the b term in the equation linking RPI and sterling M3 should be positive.

In assessing and using a regression model a number of final points should be considered. First, regression cannot be used to prove that a theory is correct. It simply provides statistical evidence as to whether observed movements in a variable are consistent with the theoretical predictions, that is, whether the data are consistent with the appropriate economic theory. For the example used in this chapter, our conclusion is that the available data (on sterling M3 and the RPI) are not inconsistent, at the 95 per cent confidence level, with the predictions of the quantity theory of money that prices will rise if the money supply increases. As we have consistently stressed, this is *not* the same as saying that the quantity theory is correct.

Second, regression cannot prove 'cause and effect'. The fact that two variables are significantly correlated does not indicate that one 'causes' the other. Again, it is economic theory which must be used to justify such a cause–effect pattern.

Third, in practice the reliability of the technique's results depends largely on the quality of the data used. The choice of variables, the data definitions and—for time-series data—the choice of historical period must all be made with care and with appropriate theoretical justification.

Fourth, considerable care must be taken when using regression results for forecasting and due attention paid to the implicit assumptions of the simple linear regression approach: that the relationship is a linear one; that there is only one (major) explanatory variable; that the relationship between the two variables is constant over time.

Implicitly in a regression model we make the usual assumption of *ceteris paribus*. When forecasting future movements in the Y variable this assumption—that all other factors not included in the equation remain constant—becomes increasingly difficult to accept. This is one of the major reasons why as distinction is made between forecasts based on *interpolation* and those on *extrapolation*. The distinction is simple. An interpolated forecast is based on the use of a value for the X variable that falls within limits that have already been observed, while an extrapolated forecast is based on an X value that falls outside the observed range. In both the examples above, the forecasts are based on extrapolated values. Thus, when forecasting RPI when sterling M3 takes a value of 150 we are forecasting for a money supply value that is outside the observed range of values and as such deserves to be treated with extra caution no matter how statistically reliable the regression equation appears.

In spite of these points the usefulness of regression to the economist and to business in general should not be underestimated. It provides one of the most powerful quantitative tools for economic analysis.

26-8 SUMMARY

The *line of best fit* is the linear equation that comes closest to the observed set of data points.

The *method of least squares* is the method used to estimate the regression line from the observed data.

The *explained variation* is that part of the total variation in the Y values that can be associated with the estimated regression equation, while the *unexplained variation* is that part of total variation that remains unaccounted for by the equation.

The *coefficient of determination* is a measure of the variation in the Y variable that can be accounted for by variation in the X variable. It is a statistic which measures how close the regression line fits the data.

EXERCISES

26-1 The data below relate to the example used in Chapter 4 and show the new registrations of cars (expressed as

	New car registrations (thousands)	Income *per capita* (£)
1970	91.4	2204
1971	108.4	2222
1972	138.6	2402
1973	137.1	2561
1974	102.8	2540
1975	98.5	2549
1976	106.5	2536
1977	109.4	2509
1978	131.6	2682
1979	142.1	2823
1980	126.6	2869
1981	124.5	2803
1982	132.0	2815
1983	150.5	2881
1984	146.6	2945
1985	153.5	3020

Source: Economic Trends Annual Supplement.

an average of the monthly figures and measured in thousands), and *per capita* real personal disposable income measured in pounds at 1980 prices.

(*a*) Draw a scatter diagram for the data.
(*b*) What evidence is there for a linear relationship?
(*c*) What (economic) reasons can you suggest for the fact that the data do not all lie on a straight line?
(*d*) Carry out a regression analysis on the data.
(*e*) How do you interpret the slope of the line you have estimated?
(*f*) Test the significance of your regression results. What statistical conclusions do you come to about the reliability of the equation?
(*g*) What economic reasons can you suggest as to why the equation may be unreliable for forecasting?
(*h*) Collect data on the two variables to bring them up to date. Using the latest income data, forecast the number of cars registered.
(*i*) Compare your forecast value with the actual value. How do you account for the differences?

26-2 Using the data in Exercise 26-1 determine the trend line and assess your results statistically. Forecast the number of cars registered using the trend line for the same year as you produced a forecast in 26-1(*h*). Which equation (that derived in Exercise 26-1 or the trend line) would you prefer to use for forecasting purposes?

26-3 The data below relate to the example used in Chapter 2 and show the percentage of households in a particular income group with a caravan and the average normal weekly disposable household income for households in that income group.

Percentage of housholds with a car/van	Average normal weekly disposable househood income (£)
9.8	33.93
6.1	44.11
18.2	57.75
26.4	70.78
41.5	86.46
47.7	102.89
61.2	120.32
69.2	137.40
71.3	155.16
79.1	172.52
80.1	190.29
88.4	216.28
89.5	252.66
93.5	292.01
95.5	338.01
97.8	502.82

(*a*) Carry out a regression analysis for these data.
(*b*) Assess your results statistically. What conclusion do you come to about the usefulness of the equation?
(*c*) Assess the equation in economic terms. How useful is it?
(*d*) Forecast the percentage of car ownership when income is £200 and when income is £600. Which represents an interpolation and which an extrapolation? Which would you regard as more reliable?

26-4 Collect data on the annual energy consumption by industry for the last 15 years. Collect comparative data on the Index of Industrial Production. Let Energy be the dependent variable.

(*a*) What value (positive/negative) would you expect for the *b* term of a regression equation based on these data?
(*b*) Carry out a regression analysis using Energy as the dependent variable.
(*c*) Assess your results.
(*d*) Assume you are working for the Department of Energy. Draft a report summarizing your findings and discussing the reliability of using the results to forecast future energy demand by industry.

27

THE SUPPLY OF MONEY AND ITS CONTROL

27-1 INTRODUCTION

Now that the importance of the money supply for macro-economic policy has been established, this chapter explains, first, how the money supply can grow, and second, how that growth can be controlled. From the point of view of the monetarists, these matters are of substantial importance since the first relates to the cause of inflation while the second pertains to its prevention. This work necessitates a brief examination of the structure of the financial system.

27-2 FINANCIAL INTERMEDIATION

Income and expenditure are rarely in balance for most households and firms. Some will have an excess of expenditure over income, and thus need to borrow, while others will be in surplus. For the economy as a whole, the historical pattern has been for private households, in aggregate, to be net savers while the government and industrial and commercial companies tend to record deficits.

These surpluses and deficits are balanced out by savers lending funds to those in deficit. It is, of course, unusual for lenders to pass funds directly to borrowers. More commonly, money is placed in an institution like a bank or building society which in turn lends the money on to the final borrower. This process of *financial intermediation* brings advantages in that financial institutions can pool the often small savings of a number of people into a substantial sum. For example, building societies typically need the deposits of five savers to finance each loan. Another advantage of using financial intermediaries is that risks can be spread. In the case of company shares, it is widely accepted that a portfolio should include

278

shares in about 20 companies to reduce risk to a reasonable level. Because of brokerage charges, it would be very expensive to hold a wide range of shares. Nevertheless, a small saver can overcome this problem by placing his or her money with a unit trust or a life assurance company, which can use the money together with that of its other clients to purchase a range of assets.

The relationship between private households and their banks and building societies can be likened to retailing, in that the organizations concerned undertake an extremely large number of small-scale transactions through extensive networks of local branches. There is, analogously, a wholesale trade in funds in which financial institutions use the funds gathered through their retail operations to buy large blocks of securities. The markets on which these assets are traded are known collectively as the *capital market* (sometimes known as the 'City'). Formerly, much of the trade in securities was conducted in the Stock Exchange, but the advent of computerized systems means that the market is now the network of electronically linked dealing rooms which extend throughout the City of London and beyond. It may be useful to examine some of the major types of securities traded there.

First, there are company shares or *equities*. These entitle the holder both to vote at the annual general meeting of the company and to receive a *dividend*—a share in the company's profit that is distributed to shareholders rather than retained by the company to finance future investment. Dividends fluctuate according to the profitability of the company.

Second, *bonds* differ from company shares in two respects: they are issued for a finite period of time, at the end of which they are 'redeemed', that is, bought back by the issuing organization at their face value; and they pay a fixed return every year. This fixed return is known as a *coupon* and is expressed as a percentage rate. Although companies issue bonds, the largest source is the government, whose bonds are known as 'gilt-edged stocks', 'government stocks' or just *gilts*. Gilts often run for 25 years from issue to redemption, though after the elapse of time, a stock matures into a *medium* and, when its redemption date draws close, into a *short*. The total value of gilt-edged stock that is outstanding is known as the *National Debt*.

The final main category of security is *bills*, which are issued by companies, local authorities and the government. Bills generally only run for three months from issue to redemption, and are thus short-term securities. The buyer or holder is not entitled to receive any payment other than that for redemption. The organization buying bills can, therefore, only earn a return by buying bills at a price below their face value, a practice known as *discounting*. The most important bills—for reasons which will be examined later in this chapter—are the Treasury bills issued by the government. The markets on which bills are traded are termed the *money markets*.

The general characteristics of these securities are that they consist essentially of promises to make payments at some time in the future. In the case of shares, the promises are notably vague, there being no guarantee that a company will either make a profit or distribute a dividend. Bonds and bills, by contrast, carry highly specific promises to pay either redemption moneys or coupons (or both). All securities can be bought and sold at prices which are naturally determined by the future payments which they are expected to earn. This relationship between price and payments is examined in Chapter 28.

Borrowers can raise new funds on the capital markets by issuing new securities for sale. The capital markets thus perform the important economic function of channelling funds from savers into investment in capital equipment. It should be stressed, however, that it is not usual for investors to buy a security and hold it until it falls due for redemption. More commonly, securities are bought and sold several times during their lives because, perhaps, the original holder's circumstances change and he or she needs money rather than the security. Keynesian economists in particular stress the way that investors continually make choices between holding money and holding securities. Indeed, the trade in 'old' securities quite overshadows the issue of new securities. Naturally, new securities have to offer returns which are commensurate with those on existing securities, so that the fluctuating prices and interest rates on old securities dictate the terms on which new borrowers may borrow.

27-3 THE BANKING MECHANISM

Within this general framework of borrowing, financial intermediation and lending, the banks play a rather distinctive role in two related respects. First, their business consists to a large degree of making loans rather than dealing in existing securities. Second, the deposits which the public place with them constitute the bulk of the stock of money in the economy (as readers will recall from Chapter 25). This section looks at the three main subsections of the banking system in turn: the central bank, the banks proper and the discount houses.

The central bank

The linchpin of the banking system of any market economy is its central bank. In the United Kingdom, this is the Bank of England, which was established in 1694 and taken into public ownership in 1945. Besides having a general responsibility for maintaining the various regulations which govern the City, the Bank has a number of important economic functions. First, the government's accounts, into which taxation is paid and from which expenditure is financed, are held at the Bank of England. Second, the Bank undertakes the borrowing which governments frequently need to make up the difference between income and expenditure. (The technical term for this shortfall is the *Public Sector Borrowing Requirement* or PSBR.) The Bank of England thus has the task of undertaking the borrowing by issuing Treasury bills, National Savings and gilts. Third, it serves as the banker to the ordinary banks, all of whom maintain accounts at the Bank of England. Fourth, it issues notes and coin to the public via the banks. Fifth, it intervenes in the foreign exchange market (a topic which is examined in Chapter 32).

The sixth function is in some ways the most important. The Bank of England, like all central banks, acts as the *lender of last resort*. The need for a body to act in this capacity arises from the fact that the banks' reserves of notes and coin are smaller than the deposits which the public place with them. Should all the depositors at one bank come to the conclusion that it was unreliable in some way, they might decide to withdraw their money (thus, of course, precipitating the very crisis they feared). The bank concerned would have to raise the necessary cash by borrowing from other banks. If, however, the panic were general, all the banks would be in the same situation and there would be a shortage of cash throughout the banking system. Some banks would be unable to meet the public's demand for cash and would therefore have to close down (as many did during the Depression of the 1930s). By standing ready to supply cash in an emergency, the Bank of England thus makes a loss of confidence in the banking system less likely.

This 'last resort' money is available only at a high ('penal') rate of interest. This was, in previous years, published as 'Minimum Lending Rate' (MLR). More recently, however, the Bank has ceased to disclose its penal rate, and the financial markets are thus placed in the position of having to guess its level. All central banks operate such 'discount' rates. Although the privilege of borrowing at least resort from the Bank of England is restricted to the discount houses (see below), MLR nevertheless influences interest rates throughout the financial system. Together with the other five functions, the role of lender of last resort places the Bank of England in a position to exert much control over interest rates and the money stock, that is, to operate monetary policy.

The banks

The second element in the banking mechanism is the banks themselves. Perhaps the easiest method of analysing these institutions is by considering the main items in their balance sheets, that is, their *assets* and *liabilities*. Liabilities are the name given to any debts which a firm owes, while assets are the wealth which can be used to meet those debts. Bank deposits, from the point of view of the individuals and firms who hold them, are to be counted as assets. From the standpoint of the banks, however, they are claims which people can make against the banks and must accordingly be classed as liabilities.

On the assets side, banks are naturally free to earn profits by holding interest-bearing securities. In practice, however, their main business lies in advancing loans to borrowers. The problem here is the conflict between liquidity and profitability. While loans earn interest, it is not usually possible to make borrowers repay their loans at short notice. By contrast, banks are obliged to provide cash for any depositor wishing to withdraw funds on demand. Banks thus borrow short and lend long. The difficulty which attends this policy is that there is no guarantee that banks will have sufficient cash reserves to meet a surge in withdrawals.

The solution to this problem is a compromise between the conflicting principles of liquidity and profitability. While most assets are held, profitability, in the form of loans, a certain proportion is kept in the form of cash or other liquid assets as a contingency reserve. In effect, the banks rely on the probability that only a small proportion of their customers will wish to withdraw funds on any one day. The policy is known as *fractional reserve banking*, and the ratio of liquid (or *reserve*) assets to total assets is termed the *liquidity ratio*. In February 1988, for instance, the liquidity ratio for the banks taken together was 32 per cent. Figure 27-1 shows a highly simplified version of the balance sheet of a bank observing a liquidity ratio of 20 per cent. (Readers who find the sums unconvincingly small are invited to think of them as referring to millions of pounds.)

From the point of view of understanding the banking mechanism one topic is of critical importance. This is the method by which payments are made between the customers of different banks. It involves the use of the balances which the banks hold at the Bank of

Liabilities		*Assets*	
Deposits	£100	Liquid assets	£20
		Loans	£80

Figure 27-1 An illustrative bank balance sheet

England (which may for convenience be called 'bankers' balances'). To illustrate the process, let us imagine that a consumer who banks at, say, Lloyds buys £100 worth of goods (by cheque) from a shopkeeper who banks at another bank, say, Barclays. It is clear that £100 must be added to the shopkeeper's account (at Barclays) while £100 must be deducted from the customer's account (at Lloyds). These two changes would amount simply to a transfer of liabilities from Lloyds to Barclays. By themselves, however, these adjustments would be insufficient, since assets and liabilities must be equal for the two banks. It is thus necessary for a transfer of assets to accompany the transfer of liabilities: some payment must be made by Lloyds (the consumer's bank) to Barclays (the shopkeeper's). Payments between banks are in fact made by means of the bankers' balances at the Bank of England. This, indeed, is the purpose for which these accounts are held. In the example above, the cheque written by the consumer would be settled by Lloyds' paying £100 from their account at the Bank of England into Barclays' account there.

(It is also worth noting that inter-bank settlements are kept to a minimum by the process of *clearing*, whereby payments from the customers of one bank to those of another are balanced against those in the reverse direction. By this means, inter-bank payments are restricted to *net amounts*. Banks participating in the clearing system are called the *clearing banks*. They are also sometimes called the 'high street banks' because of their large branch networks.)

The discount houses

This small group of long-established companies operate in the 'wholesale' financial markets. The name arises from their traditional business of lending money by means of discounting bills. The money for this lending has always been borrowed from the larger banks on condition that it be repayable virtually at a moment's notice, and these loans are known in consequence as *money at call*.

From the point of view of the banks, money at call is useful in that it earns interest (unlike bankers' balances) while remaining very liquid because of the short notice required for repayment. The banks exploit this liquidity by switching funds between their bankers' balances and money at call as circumstances dictate. When the customers of a particular bank are, in aggregate, receiving payments from people who are customers at other banks, the first bank will find that its Bank of England balance is growing. It may then lend out any excess to the discount houses. Conversely, when a bank's balance at the Bank of England is depleted (perhaps because customers are paying money out of their accounts) the bank will rebuild it by recalling these loans. Loans to the discount market can thus be used to compensate for fluctuations in the settlement of payments between banks.

It might appear that the existence of the discount houses is rather precarious in that they have very little notice for the repayment of their borrowed funds. In practice, however, each discount house borrows from several different banks. It is thus able to rely on the probability that while one bank may be recalling loans because it is losing funds, others will be gaining and will therefore be willing to increase their lending. Indeed, the discount houses will only find themselves short of funds when all the banks face withdrawals at the same time. Under these circumstances, of course, the discount houses would approach the Bank of England as the lender of last resort.

The service which the discount houses render in return for their privileged access to the

Banks is to purchase the weekly issue of Treasury bills. In practice, the discount houses buy Treasury bills when they are newly issued and then sell them, often to the banks, when they are a few weeks old. Although anyone can bid for Treasury bills, the discount houses stand ready to take up any which remain unsold, and the government is thereby assured that it will be able to raise as much money as it wishes by this means. As later sections will show, the extent to which governments rely on the issue of Treasury bills to finance their spending plans has a critical influence on the ability of the banking system to create money.

27-4 CREDIT CREATION

It was noted above that banks occupy a special position in the financial system in that their liabilities (bank deposits) constitute the bulk of the supply of money in the economy. This feature raises the question of how banks can make the money supply expand. Where, in other words, do bank deposits come from?

For individuals, the easiest way to increase the amount of money in their bank deposits is to save. This means reducing expenditure by, say, walking to work rather than taking the bus. The net result, however, is that while the saver's bank account grows, that of the bus company will decrease. All that is achieved is the transfer of money from one account to another. Similar reasoning may be applied to the raising of money through the sale of a house or a car: the bank account of the seller rises, but that of the buyer goes down. Indeed, the same effects follow from the borrowing of money by the issue of securities. The bank account of the person or company borrowing the money goes up, while those of the people buying the securities fall. The conclusion must be that the ordinary business of buying and selling or saving and lending cannot increase the total stock of bank deposits in the system as a whole.

To investigate the process whereby the money supply of the entire economy expands, let us assume that there are 10 banks, all of which are identical copies of the bank whose balance sheet was set out in Fig. 27-1. All are assumed to follow a liquidity ratio of 20 per cent. Figure 27-2 shows the consolidated balance sheet for the entire banking system (excluding the central bank). Ignoring notes and coins in the hands of the public, the money supply of this economy amounts to its aggregate bank deposits, that is, £1 billion.

Let us now make the assumption that a customer was to arrive at one bank—let it be Bank 1—with a Treasury bill to the value of £10 million in his possession and the request that the bank take charge of it, crediting his account by the equivalent amount. Such a transaction would place the bank in the position shown in Fig. 27-3. With deposits of £110

Liabilities		Assets	
Deposits	1000	Liquid assets	200
		Loans	800

Figure 27-2 Consolidated balance sheet of all banks (£ million)

Liabilities		Assets	
Deposits	110	Liquid assets	30
		Loans	80

Figure 27-3 Bank 1 after the deposit (£ million)

Liabilities		*Assets*	
Deposits	118	Liquid assets	30
		Loans	88

Figure 27-4 Bank 1 after lending (£ million)

million this bank would have a need for only £22 million in liquid assets (20 per cent of £110 million), rather than the £30 million it actually has. This position would be unsatisfactory for the bank since liquid assets earn lower returns than other assets like loans, and the bank's managers will clearly wish to keep reserve assets down to a minimum, while loans ought to be raised to a maximum. Ideally, the bank would like to switch £8 million from liquid assets to loans.

Performing such a transformation is fairly straightforward in principle, when two points are borne in mind. First, it was noted above that one liquid asset in particular, bankers' balances at the Bank of England, were used in settling payments between banks. By having an excess of liquid assets, Bank 1 is able to afford a loss of £8 million in the settlement process. Second, the bank is able, within the bounds set by the liquidity ratio, to increase its own lending, that is, to add loans to its balance sheet.

In the context of these two points, the policy of the bank would be to advance a loan of £8 million to one of its customers. (It is clearly essential for this process that there should be customers who are willing to borrow from the bank, and we shall accordingly assume that such people exist.) When a loan is made, the borrower's account is credited immediately, so that the bank's balance sheet would look as shown in Fig. 27-4. This position will not, it may be reasonable to assume, persist for long. The borrower will spend the loan, and the probability is that the seller of the goods will bank not at Bank 1 but elsewhere—call his bank Bank 2. When the money is spent, Bank 1 will find itself with a lower stock of deposits (by £8 million) and with a correspondingly lower level of liquid assets. Its position is as shown in Fig. 27-5, with the reallocation of assets now complete.

For Bank 2, however, the process is only just beginning. Its new balance sheet is shown in Fig. 27-6. Bank 2 is now in position similar to that of Bank 1 in Fig. 27-3, that is, with an excess of liquid assets. In this case, the excess is rather smaller, at £6.4 million (£21.6 million being the required level of liquid assets). It could also therefore engage in the business of switching its assets by advancing a loan of £6.4 million and seeing its liquid assets diminished by the settlement process. The bank receiving the liquid assets would naturally repeat the process on a smaller scale, thus transferring the liquid assets to yet another bank.

Liabilities		*Assets*	
Deposits	110	Liquid assets	22
		Loans	88

Figure 27-5 Bank 1 after settlement (£ million)

Liabilities		*Assets*	
Deposits	108	Liquid assets	28
		Loans	80

Figure 27-6 Bank 2 after settlement (£ million)

Liabilities		Assets	
Deposits	1050	Liquid assets	210
		Loans	840

Figure 27-7 Consolidated balance sheet of all banks (£ million)

The advancing of loans would continue, diminishing at every round, until a new equilibrium for the entire banking system, in which all banks were back at a liquidity ratio of 20 per cent, had been reached (Fig. 27-7). The money supply in the new equilibrium, it will be noted, is up by £50 million. This is the sum of the loans advanced by the various banks during the process: £8 million by Bank 1, £6.4 million by Bank 2 and so on together with the original deposit of £10 million for the person with the Treasury bill. This ability of a relatively small injection of liquid assets into the banking system to engender much larger amounts of bank lending and thus the creation of money is termed the *banking multiplier*.

This example has underlined a number of important points. First, *bank deposits grow by means of bank lending*. Since bank deposits are the main constituent of the money supply, the main mechanism by which the money supply grows is through bank lending. Second, it has been established that banks lend when they have an abundance of liquid assets, that is, that the condition for the expansion of the money supply is an excess of liquid assets such as Bank of England balances. Indeed, bankers' balances are often referred to as the *monetary base* of the banking system.

The next stage in the analysis must plainly be to discover how the banks can obtain extra liquid assets like the Treasury bill in the example above.

27-5 THE PUBLIC SECTOR AND THE BANKING SYSTEM

So far, liquid assets have been presented as consisting simply of bankers' balances and money at call. There are in fact several other categories of liquid assets and a fuller list might include the following: balances at the Bank of England; money at call; treasury bills; short-dated gilt-edged stock; local authority bills; and other bills. The origin of increases in these liquid assets is the public sector. It will be recalled that the Bank of England acts as banker to the government, and it therefore participates in the system of settling payments between banks like any other bank. When, for example, the government buys a frigate for the Navy, it pays the shipbuilder with a cheque drawn on its account at the Bank of England. The shipbuilder presents the cheque to its bank, say, Barclays. The shipbuilder's account must be duly credited and the cheque must be settled, like any other cheque, by the transfer of cash between the two banks concerned. In this case the paying bank is the Bank of England and the receiving bank is a clearing bank. An increase in the liquid assets held by the clearing banks would thus be the net result of this transaction (or indeed, of any public expenditure whatsoever).

While public spending has the effect of adding to these liquid assets, payments *from* the general public to the government work in the opposite fashion. Thus taxes involve the payment of cheques from members of the public to the government. In the process of settling these cheques, balances have to be transferred from the payers' banks to the Bank of England, and the banks as a whole suffer a loss of bankers' balances as a result. Thus if all public spending were balanced by taxation, the net result would be to leave bankers' holdings of liquid assets unchanged.

Taxation is rarely adequate to cover all the government's spending needs. To finance the rest—the PSBR—the government borrows by issuing securities. The main securities issued by the government are as follows: National Savings certificates, which are medium-term securities sold mainly to private individuals; gilt-edged stocks, which are long-term securities sold largely to financial intermediaries like pension funds; shares in privatized companies, which, while securities issued by the government, are not really loans in that they are not redeemable (they are taken up by both individuals and financial institutions); and treasury bills, which are bought primarily by the discount houses (since the discount houses buy the bills with money borrowed from the banks, treasury bills may in effect be considered as being sold to the banks themselves).

The monetary effects of expenditure which is financed by the issue of Treasury bills (or more generally by borrowing from the banking system) is rather different from the effects of that which is financed by borrowing from the public or from companies. As far as the banks are concerned, sales of the first three types of government securities have the same effect, that is, they reduce bankers' balances at the Bank of England. This is because these securities are paid for by cheques in favour of the government, and the settlement of these cheques reduces bankers' stocks of liquid assets just as much as does taxation. Thus if the frigate were financed by issuing gilts, the net result would be the same as if it had been paid for out of taxation: bankers' liquid assets would remain unchanged.

Rather different results would follow, however, if the expenditure were to be financed by the sale of a Treasury Bill to Barclays Bank. Although the Treasury bill would have to be paid for by a deduction of, say, £500 million from Barclays' balance at the Bank of England, Barclays would naturally be in possession of the bill itself. This of course would be counted as a liquid asset. The bank's total liquid assets, having risen by £500 million as a result of the payment for the frigate, would therefore remain at the new high level. In sum, public expenditure which is financed by borrowing from the banks—normally by means of the issue of Treasury bills—has the net effect of pumping extra liquid assets into the banks' balance sheets.

Borrowing from the banks to finance public expenditure is, in the short term, an attractive option. The two principal ways to paying for public expenditure, taxation and borrowing, both have problems in that taxation is usually unpopular while borrowing will make interest rates rise, pushing up mortgage payments and depressing investment. Selling Treasury bills, however, seems to be a way of avoiding both of these difficulties. In this respect, it is the modern equivalent of the ancient practice of printing new banknotes to pay for public apending. The drawback, however, is that it leaves the banks with larger bankers' balances. This, as we have seen, places them in a position to lend to their customers. Since bank lending is the means by which bank deposits (that is, money) are created, the ultimate result of paying for public spending by selling Treasury bills to the banking system is that the money supply rises. This in turn—the monetarists argue—leads to inflation.

27-6 MONETARY POLICY AND THE CONTROL OF THE MONEY SUPPLY

Governments have long been concerned with reducing inflation. As Chapter 25 showed, the monetarist analysis of the problem suggests that the cause of rising prices is an expansion in the money supply. The mechanism which produces a higher stock of money runs, it appears, from excessive public spending through public borrowing from the banks and higher bank lending to the growth of bank deposits. This mechanism has been the focus of several instruments of policy designed to affect either the quantity of money or interest rates, and they are thus known collectively as *monetary policy*. Monetary policy is usually administered by the Treasury and the Bank of England, who are sometimes described jointly as the *monetary authorities*.

The most fundamental policy open to the government is to reduce its need to borrow from the banking system in the first place. This implies limiting public expenditure more or less to the level that can be supported by an acceptable level of taxation. Although the relationship between public expenditure and revenue is more properly described as fiscal policy, the implications of public borrowing for banks' holdings of liquid assets are so important that it must also be considered in the context of controlling the money supply. It is for this reason that cuts in public expenditure are advocated as a means of reducing inflation. Such a policy would minimize the PSBR, which could then be financed by issuing gilts and National Savings. The result would be that the banks holdings of liquid assets would be kept stable. (It may be noted that controlling liquid assets is not easy when the Bank of England acts as lender of last resort, since this role obliges the Bank to supply liquidity to the banking system upon request. The Bank's only option is to set costly terms—a high MLR—if it wishes to discourage the use of this facility.)

If a government is committed for political reasons to certain levels of expenditure and taxation, then clearly it must borrow to finance its deficit. If inflation is to be avoided, the government cannot borrow from the banks since this would allow the monetary base to expand. It would therefore have to borrow from the general public (sometimes called the *non-bank public* in this context). One option here would be to attract the savings of the general public into National Savings. Another, known in the United States as 'open market operations' and in the United Kingdom as *funding*, is to sell large volumes of gilt-edged stock.

A third policy is to influence interest rates. Here the government has two instruments at its disposal. One is to alter MLR, which naturally influences the rates charged by banks and building societies. Another is to raise or lower the rate of interest on both National Savings and gilts. The rates chosen will of course be determined in part by the government's intended sales. If it has a large PSBR to finance, then rates will have to be set at a high level in order to attract funds. Indeed, a substantial programme of funding will be a way of driving interest rates up. Higher rates on bank loans will of course make people less ready to borrow from the banks, and this will also tend to slow the rate of growth of the money supply.

Besides influencing the general conditions in financial markets, the authorities have also tried to influence the decisions of banks themselves. During the 1960s, governments made direct appeals to the banks to forgo opportunities for profitable business by voluntarily restricting their lending. Unpopular and difficult to enforce, these tactics have long been discarded. More recently, governments have sometimes called for 'Special Deposits' which banks are required to lodge with the Bank of England. Thus a certain proportion of bankers' existing deposits at the Bank of England has to be transferred to a special account which may not be used like ordinary bankers' balances as the basis for lending. The effect is to reduce the monetary base of the banking system and the intention behind calls for Special Deposits is that the banks' lending operations will be curtailed by this loss.

27-7 SUMMARY

Financial intermediation is the process whereby specialist organizations accept 'retail' deposits or payments from the public, pool them and use them to buy securities. When the securities so bought are newly issued, the savings of the public are channelled into capital investment.

The banking mechanism consists of the central bank, the banks and the discount houses. The central bank acts as lender of last resort and operates monetary policy, that is, the control of the money supply and the setting of interest rates.

The banks use their balances at the central bank for settling payments between themselves. They also follow a prudential *liquidity ratio*.

Credit creation is the means by which the supply of money increases. Since the principal component in the money supply is bank deposits, the money supply rises by means of bank lending. Banks only lend, however, when their holdings of liquid assets exceed their liquidity ratio. New liquid assets come from public spending which is financed not by taxation or the issues of securities to the public but by borrowing from the banks. This is normally done through the issue of Treasury bills, and is equivalent to printing money.

Montary policy means the control of the money supply by through reducing PSBR, funding and raising interest rates.

EXERCISES

27-1 In example used in this chapter, Bank 1 extended £8 million in new loans while Bank 2 extended £6.4 million. Had the process gone on to include Banks 3, 4 and 5, how much would they have lent?

27-2 The diagram below shows the consolidated balance sheet for the banking system of a country. Interest rates stand at 10 per cent. How would it change in the following circumstances:

Liabilities		Assets	
Deposits	24 000	Liquid assets	4 000
		Loans	20 000

(*a*) a rise in the liquidity ratio to 20 per cent;
(*b*) a fall in the liquidity ratio to 12.5 per cent;
(*c*) a rise in interest rates to 16 per cent;
(*d*) a £1000 programme of public spending financed by taxation;
(*e*) a similar programme of public spending financed by issuing Treasury bills to banks.

27-3 You are the bank manager of branch which has 500 customers. You have the following data:

Mean number of visits per customer per week = 0.6   SD = 0.25
Mean amount of cash withdrawn each visit = £40   SD = £8
Mean amount of cash deposited each visit = £12

You can only replenish your stocks of cash once a day (after close of business). Calculate how much cash you would need to hold to meet 99 per cent of daily needs for cash.

27-4 Some members of the students' union of your college want to spend £500 supporting a demonstration in favour of more public spending on education. The finance officer thinks this a waste of money, given the attitude of the government to inflation. She asks you to draft the outline of a speech she will make explaining, if not defending, the government's view of the dangers of public spending.

27-5 The Anglo-Ruritanian Trade Society is an association of British firms who do business with Ruritania. Some own manufacturing subsidiaries there, some invest in Ruritanian securities and some are engaged in civil engineering work for the government. A new Prime Minister is elected, committed to restraining Ruritania's inflation by monetarist means. Write a circular to members of the Society, outlining the likely policies to be pursued and their consequences for the Society's members.

28

FINANCIAL MATHEMATICS

28-1 INTRODUCTION

In Chapter 27 the principal features of the banking and financial system of the United Kingdom were discussed; the financial sector was shown to operate as an intermediary between those wishing to save and those wishing to borrow. The financial markets, like any other market, operate in terms of supply, demand and price. In a financial context, the price which equates supply and demand for money is the rate of interest.

At the micro-economic level both individuals and firms are affected by levels of interest. Individuals will look for the most financially rewarding opportunities for investing savings while those seeking credit will look for the cheapest source of such credit. For the firm similar considerations apply with respect to the future use of company profits, future investments and the raising of outside capital to finance company expansion. An adequate understanding of the appropriate financial calculations is necessary for rational economic behaviour. At the macro-economic level the government, through the monetary authorities, operates monetary policy by intervening in the financial markets to control the money supply and the price of money—the rate of interest.

This chapter will introduce the basic mathematics needed to deal with such financial transactions.

28-2 TIME PREFERENCE

The fundamentals of financial mathematics are based on a simple feature of rational economic behaviour. If you were offered the choice of receiving £50 today or £50 in 12 months' time you would, quite rightly, opt for the £50 now. Even ignoring the possibility of inflation over the next year, you would probably argue that £50 now has more value to you than £50 in 12 months'. After all, you could use the money now to purchase some item from which you derive immediate use and satisfaction. Similarly, there may be uncertainties over your circumstances in one year's time. You may, by then, have won a fortune on the premium bonds or football pools in which case the future £50 will have little value compared with the rest of your wealth. Equally, in a year's time you may be dead. This preference for payment in the present rather than payment in the future is known as *time preference*.

Because consumption in the present is preferable to consumption in the future anyone who defers consumption (by lending the money they would have spent) suffers a loss of welfare for which they require compensation. Hence anyone wishing to borrow money will have to offer some reward—interest—to the lender.

28-3 INTEREST RATES

Suppose you had the sum of £100 in a bank or building society account. Such an account we will suppose has an interest rate of 10 per cent per year (per annum). What does this mean and how is the interest calculated?

The £100 you deposited is referred to as the *principal* and it is obviously this sum that will attract interest at a rate of 10 per cent p.a. So, at the end of the first year your account would be credited with a further £10 representing the interest awarded. But what would happen if you left the money in your account for a second year? What would be your reaction if the bank credited your account with a further £10 interest at the end of that year?

Naturally, you would not be satisfied with such an arrangement. The second £10 reflects interest paid on the principal for the second year, which is fair enough. But you have had no reward for leaving your first year's interest untouched in the account. This, too, should attract interest. The appropriate interest credited at the end of the second year should therefore have been £10 which is 10 per cent of the principal, plus £1 which is 10 per cent of the interest from the first year. So, the interest paid should be £11. The same principle can be extended to subsequent years. Table 28-1 shows the initial principal sum and the interest earned at the end of each year which is then added to the principal for the following year. So at the end of a five-year period the original £100 will have increased to £161.05.

Table 28-1 Interest calculations

Principal of £100, interest rate 10 per cent p.a.

Year	Principal at beginning of year	Interest on principal	Principal at end of year
1	£100	£10	£110
2	£110	£11	£121
3	£121	£12.10	£133.10
4	£133.10	£13.31	£146.41
5	£146.41	£14.64	£161.05

Table 28-2 Interest calculation, principal P, interest rate r

Year	Principal at beginning of year	Interest on principal	Principal at end of year
1	P	Pr	$P + Pr = P(1 + r)$
2	$P(1 + r)$	$P(1 + r)r$	$P(1 + r) + P(1 + r)r$ $= (P + Pr)(1 + r)$ $= P(1 + r)(1 + r)$ $= P(1 + r)^2$
3	$P(1 + r)^2$	$P(1 + r)^2 r$	$P(1 + r)^2 + P(1 + r)^2 r$ $= (P + Pr)(1 + r)^2$ $= P(1 + r)(1 + r)^2$ $= P(1 + r)^3$

Such a method of interest calculation, where the interest from one period itself earns interest, is known as *compound interest*. (If interest were based only on the original principal and not subsequent interest payments as well it would be known as *simple interest*.)

Although the step-by-step calculations in Table 28-1 are straightforward they can become a little long-winded if interest is being worked out for long periods of time. Calculating the final total for, say, a 20-year period would be tedious. Instead we can derive and use a formula for compound interest calculations.

If we let the variable P represent the original principal sum, and r the rate of interest, we can express the calculations in Table 28-1 as a series of formulae, as in Table 28.2. It is apparent from the table that there is a pattern to the compound interest calculations. The value, V, of the principal at the end of the tth year is

$$V = P(1 + r)^t$$

where P is the original principal sum, r is the annual rate of interest expressed as a decimal, and t is the appropriate number of years. Hence, for our principal of £100 we could have calculated the value of the principal at the end of the five-year period as $£100(1 + 0.1)^5$ $= £101(1.1)^5 = £161.05$. At the end of a 10-year period a similar calculation would show that the original investment would increase to £259.37.

The formula for compound interest can be used for any combination of P, r and t. In the above example we assumed for simplicity that interest was added to the account at the end of each year. This will not necessarily be the case. Interest may be credited biannually, quarterly, monthly even daily. The same formula can still be used. Assume that, instead of paying interest annually, the same account credited the accrued interest to your account on a quarterly basis. What would the final value of your account be in 10 years? Keeping P at £100, but with r now at 2.5 per cent (0.025 as a decimal) per quarter, and t equal to 40 (4 quarters × 10 years), now the value of your account after 10 years would be $£100(1.025)^{40}$ $= £268.51$.

The same formula can also be used in reverse. Frequently, for purposes of investment appraisal, we may wish to know the rate of interest associated with the financial return from some investment. Assume you have the opportunity of investing £100 in some project now that offers to pay you £150 back in four years' time. What annual rate of interest is your investment actually earning?

We need to rearrange our formula for the value of the principal after t years, $V = P(1 + r)^t$, to give us an expression for the annual rate of interest r. This is done as follows:

$$V = P(1 + r)^t$$

$$\frac{V}{P} = (1 + r)^t$$

$$\sqrt[t]{\frac{V}{P}} = 1 + r$$

$$r = \sqrt[t]{\frac{V}{P}} - 1$$

We can now substitute the figures given in the problem:

$$r = \sqrt[4]{\frac{150}{100}} - 1$$

$$= \sqrt[4]{1.5} - 1$$

$$= 1.1067 - 1$$

$$= 0.1067 = 10.67 \text{ per cent}$$

This investment, therefore, attracts a rate of interest of 10.67 per cent p.a. This is referred to as the *yield* on the investment.

28-4 PRESENT VALUE

One particularly important use of compound interest principles lies at the heart of investment appraisal techniques—the calculation of *present value* and the technique of *discounting* cash flows.

The principle of present value is already established. *Ceteris paribus*, you would prefer £100 now to £100 in one year. But suppose you were offered not £100 in a year's time but rather £110? Would your preference still be to take the £100 now or the £110 in the future? The answer will obviously depend primarily on the prevailing interest rate that the £100 now could earn over the next 12 months. At a rate of interest of, say, 10 per cent you would regard the two alternatives as equal. In the terminology of finance, £100 is seen as the *present value* of £110. That is, £100 is the sum you would need at present, given a rate of interest of 10 per cent, to generate a value of £110 in one year's time.

The general calculation of a present value can be derived from the compound interest formula derived earlier.

$$V = P(1 + r)^t$$

Table 28-3 Project comparison

Time	Project 1		Project 2	
	Cost (£)	Revenue (£)	Cost (£)	Revenue (£)
Now	8 000		8 000	
End of Period 1		2 000		
End of Period 2		3 000		1 000
End of Period 3		4 000		2 000
End of Period 4		2 000		4 000
End of Period 5		1 000		6 000
Total	8 000	12 000	8 000	13 000

Rearranging gives:

$$P = \frac{V}{(1 + r)^t}$$

where P represents the present value of a future sum at a specific rate of interest. So, for example, at an interest rate of 10 per cent a project which provided £500 in five years' time would have a present value of:

$$P = \frac{£500}{(1.10)^5} = £310.46$$

That is, a sum of £310.46 *now* and a sum of £500 in five years' time are regarded as equal and an individual would have no particular preference for one or the other. Naturally, should interest rates change present values will also change.

Present value calculations can be used in the appraisal of investments. Typically, an organization or individual will be faced with alternative uses for fixed resources. A firm, for example, may be able to invest the same sum in two different projects and it is likely that the projects will generate different cash flows over time. Let us suppose the firm is faced with the situation in Table 28-3. There are two alternative projects, both with an initial cost of £8000. The two projects, however, generate future revenue flows in two different ways. On the face of it Project 2 appears more attractive as the project profit is £5000, compared with £4000 for Project 1.

It should be apparent, however, that the simple profit calculation fails to take into account the fact that the two projects generate revenue at different times and for a more appropriate comparison we must take this time element into our calculations. That is, we must discount future revenue flows to the present value. We can do this for each year for each of the two projects using the formula derived earlier. The results are shown in Table 28-4.

Interpretation of the individual results is as before. Let us take the figure, say, for Period 3 for Project 1 of £3005. This is the present value of the revenue of £4000 arising in that year. In other words, £3005 now and £4000 at the end of Period 3 are exactly equivalent, at a discount rate of 10 per cent.

From the total discounted value for Project 1 of £9289 we have a means of assessing the

Table 28-4 Project comparison with discounted values at 10 per cent discount rate

Time	Project 1		Project 2	
	Revenue (£)	Discounted revenue* (£)	Revenue (£)	Discounted revenue* (£)
End of Period 1	2 000	1 818	0	0
End of Period 2	3 000	2 479	1 000	826
End of Period 3	4 000	3 005	2 000	1 503
End of Period 4	2 000	1 366	4 000	2 732
End of Period 5	1 000	621	6 000	3 726
Total	12 000	9 289	13 000	8 787

* Discounted values have been rounded to whole numbers.

profitability of this project in present value terms. This figure indicates that the present value of the £12 000 of revenue flows for Project 1 is £9289. That is, £9289 now is exactly equivalent to £12 000 spread as shown over the next five years. Given that, for Project 1, we must spend £8000 now to achieve this present value of £9289 logic suggests that this project is worthwhile.

Exactly the same procedure is applied to Project 2. It also has a present value (£8787) greater than the present cost of £8000, so it too is potentially worthwhile. The difference for each project between the present value of the revenues and the present values of the costs is known as the 'net' present value.

But, given that we can only invest in one project which should it be? Again, logic suggests that we should choose the project with the highest net present value, *ceteris paribus*. Here, contrary to the original impression, this would be Project 1. The technique allows for the fact that Project 1 has a more favourable time distribution of revenue flows.

While calculations like this are extremely common in investment appraisal, no decision-maker will, of course, rely solely on such calculations. Other factors, such as risk, uncertainty and the possibility of interest rate changes, will also have to be taken into account before reaching a decision.

The use of present value techniques can be applied to any alternative uses of funds. Typically, an organization may be comparising the present value of some investment project—say, expanding its factory or production line—with an alternative use of the same funds—say, investing in gilt-edged securities. A comparison of the relative present values will help the organization choose between such alternatives. In fact, the relationship between present value, the price of stocks and shares and the rate of interest is a critical one.

28-5 INTEREST RATES AND SECURITY PRICES

A further important use of financial appraisal techniques brings us back to some of the key concepts introduced in the previous chapters on macro-economic theory. This concerns the relationship between the prices of financial securities—like company shares, Treasury bills and gild-edged stocks—and the rate of interest. The discussion which follows centres on gilts but the principles of present value which are presented are equally applicable to other forms of securities.

Readers will recall that the monetary authorities issue gilts at a fixed rate of interest to the public and, more importantly, to the financial sector. The purchase of such a stock is, essentially, a loan of the purchase price to the government for some fixed period. The owner of the stock is paid the fixed rate of interest on an annual basis by the Treasury and is also repaid the purchase price of the stock when it is redeemed at a specified future date.

Thus, if you bought £1000 of 1995 Treasury stock at 8% the Treasury would receive your £1000 and in return would pay you £80 interest each year until 1995 when it would pay you back your £1000 principal. It is important to note that gilts are transferrable. That is, should you wish, you could sell your stock to someone else during this time. They would then receive any future interest payments and the eventual repayment of the original £1000. In practice, the trade in such stocks—'old' securities—forms the major part of the business of financial markets.

To illustrate the link between the price of securities and their yields, suppose that you were the proud owner of a £1000 stock issued at 8 per cent p.a. that was redeemable in five years' time. What would you regard as a fair selling price for the stock? Conversely, what would you regard as a fair price for such a stock if you were seeking to invest some of your spare cash? It is apparent that the use of discounted cash flows to determine the present value of the stock would be appropriate here. Effectively you are faced with the situation detailed below.

Time	Coupon (interest) (£)	Redemption value (£)	Total cash flow (£)
Now			
End of Year 1	80		80
End of Year 2	80		80
End of Year 3	80		80
End of Year 4	80		80
End of Year 5	80	1000	1080

It is now a simple matter of calculating the present value of this income stream. It is, of course, appropriate to use the prevailing rate of interest as the discount rate. This is likely to differ from the coupon paid on the stock, which may have been issued several years previously. Let us suppose the current rate of interest is 9 per cent p.a. The present value of this income stream would then be £961.09 (you should confirm this calculation for yourself). That is, if you put your stock up for sale (and the future income it generates) the market will set a price of £961.09.

However, let us now assume that you expect interest rates to change in the near future. Let us assume you think the rate of interest will rise to 10 per cent. Table 28-5 shows that, if interest rates rise, the present value of the stock will fall (to £924.20). Accordingly, if you had sufficient confidence in your expectations you would try to sell the stock *now* in anticipation of the increase in interest rates and the corresponding fall in the price of the stock.

It is evident that you will be successful in selling your stock at the current price *only if*

Table 28-5 Present value of 8% £1000 stock redeemable in five years' time (£)

Year	Cash flow	Interest rate (% p.a.)					
		5	6	7	8	9	10
1	80	76.19	75.47	74.77	74.07	73.39	72.73
2	80	72.56	71.20	69.88	68.59	67.33	66.12
3	80	69.11	67.17	65.30	63.51	61.77	60.11
4	80	65.82	63.37	61.03	58.80	56.67	54.64
5	1080	846.21	807.04	770.03	735.03	701.93	670.60
Present value		1129.89	1084.25	1041.01	1000.00	961.09	924.20

you can find a buyer whose expectations are different from your own. If everyone expects interest rates to rise no one will be willing to buy the stock from you at the current price.

Table 28-5 shows a range of present values for differing rates of interest. As in readily seen, there is an obvious pattern between expected future rates of interest and such security prices. As interest rates increase, stock prices, based on discounted present values, will fall. Conversely, lower interest rates mean higher prices for such securities.

It can be seen, therefore, how the price of securities is inversely linked to the rate of interest. The price of such securities is, simply, the present value of the expected revenue stream in the form of annual coupon payments together with the redemption money. If interest rates were to fall then these future revenue streams would have to be discounted at the lower rate of interest and, therefore, would have higher prices. Similarly, a change in the price of such securities would imply a change in the prevailing market interest rate. Thus security prices, yields and interest rates are determined *simultaneously*.

This relationship can also be examined from another direction by considering securities as having supply and demand schedules like any other item. The supply of securities will consist of the stock of all previously issued securities together with the flow of new issues. Although the former is largely static the latter will respond to changes in prices and interest rates. At high rates of interest few businesses will wish to borrow money to invest in new ventures and few new securities will be issued. Conversely, at low rates of interest more projects will become profitable (their net present value will rise) and more businesses will borrow by issuing new securities. Thus the supply of securities will expand at lower rates of interest. Since *lower* interest rates correspond to *higher* security prices, this suggests that the supply of securities will be greater when their prices are higher. This, of course, resembles the way in which the supply of other goods expands as their prices rise, *ceteris paribus*.

The demand for securities likewise depends upon their price. When securities prices are high (that is, when interest rates are low) few savers will wish to buy. If, however, securities were to become cheaper (but still offer the same yield) then demand would increase. The demand curve for securities will, therefore, slope downward from left to right, as do other demand curves.

The intersection of the two curves—that for supply and that for demand—determines the equilibrium price for securities and therefore, simultaneously the prevailing rate of interest.

The implications for monetary policy are evident. If the monetary authorities wished interest rates to rise they would have to drive the price of securities *down* by changing the supply: that is, by issuing large quantities of gilt-edged stock. If, on the other hand, they wanted interest rates to fall they would have to push the price of securities *up* by increasing the demand. This could be achieved by purchasing large quantities of gilts from existing holders.

28-6 SUMMARY

The *present value* represents the current value of a future stream of income at a specified rate of interest.

In *compound interest*, interest is added both to the principal sum and any past interest earned and not withdrawn. *Simple interest* adds interest only to the principal.

Time preference indicates that, other things equal, an individual will prefer to hold a sum of money now rather than in the future.

EXERCISES

28-1 The company for which you work is considering three potential projects for investment purposes. All three projects require an initial investment of £10 000 and will generate the cash flows shown below:

Year	Project 1 (£)	Project 2 (£)	Project 3 (£)
1	4 000	0	1 000
2	3 000	0	2 000
3	3 000	0	3 000
4	3 000	0	4 000
5	0	5 000	4 000
6	0	5 000	0
7	0	5 000	0
Total	13 000	15 000	14 000

(a) Assuming a rate of interest of 5 per cent per annum, calculate the discounted cash flow for each project using a computer spreadsheet.
(b) On the basis of your calculations which project would you recommend?
(c) Draft a report to the company accountant explaining why you would not support Project 2 even though it generates the highest profit on the original investment.
(d) What other factors would you wish to consider before making a final choice between the three projects?
(e) If you thought the rate of interest was due to increase to 7 per cent explain what effect you would expect this to have on the net present value figures. Calculate the new NPV figures and see if you were correct.

28-2 You currently hold a government security issued for £1000 at 7 per cent p.a. which is redeemable in six years' time.

(a) If the current market rate of interest is 10 per cent what price would you be prepared to accept for selling the security?
(b) You have a hunch that the market rate of interest will shortly fall to 8 per cent. Explain how this will affect your answer to (a).

(c) Assume that you are the only person who thinks the rate of interest will fall. What are the implications for your selling the security?

(d) Assume that everyone else also feels the rate will fall. What are the implications now?

28-3 You are employed as an investment adviser to a firm of stockbrokers. From the latest edition of the *Financial Times* (or an equivalent) obtain data on one of the government security issues and its current price. Draft a report arguing what you think will happen to the market rate of interest over the next three months and justifying an appropriate policy for buying or selling such securities for your company.

29

THEORIES OF THE MACRO ECONOMY: II
KEYNESIANISM

29-1 INTRODUCTION

The debate between monetarist economists and Keynesians is one of the most important in economics in terms of both theory and policy. The objective of the present chapter is therefore to examine Keynesian macro-economics and the policies which flow from it. Points of contrast with monetarist economics will emerge as we proceed.

The inception of Keynesian economics is conventionally dated from the publication of *The General Theory of Money, Interest and Employment* by John Maynard (later Lord) Keynes in 1936. The world economy at that time lay deep in depression: factories stood idle and millions were without jobs. (It may be noted that the words 'depression', 'recession' and 'slump' can be used interchangeably in this context.) The predominant economic ideas of the time, the 'classical' school of economics, suggested that the best way for government to proceed was to leave matters to the market. (Many ideas from classical economics, of course, have been carried forward into today's neo-classical/monetarist economics.) It was argued, for example, that unemployment could be cured by allowing wages to fall so that labour would be cheaper to employ, and that the fall in demand for loans would so depress interest rates that business would once again become profitable and investment would revive. Indeed, the government's position (known as the 'Treasury view') was that any attempt to reduce unemployment by, perhaps, initiating a programme of public works, would be bound to fail. The thinking behind this conclusion was that any borrowing by the government would drive interest rates up, thus depressing private investment.

Many economists of the time found the Treasury view difficult to accept. Keynes's contribution was to provide a new theoretical approach which demonstrated that the government *could* successfully reduce unemployment by direct intervention. How the analysis arrived at this conclusion is explained in the following sections.

29-2 THE CIRCULAR FLOW OF INCOME AND EXPENDITURE

The central concept of monetarist economics, as we have seen, is the quantity of money. Monetarists believe the relationship between money supply and expenditure to be firm, stable and direct, with money changing hands at a reasonably constant rate. Keynesians, by contrast, argue that the velocity of circulation of money can fluctuate widely so that the relationship between money and expenditure is quite indeterminate. Economic behaviour can, Keynesians conclude, only be analysed by examining expenditure itself. The key role in Keynesian macro-economics is taken, therefore, by expenditure.

As outlined in Chapter 24 on national income accounting, expenditure takes place within the circular flow of income and expenditure. This phrase underlines the twofold idea that one person's expenditure is another person's income, and that a person's income is the basis for his or her expenditure. Income thus gives rise to expenditure, expenditure gives rise to income and so on. National income is, of course, related to employment in that higher levels of national income will generally be associated with lower unemployment. The level of national income which reduces unemployment to an insignificant rate is known as the 'full employment' level of national income. In the 1950s and 1960s, full employment was taken to be an unemployment level of about 3 per cent of the work-force, but many economists now believe that today the figure lies closer to 12 per cent.

Figure 29-1 shows the simple circular flow model, which is slightly more elaborate than the one set out in Chapter 24. There it was assumed, first, that consumers spent all their incomes, and second, that businesses distributed all their receipts to the owners of

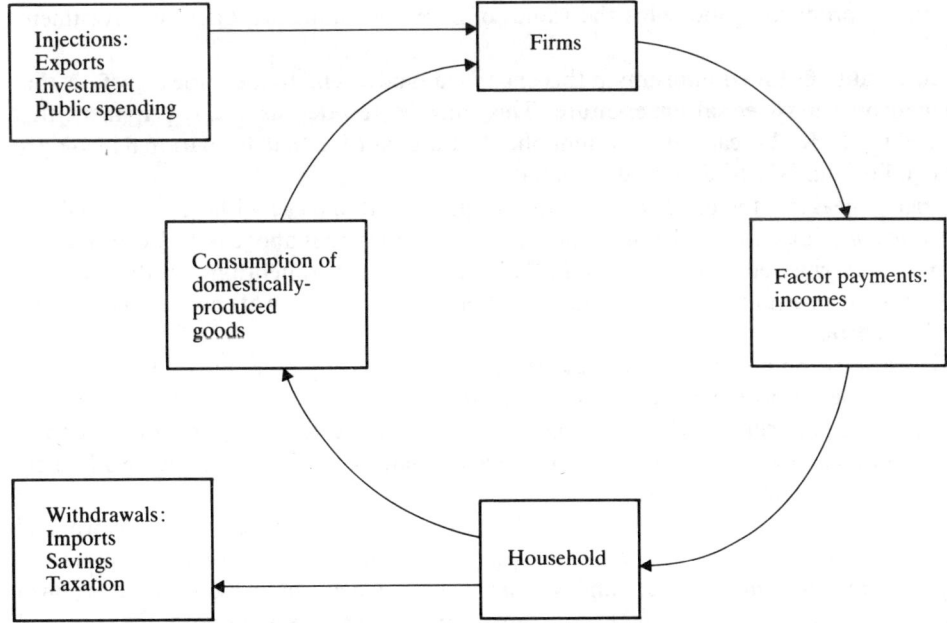

Figure 29-1 The circular flow of income and expenditure

factors of production. It followed that total incomes and total consumer expenditure would be equal. Left to itself, such a position could continue indefinitely simply because there are no forces in the situation which would bring about any change. In particular, there would be no reason to expect any change in the level of income and Keynesians therefore describe a situation in which income and expenditure are equal as one of equilibrium.

29-3 PLANNED INJECTIONS AND PLANNED WITHDRAWALS

The simple model may now be made more realistic by allowing for the fact that household income does not all remain within the circular flow. Some expenditure goes on imports (usually denoted M) and thus can no longer serve as a basis for paying factors of production in the home economy. More income is diverted into savings (denoted S) and the payment of taxation (T). These items are all described as *withdrawals* (denoted W) from the circular flow, as they do not (directly) provide incomes for anyone within the circular flow. The only segment of household income which stays inside the circular flow, in other words, is the proportion which is spent on domestically produced consumer goods (denoted C_d). Aggregate expenditure may therefore be thought of as comprising spending on domestically produced consumer goods, saving, taxation and imports: $C_d + W$.

Conversely, many kinds of expenditure originate outside the circular flow. The main instances are public spending (denoted G), spending on capital goods (investment) (I) and overseas expenditure on exports (X). These items are known as *injections* into the circular flow (J). Once spent, of course, they constitute the incomes of the people who produce the items in question just like ordinary consumer spending on domestically produced goods. Thus aggregate income (denoted Y) must be considered as being made up of the value of domestically produced goods plus the values of public spending, exports and investment: $C_d + J$.

The conditions for equilibrium in this expanded model remain the same as before, that is, that income must equal expenditure. This may be restated as the requirement that $C_d + J = C_d + W$. This can easily be simplified to the condition that, for national income to be in equilibrium, W and J should be equal.

Strictly speaking, the condition for equilibrium is that *planned* withdrawals should be equal to *planned* injections. Like most models in economics, that above is really formulated in terms not of what economic agents do but in terms of their intentions. In this case, the circular flow is in equilibrium when the plans relating to withdrawals are consistent with those for injections.

The various components of planned W and J can be clearly paired together—tax with public spending, imports with exports and saving with investment. For the purposes of arriving at an equilibrium level of national income, however, there is no need for there to be equality between the two sides of any one pair. What is important is the relationship between total withdrawals and total injections.

It is normal in Keynesian analysis to add the assumption that injections are determined by outside factors, that is, they are *exogenous*. They would not, therefore, be expected to change with income. On the other hand, withdrawals are usually assumed to be determined largely by the level of income: higher incomes mean higher taxes, imports, savings and higher consumption of domestically produced goods. Algebraically:

$$M = f(Y)$$

$$S = f(Y)$$

$$T = f(Y)$$

The relationship between income and any one of these is usually referred to as a *propensity*, and it can take one of two forms. First is the average propensity to (say) import. Thus if 30 per cent of total expenditure is devoted to imports, the economy would be described as having an average propensity to import (*APM*) of 0.3. Average propensities to pay taxes (*APT*) and to save (*APS*) could be compiled in a similar fashion, and the total of these three would be the economy's average propensity to withdraw.

The focus of interest often falls not on average propensities but on *marginal propensities* such as the marginal propensity to import (*MPM*). This is the change in imports with respect to a given change in income, and would be expressed, like an average propensity, as a decimal between 0 and 1. Algebraically it is written as:

$$MPM = \frac{\mathrm{d}M}{\mathrm{d}Y}$$

If expenditure on imports were plotted against income on a graph, the slope of the line would of course indicate the value of the marginal propensity to import. An economy's marginal propensities to save (*MPS*), to pay taxes (*MPT*) and to consume domestically produced goods (*MPC*$_d$) could all be calculated (and graphed) in similar ways. The sum of the first three would be the marginal propensity to withdraw. Clearly, the sum of all the marginal propensities must be 1.

The assumptions that planned injections are determined exogenously and that planned withdrawals vary with income can be represented on the 'Keynesian cross' diagram in Fig. 29-2. The *J* function runs horizontally, indicating that planned injections are determined

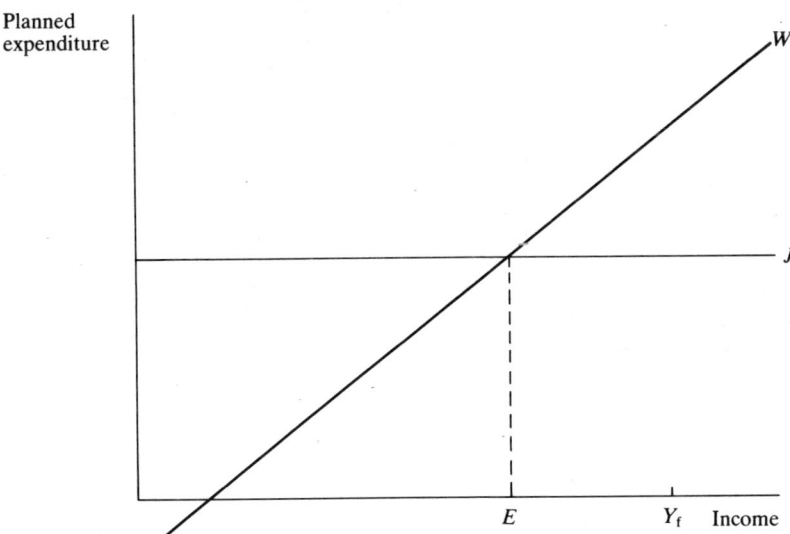

Figure 29-2 Income and expenditure: the Keynesian cross

exogenously. The W function slopes upwards to the right because higher incomes mean higher planned withdrawals. The gradient of the W function shows, of course, the share of any extra income taken by planned withdrawals; it thus shows the marginal propensity to withdraw. For simplicity, this is shown in the diagram as being constant, an assumption which produces a linear W function. Other assumptions, of course, could equally well be used but they would not materially affect the model. The diagram indicates that planned W and J are only equal at one particular level of income, E. Since equality between W and J is the condition for equilibrium, it may be deduced that E is the equilibrium level of national income.

The same principles may be expressed slightly differently by means of the 'Keynesian 45°' diagram, illustrated in Fig. 29-3. Like Fig. 29-2, the axes show income and expenditure. The line OA runs at 45° from the origin and thus indicates points of equality between income and expenditure. At points above the line, such as point H, planned expenditure would be greater than income (and the economy would be engaging in *dis*-saving). Since the condition for equilibrium is that income must equal planned expenditure, such a point could not represent an equilibrium. Conversely a point below the 45° line such as point T would imply that planned expenditure was less than income. Again, this point could not represent an equilibrium. It thus appears that OA indicates the points which are *possible* equilibria.

The other functions on the graph are as follows. JK shows the injections function, which runs horizontally across the graph because injections are exogenous. The line BC, which is termed the 'consumption function', indicates the amount that will be spent on

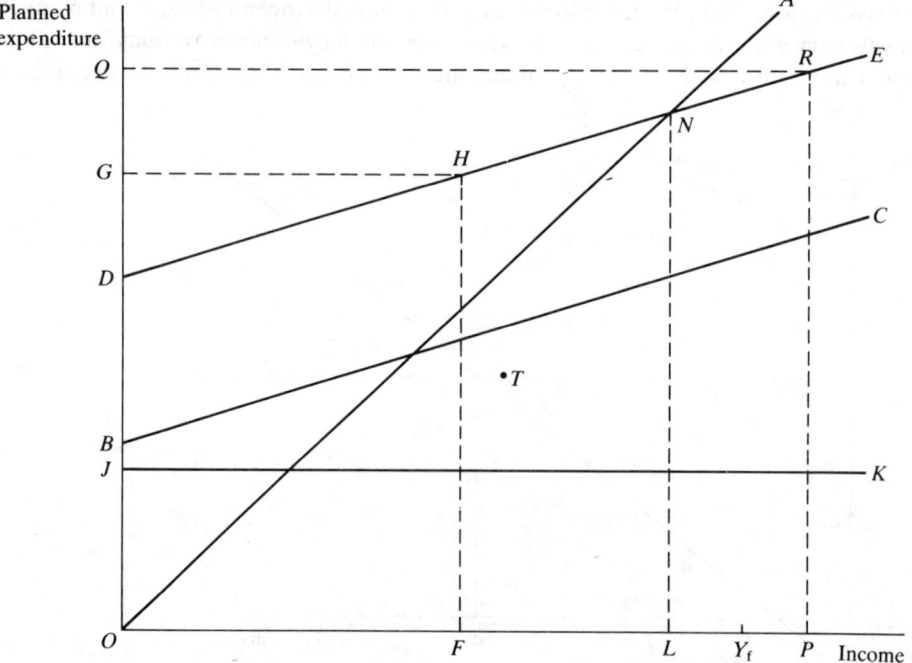

Figure 29-3 Income and expenditure: the 45° diagram

domestically produced goods at different levels of income. The gradient of this line is less than 45° because a given increase income will induce a smaller rise in expenditure, a proportion of the extra income being diverted into withdrawals ($MPC_d < 1$). The 'aggregate demand' function, DE, is simply the sum of the consumption and the injections functions, and it shows the amount of expenditure which is planned (the dependent variable) at each level of income (the independent variable). Thus an income of F would give rise to planned expenditure of G, while an income of P would induce expenditure of Q.

Since equilibrium must lie on the line OA, it is clear that neither H nor R can represent an equilibrium. At H, planned expenditure (G) exceeds income (F), while at R income (P) exceeds planned expenditure (Q). Only at L, with the aggregate demand function intersecting the 45° line at N, are the conditions for equilibrium fulfilled.

An important point to note is that equilibrium cannot exceed the limits set by the economy's physical capacity to produce, which is normally associated with the full employment level of income, Y_f. If, as in Fig. 29-3, equilibrium income were to lie above Y_f, shortages would develop and prices would rise, that is, there would be inflation. This would reduce the real value of income and planned expenditure, forcing a reduction in both in real terms. The aggregate demand function would therefore shift downward from its unsustainable position to a lower level which was more sustainable.

For Keynesians the important point about equilibrium is that within the limits set by capacity *there is no necessity for equilibrium to coincide with full employment*. In Fig. 29-2, national income is in equilibrium at a level below that required for full employment: unemployment would exceed 12 per cent.

29-4 THE ADJUSTMENT PROCESS

Having described equilibrium, the next stage is to vary the initial assumptions to see how the model responds. To do this, let us imagine an economy in which income is running at £100 billion per year. Exogenous forces determine that injections should run at a rate of £40 billion per year. Tax rates, savings habits and people's tastes for imports mean that withdrawals account for 40 per cent of expenditure: the average propensity to withdraw is 0.4. The marginal propensity to withdraw is likewise assumed to be 0.4. The average and the marginal propensities to consume domestically produced goods are, by implication, both taken to be 0.6. An income of £100 billion and an average propensity to withdraw of 0.4 suggest, of course, that £40 billion will be withdrawn from the circular flow each year. Since planned injections run at £40 billion per year, planned injections and withdrawals are equal and the economy is in equilibrium.

Let us now assume that the demand for exports rises to £60 billion per year. Planned J is now greater than planned W: national income is now in disequilibrium. This brings into operation the Keynesian adjustment mechanism. Initially, the rise of £20 billion in export sales raises domestic incomes by £20 billion. Of this, 40 per cent, or £8 billion per year, will be withdrawn from the circular flow in the form of savings, taxation or imports. The remaining £12 billion per year, however, will be spent on domestically produced consumer goods. Since this £12 billion remains within the circular flow, it provides a further boost, of £12 billion, to domestic incomes, that is, it provides a second round of extra income, over and above the initial £20 billion. When this £12 billion comes to be respent, it is naturally divided between withdrawals (40 per cent or £4.8 billion per year) and expenditure on domestically produced goods (£7.2 billion). This £7.2 billion will then also go round the circular flow, generating incomes of £7.2 billion per year, which will be divided between withdrawals and domestic spending. The process goes on, diminishing at every circuit. Table 29-1 follows its course. As round follows round the extra income generated gradually diminishes. This occurs because, at each round, some of the extra income is withdrawn, leaving less to form the next round's extra income. It can be seen that, over successive stages, the level of planned withdrawals gradually approaches that of planned injections (which stands fixed at £60 billion per year). As extra income and expenditure flow round the economy, more and more expenditure is diverted into withdrawals: 8, 4.8, 2.88 and so on. Withdrawals thus rise from their initial level of £40 billion to £48 billion, then to £52.8 billion per year and so on. The process comes to an end when the rate of withdrawals has built up to £60 billion per year. At this point, of course, planned withdrawals equal planned injections once again and equilibrium is re-established.

It is of significance that the movement from one equilibrium to another takes place by means of changes in the level of income, rather than through changes in interest rates, prices or wages. This is a major point of departure from neo-classical/monetarist economic thinking, and one to which we shall return later in this chapter.

The adjustment process could equally well have been set in train by a fall in planned

Table 29-1 The multiplier process
Initial injection of £20 billion, $MPC = 0.6$, an initial equilibrium income of £100 billion, and $W = J = £4$ billion (figures in billions of pounds)

Round	Extra income	Extra C_d	Extra W	Total W	Total income
				40.00	100.00
1	20.00	12.00	8.00	48.00	120.00
2	12.00	7.20	4.80	52.80	132.00
3	7.20	4.32	2.88	55.68	139.20
4	4.32	2.59	1.73	57.41	143.52
5	2.59	1.56	1.04	58.44	146.11
6	1.56	0.93	0.62	59.07	147.67
7	0.93	0.56	0.37	59.44	148.60
8	0.56	0.34	0.22	59.66	149.16
9	0.34	0.20	0.13	59.80	149.50
10	0.20	0.12	0.08	59.88	149.70
11	0.12	0.07	0.05	59.93	149.82
12	0.07	0.04	0.03	59.96	149.89
13	0.04	0.03	0.02	59.97	149.93
14	0.03	0.02	0.01	59.98	149.96
15	0.02	0.01	0.01	59.99	149.98
16	0.01	0.01	0.00	59.99	149.99
17	0.01	0.01	0.00	60.00	150.00
Total	50.00	30.00	20.00		

injections, changes in the levels of planned withdrawals or changes in the marginal propensity to withdraw. In each case, national income would have altered. This forms the basis of the most important conditional predictions of Keynesian economics: that national income will rise or fall in response to changes in injections or withdrawals.

29-5 THE MULTIPLIER

There is, in Keynesian economics, a fixed relationship between the initial change in either withdrawals or injections and the final effect on national income. In the example above, it was observed that the equilibrium level of national income went up by £50 billion. This rise occurred in response to an increase in injections of £20 billion. In other words, an increase in injections induced a rise in income 2.5 times its own size. This relationship is termed the *multiplier*, and it may be formally defined as

$$\text{Multiplier} = \frac{\text{change in the equilibrium level of national income}}{\text{change in injections}}$$

The value of the multiplier is determined directly by the share of income that is devoted to the consumption of domestically produced goods and can be calculated using the formula:

$$\text{Multiplier} = \frac{1}{1 - MPC_d}$$

In our example $MPC_d = 0.6$, so the multiplier is $1/(1 - 0.6) = 1/0.4 = 2.5$. If the marginal propensity to consume were very low, then the process of building withdrawals up to match a given change in injections will take a large number of 'rounds' of expenditure with each round adding extra income. Thus a low marginal propensity to withdraw implies a high value for the multiplier.

The mathematical derivation of the multiplier formula is straightforward. Earlier, we defined aggregate income as the sum of expenditure on domestically produced consumer goods, exports, investment and public spending: $C_d + J$. Denoting Y as income, we thus have:

$$Y = C_d + J$$

It is also evident that income will be the major determinant of C_d, that is:

$$C_d = f(Y)$$

If we assume, for simplicity, a linear relationship between the two we have:

$$C_d = a + bY$$

(where b, the slope, is the marginal propensity to consume). Thus:

$$Y = C_d + J$$
$$Y = (a + bY) + J$$
$$Y - (bY) = a + J$$
$$Y(1 - b) = a + J$$
$$Y = \frac{a}{1 - b} + \frac{J}{1 - b}$$

The multiplier process acts on a change in J over two periods of time. Let us denote to the variables Y and J in the first period—period t—as Y_t and J_t, and those in the second period as Y_{t+1} and J_{t+1}. Thus, our equilibrium aggregate income equation becomes:

$$Y_t = \frac{a}{1-b} + \frac{J_t}{1-b}$$

If we assume, as we did earlier, that there is some change in J, then through the multiplier process there will be some change in Y. Accordingly, the new equilibrium at period $(t+1)$ will be:

$$Y_{t+1} = \frac{a}{1-b} + \frac{J_{t+1}}{1-b}$$

Thus we can denote the change in equilibrium income over the two periods as:

$$Y_{t+1} - Y_t = \frac{a + J_{t+1}}{1-b} - \frac{a + J_t}{1-b}$$

$$= \frac{J_{t+1} - J_t}{1-b}$$

$$= \frac{1}{1-b}(J_{t+1} - J_t)$$

In the example used earlier we assumed a change in J of £20 billion and an *MPC* value of 0.6. Using the derived formula we thus have:

$$(Y_{t+1} - Y_t) = \frac{1}{1-0.6}(20) = 2.5(20) = 50$$

Thus a rise in J of £20 billion gives rise to an increase in income of £50 billion, as before.

In reality, multipliers tend to be very much lower than those in the examples above, because marginal propensities to save, pay taxes and import are rather high. When income tax, national insurance contributions and VAT were taken into account, taxation alone can take 60 per cent of any increase in income, with imports absorbing much of the rest. The consensus of modern research places the value of the multiplier between 1.1 and 1.3. Nevertheless, it remains an aspect of the macro-economy which policy makers cannot afford to ignore when calculating the likely effects of any decisions about, say, public expenditure.

29-6 THE PERSISTENCE OF ECONOMIC DEPRESSIONS: STICKY WAGES AND THE LIQUIDITY TRAP

One characteristic of economic life throughout the nineteenth and early twentieth centuries was the trade cycle. Economies went successively through slump, recovery and boom before falling back into slump, the entire cycle usually lasting some ten years.

On the basis of this experience, the classical economists believed that the economy contained mechanisms which could move it from one stage of the cycle to the next automatically. One such mechanism was the capital market, where it was felt that the demands of businessmen for investment funds would, in times of boom, tend to push interest rates upwards. Since interest payments are deducted from profits, this would make business less profitable, inducing a downturn in investment. A decline in order for capital goods would depress demand, factories would shut and the slump phase would begin. During the slump itself, few businessmen would seek to expand their operations and the demand for loanable funds would collapse. Would-be lenders would compete against each other by offering easier and easier terms. In these circumstances, interest rates would naturally fall. The classical economists drew the conclusion that this process would reduce interest rates sufficiently to restore business profitability, thus promoting the recovery of the economy and rekindling the demand for loans. Another corrective mechanism was felt to be the labour market, in which wages rose and fell in response to supply and demand. During the boom, labour would become scarce and wages would rise. Like rising interest rates, this would cut into profitability, inducing business failures and bringing the boom to an end. The ensuing slump, however, would allow employers to cut wages, once again restoring profits and inducing a recovery. Interest rates and wages thus played critical roles in the classicists' belief that the boom phase of the cycle contained the seeds of the slump, while the slump prepared the way for the coming boom.

These ideas differ markedly from those of Keynes. In Keynesian macro-economics, there are no forces inside the circular flow of income and expenditure which can move the economy from one level of national income to another. All movements are the result of the exogenous forces which govern planed injections and withdrawals. Should these plans shift the economy to a position of high unemployment, it will remain there until those plans are revised. The central point is that there are no forces within the circular flow of income and expenditure itself that will necessarily induce those changes. A peculiar feature of the slump which began with the Wall Street Crash of 1929, in fact, was the lack of any sign of recovery for over a decade. The corrective mechanisms postulated by the classicists seemed to be inoperative. Keynes, however, was able to offer an explanation using the ideas set out earlier: persistent unemployment could be seen as the effect of a rise in planned withdrawals or a cut in planned injections. Keynes was naturally obliged to explain how it was that the corrective mechanisms of classical economics were prevented from working. With regard to the labour market, he argued that pay would not tend to fall during a slump partly because of the power of trade unions and partly because workers' living standards were heavily influenced by social conventions which required that different occupations be accorded their traditional remuneration, regardless of the level of unemployment. Wages were, he maintained, 'sticky'. Indeed, a salient feature of the inter-war years in the United Kingdom was the fact that wage rates fell by less than 1 per cent per year despite heavy unemployment.

The second corrective mechanism was the capital market. Both Keynes and the classicals accepted that lenders would tend to hold their funds in the form of bank balances until they found securities to buy. They also shared the view that, during the slump phase, interest rates would tend to fall. The classical economists, as we have seen, drew the conclusion that this process would reduce interest rates sufficiently to rekindle demand for loans. It was at this point that Keynes and the classical economists parted company. Keynes argued that lenders tended to base their decisions on some expectation of a 'normal' rate, or range of rates, of interest. Let us assume this to be 4–6 per cent, while, because of a slump, actual rates had gone down to 2 per cent and were still falling. Let us further assume, however, that a rate of 1 per cent would have been necessary to revive investment. At 2 per cent, according to Keynes, lenders would be expecting the fall to go into reverse with rates climbing back into their normal range. This expectation would lead them to view bonds which were on offer with a yield of 2 per cent as being extremely risky. Readers will recall from Chapter 28 that an upward movement in interest rates implies a downward movement in security prices. Anyone buying a bond that offered 2 per cent would, if rates rose, suffer a substantial capital loss. Keynes concluded that the risk of such losses would make lenders refuse to buy securities at these rates of interest—they would, he suggested, prefer to keep their money in the bank as what he termed 'speculative balances', awaiting the upturn in interest rates. As a result, the demand for money at low interest rates would become infinitely elastic, as illustrated in Fig. 29-4.

For the macro-economy, the implications of this line of reasoning are significant. Entrepreneurs who would have borrowed money at 1 per cent will be turned away from the capital markets, the money will remain unspent and business ventures will not be started. The economy will remain in depression. This logic does not however suggest that the capital market will be in disequilibrium during a depression. Although a slump may begin with an excess of loanable (but unlent) funds, this does not persist because the slump reduces incomes. This is turn makes savings fall and the balance between saving and investment is restored. The difference between the Keynesian and the classical account is simply this: the classical economists saw the re-establishment of equilibrium as being the work of changes in interest rates, while Keynes saw this role being performed by changes in income. It would, however, be unwise to exaggerate the differences between Keynes and the classical economists on this point, since both admitted that income and interest rates influenced decisions to save and to borrow. The difference is rather one of emphasis, with Keynes arguing that saving and borrowing were primarily dependent upon income levels rather than interest rates.

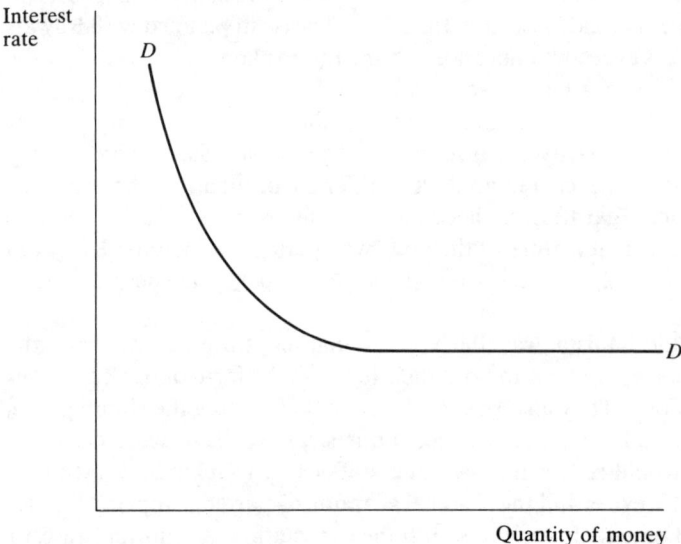

Figure 29-4 The liquidity trap

29-7 COUNTER-CYCLICAL FISCAL POLICY

Keynes's answer to the problem of depression was that income should be raised by making planned injections exceed planned withdrawals. To bring this about, Keynes argued, the government should operate an active fiscal policy, that is, it should manipulate its tax receipts and/or its levels of expenditure. In a slump, it should pursue a 'reflationary' fiscal policy by cutting taxes and so reducing withdrawals.

An alternative reflationary policy would be to raise injections by stepping up public spending (thus did Keynes legitimize a programme of public works as a cure for unemployment). Either step, of course, would raise the government's deficit, the PSBR. Borrowing the funds should present few problems, of course, because of the large speculative balances which lenders would be holding.

Naturally, the ability of a government to raise the output of the economy is limited by the capacity of the economy to produce goods and services. The existence of unemployment indicates that the economy has a degree of excess capacity. As aggregate demand rises, either through the normal processes of the business cycle or through the operation of a reflationary policy, spare capacity is brought into use. As capacity limits are reached, that is, as the economy approaches full employment, bottlenecks and shortages begin to appear, and prices begin to rise. The overstimulation of aggregate demand, in other words, can produce inflation. To deal with inflation, the appropriate policy is to 'deflate' the economy by means of higher taxes or reductions in public spending. Thus a 'counter-cyclical fiscal policy' (also known as a 'demand management policy' or 'fine-tuning') of reflation and deflation would, Keynes predicted, smooth out the fluctuations of the business cycle.

These policy implications have come under sustained attack over the years from economists of the neo-classical/monetarist school. One argument put forward is that an expansion of public spending and borrowing in a slump would drive up both pay rates and interest rates. The private sector of the economy would thus be 'crowded out' of both the labour and the capital markets. It is plain that this reasoning has much in common with the Treasury view of the 1930s.

29-8 THE IMPORTANCE OF KEYNESIAN ECONOMICS

On a theoretical level, Keynesianism represents an important strand in economic thought because it challenges the idea that markets will, if left to themselves, arrive at the optimum position. Whereas monetarists and the classical economists have faith in the ability of markets to move swiftly from one equilibrium to another, Keynesians argue that neither the labour nor the capital market can be relied upon to do this. In consequence of their pivotal roles in the economic system as a whole, the failures of these markets can mean the persistence of mass unemployment. In practical terms, Keynes offered governments a way of keeping unemployment under control. This prospect arose from the conditional predictions which the theory generated: if the government could engineer an excess of planned injections over planned withdrawals, national income would expand and unemployment would fall. Conversely, if the government created an excess of planned withdrawals over planned injections, national income would fall and unemployment would rise. Keynes's recommendations were adopted at the end of the Second World War and formed the basis for policy for the next three decades. How successful the theory was, how reliable its conditional predictions proved to be, is a topic to be examined in later chapters.

29-9 SUMMARY

Aggregate expenditure determines, within the limits of the capacity of the economy, the level of economic activity and thus of employment.

Injections are items of expenditure which are added to the circular flow from outside, like export sales, public spending and investment spending.

Withdrawals are items of expenditure which leave the circular flow such as taxation, imports and savings.

Equilibrium national income is attained when planned injections equal planned withdrawals. This need not coincide with full employment.

Adjustment occurs when planned injections and planned withdrawals are not equal, and it takes place through changes in national income. This Keynesian account is different from adjustment processes as described by neo-classical economists, who stress the importance of interest rates and exchange rates in bringing injections and withdrawals into line. The *liquidity trap* is the supposed refusal of investors to buy bonds at low interest rates for fear of suffering a capital loss in the eventuality of a rise in rates. At low interest rates, according to Keynesians, the demand for money becomes infinite, preventing rates from falling sufficiently to rekindle business activity. *Fiscal policy* is the manipulation of taxation and public spending. Keynesians advocate a *counter-cyclical* fiscal policy to even out booms and slumps.

Crowding out refers to the alleged effect of an expansionary fiscal policy in driving up pay or interest rates.

EXERCISES

29-1 Below are two expressions showing the demand for loanable funds:

$$D = a + 16i + 0.1Y$$

$$D = a + 0.1i + 16Y$$

where i is the rate of interest and Y is aggregate national income. Which equation is monetarist and which Keynesian, and why? Compare and contrast the monetarist and Keynesian views of the demand for money.

29-2 Collect data for the last 10 years on consumers' expenditure in real terms and personal disposable income in real terms.

(*a*) Determine, using regression techniques, the appropriate linear equation for the consumption function.
(*b*) How, in economic terms, would you interpret the a and b parameters you have estimated?

29-3 Assume that the levels of injections of expenditure into an economy are determined exogenously and are currently running at £50 billion. The consumption function is currently:

$$C_d = 100 + 0.75Y$$

(*a*) Determine the equilibrium level of income
  (*i*) graphically   (*ii*) algebraically

(b) The level of injections now increases by £10 billion. Determine the new equilibrium level of income:
   (i) graphically   (ii) algebraically
(c) Using a computer spreadsheet determine the round-by-round effect of the increase in the level of injections. How many rounds does it take before withdrawals are effectively equal to injections?

29-4 The marginal propensity to consume (MPC) of the consumption function given in Exercise 29.3 changes to 0.75.

(a) Determine the change in equilibrium income from the original level (in Exercise 29-3(a)).
(b) Explain why the equilibrium level of income has changed.
(c) What factors might cause the MPC to change?

29-5 The economy of Ruritania is suffering from unemployment, and a government supporting Keynesian policies has just been elected. As secretary of the Anglo-Ruritanian Trade Society (described in Exercise 27-4 at the end of Chapter 27), draft a one-page circular explaining the likely policies to be followed and their possible effects on your members' businesses.

30

UNEMPLOYMENT

30-1 INTRODUCTION

In the previous chapter it was seen that the control of unemployment is one of the central concerns of Keynesian economic policies. Indeed, the level of unemployment in an economy is a major focus of attention for economic commentators and policy-makers. Unemployment, of course, is a highly visible indicator of the level of economic activity in an economy. This chapter examines the way in which unemployment is measured and the problems associated with the interpretation of the unemployment figures.

Figure 30-1 shows the levels of unemployment in the United Kingdom and the rate of unemployment from 1950 to 1985. Also shown is the level of real national income over the same period. It is apparent both that unemployment has fluctuated widely over the period and that there is some apparent correlation between movements in unemployment levels and in national income.

30-2 MEASURING UNEMPLOYMENT

While observed movement in unemployment levels may seem self-evident, as in Fig. 30-1, considerable care has to be taken when interpreting unemployment data. Definitions of, and methods of measuring, unemployment vary considerably.

The first distinction to be made is between those who wish to earn an income and those who do not, because they undertake unpaid work at home, or because they are retired or disabled or for some other reason. The former group are said to *participate* in the labour market, and the *participation rate* refers to the proportion of the population who form the labour force. 'Unemployment', naturally, does not refer to non-participants but is restricted

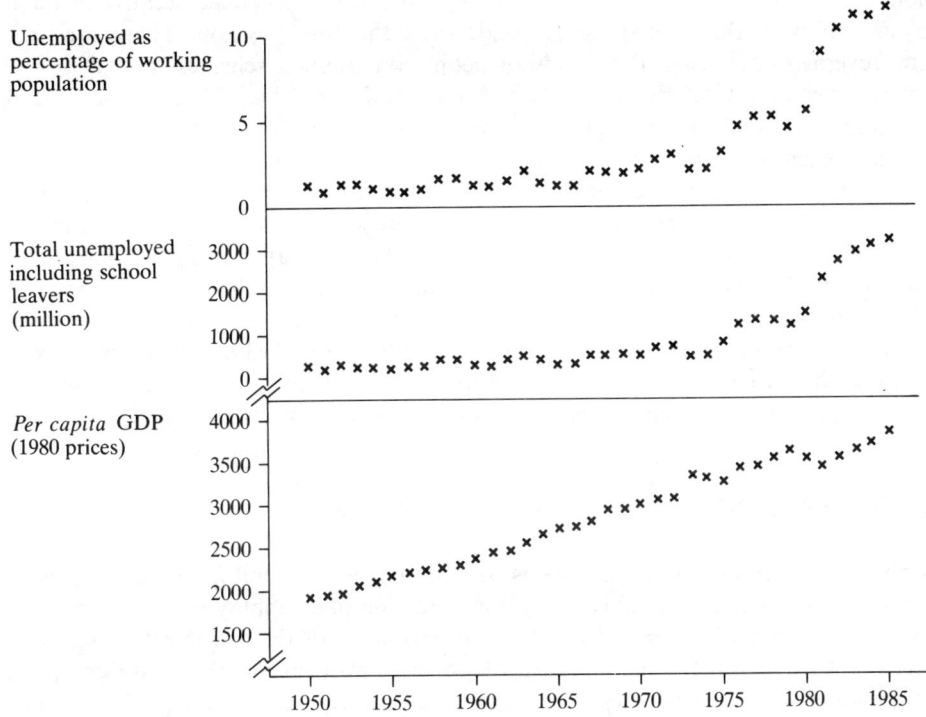

Figure 30-1 Unemployment and per capita GDP, 1950–85 (*Source: ETAS*)

to those who are willing and able to work at the going rate of pay, but who do not have employment. It is sometimes described more accurately as 'involuntary unemployment'.

Arriving at an objective measure of this concept is by no means straightforward. The procedure of the Department of Employment (DE), which produces the unemployment figures for the United Kingdom, is to count the number of people who register at their offices as being in search of work. Registration at once ensures that a person will be informed of any vacancies and entitles that person to unemployment benefit. Benefits are, of course, restricted to those who have been paying National Insurance contributions when they were in work. This approach is, however, problematic on two grounds.

First, the DE's definition counts as unemployed many people who register so as to qualify for benefits when they are not in fact available for work, like some disabled people and many who have taken premature retirement. The DE cannot therefore simply report the crude number of those registering but is obliged to decide whom to exclude. During the course of the 1980s, the rules for compiling the unemployment total have been altered some 19 times. Although statistical accuracy is to be applauded, there can be no doubt that changes of this frequency can only be a hindrance to the economist's work of testing and falsifying hypotheses.

The second problem with the DE's approach is that many people who see themselves as being unemployed are not entitled to register because they have not been paying National Insurance contributions. Married women and people who have newly completed their education are instances of these groups. Critics of the DE argue that, because of these 'hidden' unemployed, the official figures understate the true position. There are, furthermore, several hundreds of thousands of people on training schemes funded by the government who would otherwise be classed as unemployed. Defenders of the official classification, on the other hand, argue that the errors of inclusion and those of omission tend to cancel each other out.

An alternative approach, used in the United States and other countries, is to conduct market research to find out how many people without jobs actively sought work in the previous week or month. The advantage of this method is that it includes job-seekers regardless of whether they are entitled to any benefits or not. It is, however, not without problems of its own in that it would exclude people who were in any objective sense unemployed but who had not looked for a job recently because they knew that none was to be had in their area. In addition, there arise the problems of interpreting sample information, as discussed earlier in the text in the chapters on statistical inference.

30-3 INTERPRETING UNEMPLOYMENT LEVELS

A major use of unemployment statistics is as one means of monitoring the success of government economic policy. That is to say, the reduction of unemployment is, along with controlling inflation and raising the rate of economic growth, an objective of most governments. As a result, the methods by which the statistical indicators are compiled become a matter of some sensitivity, with governments being strongly tempted to change definitions and procedures so that the figures present their policies in a more favourable light. Cynics, indeed, have elevated this to the status of a law—'Goodhart's Law'—which states that any statistical series that gains political importance will be adulterated. It may be noted that most of the changes to the unemployment figures referred to above had the effect of reducing the reported totals.

A second major function of unemployment statistics (in conjunction with other economic data) is to serve as a basis for economic policy decisions. From this point of view, it is clearly important to be able to identify the 'turning points' of the economic cycle. Besides the problems of lags and of changes in definitions, a further difficulty is caused by the fact that most economic statistics fluctuate from season to season. Unemployment levels, for example, are generally higher in the winter and lower in the summer. It is clearly possible that a recession developing in the late summer could be mistaken for a normal seasonal rise in unemployment and thus go unnoticed for several months. It is thus necessary to distinguish underlying trends from more superficial events. This is something to which we return later in the chapter.

30-4 TYPES OF UNEMPLOYMENT

It is important to realize, when using unemployment data, that—regardless of what is happening to the total level of unemployment—the *composition* of the unemployed will be constantly changing. Those recently unemployed (or recently entering the labour market) will be adding to the total while others will be leaving the unemployment register as they find work, retire or leave the labour market for other reasons. There may also be considerable change in the composition of unemployment by age, by sex, by social group and by region. Economists tend to distinguish between different classifications of unemployment.

Frictional unemployment relates to the unavoidable level of unemployment caused by dynamic economic change. People switching from one job to another, those leaving education and moving into employment, and those retraining to take advantage of new job opportunities are all examples of frictional unemployment.

Structural unemployment is a longer-run phenomenon. It refers to the major structural changes that occur in the economy over time and the associated unemployment. Shipbuilding and heavy engineering were, traditionally, large employers in the British economy. Over time, for a number of reasons, these industries have declined and others, such as micro-electronics, have expanded. Inevitably, there will be a mismatch between the skills of the workers in the declining industries and the skill requirements of the employers in the expanding industries: welders who found employment in the Glasgow shipyards are unlikely to find their skills relevant to a micro-computer manufacturer.

Demand-deficient unemployment refers to unemployment which, in Keynesian terms, is caused by equilibrium aggregate demand being lower than the full employment level of income and output.

There are obvious, and differing, policy implications for the different classifications of unemployment.

30-5 SEASONAL ADJUSTMENT

Many such series of economic variables follow a regular, and hence predictable, pattern over a 12-month period. Such a pattern is referred to as the *seasonal variation*. From Fig. 30-2, which shows unemployment in the United Kingdom on a quarterly basis from 1980, it is

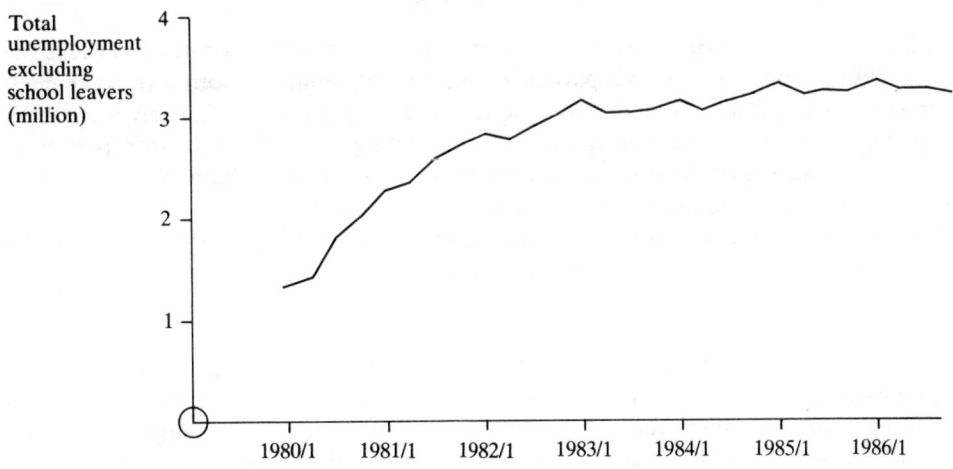

Figure 30-2 Unemployment, 1980-6 (*Source: ETAS*)

evident that, for example, the first quarter of each year regularly sees a rise in unemployment. The possible reasons for this are not difficult to surmise. Many industries connected with tourism, for example, are likely to experience a (temporary) downturn in demand at this time of the year which in turn will (temporarily) affect their employment levels. The construction sector is another obvious example of this.

It is also apparent from Fig. 30-2 that, apart from the regular seasonal variations, there is a longer-term pattern to the unemployment levels. Such a longer-term pattern is referred to as the *trend*.

It is obviously important for the policy decision-maker to be able to recognize whether a change in unemployment reflects an underlying change in the basic trend or is simply a *temporary* seasonal phenomenon. A policy reaction to a change in unemployment that is purely seasonal would be unnecessary and possibly counterproductive. As a result considerable attention is focused not on the actual data series of a variable such as unemployment but rather on the *seasonally adjusted* time series. Seasonal adjustment is a mathematical technique designed to remove the seasonal variation from a data series leaving only the underlying trend. The remainder of this chapter outlines the appropriate techniques.

It should be noted that for most officially published time-series statistics data will be available in both the original and the seasonally adjusted forms and for purposes of analysis and evaluation the adjusted series is the one to use. It must also be noted that, in practice, seasonal adjustment is a particularly complex and refined statistical and mathematical technique, although based on the methods of calculation which follow.

30-6 TIME-SERIES MODELS

In general, a time series such as unemployment can be broken into three major components (hence the alternative name for the technique of *time-series decomposition*):

$$D = T + S + R$$

where D is the original data series, T is the trend, S is the seasonal variation and R is the residual. Thus, unemployment in a particular quarter will comprise both a trend element and an element of seasonal fluctuation. The residual component is effectively a catch-all item for any random and unpredictable factors affecting unemployment in a particular period—such as strikes or the closure of a large firm—which have nothing to do with either seasonal variations or the underlying trend in unemployment.

Time-series decomposition seeks to isolate the trend and seasonal variation in the series. The seasonally adjusted data can then be calculated as:

$$D - S = T + R$$

The technique itself is straightforward (even if the assumptions behind some of the calculations are, for some series, questionable!). The first step is to calculate the trend for the series, using a set of moving averages. The trend can then be removed to find the seasonal deviation and, in turn, the seasonal variation removed from the original data to provide the seasonally adjusted series.

Calculation of the trend

Readers will remember that we view the trend as the underlying movement in the series and the seasonal fluctuation as the temporary variation that occurs over a 12-month period. It follows, therefore, that over a 12-month period the seasonal fluctuations in a series should cancel out, given that in any one quarter or month such variation is, by definition, temporary. So if we were to take a set of four quarterly unemployment figures and calculate a simple arithmetic mean then this average would contain no overall seasonal effects.

So, looking at Table 30-1, which shows the quarterly unemployment data, we could average unemployment over the first four quarters. We could then average unemployment over the next four quarters (1980/2 to 1983/1) and so on for successive sets of four quarters through the series. The problem with this is that the resulting average would be the average for the middle of the period covered—in the case of the first calculation the average would refer to the moment in time *between* Q2 and Q3—rather than to a specific quarter as we require. For this reason a slightly different method of calculating the average is required.

First of all, as before, we calculate the totals for each successive set of four quarters, just as if we were about then to divide by four to find the mean. These figures are shown in the column headed '4Q total'. As you can see from the layout of the table if we were now to calculate the mean from the 4Q total it would fall between the time periods identified. So, instead, we calculate the sum of pairs of the 4Q total values to give the figures in the column headed '8Q total'. These figures represent a total of 8 quarters' data and, as can be seen, if we were now to average these figures they would correspond to specific quarters. Given that we have totals corresponding to 8 quarters we must divide the totals by 8 to calculate the mean. This average is shown in the column headed 'Trend' and represents what is known as a 'centred moving average'. Naturally, manual calculation of such a trend is not to be recommended.

The trend values calculated show the underlying movement in the series as it is averaged over time. These trend values are shown in Fig. 30-3 and the underlying pattern of movement in unemployment is readily visible.

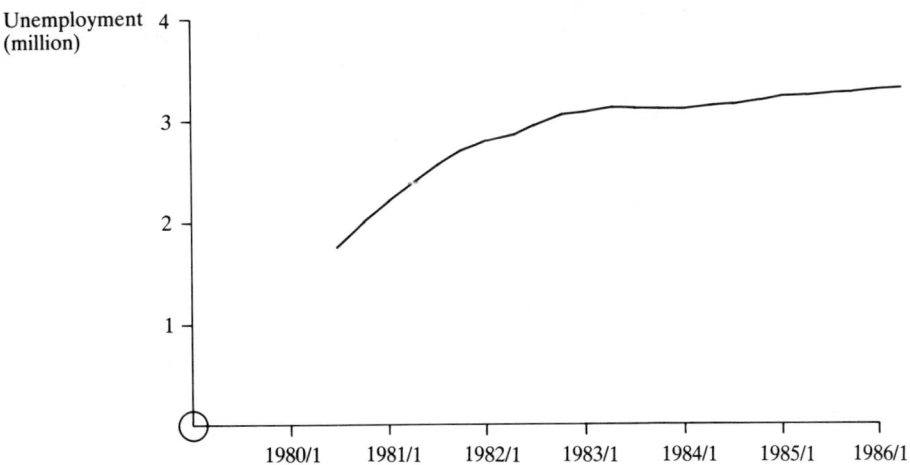

Figure 30-3 Trend in unemployment

Table 30-1 Calculation of trend and seasonal components of quarterly unemployment (thousands)

Quarter	Unemployment	4Q Total	8Q Total	Trend	Deviation	Seasonally adjusted unemployment
1980/1	1 379					1 315.85
1980/2	1 445					1 500.25
		6 659				
1980/3	1 824		14 245	1 780.62	43.375	1 833.37
		7 586				
1980/4	2 011		16 119	2 014.87	−3.875	2 009.52
		8 533				
1981/1	2 306		17 858	2 232.25	73.750	2 242.85
		9 325				
1981/2	2 392		19 407	2 425.87	−33.875	2 447.25
		10 082				
1981/3	2 616		20 720	2 590.00	26.000	2 625.37
		10 638				
1981/4	2 768		21 680	2 710.00	58.000	2 766.52
		11 042				
1982/1	2 862		22 407	2 800.87	61.125	2 798.85
		11 365				
1982/2	2 796		23 032	2 879.00	−83.000	2 851.25
		11 667				
1982/3	2 939		23 671	2 958.87	−19.875	2 948.37
		12 004				
1982/4	3 070		24 280	3 035.00	35.000	3 068.52
		12 276				
1983/1	3 199		24 679	3 084.87	114.125	3 135.85
		12 403				
1983/2	3 068		24 822	3 102.75	−34.750	3 123.25
		12 419				
1983/3	3 066		24 815	3 101.87	−35.875	3 075.37
		12 396				
1983/4	3 086		24 798	3 099.75	−13.750	3 084.52
		12 402				
1984/1	3 176		24 905	3 113.12	62.875	3 112.85
		12 503				
1984/2	3 074		25 142	3 142.75	−68.750	3 129.25
		12 639				
1984/3	3 167		25 413	3 176.63	−9.625	3 176.37
		12 774				
1984/4	3 222		25 705	3 213.13	8.875	3 220.52
		12 931				
1985/1	3 311		25 969	3 246.12	64.875	3 247.85
		13 038				
1985/2	3 231		26 124	3 265.50	−34.50	3 286.25
		13 086				
1985/3	3 274		26 217	3 277.12	−3.125	3 283.37
		13 131				
1985/4	3 270		26 306	3 288.25	−18.250	3 268.52
		13 175				
1986/1	3 356		26 374	3 296.75	59.250	3 292.85
		13 199				
1986/2	3 275		26 356	3 294.50	−19.50	3 330.25
		13 157				
1986/3	3 298					3 307.37
1986/4	3 228					3 226.52

Calculation of the seasonal variations

The trend values can now be used to derive the quarterly seasonal variations. If we ignore the residual terms (which, after all, are random and unpredictable by definition) we have:

$$D - T = S$$

That is, we can estimate the quarterly seasonal variations by removing the trend from the original series. These deviations are shown in Table 30-1. If we examine these deviations for the first quarter of each year we can see that there is a consistent pattern in that in each quarter at this time of year there is a large positive deviation. That is, at this time of year unemployment is always above the trend. But why are these deviations not constant from year to year? The answer lies in the R term. These deviations include not only the seasonal variation but also any residual or random variation. While we have no precise way of estimating the R component of a particular quarter's deviation it seems reasonable to argue that over a number of years such fluctuations will tend to cancel each other out. If, then, we were to take the individual deviations for a particular quarter and average them we would expect this to provide a reasonable estimate of the seasonal variation in this quarter.

(There is, of course, another probable cause of the inconsistency of the quarterly deviations in this case. Given that the definitions used to measure unemployment have frequently changed over this period it is likely that this is reflected in the fluctuating quarterly deviations. Unemployment figures, however, are a relatively extreme example of this problem.)

If we collect the deviations together, as we have done in Table 30-2, the average seasonal fluctuation is easily calculated. Also shown is an average deviation for each quarter. By definition such averages should sum to zero given that over a 12-month period the seasonal effects will cancel each other out. In practice, this rarely happens, so the averages need to be adjusted so that they do sum to zero. In this case, they total 38.08, so each average has a quarter of this total subtracted giving the average seasonal variations shown.

(Note again that, in this case, we have further evidence of the inconsistency of the unemployment series we are using. The deviations for the third and fourth quarters include both positive and negative values. Again, this can almost certainly be attributed to the changing definitions of the unemployment data.)

Table 30-2 Calculation of seasonal variations

			Quarter	
	1	2	3	4
1980			43.375	−3.875
1981	73.75	−33.875	26	58
1982	61.125	−83	−19.875	35
1983	114.125	−34.75	−35.875	−13.75
1984	62.875	−68.75	−9.625	8.875
1985	64.875	−34.5	−3.125	−18.25
1986	59.25	−19.5		
Average	72.6667	−45.729	0.14583	11.00
Seasonal				
variation	63.1457	−55.25	−9.3752	1.479

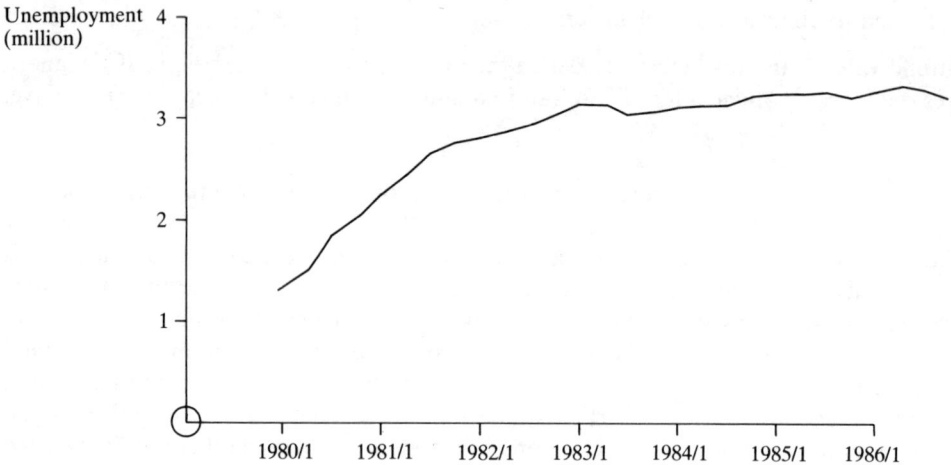

Figure 30-4 The seasonally adjusted series

The interpretation of these variations is straightforward. Looking at the first quarter, we see that, on average, unemployment rises by 63 000 at this time of year only to fall on average by 55 000 in the following quarter. It is more usual, however, to use such variations to calculate the seasonally adjusted series. This is also shown in Table 30-1 and in Fig. 30-4. The original series simply has the appropriate quarter's seasonal variation subtracted (remember that if the seasonal variation is negative this will have the effect of making the adjusted series larger than the original. In general, for analytical purposes, it is this seasonally adjusted series that we should focus on for it allows us to examine the longer-term movement in the data without being distracted by seasonal fluctuations.

30-7 USING MONTHLY DATA

Many series are available in both quarterly and monthly form. Seasonally adjusting a monthly series follows exactly the same process except for the calculation of the trend. In this case we would first work out a 12-month total (instead of a four-quarter total) and then add successive pairs of 12-month totals together to calculate a 24-month total which can then be divided by 24 (rather than 8) to provide the trend. The remaining calculations remain unchanged although a considerable amount of data will be required in order to provide several deviations for each month of the year.

30-8 ADDITIVE AND MULTIPLICATIVE MODELS

The method we have used thus far is referred to as the *additive* model, given that the components of the series are literally added together:

$$D = T + S + R$$

There is an alternative model available where the component terms are expressed in terms of multiplication:

$$D = T \times S(+R)$$

In such a case the seasonal factors would now be calculated as:

$$\frac{D}{T} = S$$

That is, the seasonal factors for the multiplicative model will be ratios rather than differences. As ratios (about the value 1.0) they will show the relative seasonal fluctuation. Thus a seasonal factor of, say, 1.07 for a data series using this model indicates that the original data are 7 per cent above the trend in this period. The sum of such ratios should be 4 (for quarterly data) and the adjustment to the ratios should be made accordingly.

The distinction between the two models is not primarily one of calculation, however. The additive model implies that the seasonal variation around the trend maintains a constant *difference*. Thus, in our example no matter what the trend we are always adjusting the first quarter of the series by the same amount of seasonal variation. The multiplicative model assumes instead that the seasonal variation is a constant *proportion*. Accordingly, this model is often more useful in situations where the trend is undergoing considerable change although for relatively short periods of time there is often little apparent difference between the two methods of calculation.

30-9 SUMMARY

Unemployment is generally classified into three broad groups. *Frictional* unemployment relates to temporary unemployment as people switch between jobs or enter and leave the labour market. *Structural* unemployment arises from the long-run changes in the economic structure. *Demand-deficient* unemployment arises when aggregate demand is less than the full employment level.

Seasonal variation is the change in a time series at a specific time of the year.

The *additive* model assumes the seasonal variation to be a constant difference from the trend whilst the *multiplicative* model assumes a constant proportional difference.

EXERCISES

30-1 Collect the latest available data on unemployment by region from the *DE Gazette*. Collect comparable data for the period 10 years ago.

(a) What regional differences are apparent?
(b) What would you infer to be the probable causes of such differences?
(c) How could you determine whether your inferences in (b) were correct?

30-2 Collect the latest available data on unemployment by duration. Collect comparable data for the period 10 years ago.

(a) Calculate the average duration of unemployment for the two periods.
(b) What observations can you make about the two averages?

(c) What evidence is there to indicate that there has been a change in the average duration of unemployment?
(d) What testable hypotheses for this change can you suggest?

30-3 Collect the latest available data on employment by industrial classification. Collect comparable data for the period 10 years ago.

(a) What observations can you make about the trends in industrial classification of the employed?
(b) What evidence is there to indicate there has been a change in the level oɪ structural unemployment?

30-4 Collect data for the past 20 years on the following:

(a) the population of working age
(b) the labour force
(c) total employed
(d) total unemployed

Assume that you work for the Department of Employment. Draft a report summarizing the past trends in these variables and assess the implications for government initiatives to reduce the level of unemployment.

30-5 Collect quarterly data on total consumers' expenditure (unadjusted) and personal income before tax (unadjusted). Seasonally adjust the data and derive the trends.

(a) What use do you think the trends data you have derived are to an economic forecaster?
(b) What factors can you suggest to explain the seasonal pattern you have derived?

31

INFLATION AND UNEMPLOYMENT

31-1 INTRODUCTION

While unemployment was the major economic problem of the inter-war years, the primary issue in recent years has been inflation. As Fig. 31-1 shows, prices rose at an accelerating rate from 1959 to 1975. Although there has been some deceleration more recently, this has

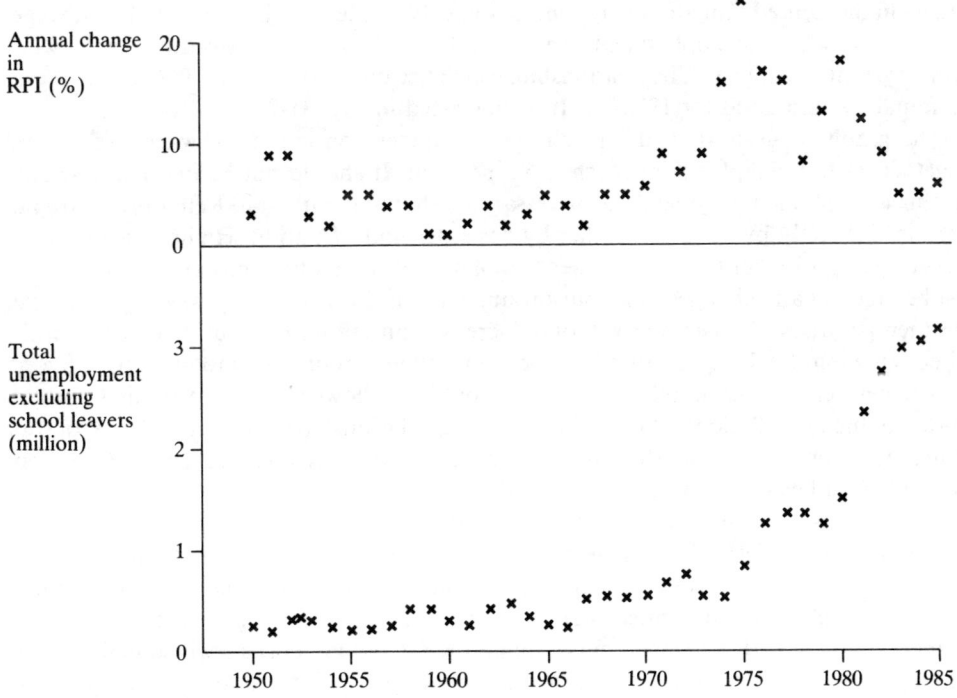

Figure 31-1 Inflation and unemployment, 1950–85 (*Source: ETAS*)

only been attained, as the graph also shows, at the cost of relatively high levels of unemployment. Significantly enough, the struggle to control inflation brought about a radical change in the theoretical basis of economic policy-making, as worsening inflation undermined the credibility of Keynesianism, the school of thought upon which government policy had been based since the end of the Second World War. During the second half of the 1970s, it was supplanted by monetarism, whose rather different policy recommendations seemed to hold greater promise. The chapter concludes by reviewing the effectiveness of these new policies.

Whatever their political persuasion, governments are obliged to attempt to control both inflation and unemployment because of the costs which these impose on society. The costs of inflation are discussed in Chapter 23, while those of unemployment are easily perceived: the economy loses the output of those unable to work, while the people concerned suffer by lacking both an income and a useful role to fulfil.

31-2 THE PHILLIPS CURVE

The problem with having the twin goals of low inflation and unemployment is that they are, to a degree, incompatible. Chapter 29 explained the Keynesian view that unemployment could be reduced by a reflationary fiscal policy, but it went on to note that if aggregate demand pressed too closely on the capacity of the economy, shortages would ensue and inflation would develop. This tension was investigated in a seminal piece of research published in 1958 by Professor A. W. Phillips, who analysed changes in the wages of workers in the United Kingdom between 1861 and 1913. He found, as expected, that wages rose quickly when unemployment was low, but advanced at a slower pace when unemployment was higher. The relationship, which became known as the *Phillips curve*, was also found to hold good for 1913–57. It is illustrated in Fig. 31-2.

The graph suggests that, during the period under consideration, wage rises ceased altogether when unemployment reached 5.5 per cent. It should not be inferred, however, that this level of unemployment was necessary to eliminate inflation. Retail prices are not determined directly by costs but rather by costs per unit of output. Higher wages do not necessarily imply higher labour costs per unit of output (unit labour costs) because account must be taken of any changes in labour productivity. If this is rising by, say, 4 per cent per year, then pay rises of 5 per cent will only increase unit labour costs by 1 per cent. In the United Kingdom the long-run trend has been for labour productivity to grow by some 2.5 per cent per year, which implies that wages could be allowed to go up by that amount without inducing inflation. On the basis of the relationships uncovered by Professor Phillips, therefore, it seemed that unemployment could be reduced to about 3 per cent before inflation began to appear.

The Phillips curve did not, of course, embody any new theories—it simply measured two variables—but derived its plausibility from the pre-existing 'demand-pull' theory of inflation. (The alternative 'cost-push' theory is examined later in this chapter.) The demand-pull theory argues that rising prices were to be attributed to excess aggregate demand. The argument, in brief, is that demand curves in all the individual markets which make up the economy would shift to the right, causing equilibrium points to shift also. The only condition that needs to be present (besides rising demand) is that supply should not be

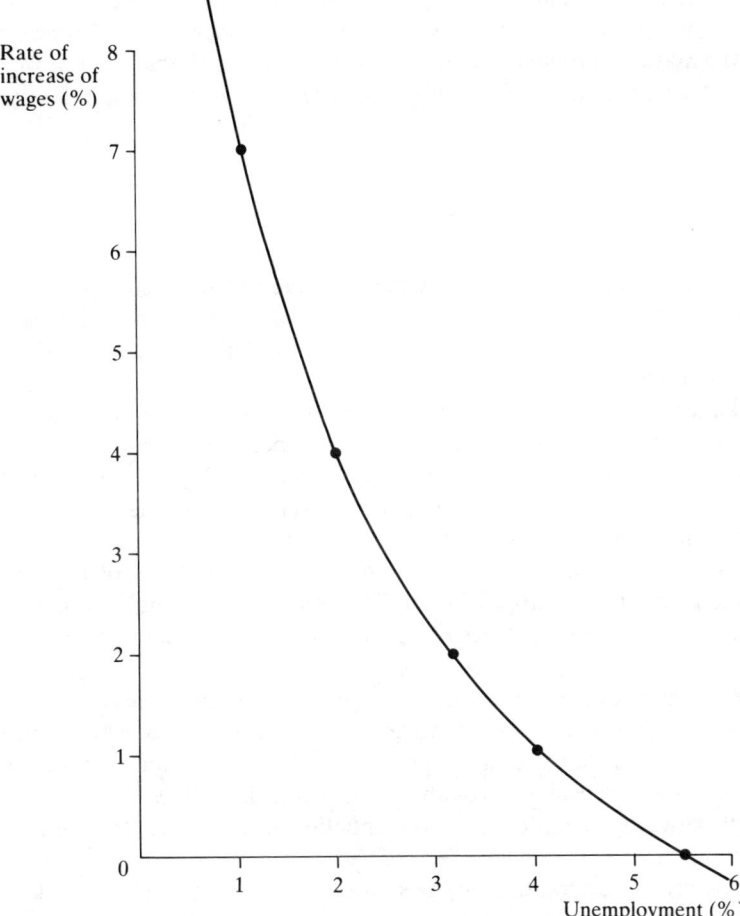

Figure 31-2 The Phillips curve

infinitely elastic. The Phillips curve seemed to confirm—that is, it failed to reject—the demand-pull approach by demonstrating that, in the labour market, the level of demand (as indicated by the rate of unemployment) determined the rate of change of the price of labour (that is, wages) and thus of the general level of prices.

From the point of view of the demand-pull school, the cause of the excess demand was unimportant—it could be expenditure by the public sector, export demand or consumers. It could equally arise from an expansion of the money supply. Indeed, the monetarist theory of inflation can, from this point of view, be interpreted as merely one type of demand-pull theory.

The monetarist view of inflation is that prices cannot go up for any length of time unless the money supply also rises. The argument is that higher prices would produce an upward shift in the demand for money, and, if this were not met with an increase in the money stock, the result would be a rise in interest rates. This in turn would choke off investment and bring the inflationary process to a halt. In technical terminology, inflation can only be sustained, in the view of monetarists, if it is *validated* by an expansion in the money supply. Professor Milton Friedman puts the matter a little more accessibly with his phrase 'inflation is always and everywhere a monetary phenomenon'. As we shall see, this view has not always commanded universal agreement.

31-3 THE PHILLIPS CURVE AND ECONOMIC POLICY

It seemed that Professor Phillips had managed to define the hitherto elusive concept of full employment as being an unemployment rate of 3 per cent. As Fig. 30-1 shows, this was rather higher than the levels which had obtained since the war. The implications of his work, however, went rather further. It seemed that policy-makers faced a range of options in relation to inflation and unemployment. Those policy-makers who were concerned with the dangers of inflation might choose to keep unemployment at 3 per cent. Those who were willing to tolerate a measure of inflation could, however, push unemployment below this rate. Governments could, in effect, choose their preferred location along the curve. The Phillips curve was thus interpreted as defining a 'trade-off' between inflation and unemployment, and was therefore incorporated into the Keynesian policies of demand management. It seemed to give concrete support to the Keynesian idea that the government could steer the economy in any direction it desired using the control levers of fiscal and monetary policy.

For most of the 1960s, pay rises conformed quite closely to the conditional predictions of the Phillips relationship. In 1968, however, wage rises were recorded which were substantially higher than would have been expected given the prevailing level of unemployment. This pattern was repeated throughout the 1970s and 1980s, as Fig. 31-1 illustrates. The trade-off between unemployment and inflation disappeared: the Phillips relationship had broken down.

The term coined to describe the simultaneous existence of stagnation (high unemployment) and inflation was *stagflation*. (The word originated in the United States, though the problem of stagflation was, in fact, world-wide.) Its appearance posed a problem of some gravity for economists of both the Keynesian and monetarist persuasions, for both schools of thought viewed inflation as the result of excess demand—their principal difference being the importance which ought to be accorded to the money supply. Now, however, inflation was running ahead despite clear indications that aggregate demand was actually falling. Indeed, between 1966 and 1972, unemployment rose from 350 000 to over 820 000. These events were not compatible with demand-pull theories of inflation of any kind. Both schools of thought were therefore forced to develop theories to account for the new developments.

31-4 THE KEYNESIAN RESPONSE: COST-PUSH THEORIES OF INFLATION

The fact that both incomes and prices were going up when there were no signs of excess demand suggested that the main shifts were occurring on the supply side of markets (including the labour market) rather than upon the demand side. To account for this, economists of the Keynesian school like Thomas (later Lord) Kaldor began to develop a cost-push theory of inflation.

The theory was based on the assumption that markets for both labour and commodities are imperfect. Labour markets are assumed to be dominated by large trade unions who are usually concerned to maintain the 'differentials' between various groups of workers. A pay rise for unskilled operatives, for example, would therefore be used as the grounds for a claim by skilled workers who would not wish to see any reduction in the gap in pay between themselves and their colleagues. Similarly, the theory assumed the markets for goods and services to be ologopolistic rather than competitive. The theory also noted that prices were influenced by taxes like VAT, and that pay claims may be affected by income-tax rates. It further assumed that economic units—unions and firms—have some target level of real income (wages or profits) which they seek to maintain.

The deduction to be made from these assumptions is that economic units have a degree of control over the prices at which they sell their goods and services. This control is used, the theory suggests, to defend their real-income targets. As long as all units receive these incomes the system remains in equilibrium.

The next stage in the argument is to assume that some external force raises the cost of living and thus reduces the real incomes of trade union members. Their reaction is a series of pay claims. Rather than face costly strikes, employers concede the claims, restoring their profits by raising their prices. This again reduces workers' real incomes, prompting another round of pay claims and so on. The process of inflation is thus a *wage-price spiral*. The theory therefore makes the conditional prediction that an economy composed of concentrated markets will experience inflation after an external shock reduces living standards.

The important point is that inflation can proceed more or less independently of the level of demand or the rate of unemployment. Eventually low demand will weaken the power of both unions and firms and the spiral will stop. Until then, however, it will continue.

The final stage in the argument is to argue that the description fitted the British economy in the 1960s and early 1970s, with the role of external shock being variously fulfilled by the devaluation of sterling in 1967 (which put up the prices of imported goods— the mechanism is described in Chapter 35), the inclusion of working-class incomes in the income-tax net or the rise in the price of oil in 1973.

The theory is naturally open to several objections. Three relate to the alleged monopoly powers of firms and unions. First, many economists, particularly Austrians, would argue that the economy was fundamentally competitive despite the fact that markets can appear concentrated (see Chapter 18). Second, it is not clear why economic units which possess monopoly power should only exercise it in response to *reductions* in their real incomes. After all, if firms could raise their prices at will, there is no real reason to delay doing so until employees have extracted a wage rise. Third, the theory of monopoly can explain why the price of a product goes up when the industry producing it becomes a monopoly, but this does not suggest that prices should rise year after year. For this to occur, the amount of monopoly power in the economy must be continually advancing—a proposition which cost-push theorists have not put forward.

The objection which monetarists lodge against the theory resembles their view of demand-pull theories outlined earlier. It is that the wage-price spiral could not operate for long without increases in the money supply, that is, without being validated. The argument is that the higher prices and wages produced by wage-price spiral would raise the demand for money since people would need more cash for their everyday transactions. If the money supply were held constant, however, the demand for it would exceed supply. Interest rates would rise, savings would increase and demand would fall. As a result, unemployment would rise, undermining the power of both unions and firms, and the wage-price spiral would eventually peter out in a recession. The spiral can only proceed, monetarists argue, if it is validated by an increase in the money supply. If, however, an expanding money supply is an essential ingredient in the process of inflation, then it ought to be recognized as such and no independent importance ought to be attached to unions or firms.

31-5 KEYNESIAN POLICIES TO CONTROL INFLATION

However convincing or otherwise the cost-push theory appeared, Keynesian policy-makers were faced with a choice over the control of inflation. Even if inflation were being caused by cost pressures, one way to control it would still be to use monetary and fiscal policy to deflate demand and so induce mass unemployment, which would undermine the power of both unions and firms and so bring the wage-price spiral to a halt. Alternatively, the government could follow the logic of the cost-push theory and intervene directly in the process of inflation. Indeed, the importance of the cost-push theory was that it seemed to offer Keynesian economic policy-makers a way of controlling inflation without imposing the social costs of unemployment. It was accordingly adopted.

Government intervention in the wage-price spiral can, in principle, take many forms. First, the basis of the spiral can be undermined by engendering more competition—by reducing entry barriers—and by curbing the powers of the unions. Second, pay settlements could be reduced either voluntarily by the unions or by the government imposing legal constraints on pay rises. A further possibility would be to restrain price rises, again either on a voluntary or on a statutory basis. Prices could also be held down by reductions in indirect taxes or by subsidies. These policies have been collectively termed *prices and incomes policies*.

Policies of this nature were followed in various forms from 1967 to 1979. The period in which they were pursued with the greatest commitment was from 1974 to 1978, when the Labour government negotiated a 'Social Contract' with the trade unions. In return for voluntary pay restraint, the government enacted changes in employment legislation (e.g. establishing rights to maternity leave and to appeal against unfair dismissal) and restrained price rises by setting up the Prices Commission and by subsidizing food, housing and the outputs of the then nationalized industries such as gas.

Although the rate of inflation declined from 1975 to 1979, it nevertheless remained unconquered. The bald fact is that, between 1967 and 1979, the general level of retail prices increased by a factor of 3.5. A feature of the period which many found disturbing was the way in which the money supply was neglected. The subsidies paid under the Social Contract led to higher public spending, which the government paid for (in part) by borrowing from the banks, that is, by printing money. Thus the Social Contract led to the money supply's rising at a rapid rate. The persistence of inflation in the context of an expanding supply of money was seen as powerful evidence in favour of monetarism. By the late 1970s, the tide of the argument was running decisively in favour of monetarism.

31-6 SUMMARY

Demand-pull theories suggested that the cause of inflation was to be found in levels of expenditure which outran the capacity of the economy. According to this line of reasoning, inflation ought to occur when unemployment was low.

The *Phillips curve* identified a negative relationship between unemployment and inflation for the period 1861–1957, as predicted by demand-pull theories. This was seen by policy-makers as describing the terms of a trade-off between these two policy objectives. In the late 1960s this relationship was no longer supported by the data.

Stagflation is the simultaneous occurrence of inflation and unemployment. Its appearance suggested that inflation was not a demand-pull phenomenon but was driven by the supply side of markets.

Cost-push theories were advanced by some Keynesian economists to explain stagflation. They were based on the assumption that markets, for both goods and labour, were concentrated so that sellers were able to raise prices (and salaries). *Prices and incomes policies* were based upon cost-push logic. They attempted to control inflation by intervening directly in the processes of pay bargaining and price setting.

EXERCISES

31-1 Cost-push theories of inflation see the militancy or strength of trade unions as an important part of the process of inflation. How do you think this could be measured and quantified? What objections could be lodged against these methods? What is their significance for cost-push theories?

31-2 Comment critically on the importance of the idea of 'validation' for cost-push theories of inflation.

31-3 The government has just instituted a policy to control pay and price increases. Some unions object to this restriction of their rights to negotiate pay rises, while some firms think it will interfere with their ability to run their businesses. The government minister responsible calls a meeting to discuss the matter with the above parties, together with representatives of consumer organizations (who approve of the policy). Write briefing notes for each of the four parties present.

31-4 Collect data for the past 15–20 years on average earnings of all employees (all manufacturing industries) and the Retail Price Index.

(a) Plot the two variables on a suitable graph.
(b) Is there any evidence of a pattern between the two?
(c) What inferences could you make about the cause–effect structure between the two variables?
(d) What are the policy implications of your inferences?
(e) How could you test the validity of these inferences?

32

STAGFLATION—THE MONETARIST VIEW

32-1 INTRODUCTION

Like Keynesians, monetarist economists were placed in a quandary by the appearance of stagflation. The general understanding which monetarists had of inflation was that it was a demand-side phenomenon: excessive growth of the money supply produced shifts in demand curves in all markets, resulting in excess demand which produced higher prices. Indeed, the only criticism which monetarists made of the demand-pull theory of inflation was that the latter understated the role of money in sustaining demand. As was suggested earlier, however, the implication of stagflation was that inflation was being produced not by shifts in demand but by shifts in supply curves. Again like the Keynesians, the monetarists began to pay more attention to ideas which explained shifts in supply.

The principal architect of the theory which emerged was Professor Milton Friedman. The theory was known as the *expectations-augmented Philips curve*. This is perhaps a curious title in view of the fact that, as we shall see, the theory in its strict form does not so much augment the Phillips curve as replace it completely.

32-2 THE EXPECTATIONS-AUGMENTED PHILLIPS CURVE

The model starts by making a number of assumptions about the labour market. This is assumed to be a competitive market in which employers and would-be workers arrange the hiring of labour. The supply of labour is assumed to be determined by people's relative preferences for income or leisure. Specifically, it is assumed that greater numbers of people can only be tempted away from their leisure pursuits or domestic duties by the offer of higher real wages. As a result, the supply curve of labour thus slopes upwards to the right.

The demand for labour is assumed to be determined by the relationship between labour costs and the prices of the goods made. It is assumed that the law of diminishing returns applies, meaning that successive workers will be less and less productive. Employers' demand for labour will therefore vary inversely with real wages: many workers will be sought when wages are low but few will be required when wage rates are high. Thus the demand curve for labour slopes downwards to the right. For simplicity, technology is taken to be constant. The labour market is thus assumed to resemble that for any ordinary commodity, and it may be deduced that it would (unless prevented) come to an equilibrium in which all the people who wished to work at the going rate of pay (or range of rates of pay) would have jobs.

The situation is complicated slightly by two further assumptions. First, the labour market is assumed to contain an element of dynamism, with firms expanding and contracting so that workers are constantly having to find new jobs. Second, it is also assumed that the participants in the labour market suffer from a degree of ignorance, with workers in particular having to search before they find a job which gives them rewards which they consider adequate. Taken together, these assumptions produced the conclusion that, even when the labour market is in equilibrium, there must be a certain level of unemployment because potential workers are engaged in a search for suitable employment. This level Friedman termed the 'natural rate' of unemployment, and it is the central concept of his theory.

This model is illustrated by Fig. 32-1, which shows a conventional demand curve for labour, *DD*. There are two parallel supply curves for labour: *GG* represents the gross supply of all potential workers at various rates of pay, while *NN* represents the proportion of those

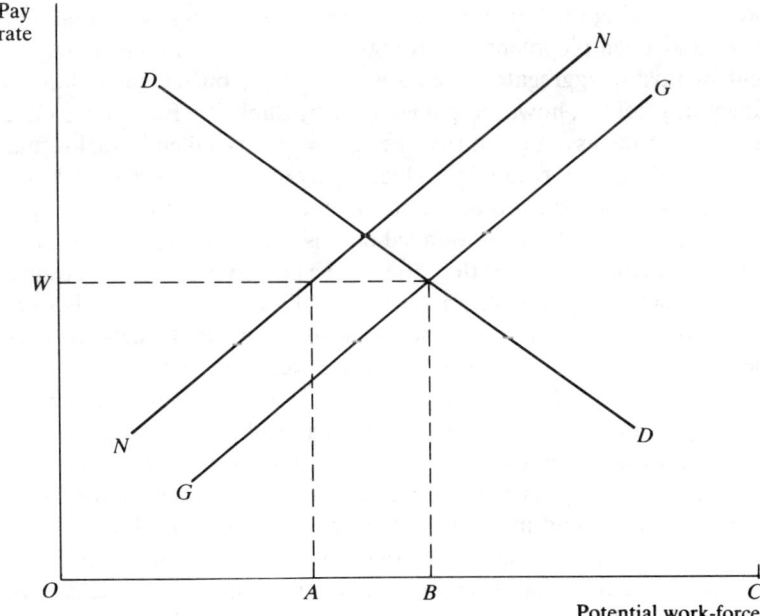

Figure 32-1 The labour market

who have found satisfactory work. The horizontal difference between *GG* and *NN* represents those would-be workers who are searching for employment. The population is thus divided into three groups: *OA*, the employed labour force; *AB*, those unemployed but searching, and *BC*, the economically inactive. The rate of unemployment—which is the natural rate when the market is in equilibrium—is clearly *AB* as a percentage of the whole labour force, *OB*.

The point to stress here is that the relative sizes of the three groups are determined by the positions of the three curves, that is, by their respective shift factors. On the demand side, the main element is the prices of the products made, that is, the general price level. If this were to rise relative to wages, employers would make more profits and the demand curve for labour would shift upwards. Falls in product prices, conversely, would make the curve shift downwards. For the gross supply of labour, people's work and leisure preferences are the main factor. The natural rate of unemployment—the difference between *GG* and *NN*—will be governed by the search process. Anything which encourages people to continue searching or which makes it more difficult for workers and employers to agree on a contract of employment will tend to raise the natural rate of unemployment. It will for example go up, *ceteris paribus*, if unemployment benefits are increased, if job-seekers have inappropriate skills or if the unemployed fail to move from one region to another to gain work.

The next step is to examine the model's reactions to changing the assumptions. Since the purpose of the theory is to explain the failure of Keynesian demand management, the changes in question will be taken to be fluctuations, induced by government economic policy, in the level of aggregate demand. Let us assume, therefore, that the government raises its spending, financing the change by printing money. The immediate effect of the higher demand is to raise product prices, making business more profitable. In effect, labour costs fall in real terms, inducing employers to seek more workers. This they do by offering higher wages. Job-seekers, mistaking the higher money wages for higher real wages, accept the offers of employment and unemployment accordingly falls. The Keynesian policy of reducing unemployment by raising aggregate demand is thus, at the outset, successful.

The reduction in unemployment is, however, gained only by duplicity. Employers have expanded their labour forces on the assumption that labour costs have fallen in real terms. This proves to be incorrect, as they are forced to offer higher pay to attract the extra labour. For their part, workers have accepted the job offers on the understanding that real wages were rising—a belief which also proved to be ill-founded because rising product prices have in reality already eroded those income gains. Both parties to the new employment contracts, in other words, have been under misapprehensions. It matters little that their beliefs were incompatible—employers thinking that real wages had gone down, while the new workers thought they had gone up. All that is important is that the beliefs were false.

After a while, the illusions are dispelled—employers realizing that real wages are higher than anticipated and employees finding them to be lower. As a result, both parties seek to undo the new employment contracts—employers by reducing their work-forces and job-seekers by resuming their search activity. The labour market thus returns to its natural rate of unemployment: the success of demand management endures only for the short run.

It would, however, be erroneous to conclude that the whole episode brings no permanent results. Whereas before there had been no inflation, now prices and wages have both gone by some amount, say, 2 per cent. The next stage in the argument which Friedman develops is to assume that employers and workers will proceed to build this level of inflation into their decisions. Job-seekers (the unemployed) thus scale up the rewards which they expect to be offered, while employers decide how many workers to employ on the assumption that prices and wages will continue rising at 2 per cent. The easiest option for the government in this situation is to validate the expectations of job-seekers and employers and allow inflation to proceed at 2 per cent per year by raising the money supply at that rate. The labour market will therefore remain in equilibrium with unemployment at its natural rate and inflation running at 2 per cent.

These events can be traced on a Phillips curve graph, as in Fig. 32-2. Initially, there is no inflation and unemployment stands at its natural rate, A. The expansion in demand reduces unemployment but causes a degree of inflation, moving the labour market along the Phillips curve to B. The discovery by both employers and job-seekers that their expectations about real wages were incorrect then takes the level of unemployment back to the natural rate, but this is now combined with a rate of inflation of 2 per cent, C. In fact, the Phillips curve is argued to be merely a short-run relationship, with the duration of the short run being set by the duration of people's misconceptions.

Different features of the model can be explored by looking at other government policies. First, let us assume that instead of increasing the money supply by 2 per cent per year, the government makes a second attempt to reduce unemployment below the natural rate. This could only be effected by increasing the money supply at a rate faster than the established 2 per cent. Since employers and job-seekers were reckoning on inflation at 2 per cent, the extra demand would again deceive them into thinking that real wages had changed. Employers, seeing prices increasing at, say, 4 per cent would again try to hire more workers. The higher wages offered would again lead job-seekers to cut short their searches and accept employment in the belief that the jobs were paying higher real wages. Eventually, however, both sides would once again see their mistakes and withdraw from the contracts of

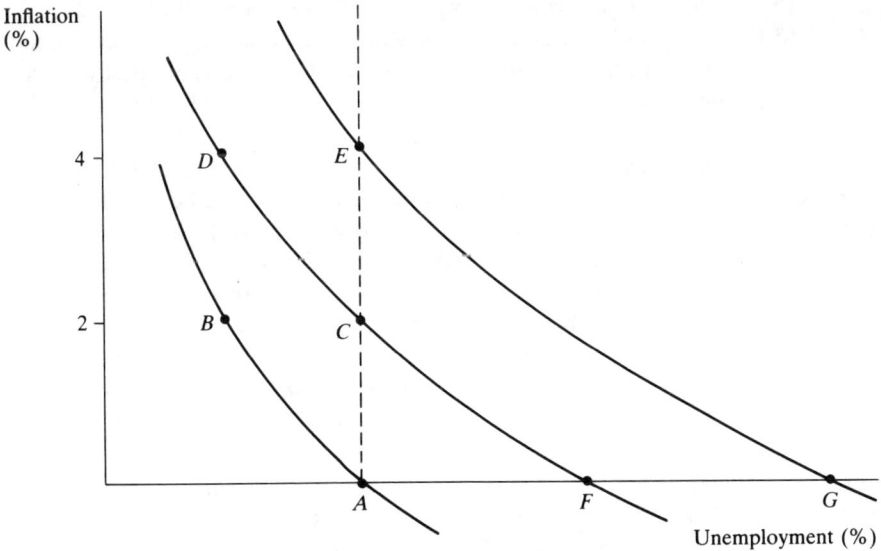

Figure 32-2 The expectations-augmented Phillips curve

employment. Unemployment would revert to the natural rate, this time against a background of 4 per cent inflation. On Fig. 32-2 this is the movement from C to D and back to E.

Further attempts to reduce unemployment below the natural rate would, by similar logic, lead merely to higher inflation. Thus unemployment can only be taken below the natural rate for extended periods of time at the cost of *accelerating* inflation, and an alternative name for the natural rate of unemployment is the *non-accelerating-inflation rate of unemployment* (NAIRU).

The converse policy would be for the government to hold the money supply constant at its new rate (2 per cent above the opening level). This would prevent prices from rising any further, that is, it would bring inflation to a halt. The trouble is that—like the unexpected inflation which came when the government expanded the money supply—the stopping of inflation would be unexpected and would therefore produce mistaken beliefs among employers and job-seekers. This time, seeing prices stabilize and, thinking that labour costs were going up relative to prices, employers would take steps to cut their labour forces. This fall in the demand for labour would slow down the growth of wages, and job-seekers, who were expecting wages (and prices) to keep on going up at 2 per cent per year would find that fewer and fewer of the jobs on offer were matching up to their expectations. In consequence they would lengthen their search periods. Unemployment would under these circumstances rise to point F.

The re-establishment of equilibrium can only occur when both groups have learned the error of their perceptions. Friedman argues that this will only occur after a period of low inflation that is lengthy enough to reassure people that prices have truly stabilized. When people are once again convinced that inflation has ceased, employment bargains will once again be struck and unemployment will fall back from F to A. (If the economy had already reached E with inflation at 4 per cent, then halting the growth of the money supply would send unemployment all the way up to G before falling back to A. Higher rates of inflation would require correspondingly higher rates of 'transitional' unemployment.)

Points D, C and F on the graph trace out a curve which bears a strong resemblance to a Phillips curve, as do points A and B. The feature common to all the points on these curves is that they involve a single assumption about inflation. Along DCF, labour-market participants expect inflation to be 2 per cent, while along AB inflation is expected to be zero. Similar lines could be drawn in for expectations of 4 per cent inflation (running through E) and for higher rates. Indeed, an infinite number of Phillips curves could be drawn, one for each expected inflation rate. The original Phillips curve now appears—from a Friedmanite perspective—to be a special case which recorded events which took place *when labour market participants were expecting zero inflation.* Seen from this perspective, expectations about inflation are a shift factor which governs the position of the Phillips curve.

The role of a Phillips curve in this model is to govern the behaviour of the market if and when there is any discrepancy between people's expectations about inflation and the actual rate. This is purely a short-run phenomenon. In the long run, no variation in unemployment is possible—it must always revert to the natural rate. The only variation which is permissible in the long run is in the rate of inflation. In other words, the economy is only free to move up or down the line ACE on the graph. The long-run trade-off between inflation and unemployment is, according to Friedman, a mirage.

32-3 CONDITIONAL PREDICTIONS OF THE MODEL

Three significant conditional predictions can be deduced directly from the model (though others could naturally be found). First, any deviation of unemployment from the NAIRU will only be short-term. Second, if unemployment is forced below the NAIRU for longer than the short term, inflation will accelerate. Third, once inflation has got under way, a policy of reducing it by controlling the money supply will give rise to unemployment which exceeds the NAIRU for some transitional period.

These three conditional predictions have one important feature in common: they depend upon the relationship between actual unemployment and the NAIRU. This, of course, creates a problem because without a clear statement of the value taken by NAIRU, the theory is not open to being falsified. In other words, there is no way of testing the theory unless the NAIRU is established.

This challenge has naturally been taken up. For many researchers, a starting point has been the fact that, between 1956 and 1966, inflation ran consistently at 2–3 per cent, implying that the labour market was, for those years, in equilibrium. Since average unemployment was then 2 per cent, the clear implication is that the NAIRU was at that time 2 per cent. In subsequent years, however, changes in unemployment benefits, employment protection legislation and other factors have caused it to rise. The results reported by Layard and Nickell,[1] for example, are shown in Table 32-1. The first two columns shows estimates of NAIRU and levels of unemployment for different periods. A comparison of the two suggests whether inflation should be expected to be accelerating or decelerating. For example, between 1967 and 1979, unemployment was below NAIRU, indicating that inflation should have accelerated. After that date, however, unemployment exceeded NAIRU and inflation should have decelerated. Apart from the fact that the deceleration was delayed until 1980, these findings are confirmed by the data on inflation shown in the third column.

It would, however, be misleading to suggest that economists had arrived at a consensus as to the value of NAIRU (and thus the rate of inflation to be expected at any given level of unemployment). Until the value of the NAIRU is established to the satisfaction of all, of course, the theory cannot really be tested.

Table 32-1 NAIRU and changes in inflation, 1956–83

Period	NAIRU (%)	Actual unemployment (%)	Inflation (%)
1956–66	1.96	1.96	3.4
1967–74	4.02	3.78	10.6
1975–79	8.20	6.79	16.5
1980–83	10.47	13.79	11.1

Source: R. Layard and S. Nickell, 'Unemployment and Inflation in the UK', *Economica Supplement*, 1986, Table 10.

32-4 POLICY IMPLICATIONS

The success of monetarism in displacing Keynesianism as the basis of eonomic policy has already been mentioned. In part this was due to the fact that, whatever the difficulties of falsifying Friedman's theory, it offered a persuasive account of the way in which demand-management policies might degenerate into stagflation. It also, of course, offered two pieces of practical advice to policy-makers faced with the seemingly intractable problem of inflation.

First, the theory implied that politicians should not attempt to reduce unemployment below NAIRU. Until the precise value of the NAIRU had been spelled out, this advice was a trifle imprecise, but the implication seemed to be that previous targets for unemployment might have been too ambitious.

Second, as a theory from the monetarist tradition, it suggested that the only way to control inflation was by restricting the growth of the money supply. This would involve, of course, the familiar tools of high interest rates, cuts in public spending and a reduced PSBR. A corollary of the theory, of course, was that prices and incomes policies would be as ineffective as Canute's efforts to restrain the incoming tide, and should accordingly be abandoned.

The theory also warned that the transition from high inflation to low or zero levels would involve heavy unemployment. This unemployment would arise, of course, because people would tend to overestimate the true rate of inflation. The government could, however, attempt to reduce this transitional unemployment if it could convince people that their expectations of inflation were too high. In other words, governments could attempt to 'talk down' the rate of inflation.

32-5 KEYNESIAN AND MONETARIST COUNTER-INFLATION POLICIES COMPARED

The divergence between Keynesian and monetarist approaches to inflation was vividly illustrated during the late 1970s. In 1975, policy was clearly Keynesian: there were legal controls on prices and voluntary restraints on pay rises. Tolerance was shown towards the expanding money supply. By 1979, following the 1976 sterling crisis and the election of a new government, the emphasis of policy had switched to the control of the money supply by means of high interest rates and cuts in public spending. The statutory control of prices was ended, and, in so far as it was possible for the government to distance itself from pay negotiations when the public sector employs some 32 per cent of the nation's work-force, incomes policies were abandoned.

The change in policy reflected the divergent interpretations of economic events offered by Keynesianism and monetarism. Keynesian economics sees markets—for goods, for capital and labour—as being imperfect. Flaws arise from high degrees of concentration in product markets and, to a greater degree, from the limited information that is available to all buyers and sellers, borrowers and lenders. As a direct result, the market system cannot, in Keynesian eyes, be guaranteed to produce full employment. This failure obliges governments to correct the workings of the market by *intervening*: demand management and prices and incomes policies are its practical consequences.

Monetarist economics, as a constituent element of the neo-classical tradition, affirms the perfection (or rather the perfectibility) of markets. The vital conditions for true equilibrium is that governments should refrain from interfering: *laissez-faire*, not intervention, is the watchword. As far as monetarists are concerned, the labour market should be allowed to find its own equilibrium, with the government's role being restricted to seeing that the growth of the money supply is kept under control. Indeed, the economic system is seen as being quite outside the control of governments, whose efforts at directing economic events can never help but only hinder.

There was, however, one point upon which monetarists and Keynesians concurred: even if the causes of inflation lay on the supply side of markets, high unemployment could nevertheless be expected to bring it down. This expectation was duly confirmed. The restrictive monetary policies of the new Conservative government of 1979 reduced aggregate demand, GDP contracted and unemployment rose from just over 1.2 million (5 per cent) in 1979 to just over 3 million (13 per cent) by 1984. If the figures produced by Layard and Nickell are accepted, of course, the significant point was that in 1980 unemployment finally exceed the NAIRU for the first time. The result was that inflation, which had been running at 13 per cent in 1979, fell back to 5 per cent in 1984.

Despite these efforts, it would nevertheless be difficult to claim that the policy has met with unalloyed success. Pay rises in 1986—despite both record unemployment and inflation of 5 per cent or less—continued to run at an average of 7.5 per cent. In default of an accepted value for NAIRU, these events are open to several interpretations. For some, they are an indication that cost-push pressures are still at work and many, including Layard and Nickell, have canvassed the idea that income policies should be readopted. Others see the fact that inflation and pay rises have both remained steady at about 5 and 7.5 per cent, respectively, for five years (1982–7) as confirming their view that the NAIRU has moved to 13 per cent, implying that any further reduction in inflation will require even higher unemployment. If it is accepted that NAIRU has increased because of factors like that mismatch between the skills of the unemployed and the kinds of vacancies offered, the clear implication is that policy should be directed towards the ways—such as training—by which these developments can be reversed. Thus micro-level policies (such as training) may have to be called upon if the two-sided problem of inflation and unemployment is to be addressed.

32-6 SUMMARY

The natural rate of unemployment (*NAIRU*) is the residual unemployment to be found when the labour market has cleared. It will reflect the search activity of job-seekers.

A short-run trade off can be made between unemployment and inflation by creating or raising inflation. Job-seekers accept employment, and a Phillips curve is traced out. The jobs are, however, taken under a misconception and in the long run unemployment reverts to its natural level.

The *expectations-augmented Phillips curve* is the long-run trade-off between unemployment and inflation. It is, in fact, a vertical line at the NAIRU: there is no real trade-off, because holding unemployment below this level will, the theory predicts, lead to accelerating inflation.

Transitional unemployment is the unemployment which ensues when a government begins to curb the money supply after a period of inflation. As long as people expect high inflation, job search is prolonged and unemployment rises.

EXERCISES

32.1 Explain the role of misconceptions in Friedman's model of unemployment and inflation. Why was Friedmans model so attractive as an explanation of inflation?

32-2 You are a consultant economist recently recruited to the Ministry of Economic Affairs of an emerging country. You are of a monetarist persuasion. The data on unemployment and inflation for the past nine years are as follows:

Year	1	2	3	4	5	6	7	8	9
Unemployment (%)	3	3	3	6	6	10	12	11	14
Inflation (%)	2	2	2	4	7	13	13	15	13

Write a report for the Minister for Economic Affairs,

(a) explaining these past trends;
(b) recommending policies;
(c) anticipating the effects of those policies.

32-3 You are working for an economic research unit. Collect appropriate data for the last 10 years on the Retail Price Index, the money supply, and the rate of unemployment. You will have been forced to choose from among several different measures of these variables.

(a) Justify your choices.
(b) Using the data collected, draft a report to the unit's head comparing and contrasting the Keynesian and monetarist approaches to the unemployment/inflation issue.
(c) Use regression analysis where appropriate to support the arguments you use in your report.

32-4 You are a senior Civil Servant in the Treasury. An election is about to be held, in which the main parties are monetarists and Keynesians. Inflation is running at 7 per cent. An inter-departmental committee is to meet to discuss the programmes of legislation and other matters which Civil Servants could put before the new government. Naturally, two alternative programmes must be prepared! You will represent the Treasury. Draft some briefing notes to take with you.

REFERENCE

1. Layard, R. and S. Nickell, 'Unemployment and inflation in the UK', *Economica Supplement*, 1986.

INTERNATIONAL TRADE

33-1 INTRODUCTION: THE IMPORTANCE OF TRADE

It is apparent that the important macro-economic concepts that we have discussed over the last few chapters—unemployment, inflation, macro-economic management policies—cannot be examined or understood in isolation. All economies trade with other economies and trade will obviously have implications for the domestic policy-maker at both the macro and micro levels.

British imports of goods and services are running at around 30 per cent of total domestic expenditure and have been steadily increasing in real terms for the last three or four decades. Similar patterns are visible in British exports where, again, around one-third of the goods and services produced in the United Kingdom are destined for overseas markets—implying that a considerable number of jobs are directly dependent upon the ability of British firms to win orders abroad. The UK, furthermore, is intimately linked to the international financial network, with the City being the principal market for securities in Europe. The British economy is thus described as being *open*, in contrast to *closed* economies which are less heavily involved in the international economic system. The purpose of this chapter and those which follow is to examine these international economic relationships and to review their consequences for business and government in the UK. In this chapter we look at the benefits, in terms of higher output and income, which can accrue to nations participating in international trade.

33-2 THE PRINCIPLES OF ABSOLUTE AND COMPARATIVE ADVANTAGE

Absolute advantage

It is evident that some economies have an advantage over others in the production of certain goods and services. In some cases such an advantage may be total or absolute because of climate, endowment of natural resources, geographical position and so on. Equally, an economy may be in a position of absolute advantage in the provision of one product and an absolute disadvantage in the provision of another. If this first economy can match with a second where the advantages are reversed then trade obviously becomes mutually beneficial. The UK, for example, has an absolute advantage in the provision of financial services over, say, the Ivory Coast in West Africa. Equally, the Ivory Coast has an absolute advantage in the production of fresh pineapples. While the UK could potentially satisfy its demand for pineapples through domestic production, and the Ivory Coast develop its own stock exchange and multinational financial services, the cost of doing this—particularly in opportunity-cost terms—would clearly be prohibitive. It is readily accepted that under such conditions of absolute advantage trade would be mutually beneficial.

However, absolute advantage does not explain the bulk of world trade patterns. The UK, for example, imports a considerable quantity of goods that could equally well be produced domestically. Cars, stereos, colour TVs, compact disc players, home computers and so on are all examples. There is considerable concern over the deindustrialization of the British economy—the movement towards importing many goods that, traditionally, were produced domestically. This, however, is not solely a British phenomenon. Most industrialized economies will import products that could have been produced domestically. The economic principles behind such trade patterns are explained by *comparative advantage*.

Comparative advantage

The theory of comparative advantage states that trade is likely to be mutually beneficial even under conditions where one economy can produce every good at a lower cost—in terms of resources—than another. At first sight, this theory seems a little surprising. If, say, Japan can produce *all* items more efficiently than the UK how can it be to Japan's advantage to trade with the UK? The answer lies with the related opportunity costs. An example will serve to illustrate the reasoning behind the theory.

For simplicity, let us assume that we are dealing with just two economies—say, the UK and Japan—and with just two products—say, food and cars. Let us also suppose that we have data relating to the production resource requirements of the two products in the two economies. The resource requirements, we will further assume, relate to the supply of resources to the two alternative areas of production. Thus, a resource unit can be thought of as some mixture of land, labour and capital that will be required in the production process. These are illustrated in Table 33-1. Thus, in the UK if we make one resource unit available (a combination of land, labour and capital) we could produce either 10 units of food or 15 units of cars. Natually, given the finite supply of resources, the British economy would be seeking to use these fixed resources to produce an optimum combination of the two products. A similar situation occurs in Japan, with one resource unit generating either 12 units of food or 20 units of cars.

It is apparent from Table 33-1 that Japan is more efficient than the UK in the production of both food and cars. In both cases output in Japan is greater than that in the UK with the same resource input. The question we raised originally was: why should trade between the two economies take place given that Japan is a more efficient producer of both products? Bluntly, is there anything in it for Japan?

Table 33-1 Production from one resource unit

	Product Food (units)	Cars (units)
UK	10	15
Japan	12	20

The answer is that, under the appropriate conditions, both economies can benefit from increased spcialization by concentrating on producing that product in which it has the *greatest comparative advantage*. To see the logic of this let us examine Table 33-1 further.

Assume, for the moment, that each economy wished to increase its output of cars by 300 units. Given that resources are fixed in supply then this can only be achieved by switching resources away from food. In the case of the UK, producing an extra 300 units of cars would require 20 resource units. These would have to be diverted away from food production which would therefore decrease by 200 units. In Japan, on the other hand, the increase in car output would require only 15 resource units to be diverted from food production which would, therefore, decrease by only 180 units. Readers will be aware that these sacrifices of food production for car production are the relevant opportunity costs of car production in the two economies.

Now, assume that we could, somehow, persuade both the UK and Japan to reallocate resources in the following way: Japan would switch 15 resource units from food to car production while the UK would switch 20 resource units away from cars to food production. The effects of this on production would be as shown in Table 33-2. World output increases. In our example, the reallocation of resources has left total car production unchanged while food production has increased by 20 units. Naturally such resource allocation will not happen because of agreements between two economies. Rather, it will be left to the market, and specifically to entrepreneurs, to discover the potential of such trade. The operations of supply, demand and price will now take place on an international scale and not just domestically.

Suppose the UK agrees to buy 300 cars from Japan. A trade agreement with Japan, whereby Japan agreed to supply the cars in return, say, for 190 units of food would leave both economies better off. Japan could now divert its 15 resource units to car production knowing full well that the 190 food units it will receive from the trading process are more than could have been produced domestically with the 15 resource units. Similarly, the UK has also benefited: by reallocating 20 resource units from cars it will receive the 300 cars it could have produced domestically but will still have a surplus of 10 units of food after paying Japan for the cars.

Table 33-2 Change in production

	Food (units)	Cars (units)
UK	+200	-300
Japan	-180	+300
Net change	+20	0

Table 33-3 Comparative advantage ratios

	Food	Cars
UK	15/10 = 1.5	10/15 = 0.67
Japan	20/12 = 1.67	12/20 = 0.6

Naturally, our example is, like all models, an oversimplification of the real world but it readily illustrates the basic principles involved. Each economy has specialized in the production of the good where it has a comparative advantage, even though Japan has an absolute advantage in both areas of production. Effectively, each economy has specialized where it has the greatest relative efficiency.

Such comparative advantage is easily calculated. The comparative advantage ratios are calculated in terms of the units of the other product that must be sacrificed in an economy in order to increase production of the other product by one unit. Plainly, this is the opportunity cost. These ratios confirm the logic of the trade pattern.

If we look at the opportunity cost of cars first, we can see that Japan clearly has a comparative advantage over the United Kingdom in the production of cars. The opportunity cost—expressed in terms of food production that would be forgone—is lower for Japan than for the UK. Clearly, it is better, in terms of world production, for Japan to produce cars given that, relatively, it must sacrifice less in terms of food production forgone than the UK.

Equally, for food production it is the UK that has the comparative advantage, sacrificing less in terms of car production forgone than Japan. Thus, even though Japan is *absolutely* more efficient than the UK in both areas, its *relative* advantage is greater in car production. The same conclusion is illustrated if we examine the relative efficiency ratios for the two areas of production. Japan is 20 per cent (12/10) more efficient than the UK in food production but is 33 per cent (20/15) more efficient in car production. Japan will, therefore, specialize in car production where its relative efficiency is highest.

Terms of trade

In practice, of course, international trade is undertaken in financial rather than barter terms and the mechanisms by which such international financial transactions take place are discussed in subsequent chapters. Although in principle it is to their mutual benefit to trade internationally, trade between economies will only occur only under the right conditions. The extent to which trade is beneficial to an economy will depend upon the *terms of trade*— the rate at which we can trade our domestic products for those of another economy.

To illustrate let us return to the British–Japanese trade of food for cars. The UK wants the 300 cars produced by Japan. How much, in terms of food, will the UK be willing to pay for these cars? The answer is up to 200 units of food. Any more than this and it will not be in the UK's interests to trade. If Japan required, say 210 units of food in exchange, it would be cheaper, in opportunity cost terms, for the UK itself to switch productive resources from food to cars.

Conversely, the question arises: how much will Japan want for the 300 cars produced? Again, the answer is apparent: anything over 180 units of food will be acceptable. Any less than this and again, in opportunity cost terms, it would be better for Japan to produce its own food by reallocating productive resources away from cars.

Thus, the terms of trade would exist between the two economies for the two products would be one car for between 180/300 and 200/300 units of food, i.e. between 0.60 and 0.67 units. The exact rate of exchange will obviously depend on a number of other factors such as transport costs and the demand and supply by other economies not considered by our simple model. The conclusions, however, are straightforward. If the terms of trade are high in favour of food then the food producing economy will benefit. Conversely, if the food prices are low then the car-producing economy will benefit.

Equally, trade will only occur when the terms of trade are somewhere within the limits which make trade mutually beneficial. If the terms of trade, for whatever reason, lie outside these limits the economies will not specialize but will seek to become self-sufficient in all items.

33-3 CONCLUSION

The theory of comparative advantage provides an explanation for most international trade patterns. It explains why it can be beneficial to an economy to trade with other economies regardless of the level of its productive efficiency.

The theory does not, however, take into account other factors that may be important to the decision-maker. There may be strong arguments on *normative* grounds to erect trade barriers to prevent, for example, the demise of a domestic car industry. Economic theory may show that a particular economy does not have a comparative advantage in this area and would benefit, at the macro level, from free trade through the differing opportunity-cost structures. However, there may well be other (non-economic) justifications for supporting such a domestic industry. The policies of governments towards international trade will be examined in further detail in Chapter 35.

33-4 SUMMARY

Absolute advantage occurs when one economy is more efficient at producing some item than another economy. *Comparative advantage* occurs when one economy is more efficient at producing all items than another economy but where opportunity costs differ. Both economies will produce and trade those items where they are *relatively* most efficient.

Terms of trade relates to the rates at which goods are traded for each other internationally.

EXERCISES

33-1 Assume the following production schedule for two economies, in terms of units of the product produced with one resource unit:

	Product X	Product Y
Country A	18	24
Country B	15	30

(a) Which country will produce which product?

(b) What will be the terms of trade?

(c) Assume that Country B now becomes more efficient in producing Product X so that one resource unit will now generate 20 units of the product. What will happen to the trade patterns? Explain why this happens.

33-2 From the *Monthly Digest of Statistics* (or an equivalent source) collect data on the level of British imports and exports with the following groups of economies:

European Communities
Rest of Western Europe
North America
Oil-exporting countries
Other developed countries
Other developing countries
Centrally planned economies

Collect the data for the latest year available and for the period 10 years (or longer) ago. Using a computer spreadsheet, work out the changes in exports and imports that have occurred over this period. What inferences can you make about the United Kingdom's comparative advantage with respect to the other groups of economies?

33-3 Collect data for the following series over the past 10–15 years:

(a) Imports of leather goods, textiles and made-up articles.

(b) Exports of leather goods, textiles and made-up articles.

(c) Employment in the textiles, leather, footwear and clothing sector.

Assume you have been commissioned by a joint group of British companies and trade unions operating in this industry to produce a briefing report for it to use in lobbying the government to impose a variety of trade barriers to stop such imports. Include in your report the arguments that may well be used *against* such barriers by the Department of Trade.

THE BALANCE OF PAYMENTS AND THE FOREIGN EXCHANGE MARKET

34-1 INTRODUCTION

Chapter 33 analysed the way in which trade allowed countries to benefit from the fact that their respective comparative advantages lie in the production of different goods and services. This chapter will carry the examination of international economic relations forward by looking at the ways in which these underlying factors manifest themselves in financial terms, that is, in terms of international payments and foreign exchange rates.

34-2 THE BALANCE OF PAYMENTS ACCOUNTS

All transactions between the United Kingdom and the rest of the world are recorded in the balance of payments accounts. The three principal sections of the accounts relate respectively to transactions in goods, in services and in assets. Transactions in goods are familiar to most people as imports and exports. Together they are known as the country's *visible* trade, to distinguish it from *invisible* trade, which relates to transactions in services like tourism, banking, insurance, brokerage services and transport. Also included under the heading of invisibles are transfers (such as money sent to relatives abroad) and receipts of interest, profit and dividends earned by overseas investments. (Readers will recall meeting this last item under the name of 'property income from abroad' in Chapter 24 on national income accounting.) Although sales of services are sometimes referred to as 'invisible exports' and purchases as 'invisible imports', they are described in the official accounts as credit and debit items respectively. Visible and invisible trade together constitute the *current account* of the balance of payments.

Transactions in assets, sometimes termed the *capital account* of the balance of payments, consist of the purchase and sale of physical assets like land and buildings together with borrowing and lending. Included in the capital account are items like the granting of trade credit (that is, allowing a customer some time in which to settle a bill), lending by banks and the purchase and sale of securities like company shares, Treasury bills and gilts. The purchase of British assets by overseas residents is known as *inward* investment, since funds flow into the UK, while the purchase of foreign assets by British residents is termed *outward* investment. Transactions in physical assets are known as *direct* investment, while borrowing, lending and transactions in securities are termed *indirect*. Table 34-1 shows the UK's balance of payments for 1986.

Although the international transactions of an economy like the British are undertaken by millions of separate individuals, the balance of payments accounts invariably balance. This is due fundamentally to the methods of drawing up the accounts, which follow the conventions similar to those of double-entry bookkeeping. To illustrate this point, let us imagine that a British firm sends a consignment of, say, motor vehicles to the United States. The cars go to car dealers who, we may further assume, only pay for the cars when they have actually sold them to consumers. These various transactions would appear in the accounts in the following way. First, the despatch of the consignment would naturally count as an export of, say, £1 million. Second, the car maker would be considered to have extended trade credit of £1 million to the dealers, that is, to have lent them the money to purchase the stock. Since trade credit is counted as an outflow of funds on capital account, there is a debit item to set against the credit item of the export consignment. When the cars are sold, the car dealers pay off their debts to the car making payment in the form of dollars. These funds will initially be paid into an account in the car maker's name in a bank in the USA. At this point, the trade credit will be deleted from the balance of payments accounts, but another item will appear: the car manufacturer will be deemed to have invested in an overseas bank deposit. (If the money is used to buy, say, American Treasury bills, it will be reclassified accordingly.)

Table 34-1 United Kingdom balance of payments, 1986 (£ billion)

Visibles			
Exports	72 843		
Imports	81 306		
Visible balance		−8 463	
Invisibles			
Services	4 990		
Interest, profit and dividends	4 686		
Transfers	−2 193		
Invisible balance		7 483	
Current balance			−980
Net transactions in UK assets and liabilities			−10 747
Balancing item			11 727

Source: UK National Accounts, 1987.

In summary, the car firm is counted as, first, having created a credit entry for the balance of payments accounts by exporting the goods to an overseas market, and second, having created a debit item by investing the proceeds of the sale overseas in some way.

The story is, of course, unlikely to end at this point since the objective of the vehicle manufacturer would not be to accumulate funds in bank deposits in the USA but rather to bring the funds back to the UK to pay wages and dividends. He would therefore attempt to exchange his dollars for sterling. The question is: who might be willing to make such an exchange?

One possibility is that the dollars could be desired by a British business person who had the intention of buying goods from the USA. She would, of course, be obliged to pay her American supplier not in sterling but in dollars. Similarly, the dollars might be sold to a British-based holiday company which was running packaged tours in the USA and which had to pay the American hoteliers in dollars. Yet another possibility might be that the dollars could be bought by a unit trust which wished to buy American company shares. In short, any transaction related to a *debit* item in the balance of payments would require the purchase of dollars.

Eventually, the dollars are sold via the foreign exchange market to someone desiring to buy goods, services or assets from the USA. The car company's 'overseas investment' could then be deleted from the balance of payments accounts. This would leave only the car exports on the credit side of the accounts and the debit item—the packaged holidays or whatever—on the other. Again, the accounts would balance.

Although the overall accounts must balance, it should be noted that there is no necessity for any particular section to balance. A country can have a surplus on its visible trade or current account that is balanced by a deficit on the investment account (or vice versa).

(Despite the principles set out above the accounts frequently *fail* to balance in practice because some transactions are not recorded. The statisticians, therefore, add in a 'balancing item' to ensure the accounts balance as they should. Usually this is quite small, but due to rapid changes in the financial system this item was much larger than usual in 1986.)

34-3 THE FOREIGN EXCHANGE MARKET

From the point of view of economic analysis, the focus of interest falls not so much on the accounting procedures of the balance of payments figures as on the underlying financial and economic relationships. The vital link here is provided by the foreign exchange market, in which different currencies are bought and sold. Like many financial markets today, the foreign exchange market has no physical location but is simply the network of dealers' offices in financial centres around the world.

Like ordinary markets, the foreign exchange market sets prices for the commodities traded—in this case, the prices of the world's currencies. Since there is no world currency in which to express the prices of national currencies, the practice is to quote prices as ratio of *foreign exchange rates*. The value of the pound sterling, for example, is usually expressed as so many US dollars. When one pound exchanges for a relatively large number of dollars, sterling's exchange rate is described as being 'high', while when the pound buys rather fewer dollars, its rate is said to be 'low'. Thus a rate of $1.85 to £1 is higher than a rate of $1.65 to £1.

Plainly, sterling will have a variety of exchange rates since it is traded against a number of other currencies, and it is in consequence not easy to measure its international value. One approach is to rely simply on the exchange rate between sterling and the US dollar (this being the most widely traded currency), while another is to calculate an index—a weighted average of sterling's various exchange rates—using the various nations' shares in the UK's overseas trade for the weights.

34-4 EXCHANGE RATES AND BUSINESS

To understand the significance of the foreign exchange rate of a currency, let us consider the role which the foreign exchange rate of sterling would have played for the business people in the illustration above, starting with the car manufacturer. Clearly, his primary concern was with the amount of sterling which he could obtain for his cars—the nationality of his customers being of little importance (beyond the fact that more distant locations will involve higher transport costs. For simplicity, these will be ignored.) Let us assume that the consignment of cars cost £1 million to produce (including some allowance of normal profit). The question, therefore, is: can this consignment be sold at a profit in the American market?

The answer will depend upon two factors. The first is the dollar price of the cars. We may assume that the car market in the USA is imperfectly competitive, implying that the company has some choice over the prices which it charges but in general demand is elastic—higher prices will mean lower revenue. Let us assume that, initially, the consignment sells for $1.5 million.

The second factor is the number of pounds which the sales revenue can be exchanged for. If the exchange rate were to stand initially at $1.50 for £1, then the $1.5 million which the cars had earned would raise £1 million on the foreign exchange market and the company would have secured a normal profit on the sale.

Let us now suppose that the exchange rate were to rise to $2 to £1. With the cost of a consignment still £1 million, the car manufacturer would have to raise the price for the consignment from $1.5 million to $2 million. Since demand is elastic, sales fall.

Converse results follow from a fall in the exchange rate. At, say, $1 to £1, the car manufacturer can afford to cut the American price for his consignment to $1 million. As a result, cars become easier to sell and sales revenue rise. Indeed, the general rule is that a lower exchange rate for sterling tends to stimulate British exports.

The converse argument applies to importers. They will normally be paying their overseas suppliers—let us assume that these are American—in US dollars. The costs which they will face will depend therefore upon the prices charged by their American suppliers (in dollars) and the number of pounds sterling needed to buy those dollars. For example, a firm buying a consignment of 100 000 textbooks from the United States may face a bill for, say, $1.8 million, that is, $18 per book. Were the exchange rate to stand at the low rate of $1 to £1, the firm would have to charge £18 per book. If, however, the exchange rate were to rise to $2 to £1, the company would be able to cut the price of its textbook to £9. In other words, a high exchange rate reduces the sterling price of imported goods and thus makes importing easier, while a low exchange rate makes imports more expensive on the British market.

Taken together, these effects mean that a low exchange rate will tend to increase exports and retard imports, producing a trade surplus. A high rate, on the other hand, will stimulate imports and hold back exports, leading to a trade deficit.

Similar effects apply to the sale of services and assets. For example, overseas tourists will be attracted to the UK if the value of sterling is low since their foreign currency will go further, while a high exchange rate will enable British residents to obtain a relatively large amount of foreign currency for their pounds, and will therefore tempt them into taking rather more foreign holidays. Again, with regard to assets, a low exchange rate will make it easier to attract overseas investors to a country, in that the investor's budget will be able to buy more in terms of land, buildings or even company shares, while a high rate will make it easier for Britons to buy, say, houses on the Spanish coast. In short, a low exchange rate encourages all the transactions associated with credit items in the balance of payments accounts, that is, the sale of a country's goods, services and assets on the world market, while a high rate promotes transactions which generate debit items in the balance of payments accounts.

34-5 SUPPLY AND DEMAND IN THE FOREIGN EXCHANGE MARKET

It may thus appear that a low exchange rate would be unambiguously beneficial for British business, for not only would it keep foreign competition out of the home market, it would make exporting more profitable. In reality, however, a rate which was unduly low would be rendered unsustainable by underlying economic forces. These may be examined with the help of a supply and demand model.

Figure 34-1 is a graphical representation of a model of the forces at work in the foreign exchange market for sterling. The vertical axis measures the price of sterling, that is, its exchange rate, while the horizontal axis shows the quantity of sterling being brought to the market. The supply of sterling to the market is associated with imports and other debit items of the balance of payments accounts, because firms which are selling foreign manufactures in the UK will have receipts in sterling which they will wish to change into, say, US dollars. As we have seen, a high exchange rate encourages importers, with the effect that the supply of sterling to the foreign exchange market becomes greater as the exchange rate increases. Thus the supply curve slopes upward to the right. Conversely, the demand for sterling arises from exporters who, like the car manufacturer in the example above, have dollar receipts which they wish to convert into sterling. Again, as we have seen, a low exchange rate will encourage exporters, with the effect that the demand curve for sterling slopes downwards to the right.

Let us now investigate the way in which these curves move produce an equilibrium exchange rate. We will begin by assuming that the rate is below equilibrium at, say, $1 to £1. At this low rate there would be very few imports from the outside world into the British market, while British exports to overseas markets would run at a very substantial level. There would thus be a current account surplus and, *ceteris paribus*, an excess demand for sterling on the foreign exchange market. The consequences of this for the exchange rate may be illustrated by returning to the example of the British car exporter which had sold its cars in the USA for $1.5 million. If there were a shortage of sterling on the foreign exchange market, the car company (or rather its bank) would then be obliged to offer better terms to

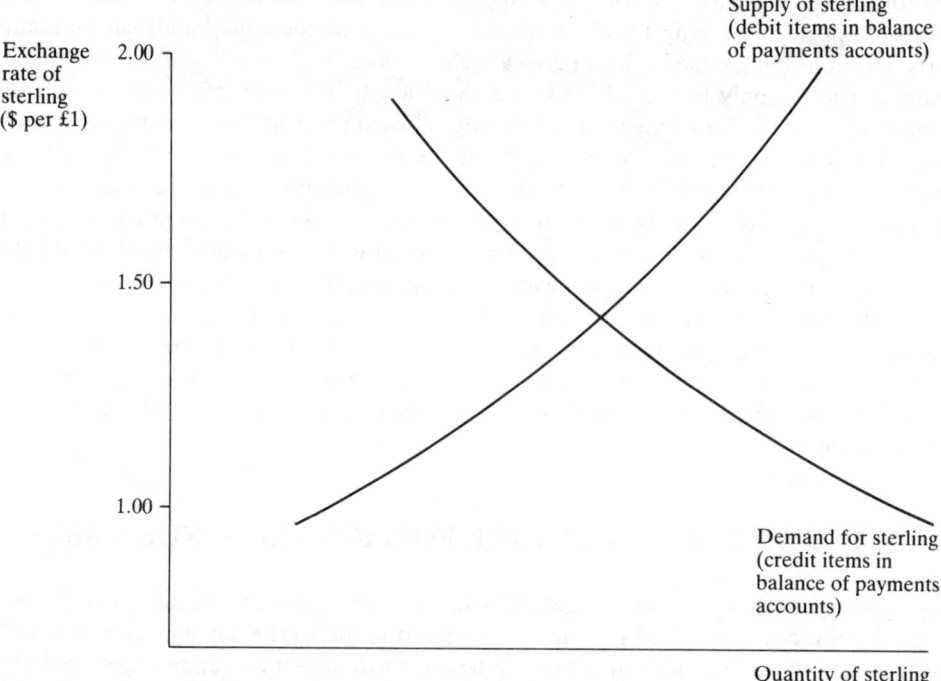

Figure 34-1 The foreign exchange market

holders of sterling to induce them to sell. That is, instead of offering to swap its $1.5 million for £1.5 million, they might have to declare that they were willing to accept £1.4 million. This would, in effect, drive up the value of £1 sterling from $1 to $1.07. In other words, an unduly low exchange rate is simply unsustainable: it sets in motion forces which tend to make the rate move towards its equilibrium level. (A similar process would naturally operate if the rate were unduly high.)

The rise in the exchange rate described above would have the effect of reducing exports (and all other credit transactions) while promoting imports (and other debit transactions). The excess demand would thus diminish as the rate climbed until, finally, the market came to equilibrium.

The characteristic of equilibrium is that the forces of supply and demand should be in balance. This does not imply that no sterling should be held outside the British economy, for clearly trading companies located perhaps in overseas financial centres will need working balances in different currencies. Rather, equilibrium implies that all currency which is held externally should be held *willingly*.

The above definition of equilibrium may shed some light on the notion of balance in the UK's external payments. Although the balance of payments accounts must be in balance, the Press often carries reports of payments surpluses or deficits. The underlying reality of these reports is usually that, first, the current account is in surplus or deficit, that is, investment flows are not considered, and second, unwanted balances of foreign currency or sterling are building up on the foreign exchange market and are tending to force the exchange rate up (or down). In other words, the surplus or deficit is to be found not in the international payments accounts but in the foreign exchange market.

34-6 SHIFT FACTORS IN THE FOREIGN EXCHANGE MARKET

As with all models of this type, the supply and demand curves are constructed on the assumption that various factors are held constant, and any change in these factors will have the effect of shifting the curves and so altering the equilibrium position. The assessment of future movements in these factors allows changes in those rates to be predicted, and financial institutions employ economists and statisticians expressly for this purpose.

The first shift factor is the ability of the economy to produce various goods and services. The costs and productivity levels of any national economy will naturally vary from industry to industry, and the previous chapter explained that nations would specialize in the production of goods in which they enjoyed a comparative advantage. Should these comparative advantages alter, the supply and demand for foreign currency would alter also. An example is provided by the development of British North Sea oil during the late 1970s and early 1980s. At that time, oil was relatively expensive, and the development of the oilfields amounted to an addition to the range of goods and services in which the UK had a comparative advantage. As a result, less sterling came onto the foreign exchange market (fewer imports of overseas oil were required) and more sterling was demanded (by overseas companies anxious to buy oil from British operators). Both the supply and the demand curves for sterling therefore shifted upwards and the equilibrium exchange rate rose. (In fact, the value of sterling rose from $1.92 in 1978 to $2.32 in 1980, though it is only fair to add that other factors such as higher interest rates were involved in this movement.) Conversely, a diminution in a country's comparative advantage, due perhaps to the failure of a farm crop that was exported, would reduce the exchange rate. Similar considerations apply to the other side of the market, that is, to an economy's willingness to buy imported goods. If tastes were to shift from domestic goods to foreign manufactures, the supply of currency on to the foreign exchange market at all levels of the exchange rate would be greater and the equilibrium exchange rate would be reduced.

In practice, of course, consumer tastes and comparative advantages in production are difficult to disentangle, since an economy which is adept at innovation will create for itself a comparative advantage in the production of goods which consumers, both at home and abroad, prefer. It may therefore be useful to consider the two elements together as 'real' factors in the supply of and demand for sterling on the foreign exchange market.

Real factors, it may be noted, do not affect an economy's visible trade alone. If the productivity of a national economy is high, its firms will be competitive, visible and invisible exports will be in strong demand abroad and overseas investors will be anxious to buy shares in those companies. Conversely, a low-productivity economy will both have difficulties in selling goods and services on the world market and experience an outflow of investment funds. Thus all sections of the country's international payments accounts will give rise to disequilibrium in the foreign exchange market.

The second shift factor is inflation. Even though the 'real' features of an economy (like tastes and comparative advantages) remain unchanged, the costs and prices in which they are expressed may well rise through the process of inflation. The result of domestic inflation, of course, is to make exporting more difficult: firms which are price-takers in overseas markets will find their profits being squeezed by rising domestic costs while firms which are able to set their own prices will be forced to increase them and will therefore lose customers. At the same time, British firms will find themselves being undercut by importers in domestic markets. In sum, exports will fall and imports will increase, producing a deficit in the current account of the balance of payments. In terms of Fig. 34-1, each level of the exchange rate will be associated with a lower level of exports (a smaller demand for sterling) and a greater level of imports (a greater supply). Both curves will therefore shift downwards.

It may be noted that the important variable in the above analysis is not the absolute rate of inflation in an economy but its rate of inflation relative to that of its trading partners. Clearly an economy which was inflating at 5 per cent per year would, *ceteris paribus*, run a trade surplus if its competitors were experiencing 15 per cent inflation.

The third shift factor is the level of interest rates. These are of particular importance to the supply and demand for currency for investment purposes, because investors usually compare the returns which are available on different securities on an international basis. Should UK gilts provide higher yields than comparable securities in other countries, investors will tend to sell their holdings of alternative securities (say, American government bonds) and move into UK gilts. To do this, they will need to sell dollars and buy sterling: the demand curve for sterling will shift upwards and the equilibrium exchange rate will rise. It may be noted that, in the short term, investment flows intended to take advantage of interest-rate differences can be far more important influences upon the exchange rate than visible or invisible trade.

The final factors is expectations on the part of investors and foreign exchange dealers about the future value of a currency. These judgements, sometimes referred to as 'market sentiments', are based largely on assessments of movements in 'market fundamentals', that is, trends in trade, inflation and interest rates, both current and expected. Sentiment is also influenced by dealers' judgement of a government's general policy stance, so that, for instance, the election of a government which seemed willing to tolerate inflation would be likely to induce sales of the currency (sometimes called a 'run on the pound') and thus a fall in the exchange rate even before any policies had been initiated. Because the financial markets hold extensive stocks of currencies as working balances, a change in expectations can completely swamp the supply of and demand for foreign currency arising from the normal business of importing and exporting. It should be noted that changes in sentiment can be self-fulfilling: if dealers expect a currency to depreciate (that is, to fall in value), they will sell and the expected depreciation will duly occur.

34-7 INFLATION AND EXCHANGE RATES: THE DEPRECIATION MECHANCISM

A change in one of the factors described above would cause the supply and demand curves for the currency to move and would thus affect the exchange rate. It was noted above that, *ceteris paribus*, higher inflation in the UK woud lead to a trade deficit, an excess supply of sterling to the foreign exchange market and thus to depreciation. The result of this depreciation will naturally be to stimulate exports and depress imports, with the consequence that the trade deficit induced by inflation is eliminated. The sequence of events whereby the depreciation of the currency compensates for domestic inflation and restores external balance is termed the *depreciation mechanism*. (There is, conversely an *appreciation mechanism* which operates when countries have surpluses.)

The effect of depreciation is to raise the prices of imported goods for consumers, adding to domestic inflation and depressing real incomes. Since export industries are made more profitable, they are able to expand. The net effect, therefore, is a transfer of resources away from consumers into exports.

It should be noted that the depreciation mechanism is less effective in the case of an 'open' economy which, like the British, purchases a large proportion of its inputs from other countries. Let us return to the example of the exported consignment of motor vehicles which was produced at a cost of £1 million. With an exchange rate of $2 to £1, the consignment would be priced at $2 million in the USA, and a 25 per cent depreciation to $1.50 to £1 might be expected to reduce the price in the USA to $1.5 million. Let us now assume that the consignment required foreign components which cost £600 000 (when the exchange rate was at $2 to £1). A depreciation to $1.50 to £1 would increase their cost to £800 000. This would add £200 000 to costs, pushing the sterling cost of the consignment up to £1.2 million. In order to cover these costs at the new exchange rate of $1.50 to £1, the company would have to sell the consignment for $1.8 million. Thus as 25 per cent depreciation would have led only to fall in price of 10 per cent. This was because over half of the value of the cars was made up of components bought from abroad. If a greater proportion of the value of the cars had been attributable to foreign components, the scope for cutting their dollar price through a depreciation would have been even smaller. More generally, the depreciation of the currency can only affect that proportion of the value of exports which is attributable to domestic production.

A feature of the depreciation mechanism which has created problems for policy-makers is that it may actually make the balance of trade worse for a period before any improvement becomes apparent. To illustrate this, let us return to the example of the importer buying 100 000 books at a cost of $1.8 million. Let us imagine that, just as the books arrive, the value of the pound falls from, say, $2 to $1. The imports must now be valued not at £0.9 million but at £1.8 million. In other words, the immediate effect of a fall in the exchange rate is an increase in the value of imports and thus a *worsening* of the trade deficit. Over the months, of course, it would be reasonable to expect the deficit to fall as consumers switched away from the more expensive imports to cheaper domestic suppliers—the bookseller would presumably look to British publishers, for example. There is thus a sequence of deterioration followed by improvement. The graphical representation of this phenomenon has led it to be called the *J-curve* effect.

The depreciation mechanism relies upon a fall in the price of a country's exports to increase the amount of its currency that is demanded on the foreign exchange market (and upon a rise in the price of imports to reduce the amount that is supplied to the foreign exchange markets). It thus requires the demand for both imports and exports to be elastic, and would fail to work if demand for either were inelastic. For example, if the demand for imports were inelastic, then raising their price on the domestic market would simply have the effect of increasing the amount of money spent upon them. This would have the perverse effect of worsening, rather than improving, the trade balance. This logic is summarized in the Marshall–Lerner theorem, which states that the condition for a successful depreciation is that the sum of the elasticities of demand for imports and exports be greater than one.

In the limiting case of infinitely elastic demand, countries would in effect be price-takers on world markets. Thus the car manufacturer in the example above would, in these circumstances, be obliged to sell his cars at the market price. If British inflation were running at, say, 10 per cent, his profits would be reduced and he would be forced to cease exporting. Sales to overseas markets would only be restored to their previous level when sterling had depreciated by 10 per cent, for then the car manufacturer, by selling at the previous dollar price, would receive 10 per cent more pounds with which to pay his costs in the UK. The argument that rates of inflation and movements in exchange rates will be inversely related is known to economists as the 'purchasing power parity' theorem. Many monetarists go further, arguing that inflation and currency depreciation arise from a common cause, namely, the growth of the money supply. For them, the expansion of the money stock is an indication of the future depreciation of the currency.

Keynesians perceive the relationship between the exchange rate and domestic inflation differently. Rather than viewing domestic inflation and depreciation as two parallel consequences of monetary expansion, they see currency depreciation as contributing to inflation through the medium of raising prices for imports. In consequence, Keynesians have on occasion sought to restrain inflation by pursuing policies designed to resist the depreciation of the exchange rate.

34-8 THE MANAGEMENT OF THE EXCHANGE RATE

Since the exchange rate is of substantial importance to the profitability of business, it has often been, along with unemployment and inflation, the subject of government economic policy. This can take several forms.

Fixed exchange rates

At the end of the Second World War, the industrial countries of the West decided that, in order to promote international trade, exchange rates ought to be stabilized. They therefore undertook to maintain the so-called 'par' values of their currencies against the US dollar. This arrangement was known as the Bretton Woods system, after the location of the conference at which the plan was adopted. The pound sterling, for instance, was (for most of the time the system was in operation) intended to stand at $2.40.

The mechanism by which rates were fixed involved intervention by governments in the foreign exchange market. When, for example, sterling appreciated (that is, its value rose above par), the government (via the Bank of England) sold sterling on the foreign exchange market so as to drive the exchange rate down again. Conversely, when the rate fell below par, the Bank was obliged to buy sterling with dollars. This system clearly required government to hold stocks of foreign currency (the 'reserves') in order to undertake this intervention. It was also possible to augment these reserves by borrowing foreign currency from other countries or from the International Fund (IMF), a body established under the Bretton Woods agreement for that purpose.

Fixed exchange-rate systems are not without their difficulties. These may not be apparent if the par rate of a currency is equal to the equilibrium exchange rate, for then intervention will consist of simply smoothing out small fluctuations, with the reserves tending to hover around their initial level. If the equilibrium rate were to fall below the par rate (because of the operation of the shift factors listed above), the monetary authorities of the country concerned would find that the reserves were running down. This, indeed, was the experience of British governments during the 1950s and 1960s, when relatively poor trends in inflation and productivity meant that the British balance of trade was chronically in deficit. The Bank of England was therefore constantly having to use the reserves to support the exchange rate. Because of the deficits, investors formed the expectation that the exchange rate would fall and began to sell their sterling. This speculative selling added to the downward pressure on the rate and eventually the UK was forced to reduce the par value for sterling (a move known as *devaluation*) in recognition of the change in market fundamentals.

While the UK faced the problem of managing a weak currency, most other industrial nations ran consistent trade surpluses and hence had strong currencies. These nations also, however, had problems under the Bretton Woods system. Because their currencies were tending to 'appreciate' (that is, to rise), their governments had to supply domestic currency to the foreign exchange market. This money had either to be borrowed, in which case it added to the various governments' PSBRs, or printed. Both policies, of course, hindered the task of controlling the money supplies of the countries concerned.

The interventionist nature of the system betrays its origins in Keynesian economic thinking. The rationale for fixing exchange rates is indeed typically Keynesian: that, if left to their own devices, foreign exchange rates would fluctuate to a pronounced degree, to the detriment of international trade. Monetarists naturally favour freely floating rates, arguing both that intervention is doomed to fail in the long run because 'fundamentals' must prevail, and that abruptly taken decisions to devalue a currency can be quite as unsettling to international trade as market-based fluctuations in exchange rates. In practice, the problems described above contributed to the abandonment of the Bretton Woods system in 1973 and its replacement by a mixed system in which currencies have no official par values yet monetary authorities intervene to restrain market-based changes which they feel to be ill-founded. The main survivor of the Bretton Woods system is the European Monetary System (EMS), which is a system of fixed exchange rates involving most members of the EC.

Interest rates

It was explained earlier that interest rates were one of the shift factors operating on the supply and demand curves for a currency. This can be exploited by using monetary policy to manage the exchange rate. Thus when the government wishes to stop the rate from depreciating, it can raise interest rates and so attract foreign funds. Indeed, it was common practice during the operation of the Bretton Woods system to use interest rates as well as reserves to defend par values, while in more recent years interest rates have been used to control the exchange rate movements as often as to control the money supply. For Britain this meant that rates were often high, with the effect that investment in new plant and equipment was held back.

Fiscal policy

Since the demand for imports is usually related to the level of income, one way to cut imports is to reduce income by deflating the economy by fiscal (or indeed monetary) means. The disadvantage of such policies is that they raise unemployment and undermine business confidence. They would only be appropriate, therefore, for use in the short term. The remedy for a chronically weak trade balance is, of course, a depreciation in the exchange rate.

Benign neglect

Governments can choose to frame policy entirely with regard to domestic considerations like the rate of inflation, with the exchange rate being left to find its own level. The expectation would be, of course, that a policy of strict monetary control would be a more effective defence of a given exchange rate than any direct intervention. This is the policy favoured by many monetarists.

34-9 SUMMARY

The *balance of payments accounts* record transactions between the United Kingdom and the rest of the world. The accounts are divided into sections dealing with *visible* trade (imports and exports), *invisibles* (trade in services) and investment flows (which relate to borrowing and lending and transactions in assets).

The *foreign exchange market* sets the rates of exchange between the world's different currencies. The demand for a currency on the market arises from its exports (and other credit items in its balance of payments) while the supply of its currency arises from its imports (and other debit items). The foreign exchange market is in equilibrium when all currency is held willingly.

Market fundamentals are the various factors which cause shifts in the supply of and demand for a currency and thus alter its equilibrium rate: a country's comparative advantages, its relative rate of inflation and interest rates.

The *depreciation mechanism* eliminates a deficit in a nation's external payments by means of a fall in the value of the currency.

The *Marshal–Lerner condition* states that the depreciation mechanism will only work if the sum of the elasticities of demand for imports and exports exceeds one.

The *purchasing-power parity theorem* states that, over the long run, inflation and currency depreciation should balance, so that the prices of any given commodity in different countries should all be equivalent to one another.

The *Bretton Woods system* of fixed exchange rates involved intervention to maintain par values for currencies. Divergent trends in productivity and inflation, however, led to chronic surpluses for some countries and chronic deficits for others. Fixed rates were eventually replaced by floating rates, although governments still attempt to manage rates by using interest rates and other instruments.

EXERCISES

34-1 'The balance of payments always balances, ergo, there can be no balance of payments problems.' Explain and discuss.

34-2 Place the following in their correct category in the balance of payments accounts:

(a) pocket money spent on an overseas holiday;
(b) buying the latest series of *Hill Street Blues* for Channel 4;
(c) buying a flat on the Costa del Sol;
(d) receiving interest payments from your investment in an American oil company;
(e) buying a Volkswagen car.

34-3 You are a senior researcher in a bank which deals in foreign exchange. A new recruit has just joined the department and has been given the job of producing a forecast for the exchange rate of sterling for the next year. You are requested to write a note describing the things she will need to examine in producing such a forecast.

34-4 Write a report on the outlook for the currency of a Third World country on the basis of the following information:

(a) Consumers are adopting Western lifestyles and acquiring tastes for European goods.
(b) The dams which provide hydro-electric power require extensive repairs.
(c) Population is rising at 2.5 per cent per year.
(d) There is considerable soil erosion.
(e) Inflation is running at 24 per cent.
(f) Demand for its main export is rising.
(g) A multinational company has recently decided to locate its regional manufacturing plant in the country.
(h) A monetarist government has just been returned to power.
(i) The country owes $12 billion to Western banks.
(j) Interest rates are currently 4 per cent.

35

INTERNATIONAL TRADE POLICY

35-1 INTRODUCTION

International trade exerts a powerful influence over national economies. Opportunities for specialization in some fields are opened up, while others are foreclosed, depending on the industries in which a country's comparative advantage lies. Export sales can provide the basis for the development of whole new industries, which, when competition arises, can then be forced into decline. These fluctuations in prosperity have given rise, periodically, to calls for foreign products to be excluded from home markets, and the objective of this chapter is to review the arguments for and against allowing overseas suppliers unrestricted access to a country's home market, that is, the policy of free trade.

35-2 THE COMMITMENT TO FREE TRADE

Until the nineteenth century, most governments used tariffs to discourage merchants from other nations from trading both in home markets and in their colonies. Britain was no exception, maintaining extensive import duties on both manufactured goods and on wheat, some 10–15 per cent of which was imported. Between 1842 and 1849, however, these duties were abolished. Other countries followed suit, and for a brief period, free trade became the norm. Later in the nineteenth century, however, the newly industrializing nations such as the United States and Germany imposed tariffs on imports in order to reserve their home markets for their own producers.

After efforts to restore free trade at the end of the First World War, the world economy took a decisive step towards protectionism in 1930 with the enactment by the American Senate of the Smoot–Hawley Tariff, which imposed heavy import duties on European products. The Europeans retaliated immediately, with the result that exporting industries in both the USA and Europe lost their markets and were forced to lay off workers. Being forced to buy from less efficient local suppliers naturally reduced real incomes. This in turn reduced demand; in the context of a gathering depression, this development was clearly less than helpful. Thus protectionism seemed to have helped precipitate the downturn, and at the end of the Second World War the Western nations redoubled their efforts to re-establish free trade. The result was an international treaty, the General Agreement on Trade and Tariffs (GATT), which made it illegal for countries to apply selective, discriminatory tariffs to the goods of any single trade partner. More importantly, GATT also acted as a forum for the negotiation of mutual reductions in tariffs. There have, in consequence, been a series of tariff cuts on manufactured goods, which are now for the most part subject to only minimum duties. The same, however, cannot be said of agricultural goods, with both the European Communities (EC) and the USA operating strict policies to prevent imports.

Despite cuts in tariffs, there are still many barriers to trade between countries. Apart from the question of language, there are international differences in consumer tastes, labelling laws, safety standards and so on. Sometimes goods may be subject to quotas, which set physical limits to the volume of goods which may be allowed into a country. Many textile products from the Third World are limited in this way, for example. Occasionally, quotas may be established voluntarily, as when Japanese car manufacturers agreed to restrict their sales to only 11 per cent of the British market in the early 1980s. (The motive for this move was a wish to avoid the possibility that stringent tariffs might be imposed.) Countries may also institute 'non-tariff barriers' by, for example, setting safety standards or labelling requirements which overseas producers would find difficult to meet. Subsidies to domestic producers also place overseas firms at a disadvantage. Finally, many governments buy goods—especially defence equipment—only from domestic firms, thus effectively closing those markets to overseas competitors.

The above practices notwithstanding, the principle of free trade enjoys a wide degree of official international support. The contrast with the early nineteenth century could hardly be more marked. To a large degree, this acceptance of free trade is due to the arguments advanced by economists (as set out in Chapter 33). In the light of these analyses of the 'gains from trade', the onus lies on those who would erect barriers to trade to justify their position.

35-3 JUSTIFICATION FOR PROTECTIONISM

The reason most commonly advanced for instituting trade barriers is to preserve jobs. Tariffs, that is, are seen as a way of maintaining demand for the output of an industry when foreign competition is eroding its share of the market. The argument rests implicitly upon a simple supply and demand model, that is, it assumes that tariffs will shift the demand curve for the products of domestic industry to the right (or at any rate slow its drift to the left).

The main objection to this policy is that it involves costs to the rest of the economy. First, tariffs would raise prices to consumers, who would be forced either to buy the more expensive home-produced item or to purchase the foreign product at a price which included the tariff. Second, to the extent that foreign goods were shut out of the market altogether, as they might be if the tariff were very high, consumer choice would be diminished. Thus the gain in jobs for one section of the labour force would be paid for by lower real incomes for other workers. It is, of course, possible to calculate the costs to consumers and the numbers of jobs preserved. For example, Silberston[1] estimated that the imposition of quotas to maintain jobs in the textile industry cost consumers an extra 5 per cent or £500 million per annum for clothing. The research also estimated that quotas had raised employment by some 48 000 jobs. At an implied cost per job of over £10 000, the study concluded that the workers concerned could have been retrained for other work rather more cheaply.

The argument above becomes more powerful when the industry in question produces goods which are used not by consumers but by other industries. If, for example, steel were subject to tariffs (in an attempt to bolster jobs in the steel industry), all metal-using industries from engineering to motor-vehicle production would face higher costs and would therefore be rather less competitive in world markets. As a result, these industries might both shed jobs and reduce their demand for steel, leading in turn to a fall in employment in steel-making. The net gain in jobs may thus be rather smaller than originally anticipated—it may even be negative.

The jobs-preservation argument can sometimes be based on the allegation that the foreign goods are selling at prices which do not truly reflect costs. It may be suggested, for example, that foreign firms are cross-subsidizing their products by overcharging in some markets so as to undercharge in others. Alternatively, the overseas supplier may be accused of *dumping*, that is, of selling at a discount goods which are surplus to its main markets. The central idea is that the prices set by the importer are not 'fair', and tariffs are needed to restore *fair trade*.

Even if it is proven that the prices set are below costs, it does not follow that tariffs should be imposed. The case rests ultimately upon an assessment of the length of time for which the practice is to be continued. If one economy is prepared to sell products to another at subsidized prices indefinitely, then the receiving economy would be best to accept what is, in effect, the gift of some resources and to readjust its economy accordingly. There is, after all, little purpose in producing butter at considerable expense when somebody else is always ready to supply it at subsidized prices. The only occasion on which the argument has any force is when the availability of cheap goods is likely to be purely transitory. In this case, domestic firms could be driven out of business, only to be forced to reopen again when the dumped goods had all been sold off. Accordingly, GATT recognizes states' rights to impose duties in cases of dumping. In practice, however, this right is rather difficult to invoke as the duration of any dumping can never be established in advance.

Historically, a major justification for tariffs has been the 'infant industry' argument: that foreign goods should be excluded from the home market while domestic producers acquire the necessary expertise and capital equipment. The validity of this argument was demonstrated in the cases of late nineteenth century Germany and America, whose industries developed rapidly behind tariff walls until they were strong enough to meet overseas competition without protection. What these cases fail to prove, of course, is the applicability of the argument to all circumstances. Nevertheless, versions of this argument are often used to advocate protection for industries in which it is felt the United Kingdom should retain some expertise. For example, governments have been urged to place orders for nuclear power stations so that design teams can be kept in being. Once dispersed, the argument goes on, these teams could never be reconstituted and the UK would not be able to engage in nuclear engineering in the future.

A macro-economic argument that has been put forward in favour of the imposition of quotas on virtually all British imports rests on the proposition that the United Kingdom has a marginal propensity to import which is rather high. The effect is to undermine any attempt to raise the aggregate level of demand in the economy, because any increase in expenditure would simply spill over into imports, leaving the output of domestic industries static. The policy would therefore fail to move the economy to full employment, which has, so the argument runs, been rendered unattainable by consumers' preferences for overseas goods. It follows that the solution would be to restrict imports to current levels so that the benefits of any growth in demand were directed towards home producers. Although the advocates of this policy concede that it would raise prices and restrict consumer choice, they argue that it would permit the economy to expand, more than offsetting the loss in real incomes. The objections to this argument may, perhaps, be best considered in the context of a wider discussion of the disadvantages of protectionism.

The final reason for protecting domestic industries is not economic but military. Many states take the view that some importance attaches to the capability to manufacture defence equipment domestically. Thus orders for new warships, tanks and planes tend to be awarded to a country's own defence manufacturers rather than permitting overseas firms to tender. The result is that costs tend to be higher, but those governments which pursue the practice clearly find this acceptable.

35-4 THE PROBLEMS OF PROTECTIONISM

The first set of objections to protectionism are based as much on history and politics as on economic theory. First among them is the fact that, quite simply, tariffs are illegal. The UK is a member of the EC, and the terms of membership preclude the imposition of tariffs and quotas by any single state. Tariffs can only be imposed by the EC as a whole, and any British policy would therefore have to gain the approval of the other member states. Moreover, any action by the EC would (unless it could be justified on the grounds that it was necessary to prevent dumping) be contrary to international treaty obligations under GATT.

The second objection to protectionism from this general area is the argument that it may well invite retaliation. Since the British economy depends upon international trade, the counterimposition of tariffs by other countries would be costly. There is, however, an even graver danger that protectionism would initiate a trade war, with states imposing tariffs on wider and wider ranges of goods. This could plunge the world into depression, as it did in the 1930s.

Third, it may be noted that protectionism is rather easier to write about than to implement in today's interdependent world economy. Consider a decision to impose tariffs on Swedish cars with the objective of assisting British car manufacturers. If, however, Swedish cars are made with British components then a fall in their sales will mean fewer jobs in the British components-manufacturing factories. Then again, foreign manufacturers may establish plants in the UK so that their goods can be described as 'British made'. These factories may well, of course, be merely 'screwdriver' plants which simply assemble parts supplied from overseas. Protectionist measures may thus be either counterproductive or unenforceable.

The purely economic arguments against protection fall under two main headings: static and dynamic. They derive respectively from neo-classical and Austrian approaches.

Many of the static arguments have been explored in our discussion above of the justifications for protectionism. These were the effects on prices to both consumers and user-industries and on the ranges of goods available for consumers to choose from. To these may be added the point that goods intended for importation into the UK may be, as a result of protection, diverted to different markets where they may also compete with British products. Thus Japanese cars diverted from the UK may undercut British car exports in, say, Brazil. Competition, in other words, may be thought of as extending over the entire world, and while it may be possible to exclude overseas producers from the British market, there is no means by which British tariffs can affect the rest of the world market.

The dynamic arguments against protectionism draw, as was noted above, on Austrian economic ideas which stress the importance of the *process of adjustment*. Tariffs, so the argument runs, may very well not be effective in promoting the kinds of adjustment which an economy may need in order to be efficient and competitive. When overseas competition threatens to take away an industry's markets, what is required is enterprise in seeking out new markets to serve or new products to make. The erection of a tariff wall will, however, simply make it easier to avoid making changes, encouraging firms simply to consolidate. Austrian economists would thus look with some suspicion upon the 'infant industry' argument. While they would probably be forced to concede that tariffs had not harmed the development of German and American industry in the late nineteenth century, they would doubtless argue that there were exceptional factors present, like the energy, aggressiveness and industriousness of those societies at that particular time. As a general rule, Austrian economists would argue that competition, including overseas competition, was necessary to prevent business from sliding into inefficiency.

A related argument is that tariffs will fail to preserve jobs over time if productivity is increasing. Even an industry with a home market that is guaranteed by tariff barriers will tend to replace workers by machines as technology advances, and this will mean reductions in employment unless new markets are found. Employment can only be maintained, therefore, not by trying to preserve existing business but by discovering new business opportunities.

The final point relates to the foreign exchange market and the depreciation mechanism, and it can be understood by following the consequences of an imbalance in trade between say, Japan and the UK in manufactured goods like cars. The immediate effect would be that Japanese firms would find themselves holding large amounts of sterling, which they would presumably attempt to sell on the foreign exchange market. This would naturally make the pound depreciate against the yen and all other currencies, with the effect that other industries in the UK would be enabled to compete more effectively on the world market and so expand. In other words, the depreciation mechanism can, in principle, be relied on to protect employment even more effectively than tariffs and quotas.

35-5 SUMMARY

Free trade is the policy of allowing overseas producers unrestricted access to the domestic market. GATT is an international treaty designed to promote free trade.

Protectionism is the use of *tariffs* (import taxes), *quotas* (physical limits) and other barriers to deter imports. These involve costs to users of the products involved in terms of higher prices, restricted choice and the discouragement of dynamism.

The *infant-industry* argument for protecting industries until they have achieved some maturity rests on the debatable assumption that the spur of overseas competition is not necessary to maintain the pace of development.

EXERCISES

35-1 The EC protects the agricultural sector, keeping imports out and prices up. Explain why you think this policy has been adopted. Explain the consequences of the policy for

(*a*) consumers
(*b*) European food manufacturers
(*c*) the foreign exchange markets for European currencies.

Support your arguments wherever possible with statistical evidence.

35-2 What justification could be advanced for protecting British computer-software firms from foreign competition? What forms of protection would you suggest? What effect would such protection have on British commerce and industry?

35-3 Using the *Annual Abstract of Statistics* (plus any other relevant sources) for relevant years, trace the output of motor vehicles in the United Kingdom and the number of people employed in the motor industry from 1974 to a recent year. Comment on the policy of voluntary import restrictions negotiated with the Japanese manufacturers.

35-4 The official policy of the government is free trade, but the unions in the coal-mining industry are demanding the imposition of tariffs on foreign coal. There is shortly to be a meeting between ministers and trade-union officials to discuss the union's demands.

(*a*) As a research officer for the union concerned, write briefing notes for your officials. Include data which you consider relevant.
(*b*) As a Civil Servant, write briefing notes for the Secretary of State for Trade and Industry. Include data which you consider relevant.

REFERENCE

1. Silberston, Z. A., *The Multi-Fibre Arrangement and the UK Economy*, HMSO, London, 1984.

36

ECONOMIC GROWTH AND ECONOMIC MANAGEMENT: AN AGENDA FOR ECONOMISTS

36-1 INTRODUCTION

As has continually been stressed in this text, economics is used to assist decision-making by individuals, firms and governments. The purpose of this chapter is to suggest areas of investigation which could be of particular importance in the future. Rather than examining the manifold questions facing different business organizations, the focus is restricted to issues of universal concern to governments and electors. Where relevant, the lessons of past experience will be outlined. The agenda contains items at micro, macro and international levels.

36-2 MICRO-ECONOMIC MANAGEMENT: INDUSTRIAL POLICY AND ENTERPRISE

For much of the present century, but particularly since the end of the Second World War, the British economy has been in relative decline: its share of world exports diminished from over 30 per cent in 1913 to 9.5 per cent in 1950. By 1980 it was down to 5.8 per cent. Industrial plant was often old-fashioned and inefficient, products were poorly designed and uncompetitive. Britain, once the workshop of the world, ran a deficit on trade in manufactured goods from 1983. Above all, British labour productivity grew more slowly than that in other industrial countries, as Table 36-1 shows.

Table 36-1 Growth of GDP *per capita* in real terms, 1960–80

Country	1960–70 (%)	1970–80 (%)
Japan	157	44
France	58	38
West Germany	52	33
Italy	61	28
United Kingdom	22	24

Sources: *UN Yearbook of National Accounts Statistics*, 1981, Table 7; and *UN Statistical Yearbook*, 1972, Table 179.

These problems have prompted governments to take a number of differing approaches towards industry. The basic attitude was one of *laissez-faire*, of allowing entrepreneurs to follow their own judgement without interference from government. During the 1980s this approach received renewed emphasis, with the Conservative governments of Mrs Thatcher placing enterprise at the centre of micro-economic policy. The encouragement of enterprise has taken many forms: liberalization, privatization, the reduction of direct taxation, subsidies for the formation of new firms and the teaching of enterprise-related skills in schools and colleges.

From 1945 to 1979, however, more interventionist approaches were pursued. Many industries were taken into public ownership. Others were subject to detailed intervention from bodies like the Industrial Reorganization Corporation, which was set up in 1965 to promote mergers between industrial companies. The intention was to form larger groupings which would be better able to compete in the world market. In a similar vein, a National Enterprise Board (NEB) was set up in 1975 with the brief of channelling public funds into new, growing firms at the forefront of technological development—a policy of 'picking winners'. The NEB, however, was diverted into subsidizing firms which were threatened with closure such as British Leyland (now the Rover Group). Such moves proved to be futile and served to discredit the interventionist approach.

Although the issue may appear to be clear-cut, it is instructive to recall the context in which interventionist approach gained favour. This consisted of two fundamental facts. One was the indisputable backwardness of British industry compared to that of its European neighbours. The other was the point that the decisions which had brought this state of affairs about had been taken not by Civil Servants or trade-union officials but by private entrepreneurs. Responsibility for Britain's relative decline seemed to lie with her businessmen.

Public intervention seemed to offer the way forward. During two world wars, many industries had been supervised not by private entrepreneurs alone but by committees with strong government influence. These bodies had in many cases forced the industries to modernize. Similarly, the electricity industry had been taken into public control during the 1920s and turned into the most modern system in Europe.

These considerations suggest that virtue may not reside solely with one approach or another. Different policies towards industry should be examined not in the light of pre-formed doctrines but of carefully researched evidence. A challenge to economists, therefore, is to devise ways of explaining and measuring the performance of the British economy in terms of productivity, share of world trade and output.

A further issue relates to the provision which ought to be made for the future economic strength of the British economy. Although the promotion of flexibility and enterprise have brought notable gains in terms of productivity, it remains unclear how far this can persist without being underpinned both by education and training and by extensive research and development activities. Despite the fact that, as North Sea oil runs out, the United Kingdom's prosperity will depend solely upon the expertise of its work-force, the British record on both the above counts is considerably worse than that of its major industrial competitors, and the necessity for raising both the quantity and quality of education, training and research is widely recognized. There is, however, less consensus over the most appropriate methods by which to proceed. One option would be to give firms tax rebates for undertaking training or R&D, while another would be for the government to put the work out to tender and allow colleges, private training establishments and research institutes to compete for the contracts. For economists, one challenge would be to investigate the implications of the different approaches.

36-3 MACRO-ECONOMIC MANAGEMENT

This aspect of economic policy has seen, perhaps, more experimentation than any other. During the first half of the century, policy was guided by the Treasury view that a counter-cyclical policy would not work and that the market system would find its own way out of recession. This philosophy was, as we have seen, replaced by a Keynesian, interventionist approach from the end of the Second World War until the late 1970s. This period saw, besides the active management of demand through fiscal and monetary policy, intervention to stabilize exchange rates and prices and incomes policies intended to restrain inflation.

The details of one of the latest attempts to restrain inflation in this manner are important as they indicate some of the limits to government policy. The events in question began in 1974 with the election of a Labour government committed to containing inflation by securing the voluntary cooperation of the trade unions. They thus negotiated a 'Social Contract' with the Trades Union Congress, which undertook to restrain pay increases. In return, the government imposed legal restraints on companies' rights to raise prices and attempted to keep down the cost of living by subsidizing food, housing and the outputs of the nationalized industries. Employment law was made more favourable to workers and the NEB was set up.

These measures—particularly the subsidies to the nationalized industries and the expenditure of the NEB—imposed a burden on the Exchequer, and although the government raised taxes, the PSBR rose from £4 billion in 1973 to £6.4 billion in 1974 and £10.2 billion in 1975. Unable to finance this fully by selling gilts, the government was forced to issue Treasury bills, that is, to print money, and sterling M3 increased quickly. Investors, both in the United Kingdom and overseas, came to the conclusion that inflation would increase and that sterling would fall in value against other currencies. (The fact that they thought in this way indicated, of course, their acceptance of monetarist economics.) Fearing that inflation and depreciation would render their securities valueless in a few years, investors began to sell sterling, and between March and May 1976 the exchange rate fell from a little over $2 to $1.70. The falling value induced even more investors to move their funds out of sterling and the downward trend gathered pace. Similar selling occurred on the gilts market, with the result that the government had even greater difficulty in financing the PSBR. It was forced to make further resort to the issue of Treasury bills. This move, unfortunately, only served to confirm the impression that the government was fast losing control of the money supply and therefore of inflation. The fall in the exchange rate accelerated. The government found itself with a full-scale sterling crisis.

Unable to support the pound, the government was obliged to seek a loan from the IMF. The condition for the loan was an undertaking that the government would publish, and then meet, targets for the growth of the money supply. (Clearly the IMF, as well as the financial markets, accepted monetarism.) What the crisis showed, however, was that the economic policies of British governments could not ignore the views of the international investment community.

Subsequent events are also of significance for economic policy. From 1979, policy adopted an avowedly monetarist stance: targets for the growth of the money supply continued to be published, interest rates were raised to record levels and public borrowing was curtailed. The immediate result was as outlined in Chapter 25: inflation fell back but unemployment rose rapidly to some 3 million.

In one sense, the policy of monetary restraint met with success: inflation came down from an annual rate of 14 per cent during the six months before the Conservatives entered office to 9 per cent in 1982 and 4 per cent in 1987. These results were not, however, without their negative aspects.

First, the levels of both inflation and unemployment could hardly be regarded as satisfactory. While prices in the United Kingdom rose more slowly during the mid-1980s than they had during the 1970s, British inflation was still worse than that of the United States, Japan and most Western European countries. Indeed, the persistence of inflation at about 5 per cent for five years (1983–7) at the same time as unemployment hovered around the 12–13 per cent mark seemed to suggest that the British economy had finally reached its NAIRU. Were this to be the case, there would appear to be little possibility of reducing unemployment since such a move would cause inflation to accelerate. For economists, the challenge, therefore, would seem to be to identify those factors which have made the NAIRU so high, and then to devise policies which would reduce it.

Another important question relates to the reliability of the monetarist approach to inflation. While inflation fell during the 1980s, money supply rose at a brisk pace. Between 1982 and 1987, M4 increased by 88 per cent, although money GDP at market prices rose by only 51 per cent. The clear implication was that the demand for money, far from remaining stable, had risen considerably. This was, of course, quite contrary to monetarist theory, which rest upon the assumption that the demand for money is stable. A further challenge to economists, therefore, is to advance (and test) hypotheses which could account for these developments.

36-4 ENVIRONMENT AND INTERNATIONAL DEBT

Besides the primarily national questions of innovation, efficiency and inflation, there are difficulties which affect the whole international economic system. Foremost among these is the fact that many Third World countries are deeply in debt. Brazil, for example, owes $68 billion to overseas creditors, while Mexico and Argentina owe $32 million and $11 billion respectively. For the developing countries (outside OPEC) as a whole, debt rose from $222 billion in 1977 to £437 billion in 1981. The problem is that servicing this debt (that is, paying interest and repaying the capital) is accounting for an expanding proportion of the countries' export earnings. For Brazil and Mexico, for example, the figures are 35 per cent and 64 per cent, respectively. Many countries have forced the banks to 'reschedule' repayments, that is, to allow repayments to be deferred. Behind these moves lies the threat that countries may simply default.

The problem for the world economy of such defaulting is that the banks which have lent the money would make substantial losses and would, in many cases, be forced into liquidation. Other depositors would therefore lose their money and confidence in the banking system would be undermined. If a panic were to set in, with all depositors seeking to withdraw their funds at the same time, more banks would close, the money supply would decline and the world economy could be thrown into depression.

Behind the debts of many Third World countries lies the problem of poverty and underdevelopment. Because Third World economies often lack industrial capacity, they can only repay foreign debts by exporting agricultural products. Often against a background of expanding population, these countries have thus been forced to raise agricultural output significantly. All too frequently this has meant the overexploitation of the land, leading to erosion and degradation. For example, a principal export product of many states in Central America is beef raised on pastures cleared from the rainforest. Although the rainforests are lush, the soils on which they grow are usually poor, and the fertility of the pastures lasts but a few years. Then the cattle ranchers are forced to move on, clearing more rainforest. Since 1950, two-thirds of Central America's rainforest has been cleared, and at current rates, the remainder will be gone by the year 2010. Similar instances of overworking the land in order to produce export crops can be cited from Latin America, Africa and Asia. In many instances food shortages and starvation have resulted. The situation has been described as one of 'environmental bankruptcy'.

The process clearly cannot go on indefinitely—like mining, it uses resources which cannot be replaced. The challenge for economists in this area is to help to devise policies which will promote forms of economic change and growth which can be sustained over the decades.

36-5 CONCLUSION

These and a myriad other issues—like the effects of advancing technology—change the circumstances under which business organizations in both the public and the private sectors operate. Since decision-makers in all business organizations are obliged to react to (and where possible to anticipate) such changes, all must reach some assessment of their effects. This work must involve, either formally or informally, a degree of economic analysis—always bearing in mind, of course, that there is more than one school of economic thought. It also requires the quantification of some aspect of the situation: concepts such as 'inflation', 'economic growth' or 'soil erosion' need to be translated into measurable terms in order to facilitate decision-making. In many cases, the task of constructing such statistical indicators will test the ingenuity of the researcher to the full.

It is the contention of this book that the process of using theories and statistical indicators to assess changes ought to follow certain rules, namely: it should involve the formulation of hypotheses which can, in principle, be tested; statistical evidence ought to be brought forward to confirm or refute the hypotheses; and evidence should be collected, processed and analysed using the appropriate mathematical and statistical techniques.

Set to work in this way, economic theory can prove to be useful to all business organizations. As we have tried to show throughout this book, modern economics and the supporting methods of quantitative analysis are directly applicable to an analysis of the problems faced by all decision-makers. It is the combination of theory and data which makes economics useful in today's business organizations.

EXERCISES

36-1 Collect data on the following variables:

(a) real per capita GDP
(b) total investment in real terms
(c) RPI
(d) Index of Industrial Production
(e) shares of world trade

for the last 20 years (taking figures for, say, every 5 or 10 years) for the United Kingdom and three or four other industrialized economies (e.g., Japan, the United States, France, West Germany). (For the United Kingdom, a useful source is *Economic Trends Annual Supplement (ETAS)*; for other countries see the *United Nations Statistical Yearbook*. For data on trade, see the *United Nations International Trade Statistics Yearbook*, Vol. I.)

Compare the trends in the variables for the different economies. What reasons can you suggest for the United Kingdom's comparative performance?

36-2 Collect data on British productivity (output per employee) for the economy as a whole, for the manufacturing sector and for the service sector. Calculate a productivity growth rate for the period for each elected government since 1950 (or later, depending on your data). (Again, see *ETAS*.) What are the implications of these differing growth rates in terms of the different economic policies adopted?

36-3 You are employed as an economic journalist working for a 'quality' Sunday newspaper. Write a short (1000-word) article on the macro-economic record of the Conservative government which came to power in 1979. (You will have to make comparisons between the present year and either 1979 or 1981—or both. Make your readers aware of these two possible measures and their respective merits.)

36-4 Some have argued that the World Bank and other international agencies have weakened the economies of some Third World countries by encouraging them to borrow money to finance the production of greater quantities of primary materials like agricultural crops and basic minerals. Formulate testable hypotheses from these ideas, and gather data to falsify or confirm them. (Data sources include the *United Nations International Trade Statistics Yearbook*, Vol. II.)

36-5 The Dean of your college is to participate in a televised debate on education with Members of Parliament and others from the education world. The Dean has asked you (a new economics lecturer) to write background notes for her to use in preparation. (The *National Institute Economic Review* for November 1987 contains two articles on training and industrial R&D which may be helpful.)

APPENDIX A

OFFICIAL SOURCES OF DATA

This Appendix contains a brief summary of the official sources of data likely to be of use to the economic and business analyst. The Appendix is intended only to provide an outline of the appropriate sources. The *Guide to Official Statistics* is essential reading if you wish to identify the source of a particular set of data and you wish to determine the relevant definitions and methods of data collection. Additionally, *Statistical Sources and Techniques*, by F. J. Randall and D. M. Wolf, provides a thorough coverage of the main official sources, with ample illustrations of the available data. There is, however, no substitute for actually going to look at these publications for yourself and browsing through the mass of data available.

ANNUAL ABSTRACT OF STATISTICS. Provides data on a wide range of variables including population, employment, unemployment, national income, taxation, consumption and saving, foreign trade, industrial production and so on.

DEPARTMENT OF EMPLOYMENT GAZETTE. Provides many series on employment, unemployment, wages and salaries. The *Gazette* also periodically includes relevant articles on this area of statistics.

ECONOMIC TRENDS. Provides quarterly and annual data on a large number of (mainly) economic series. The journal also regularly includes articles on selected aspects of some of the series covered. The *ECONOMIC TRENDS ANNUAL SUPPLEMENT* provides continuous series for the past 20–30 years on most of the economic variables covered.

FAMILY EXPENDITURE SURVEY. Provides details of the latest survey and comparisons over time.

FINANCIAL STATISTICS. Covers the transactions of the British financial sector including borrowing, lending, interest rates and security prices.

GENERAL HOUSEHOLD SURVEY. Provides details of the latest survey results (together with selected data from previous surveys) as well as details of the methodology.

MONTHLY DIGEST OF STATISTICS. Provides monthly details of many of the series in the *Annual Abstract* and provides further sub-division of many of the classifications used.

REGIONAL TRENDS. Published annually and provides a wide range of economic and social data on the standard regions in the United Kingdom.

SOCIAL TRENDS. Provides data on a variety of socio-economic variables.

UNITED KINGDOM NATIONAL ACCOUNTS (the 'Blue Book'). Provides data on the levels of income and expenditure for the national economy over the last 10-year period.

APPENDIX B

AREAS IN THE TAIL OF THE NORMAL DISTRIBUTION

z	.00	.01	.02	.03	.04	.05	.06	.07	.08	.09
0.0	.5000	.4960	.4920	.4880	.4840	.4801	.4761	.4721	.4681	.4641
0.1	.4602	.4562	.4522	.4483	.4443	.4404	.4364	.4325	.4286	.4247
0.2	.4207	.4168	.4129	.4090	.4052	.4013	.3974	.3936	.3897	.3859
0.3	.3821	.3783	.3745	.3707	.3669	.3632	.3594	.3557	.3520	.3483
0.4	.3446	.3409	.3372	.3336	.3300	.3264	.3228	.3192	.3156	.3121
0.5	.3085	.3050	.3015	.2981	.2946	.2912	.2877	.2843	.2810	.2776
0.6	.2743	.2709	.2676	.2643	.2611	.2578	.2546	.2514	.2483	.2451
0.7	.2420	.2389	.2358	.2327	.2296	.2266	.2236	.2206	.2177	.2148
0.8	.2119	.2090	.2061	.2033	.2005	.1977	.1949	.1922	.1894	.1867
0.9	.1841	.1814	.1788	.1762	.1736	.1711	.1685	.1660	.1635	.1611
1.0	.1587	.1562	.1539	.1515	.1492	.1469	.1446	.1423	.1401	.1379
1.1	.1357	.1335	.1314	.1292	.1271	.1251	.1230	.1210	.1190	.1170
1.2	.1151	.1131	.1112	.1093	.1075	.1056	.1038	.1020	.1003	.0985
1.3	.0968	.0951	.0934	.0918	.0901	.0885	.0869	.0853	.0838	.0823
1.4	.0808	.0793	.0778	.0764	.0749	.0735	.0721	.0708	.0694	.0681
1.5	.0668	.0655	.0643	.0630	.0618	.0606	.0594	.0582	.0571	.0559
1.6	.0548	.0537	.0526	.0516	.0505	.0495	.0485	.0475	.0465	.0455
1.7	.0446	.0436	.0427	.0418	.0409	.0401	.0392	.0384	.0375	.0367
1.8	.0359	.0351	.0344	.0336	.0329	.0322	.0314	.0307	.0301	.0294
1.9	.0287	.0281	.0274	.0268	.0262	.0256	.0250	.0244	.0239	.0233
2.0	.0228	.0222	.0217	.0212	.0207	.0202	.0197	.0192	.0188	.0183
2.1	.0179	.0174	.0170	.0166	.0162	.0158	.0154	.0150	.0146	.0143
2.2	.0139	.0136	.0132	.0129	.0125	.0122	.0119	.0116	.0133	.0110
2.3	.0107	.0104	.0102	.0099	.0096	.0094	.0091	.0089	.0087	.0084
2.4	.0082	.0080	.0078	.0075	.0073	.0071	.0069	.0068	.0066	.0064
2.5	.0062	.0060	.0059	.0057	.0055	.0054	.0052	.0051	.0049	.0048
2.6	.0047	.0045	.0044	.0043	.0041	.0040	.0039	.0038	.0037	.0036
2.7	.0035	.0034	.0033	.0032	.0031	.0030	.0029	.0028	.0027	.0026
2.8	.0026	.0025	.0024	.0023	.0023	.0022	.0021	.0021	.0020	.0019
2.9	.0019	.0018	.0018	.0017	.0016	.0016	.0015	.0015	.0014	.0014
3.0	.0014	.0013	.0013	.0012	.0012	.0011	.0011	.0011	.0010	.0010

APPENDIX C

AREAS IN THE TAIL OF THE t DISTRIBUTION

v	0.10	0.05	α 0.025	0.01	0.005
1	3.078	6.314	12.706	31.821	63.657
2	1.886	2.920	4.303	6.965	9.925
3	1.638	2.353	3.182	4.541	5.841
4	1.533	2.132	2.776	3.747	4.604
5	1.476	2.015	2.571	3.365	4.032
6	1.440	1.943	2.447	3.143	3.707
7	1.415	1.895	2.365	2.998	3.499
8	1.397	1.860	2.306	2.896	3.355
9	1.383	1.833	2.262	2.821	3.250
10	1.372	1.812	2.228	2.764	3.169
11	1.363	1.796	2.201	2.718	3.106
12	1.356	1.782	2.179	2.681	3.055
13	1.350	1.771	2.160	2.650	3.012
14	1.345	1.761	2.145	2.624	2.977
15	1.341	1.753	2.131	2.602	2.947
16	1.337	1.746	2.120	2.583	2.921
17	1.333	1.740	2.110	2.567	2.898
18	1.330	1.734	2.101	2.552	2.878
19	1.328	1.729	2.093	2.539	2.861
20	1.325	1.725	2.086	2.528	2.845
25	1.316	1.708	2.060	2.485	2.787
30	1.310	1.697	2.042	2.457	2.750
40	1.303	1.684	2.021	2.423	2.704
50	1.299	1.676	2.009	2.403	2.678
∞	1.282	1.645	1.960	2.326	2.576

APPENDIX D

AREAS IN THE TAIL OF THE χ^2 DISTRIBUTION

v	α 0.10	0.05	0.01
1	2.71	3.84	6.63
2	4.61	5.99	9.21
3	6.25	7.81	11.34
4	7.78	9.49	13.28
5	9.24	11.07	15.09
6	10.64	12.59	16.81
7	12.02	14.07	18.48
8	13.36	15.51	20.09
9	14.68	16.92	21.67
10	15.99	18.31	23.21
11	17.28	19.68	24.73
12	18.55	21.03	26.22
13	19.81	22.36	27.69
14	21.06	23.68	29.14
15	22.31	25.00	30.58
16	23.54	26.30	32.00
17	24.77	27.59	33.41
18	25.99	28.87	34.81
19	27.20	30.14	36.19
20	28.41	31.41	37.57
25	34.38	37.65	44.31
30	40.26	43.77	50.89
40	51.81	55.76	63.69
50	63.17	67.51	76.15
100	118.50	124.34	135.81

INDEX